*The* COMPLETE ILLUSTRATED
ENCYCLOPEDIA *of*

# Horses
# & Ponies

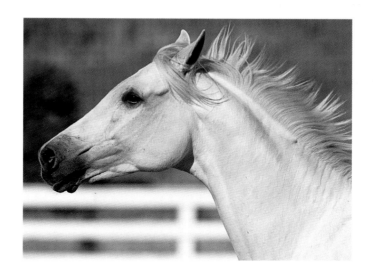

**Publisher and Creative Director:** Nick Wells
**Project Editor:** Cat Emslie
**Assistant Project Editor:** Victoria Lyle
**Picture Research:** Victoria Lyle and Gemma Walters
**Art Director:** Mike Spender
**Layout Design:** Dave Jones and Mike Spender
**Illustrator:** Ann Biggs
**Digital Design and Production:** Chris Herbert
**Copy Editor:** Siobhan O'Connor
**Proofreader:** Amanda Leigh
**Indexer:** Penny Brown

**Special thanks to**: Claire Walker, Carmen Herbert,
Fiana Muhlberger and Tamsin Pickeral

08 10 12 11 09

1 3 5 7 9 10 8 6 4 2

This edition first published 2008 by
**FLAME TREE PUBLISHING**
Crabtree Hall, Crabtree Lane
Fulham, London SW6 6TY

www.flametreepublishing.com

Flame Tree Publishing is part of the Foundry Creative Media Co. Ltd

© 2008 this edition The Foundry Creative Media Co. Ltd

ISBN 978-1-84786-228-0

A copy of the CIP data for this book is available from the British Library

Printed in China

# The COMPLETE ILLUSTRATED ENCYCLOPEDIA of Horses & Ponies

Sarah Gorrie, Pippa Roome,
Catherine Austen, Nicola Jane Swinney

**FLAME TREE
PUBLISHING**

# Contents

## History, Culture & Anatomy    10

## Care, Management & Riding    46

## The Breeds    122

# How to Use This Book

This book is divided into three main chapters, each designed to enhance an understanding of horses, their practical care, enjoyment of horses, and the various breeds that exist.

## History, Culture & Anatomy

This is an introduction to horses – their many roles throughout history and their involvement in human culture, such as art and literature, alongside their physical characteristics and behaviour.

## Care, Management & Riding

This chapter offers a practical guide to horses, taking you straight through from deciding whether and how to buy a horse, through taking care of it, to even breeding horses. If you are keen to get into the saddle, you will learn everything from the basics of tack and riding through to competing with horses.

## The Breeds

This chapter begins with a closer look at the evolution of horses into the breeds we know today. It discusses wild and feral horses, and the close relatives of horses, the Equus family – such as zebras and donkeys. It then explains what a 'breed' is and how they evolve and develop, as well as the different 'types' that horses can be classified under. This is followed by a hefty section that details almost all known breeds of horse that exist today, divided into ponies, light horses and heavy horses, organized within those sections by geographical origin and size.

Colour variations

Basic personality type

Average height

Typical uses

Similar breeds (with similar origins)

Typical temperament

Rough geographical origin

---

## LUNDY

HEIGHT: 12 hh
COLOUR: all solid colours
PERSONALITY TYPE: warm-blooded
TYPICAL USE: riding, competition

TEMPERAMENT: gentle, hardy

ORIGIN: England

SIMILAR BREEDS: Welsh, New Forest

Contrary to popular belief, the ponies of the island of Lundy, situated off the south-west coast of England, are not closely related to the area's Dartmoor and Exmoor ponies. A comparatively new equine breed, the Lundy Pony was developed in 1928 using New Forest and Welsh Section B bloodlines. The island's then owner, Martin Coles Harman, imported 34 New Forest mares and let them run with a Welsh stallion. The stallion died after only a year, having produced just one offspring.

### Height and Substance

Coles Harman's vision was a pony of style and height, a good-looking equine with quality and substance. The one colt the deceased stallion left behind proved his breeder's vision: he was a creamy dun with black points called Pepper, and was to be the foundation of the herd. Allowed to breed unchecked, the herd on the island grew until, in the 1930s, about 50 were rounded up and sent to the mainland to be sold. During the Second World War, when the shipping lanes were closed, the herd increased to about 100 ponies.

The herd was moved to the mainland in 1980, but the

### Good Doer

Still a rare breed, the Lundy Pony is attractive and hardy, with a wide, deep chest, sloping shoulders and hard, sound legs. It has a neat head and short, muscular neck. Common colours are

LEFT
The Lundy, of which there are sadly only a small number, is a well-conformed pony with a natural aptitude for jumping and a quiet temperament.

breed society formed in 1984 to the island later in the same decade. Connemara and Welsh Mountain Pony blood have been introduced, but otherwise the breed has had no outside influence.

dun, roan, palomino, bay and liver chestnut. It is a good doer and strong, but is gentle enough to be a suitable child's mount. It has a natural jumping ability, so would make a good hunting or competition pony.

## HACKNEY PONY

TEMPERAMENT: intelligent, spirited

ORIGIN: England

SIMILAR BREEDS: Fell, Hackney Horse, Thoroughbred

HEIGHT: 12–14 hh
COLOUR: bay, black, brown, chestnut
PERSONALITY TYPE: warm-blooded
TYPICAL USE: driving, show

High-stepping, elegant and spirited, the Hackney Pony is a breed in its own right, and not a scaled-down version of the Hackney Horse. It owes its existence to one man, Christopher Wilson, who bred the Hackney Horse St George to a Fell mare in 1866, then interbred the resulting offspring to make a fixed type – for some years, they were known as Wilson Ponies. Left out on the inhospitable Fells with little food or care, the breed became hardy and resilient.

### Exaggerated Action

By 1880, the Hackney Pony was an established breed, and much in demand for its stamina and good looks. The pony has a fine head with tapering muzzle and large eyes, small, neat ears, elegantly arched neck on powerful shoulders, and low

withers. Its back is compact, and it has fine legs with good joints. The feet are small and hard, and often allowed to grow long in the toe to accentuate the action. Ponies are usually bay, black or brown, with the occasional chestnut, with some white markings.

### Fascinating Facts

The Hackney Horse takes its name from the French haquenée, a language commonly spoken in the country in Medieval times, meaning a riding horse with a particularly comfortable gait.

ABOVE LEFT
The Hackney is one of the most elegant and refined pony breeds. It has a naturally extravagant, high-stepping movement and is athletically built.

The high-stepping gait is exaggerated in the Hackney Pony – it lifts its knees almost to its chest and brings its hocks right under its body. This action is not just for show: it can move at good speed with the minimum of bounce to a cart or carriage.

### Fluid and Energetic

Its showy good looks make the Hackney Pony popular, and its fluid and energetic gait is spectacular. While the breed has a tendency to pugnaciousness, its spirit and intelligence make it a joy to watch. It is the king of the show ring, exploding across the arena with piston-like

speed – head and tail carried high and proud – appearing suspended in the air for a moment at the highest point.

150

## Height

Gives the approximate height or height range of the adult horse. Most horses are measured in 'hands', which are equal to 10 cm (4 in). If a horse is, say, 14¾ hands high ('hh') it is written as '14.3' – this is not a decimal point.

**Very Small**
(< 12.3 hh/
1.28 m/51 in)

**Small**
(13 hh/1.30 m/
52 in–14.3 hh/
1.48 m/59 in)

**Medium**
(15 hh/1.50 m/
60 in–15.3 hh/
1.58 m/63 in)

**Large**
(16 hh/1.6 m/
64 in–16.3 hh
1.68 m/67 in)

**Very Large**
(17 hh/1.7 m/
68 in <)

## Colour

This gives the various possible colour and pattern combinations that the horse is known in.

 **Dun, Palomino** or **Gold**

 **Grey**

 **White, Cremello** or **Grullo**

 **Black**

 **Bay, Brown** or **Dark brown**

**Chestnut** or **Sorrel**

 **Roan** (a white-flecked coat any various possible base colours)

 **Patched** (various, including pinto – piebald, skewbald, 'coloured'; tobiano, overo, sabino, tovero)

 **Spotted** (such as Appaloosa)

 **Dual-coloured** (can be any mix)

 **All dark solid colours**

 **All colours** (can be found in any or most colours)

## Personality Type

This does not indicate the actual body temperature of the horse (which of course is a warm-blooded animal), but rather the generalized character type that the horse fits into – that is, is it a quick, high-spirited horse that originated in the warmer regions of the world, such as the hot-blooded Arabian? Is it a half-bred or part-bred horse or one that is the result of mixing hot-blooded and cold-blooded breeds; one of a more 'solid' or 'tempered' nature, and thus 'warm-blooded'? Or is it a heavy horse, known as 'cold-blooded' arguably because they often originated in colder, northern regions or because of their gentle, easy-going nature and stocky strength?

**Cold-blooded**          **Warm-blooded**          **Hot-blooded**

## Typical Use

Horses can be used for many things. These icons go some way to indicating the uses that the breed in question is put to.

 All-rounder

 All-round utility

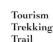 Dressage Show Competition

Polo

Racing

 Rodeo Bullfighting

 Driving Harness

 Military Police Parade

 Riding Leisure

 Tourism Trekking Trail

 Feral

 Pack Stalking

 Herding Ranching Stockhorse

 Farm Agriculture Draught

Meat

Donkey/mule production

Child's pony Mounted games

## Temperament

This gives a more detailed summary of the typical temperament of the breed – which may be helpful when choosing what horse to buy.

## Origins

Gives the rough geographical origin of the breed, if known. Sometimes this issue be debated.

## Similar Breeds

These are examples of breeds that have similar origins – such as the Fell and Dales having Friesian influences – and are often likely to be similar in appearance.

This information is followed by a more in-depth discussion of the breed, including a look at its origins, history, development and status today; its physical characteristics, temperament and behaviour, and its common uses.

## Reference Section

At the end of the encyclopedia is a list of useful addresses and contacts, from riding schools to veterinary associations; there is also a list of titles suggested for further reading. A glossary explains any terms that might be unfamiliar or sums up what you have already learnt, and a thorough index will allow you to instantly locate a particular topic.

# Introduction

'Wherever man has left his footprint in the long ascent from barbarism to civilization we will find the hoof print of the horse beside it,' wrote John Trotwood Moore.

The first section of this book will give readers an insight into this claim, and the book as a whole demonstrates the different ways in which horses have enriched the lives of human beings. Horses have been human companions for millions of years, and it is questionable whether civilization would have developed in the same way, or at the same speed, without them. Indeed, horses can be given significant credit for the development of civilization, as you will find upon further reading.

## An Ever-expanding Importance

Initially, horses were hunted for meat like the prey of Neanderthal man, but they soon found a higher place in society, to the point that even today some societies frown upon the idea of eating horse meat.

With the invention of the wheel and later domestication of the horse, humankind was provided with a method of transport that broadened its horizons tenfold. Empires were expanded and enemies defeated from the backs of horses or chariots. War may not be seen as a positive function of the horse, but think what more became possible with this new method of transport. No longer reliant only on their two feet, humans could not only travel, but also communicate over much greater distances thanks to horses and their riders, who delivered news for centuries, long before the development of the telegraph or telephone.

Being a beast of burden, the horse also aided the plight of farmers, providing a swifter and more controllable alternative to the ox prior to the development of tractors and other locomotives. The horse has helped stricken humans in the simplest ways, performing search and rescue in otherwise impassable terrain, aiding the police at riots with crowd control and centuries ago bringing aid to soldiers and the sick – the first ambulances were, after all, pulled by horses. All these services and more that have been carried out around the world throughout history are described within the book.

### Part of Human Culture

Humankind has repaid its debt to the horse by honouring this animal through art, literature, mythology and legend. The horse's importance has not been forgotten and was recognized even thousands of years ago when humans painted horses on cave walls. The horse is still the only animal seen fit to carry the monarch in most societies, or, for example, to pay tribute to a fallen president.

## Animals of Flight

Being that they are flight animals, it is a wonder that horses allow riders to mount them at all. The horse's instincts of flight have had to be conquered in order that it can carry out its roles as war horse, cart horse, police horse and so on. This behaviour and psychology is discussed in the first section of this book, too.

## Understanding Horses Today

These creatures of many roles are complicated beings, a fact that is also explored within this encyclopedia. As any horse owner will be aware, there are an awful lot of ailments that can afflict a horse, and these are described within this resource. The complicated structure of their legs, for example, as described in Anatomy and Appearance, combined with the horse's use, makes leg injuries to working animals common.

In the twenty-first century, horses are predominantly used for recreation, although in less industrialized countries they still perform the functions in agriculture, for example, that they used to in the Western world. Private individuals increasingly keep horses for recreation, and riding is a popular sport for all ages. There are riding schools around the world where anyone can learn. In this encyclopedia, you will find an explanation of the basic principles of horse riding.

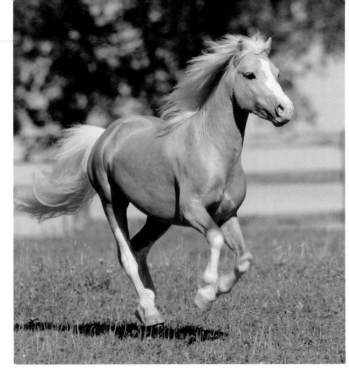

Horse riding is one of the only sports where men and women compete alongside each other, even at Olympic level. The numbers of spectators at equestrian events are growing. Racing is by far the most popular sport, with its association with gambling, but show jumping, dressage, eventing and other sports have increasing levels of support and attract increasing interest.

### Invaluable Information

Horses are not easy animals to look after, and their necessary care and manage-ment is explained in Care, Management and Riding. This section describes how a horseman or woman should keep and care for the animal, from possible ailments that might be witnessed, through an explanation of the breeding process, to tacking up the horse for riding.

You will also find an explanation of the different types of recreational and sporting activities horses are now involved in, from show jumping to gymkhanas.

The Breeds section of the encyclopedia explains in detail the hundreds of different breeds of horses that are seen today. Different types are more suitable for different tasks, and many have been specifically bred for certain purposes throughout history. Readers can discover the myriad difference between breeds, and each of their strengths and unique characteristics.

# History,
# Culture
# &
# Anatomy

# A CREATURE OF MANY ROLES

No other animal has contributed to society as much and in as many different ways as the horse. Since first being domesticated around 3000–4000 BC, horses have been utilized for transport, warfare, reconnaissance, raids, communication, hunting, logging, farming and ranching; their meat and milk have provided sustenance. They play important roles in patrol, law enforcement, search and rescue, and ceremonial duties, and are used for sport, leisure and even therapy. Possibly no other animal has been responsible for assisting the advancement of civilization to the same degree as the horse.

## War

For thousands of years, the horse's role in warfare included combat, transport, reconnaissance and raids. Types of warhorses developed over time. For example, with the advent of armoured knights in Europe, heavier horses that were able to cope with the extra weight replaced the small, swift horses chosen for their manoeuvrability.

### Early Mounted Warfare

Homer's *Iliad* describes warriors being taken to battle in chariots and fighting on foot; however, archaeological evidence suggests that the Egyptians, for example, opted early on to fight from chariots. Armies later had no choice but to fight from horseback when encountering impassable terrain. The Greek general Xenophon (c. 430–355 BC) wrote a manual on the art of horsemanship that is still referred to in the twenty-first century. The Romans' mounted army invaded Britain, but their Empire was destroyed in turn by horsemen, including the Huns. The Mongols famously raided and fought ruthlessly from horseback.

### Changing Times for Warhorses

Horses remained on the front line for centuries after the invention of firearms in the sixteenth century. Hundreds of horses were lost to gunfire at the Battle of Waterloo (1815) and again when Britain's Light Brigade advanced into Russian guns during the Crimean War (1853–56). Charging cavalry with lances took part in the First World War alongside artillery. Thousands of horses were lost to German guns in the Second World War. In recent conflicts – for example, in Afghanistan and Bosnia – horses have helped armies over difficult terrain and transported goods and refugees.

## Ceremonial Horses

Horses have performed ceremonial responsibilities for centuries in countries including China, Russia and India, where the President's Bodyguards perform ceremonial duties as well as being trained paratroopers. Most European royalty kept carriage horses for ceremonial occasions. The French cavalry regiment, the Garde Républicaine, carries out law enforcement and acts as state escort.

### American Ceremonial Horses

The Third United States Infantry Regiment, known as the Old Guard, escorts the president and serves at state and military full-honours funerals. Horses are extensively trained for this purpose so that they remain calm despite the gunfire. The regiment's horses are divided into separate groups of light and dark colours. Six horses, three of which are mounted, pull the funeral caisson. A horse without a rider, known as a caparisoned horse, is led in funeral possessions with boots placed backwards in its stirrups. Black Jack was the most famous caparisoned horse, serving in presidential funerals including that of President John F. Kennedy. President Abraham Lincoln's own horse, Old Bob, performed this duty at his funeral.

### British Royal Horses

The Household Cavalry is made up of two mounted regiments, the Life Guards and the Blues and Royals. Its role includes guarding the monarch and participating in ceremonial duties such as Trooping the Colour. Both regiments are predominantly made up of black horses. The King's Troop Royal Horse Artillery also carries out ceremonial duties and displays with six horses pulling heavy artillery at great speeds. The Windsor Greys, who are responsible for driving the sovereign, pulled the gold state coach that took Elizabeth II to her coronation in 1953. The Royal Canadian Mounted Police gave Queen Elizabeth II a charger named Burmese, whom she rode for nearly 20 years at Trooping the Colour.

ABOVE LEFT

*The British custom of 'trooping the colour' dates back to Charles II and the seventeenth century. Today it takes place annually in June to mark the Queen's birthday, and is carried out by the Household Division, on Horse Guards Parade.*

ABOVE

*The Royal race meet at Ascot lasts five days, and every day the Queen parades the straight of the mile-long course in a carriage drawn by her Windsor Greys.*

## Transport

After horses were domesticated, they were the most effective form of transport for thousands of years. With the wheel already in existence, domesticated horses were immediately used to pull chariots. Horses were also ridden, but many early types were too small to carry much weight, so two would pull a chariot together. Chariots gradually became more refined – for example,

changing from solid wheels to those with spokes. The Chinese, in particular, quickly developed effective chariots and harnesses.

### The Effects of Horse Transport

Horse transport allowed for larger battles – for example, between the Hittites and Egyptians – and for empires to extend their boundaries further than would otherwise have been possible. Transport also improved communication. Nations including those of the Mongols and Romans posted horses and riders several hours' riding distance apart, so that messages could be passed quickly over great

distances by relay. Until the advent of telegraphs, postal services around the world relied on individual riders and stagecoaches for communication. The famous Pony Express in the United States is one example of this.

### Later Forms of Horse Transport

Throughout the nineteenth and twentieth centuries, even after the invention of self-propelled vehicles, tradespeople in countries including the United Kingdon and the United States made deliveries by horse and cart. Horses also pulled buses and trams, ambulances, police and fire vehicles, funeral carriages and refuse collectors. These

animals' burdens were heavy and they had a poor life expectancy. Thousands worked as cabs in cities including New York and London. In the UK, heavier horses pulled boats along canals and large vehicles on rails, even after the invention of steam trains in the early 1800s. Throughout the Industrial Revolution and until the 1990s, ponies transported coal in mines. The wealthy kept horses and carriages or dogcarts for private use, or smaller vehicles such as gigs and phaetons.

## Fascinating Facts

The renowned American Pony Express, which carried mail from Missouri to California from 1860–61, inspired the 1950s Western *Pony Express*, starring Charlton Heston.

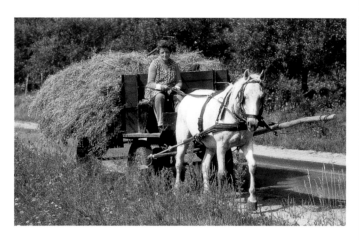

## Agriculture

Horses have played an essential role in agriculture around the world for thousands of years and still do so in areas of Eastern Europe, such as Romania, as well as parts of the developing world. The horse's role in farming changed over time and has now largely been filled by machinery. Many economies relied heavily on horse-powered agriculture until the invention of tractors, at which point millions of horses bred for farming became surplus to requirements.

### Farm Horses

Horses worked the land in countries including the United Kingdom and the United States by pulling ploughs, transporting produce and being used for logging. Other countries, such as China, used oxen and mules for farming, keeping horses for transport and military purposes. Oxen proved stronger but slower than the relatively small horses available. Countries that opted to use horses in agriculture had to breed heavier 'draught' types capable of pulling heavy ploughs and loads. They also developed lighter ploughs that the horses could cope with more easily and which suited their faster movement, therefore increasing productivity. Later on in North America, teams of horses were used to pull large combine harvesters, while other horse-drawn machinery included reapers and threshing equipment. Even in the United States, horses are still used for ranching today.

### Horse Products

Before their domestication, horses were hunted for meat and they are still slaughtered for food in parts of the world today. Countries including Mongolia consume horse

milk and produce *kumis*, which is fermented mare's milk. Horsehide is used to make a variety of leather goods, while horsetails can be used to make bows for string instruments. Parts of the horse, including their hooves and skin, can be turned into glue. In the United States, hormones are extracted from pregnant mares' urine to be used for hormone replacement therapy.

## Police

Mounted police still operate in the twenty-first century all around the world, in countries including the United States, Japan, Canada, Australia, India, the United Kingdon and many parts of Europe. They are predominantly used for patrol and crowd control. In countries including India they might be used to control crowds at a festival, while in the United Kingdon they are often seen outside football matches where they intimidate potential troublemakers. Horses also form part of search-and-rescue teams in areas that are hard to reach by vehicle.

### Police around the World

Mounted police form part of border patrols in countries such as India and the United States, where US Customs and Border Protection monitors the border of Mexico, to prevent illegal immigration and other unlawful activities. The

Royal Canadian Mounted Police (RCMP), with their distinctive red uniforms and 'Mounty' nickname, used to be solely responsible for law enforcement and keeping the peace in large areas of desolate landscape throughout Canada. Mounted police in the RCMP are still commonly seen – mostly on patrol in national parks (as are American mounted police), and they also take part in musical rides. British police horses also take part in displays, where they can be

seen jumping through hoops of fire. Police horses commonly wear protective tack, including kneepads and a clear shield across their face, when attending demonstrations where riots are predicted. Police also use horses when controlling and directing traffic in busy cities around the world.

### Training Police Horses

Police horses have to be trained to cope in loud and frightening situations where their instinct is to flee. They

undergo months of special training to ensure they will be unfazed by traffic, large crowds, loud noises, smoke and other potential hazards. Some horses with nervous dispositions never take to this line of work and are sold out of the police force.

BELOW

*The United States mounted border patrol operates primarily along the Mexican-American border to prevent illegal immigration. The horses are able to navigate terrain unsuitable for vehicles and form an essential part of the team.*

## Sport

As machinery has replaced horses in agriculture, transport and warfare in the developed world, horses are now most commonly used for leisure activities and sport. Professional horsemen and women earn money from training, selling, breeding and competing horses. The most popular horse sport, racing, with its links to gambling, has the greatest effect on the economy.

### Harness Racing

The Persians used horses for racing as early as 600 BC. Chariot racing with teams of four and two horses took place in Ancient Greece at early Olympiads, as well as racing on horseback. The Romans also held chariot

*The British Grand National is the most famous steeplechase, and one of the most challenging in the world. It attracts over 600 million viewers worldwide. See page 18.*

RIGHT

*ABOVE*

*The Kentucky Derby, a race for three-year old Thoroughbred horses, is one of the most famous flat races in the world. It is held annually on the first Saturday in May and is run over a one and a quarter mile dirt track.*

races. Harness racing is popular now in Australia, New Zealand, Russia, parts of Europe and predominantly the United States. Horses are raced at two different paces, either trotting (with the legs moving in diagonal pairs) or pacing (where the legs move in lateral pairs). The driver sits in a lightweight buggy called a 'sulky'. In Switzerland, harness races take place on snow using a sleigh instead of a wheeled vehicle.

### Flat Racing

Britain is the home of racing and, from the 1600s, British breeders developed the Thoroughbred racehorse. The United Kingdom's flat racing governing body, the Jockey Club, is located in Newmarket, which is also the most popular base for trainers. Flat races in the United Kingdom and Europe run, predominantly on grass, between March and October, although all-weather tracks are also used. The biggest flat races in the United Kingdom include the Derby, the Oaks and the St Leger. The United Kingdom's most famous flat courses include Epsom, Doncaster and Goodwood. Despite being based on the British model, flat races in the United States commonly run on dirt tracks. Lexington, Kentucky, is the home of flat racing and of the famous Kentucky Derby. In the United States, American Quarter Horses are used for the shorter, sprinting races (of just two furlongs or quarter of a mile – hence the name Quarter Horses), rather than the Thoroughbreds required in British racing. Thoroughbreds are raced in longer sprints, however.

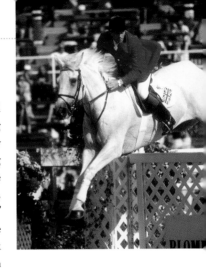

## Show Jumping

Show jumping developed from the cavalry training of horses over cross-country fences. Show-jumping competitions became more common in the late 1800s, and team events (Nations' Cups) were dominated by the military for decades. Back then, style played a part in the competition, whereas in the twenty-first century penalty marks are scored for time faults or jumping errors such as a knockdown or refusal. Show jumping is an Olympic sport affiliated to the international equestrian federation (Fédération Equestre Internationale, or

### Jump Racing

The US's Maryland Hunt Cup is a cross-country race featuring fixed fences and is a variation of steeplechasing, which is a popular sport in the UK and Ireland where horses race over obstacles built of natural materials. Steeplechases are longer than flat races, and the jumps are large, challenging and can feature drops, ditches and water. The UK's most famous steeplechase, the Grand National, has 30 impressive fences and takes place at Aintree, Liverpool, each year.

The legendary Red Rum won the Grand National a record three times. Other great steeplechases include the Cheltenham Gold Cup, held at Cheltenham racecourse in Gloucestershire, and the Pardubice, which is held in the Czech Republic. Hurdle races are similar to steeplechases, but run over smaller fences that give when the horse hits them. Point-to-pointing is a form of jump racing for amateurs organized by hunts around the UK and also takes place in Ireland.

# Fascinating Facts

Great courses such as the Hickstead Derby, in Sussex, England, feature extra, named, obstacles such as the 'Derby Bank' and 'Devil's Dyke'.

---
LEFT
---

*Opened in 1975, Spruce Meadows in Alberta, Canada, is one of the foremost equestrian facilities and holds top-level show jumping competitions between February and November.*

FEI). Competition formats vary, and classes can include several rounds. There are competitions for speed and, in puissance classes (the high jump), a wall is built up until there is only one horse remaining that can clear it. A common show-jumping track includes portable fences of coloured poles. Popular international events include those that take place at Spruce Meadows, in Alberta, Canada, and at Aachen, Germany.

## Leisure

In countries where horses are no longer required for transport and farming, they are now hired or kept for leisure purposes. Horses are playing a larger role in tourism, too – for example, being used on horseback safaris and ranching holidays. Millions of people worldwide learn horsemanship at riding schools and enjoy hiring horses for trekking excursions. Millions more

keep horses and ponies for leisure either at livery yards or on their own land. Popular activities include hacking, trail riding and hunting, plus riding club and Pony Club activities.

**Types of Leisure Riding**

Horse owners also compete for leisure, often through clubs or associations. Competition formats vary in different countries and each has their own governing body. In showing, exhibitors present their horse or pony to a judge to be assessed for conformation, movement and

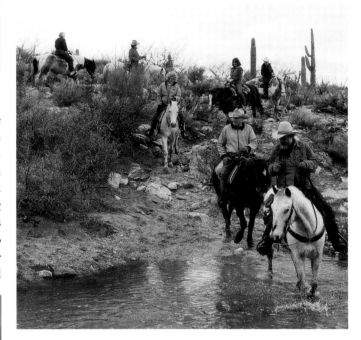

manners. Classes are split for different breeds and types. There are both in-hand and ridden classes, and handlers can also use lead reins on small ponies with very young riders. In hunter classes, competitors also jump a course of rustic fences.

Dressage is an Olympic sport, but at lower levels is a popular leisure activity. Dressage means training a horse to the highest possible level, so that it accurately

performs a number of movements at different paces in a relaxed way in response to the rider's subtle aids. Eventing is a complete competition combining dressage, show jumping and cross-country, which is a test of endurance and bravery over challenging natural fences. Events take place over one, two or three days. Other sports for leisure riders include show jumping, polo, driving and endurance.

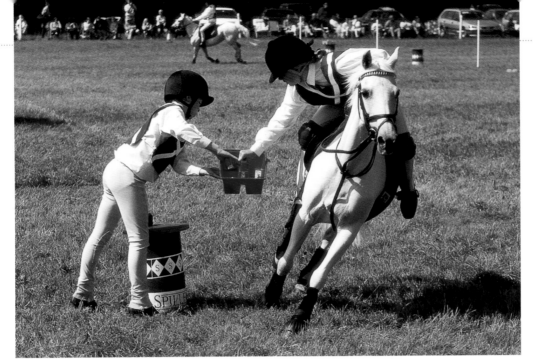

### Young Riders

Hundreds of pony clubs are active in the United Kingdom, the United States, Canada, Australia and New Zealand, teaching riding, horse management and teamwork through rallies and camps during the holidays. Countries including the UK and the US have schemes that young riders can join to concentrate on one discipline, such as show jumping, and train to compete against children from other regions or internationally. Some schools and universities also have their own riding clubs.

### Fascinating Facts

The Annual Brooksville Raid Festival has become the largest civil war re-enactment in Florida, USA, with over 3,700 re-enactors and their families participating in 2007, where they also had 32 cannons and 78 horses.

### Other Popular Activities

In the United States and Canada, and other parts of the world such as Australia and Argentina, rodeos are popular with spectators, who witness professional riders on bucking broncos, bareback riding and roping. The US Professional Rodeo Cowboys Association governs rodeos in the United States, and competition involves prize money. Women more commonly take part in barrel racing, where riders are timed racing around barrels set at points in the arena. Western classes are also more common in the United States. In these competitions, riders have to demonstrate how responsive their horses are to their aids through a variety of movements and obstacles. The level of difficulty at such events ranges from the most straightforward pleasure classes to reining, which is an international sport featuring difficult manoeuvres performed at speed.

### Hunting

Hunting on horseback, which used to be essential for food, is now a form of pest control and a leisure activity for all ages of riders in countries including the UK, Ireland, France, New Zealand and the United States. Packs of hounds most commonly hunt foxes, boar and stag, depending on the area. In places where hunts have been banned from hunting with hounds, they still follow a trail of laid scent. Hunts in the UK are currently seeking to overturn a ban. Drag hunting, where riders and hounds follow a 'line', is also a popular pastime.

### Re-enactments

Riders can combine an interest in horses with history by joining historical re-enactments of famous battles. Horses and riders are dressed in clothing and tack appropriate for the era, adding to the authenticity. In the United States, re-enactments of the Civil War are popular, and some take place on the actual battlegrounds. In the UK, common re-enactments include those of the English Civil War and campaigns from the Napoleonic era.

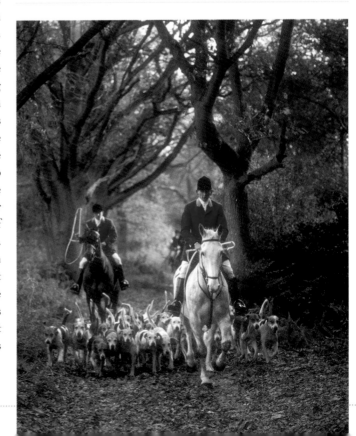

# Industry and Commerce

Around the world, horses play a significant role within world economies, whether this is through farming, transport, tourism, sport or leisure.

## The Horse's Contribution to World Economies

Ranching is still big industry in areas including North and South America, and horsemeat is a major source of income for many farmers elsewhere. Horses are used heavily in the developing world within agriculture and transport, too. In the industrialized world, horses mainly contribute to the economy through their roles in sport and leisure. Racing has a large impact on these economies, partly due to its association with gambling. In the future, horses may play a lesser role in farming and transport in developing countries, but leisure and sporting activities are likely to expand as these countries become wealthier. Jobs supported by the horse industry include areas such as retail, saddlery, farriery, grooming, veterinary and farming, as well as horse breeders, trainers and dealers.

## American and British Horse Economies

In 2005, the American Horse Council commissioned Deloitte Consulting to produce a study entitled *The Economic Impact of the Horse Industry in the United States*. This study found that the US horse industry made a $39 billion impact on the American economy. When including indirect and induced spending, this figure reached $102 billion. The report found there were

9.2 million horses in the United States, supporting 1.4 million jobs.

The British Equestrian Trade Association's (BETA) National Equestrian Survey 2006 concluded that horse owners and riders in the United Kingdom spend around £4 billion on their leisure activity. It stated that there are around 1.35 million horses in the UK. At least one person from 2.1 million British households had ridden or driven a horse regularly in the past year, and at least one person from 1 million households is responsible for a horse's upkeep.

# HORSES IN HUMAN CULTURE

The tremendous impact that horses have had on the progress of civilization is reflected in the high regard in which horses have been held throughout history. This regard has been demonstrated through both literature and art over the centuries. The fact that horses were even placed up with the gods in mythology illustrates their significance in the ancient world, and many cultures have built legends and traditions based on the importance of the horse and the reverence held for it.

## Ancient Significance around the World

Horses played a hugely significant role in ancient civilizations, changing the way people lived, worked and fought. At first, horses were solely used for meat. The first paintings of horses, dated around 30,000 BC, were found on cave walls at Chauvet, France, but bones have been found in areas where humans are known to have lived more than 50,000 years ago. Thousands more bones were found at the bottom of cliffs, suggesting that horses were hunted off steep drops.

Some scholars believe that man began keeping horses for milk and meat on the steppes of Central Asia from 4000 BC; others argue horses were not domesticated until around 2000 BC. Horses have been found with tack in chariot burials in northern Kazakhstan dating back to this era. Studies do agree that domestication may have taken place in several areas of Eurasia around the same time.

### Ride or Drive

Scholars do know that horses were being ridden before 1345 BC, when the Hittite horse master Kikkuli wrote about how to keep and train chariot horses. (It is thought that horses were not ridden in areas of the Middle East until around 1000 BC.)

The Hittites' power increased with their knowledge of horse warfare. They used horses for transport and later developed cavalry; some people believe this is because they had to breed bigger horses in order to start riding.

It may have become essential for men to ride in order to herd livestock, but it is not known exactly

when. Early bridles were like modern hackamores, with no bit through the horse's mouth, and the first mouthpieces were made of soft material such as hide. Metal bits date back to *c.* 1500 BC. As tack developed, riders would have more control over the horses whether driving or riding.

## The Roman Empire

The Roman army initially depended more on infantry, but before long there was demand for mounted troops. The Greeks began chariot racing at the Olympics from 684 BC, but the sport was even more popular with the Romans. They built the Circus Maximus in Rome, which had a capacity of around 250,000, suggestive of the importance of this sport in their lives. With their impressive roads, the Romans were also best able to utilize horses for transport.

## Chinese Invention

The Chinese developed their cavalry and began using archers on horseback to defend themselves from the Huns from around 1500 BC. China also set up advanced breeding programmes, importing stallions from Southeast Asia. The Chinese are credited with developing more effective harnesses that went around the horse's chest, as well as the first metal stirrups.

## Scythian and Greek Horsemen

The Scythians are thought to have started using archery in warfare from around 800 BC. They invaded Eurasia and settled before being removed by the Persians. Wealthy Scythians have been found buried with their horses and objects bearing images of the horse, suggesting the horse's great significance to this nation.

In Greece, riders began to replace chariots with drivers some time around 700 BC. In his writings, the Greek soldier Xenophon (c. 430–355 BC) encouraged greater sensitivity in his compatriots' riding. Alexander the Great was perhaps the most accomplished Greek horseman, having extended an empire from the back of his horse, Bucephalus.

LEFT

*Alexander the Great's heroic horse Bucephalus would only let Alexander ride him, and was said to have been a 'Thessalonian' bred horse, that is, from the plains of Thessaly. He died during battle in 327 BC at thirty years old, and was given a full, military burial.*

# Fascinating Facts

Some scholars believe that a 35,000-year-old ivory carving of a horse found in Germany had spiritual significance.

## Horses in Myth and Legend

### Greek and Roman Mythology

Horses feature heavily in Greek and Roman mythology, often in connection with the ruler of horses, Poseidon (Roman name: Neptune). One such example is Arion, the swift, immortal horse described in Homer's *Iliad*. Arion is said to be the offspring of Demeter, who turned herself into a mare to avoid the advances of Poseidon, only for Poseidon to turn himself into a horse as well.

Poseidon is said to have given two immortal horses, Balius and Xanthos (*see* below right, pictured), to Peleus, whose son Achilles drove them in the Trojan War. When Patroclus, dressed as Achilles, led the Myrmidons to fight the Trojans he was killed, and Achilles reprimanded the two horses for leaving Patroclus on the battlefield. Xanthos turned to Achilles and prophesied his death in war, having been given a voice by the goddess Hera.

At the end of this war, Greek soldiers sent the wooden Trojan horse (*see* left, pictured) that is described in Virgil's *Aeneid* as a gift to Troy. The horse held Greek soldiers who opened the gates of the city for the returning army to enter and attack while Troy celebrated the end of the war.

The winged horse Pegasus is thought to be the son of Poseidon, having formed from Medusa's blood when Perseus cut off her head (Medusa was impregnated by Poseidon). Bellerophon, who rode Pegasus when killing monsters including the Chimaera, tried to ride the horse to Mount Olympus, but Zeus made him fall to the ground, crippled. Pegasus later carried the goddess of the dawn, Eos.

Heracles (Roman name: Hercules) had to capture the flesh-eating horses of Diomedes for Eurystheus as the eighth of his 12 labours. Heracles released them on to high ground and dug a trench around them. He then killed Diomedes and fed him to the horses. Having eaten, the horses were calm and allowed Heracles to capture them.

## Norse Mythology

Odin, father of the Norse gods, was given an eight-legged horse called Sleipnir by the god Loki. Sleipnir was able to run over land and sea. Loki turned himself into a mare to lure the stallion Svadilfari away from the mason who was rebuilding the wall around Asgard that protected the gods from the giants. The mason had been promised the goddess Frigg if he completed the work in six months, and would fail without the stallion's help. Sleipnir is said to be the offspring of Loki and the stallion.

Frigg, the goddess of love, had a messenger called Gna who rode the horse Hofvarpnir, who could also run over land and water.

## Irish and Celtic Mythology

In Irish mythology, Niamh, the daughter of the sea god Manannan Mac Lir, rode a horse called Embarr. She rode him over the sea to Ireland, as the horse could run on water, and fell in love with Oisin, taking him back with her to Tir na n'Og. After three years he returned to

### ABOVE

*The myth of the centaurs, creatures with the body of a horse and the torso and head of a man, is thought to have derived from non-riding cultures of the ancient Minoan Aegean world first seeing nomadic peoples on horseback.*

Ireland, where 300 years had passed, riding Embarr. He touched the soil, which Niamh had told him not to, and became an old man.

Kelpies are a feature of Celtic myth and were feared water horses that haunted Scottish rivers. A Kelpie could turn itself into different guises, such as a grazing horse. If a man tried to ride the horse, it would run in to the water and drown him.

### Arthurian Legend

According to legend, King Arthur's horse, Llamrai, helped him to destroy the afanc, the monster of the lake Llyn Barfog. Arthur placed a chain around the lake, and he and Llamrai pulled the monster out and killed it. There is a stone near the lake known as the Stone of Arthur's Horse that is believed to carry Llamrai's hoof print.

# Fascinating Facts

According to Greek mythology, centaurs were creatures — half man and half horse — that often succumbed to their more bestial nature symbolizing the dark and unruly forces of nature.

### LEFT AND CENTRE

*The winged horse Pegasus is one of the most famous mythical horses. He is shown here, in a painting by Alexander Ivanov, with Bellerophon, as the hero sets out to defeat the Chimera. On page 24 (centre) he is ridden by Perseus carrying the head of Medusa.*

# Horses in Art

As the horse's relationship with humankind has developed, so too has the way in which it has been depicted in art. The earliest examples of horses in art are cave paintings dating back as far as 30,000 BC, such as those discovered in France during the twentieth century. There are various explanations as to why prehistoric man chose to paint horses; some believe that the images have spiritual significance, whereas others suggest that they formed a type of hunting map. The fact that horses were painted so frequently suggests their importance to prehistoric man, be it spiritual or physical.

Horses are still a popular subject for art in the twenty-first century, but less so than in the past when they featured more heavily in human civilization. Every activity that horses have taken part in, from warfare, through jousting, to racing and dressage, has been a key subject for artists of various eras.

## The Physical Development of the Horse in Art

The horse's appearance in art tells us something about their physical development, as well as their uses during different periods. As an example, light, fast sport horses pulling racing chariots were a popular feature in Roman mosaics. The Egyptians painted chariot warfare on wood, with the horses appearing petite compared to the men in their chariots. The Chinese emperor Qin Shi Huang's Terracotta Army included horses of a still small but sturdy stature (*see* page 22).

## Horses in Art in Their Different Roles

Horses have been featured in art in all their roles, even down to a mare being milked in Eugene Delacroix's (1798–1863) *Ovid among the Scythians* (1859). Agricultural horses became a more popular subject for artists from the 1700s, while hunting scenes

have been produced for centuries, from the British and French tapestries of the sixteenth and seventeenth centuries, to the oil-on-canvas Cornish hunting scenes of Alfred Munnings (1878–1959).

The most common portrayal of horses in art is at war. Famous examples include the Bayeux Tapestry, which was commissioned in the 1070s

## Fascinating Facts

Eadweard Muybridge, the inventor of the motion picture, took a series of pictures entitled *The Horse in Motion*, which answered questions about the horse's gallop, demonstrating that during mid gait all four of the horse's hooves leave the ground and tuck underneath the animal rather than extending out from the animal as previous artistic representations depicted.

after the Normans conquered England at the Battle of Hastings in 1066. Hundreds of horses in battle are stitched with wool into the linen. Another groundbreaking example, due to his use of perspective, is the *Rout of San Romano* (c. 1456) by Paolo Uccello (1397–1475), which depicts warfare between the cavalries of Siena and Florence. The English painter Alfred Munnings travelled to France to paint Canadian troops with their horses as well as battle scenes. War reporter and artist

Richard Caton Woodville (1856–1927) most famously produced the *Charge of the Light Brigade* (1854).

## The Horse as a Symbol of Greatness

Horses appeared in portraits of great kings and generals, and added prestige to these works because of their significance in the development of civilization. They acted as a symbol of strength and wealth. For example, in royal artist Anthony van Dyck's (1599–1641) *Equestrian*

*Portrait of Charles I* (c. 1637–8), the king is mounted on a huge horse and, by appearing to control the prancing beast effortlessly, symbolizes his power. British painter George Stubbs (1724–1806) was perhaps the first artist to make the horse central to a painting, rather than simply serving to add splendour to the composition. His oil on canvas *Whistlejacket* (1762) appears to be purely a tribute to the great stallion, which started a trend continued even today for immortalizing top sport horses in art.

## Horses of Legend in Art

Other popular topics for artists who incorporated horses in their work include the biblical Four Horsemen of the Apocalypse, mythical creatures such as unicorns and centaurs, and the winged horse Pegasus. Pre-Raphaelite artists, among others, also depicted horses from Arthurian legend.

*Black Beauty, the book that told the story of a horse's life, became an instant bestseller, and continues to be greatly read and loved by children around the world.*

## Horses in Literature and Film

Horses appear in literature and film in the various roles they have served humankind throughout history. In addition, there is a plethora of books and films where horses are the lead characters. These stories often tell of the hardships faced by equines at the hands of humans from the horse's perspective. Anna Sewell's *Black Beauty*, which was first published in 1877, follows the life of a black gelding. The horse tells his own story under various ownership, as well as those of his companions, including Ginger, who dies in service as a carthorse; Merrylegs, a well-behaved children's pony; and an old war horse. Through these stories, Sewell describes the often poor treatment of the workhorses of her era.

**Superior Horses in Fiction**

J.R.R. Tolkien, in his trilogy *The Lord of the Rings* (1954–5), which was brought to the big screen by Peter Jackson, describes a race of wild horses called Mearas that live in Middle-earth. These animals are superior to normal horses, live longer and are more intelligent. The kings of Rohan predominantly ride them. The chief of the Mearas is Shadowfax, who is ridden by one of the heroes of the novel, Gandalf, without a saddle or bridle. It has been suggested that Shadowfax's name derives from the horses of Norse mythology Skinfaxi and Hrinfaxi, who pulled the moon and the sun.

Jonathan Swift's *Gulliver's Travels* (1726) also features a superior race of horses called the Houyhnhnms, who are a particularly rational and intelligent species.

**Children's Books**

Horses have been a popular topic for children's stories over the past century, one example being Mary O'Hara's trilogy that began with *My Friend Flicka*, in 1941. The book follows the lives of a rancher's son, Ken McLaughlin, and his horse Flicka. This book and its two sequels, *Thunderhead, Son of Flicka* (1943) and *Green Grass of Wyoming* (1946), were adapted for film.

*The Black Stallion* was also published in 1941, being the first in a series of books by Walter Farley, and again was later made into a film. The books tell the story of a wild stallion and a boy, Alec Ramsay.

*The Silver Brumby* (1958–2003) series of children's books by Elyne Mitchell follows the adventures of a wild stallion, Thowra, and his progeny, and are set in Australia (where wild horses are known as 'brumbies'). His colour, palomino, means that other horses are hostile to Thowra, while men try to capture him.

*The iconic American hero, the Lone Ranger, rode his trusty horse Silver through endless dangers and adventures saving the day and righting injustices.*

*My Friend Flicka, the story of a young boy and his horse who he tames, has touched the hearts of children (and adults) since it was written in 1941. It was adapted for the big screen in 1943, and was also made into a television series.*

ABOVE

*Young Velvet Brown wins The Pie, a piebald gelding, in a village raffle, and goes on to win the Grand National on him in* National Velvet.

**From Book to Film**

*National Velvet* (1935), by Enid Bagnold, tells the story of a girl called Velvet Brown who, disguised as a boy, enters her horse, The Pie, in the United Kingdom's Grand National steeplechase. The novel became a popular film starring Elizabeth Taylor (1944), and in 1978 a sequel was produced called *International Velvet*, starring Tatum O'Neal.

The book *The Horse Whisperer* (1995), by Nicholas Evans, was adapted for the big screen by Robert Redford in 1998. Here a teenage girl, Grace MacLean, suffers a road accident with her horse Pilgrim. Grace loses part of one leg and the horse is scared and traumatized. Grace's mother, Annie, seeks the help of a horse whisperer, Tom Booker, to regain Pilgrim's trust and in turn aid her daughter's recovery. Nicholas Evans based the retraining of the horse in his novel on the methods of real horse trainers he met in the American West.

The story of champion American racehorse Seabiscuit (1933–1947) was made into a film in 1949, *The Story of Seabiscuit*, and again in 2003, *Seabiscuit*, which received an Oscar nomination for best picture. The story of this racehorse, who came through to win against all odds, captured the imagination of the American people during the Great Depression.

## Fascinating Facts

The 'wild' mustangs that the character Tom Smith is chasing at the beginning of the film Seabiscuit are shod.

ABOVE

*The book and film adaptation of Seabiscuit is based on the true-life story of a remarkable racehorse in America. The little horse was an unlikely champion being small, weak and lazy as a youngster, although he developed into one of the equine greats.*

LEFT

The Horse Whisperer
*A Quarter Horse called High Tower played the role of Pilgrim for the film The Horse Whisperer, although he also had several stand-in horses during filming, to give him a break. High Tower also appeared as Ginger in Black Beauty, and with Julia Roberts in Runaway Bride.*

# ANATOMY AND APPEARANCE

Physically, horses and ponies vary as much as, if not more than, humans. The different breeds and types all have their own characteristics. Although all horses may look like similar large, four-legged animals to the untrained observer, to the expert it is obvious that each equine is an individual, with its own shape, colour and personality. Biologically, the horse is a complex system. Horses have more than 200 bones, as well as a well-developed muscular system and numerous essential organs.

## POINTS OF THE HORSE

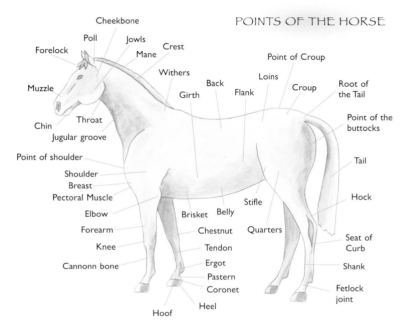

## Points, Skeleton and Organs

Before we consider the points, skeleton and organs of a horse, we should look at the straightforward aspects of height and weight.

Horses are measured at the highest point of the withers, the bony part at the base of the neck. Traditionally, horses are measured in hands, each hand being 10 cm (4 in). The common abbreviation for this is 'hh' (hands high), so a horse might be described as 15.2 hh (15 hands and 2 in). Ponies measure 14.2 hh or less. More recently, equines have started to be measured in centimetres for competitions, so, for example, some 12.2 hh classes have been replaced by 128-cm classes.

A 16.2 hh horse weighs, on average, around 600 kg (94 stones 7 pounds), depending on its type and condition.

### Points of the Horse
These are the terms used to describe certain specific external parts of the horse. The 'points' of the horse include the muzzle, poll, withers, stifle, hock, girth, quarters and tail, among others. They have several practical applications, such as in telling a vet exactly where a horse is injured or judging conformation. If used in relation to describing colour, the points of the horse refer to the mane, tail, muzzle, tips of the ears and lower legs.

### Skeleton
The horse's skeleton has two separate parts, the axial and appendicular skeletons.

The **axial** skeleton is the skull, backbone and ribcage (including the sternum and the ribs). It protects vital organs such as the brain, spinal cord, heart and lungs, and gives the body shape. The backbone does not run all the way along the top of the horse. Behind the horse's poll it curves downwards towards the underside of the neck. As the shape of the crest of the neck is determined by muscle, not bone, it can be changed by exercise.

The **appendicular** skeleton consists of the bones of the horse's legs, and the associated bones in the shoulders and hindquarters. The horse's muscles attach to the skeleton and work with ligaments and tendons to allow the animal to move.

## SKELETON OF THE HORSE

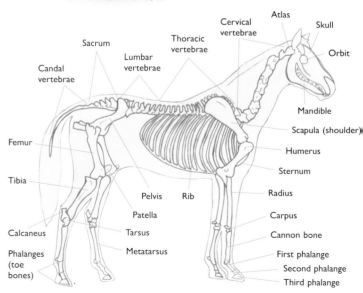

## Principal Organs and Systems

The horse's heart sits slightly to the left side of its chest and pumps blood around the body. Gaseous exchange, which sends oxygen around the body in the blood and returns carbon dioxide to the lungs to be breathed out, takes place in the lungs.

The horse's food passes from the mouth, down the oesophagus and into the stomach. The muscle at the entrance to the stomach, the cardiac sphincter, is like a one-way street: food cannot pass back through it, so horses cannot vomit.

Digestion begins in the stomach. The food gradually passes into the small intestine, which is around 22 m long, then into the shorter large intestine. As food travels along the intestines, it is broken down

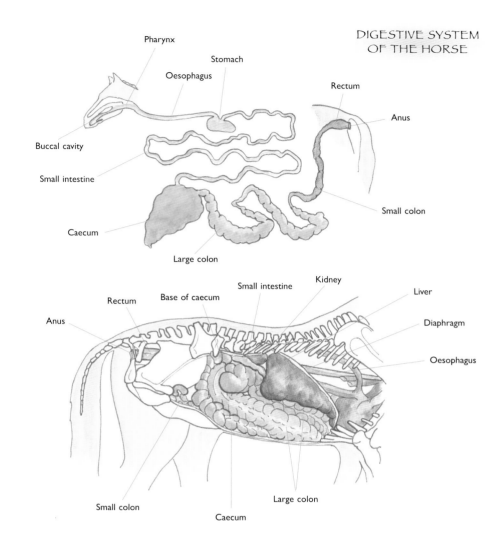

DIGESTIVE SYSTEM OF THE HORSE

Pharynx
Stomach
Oesophagus
Rectum
Anus
Buccal cavity
Small intestine
Small colon
Caecum
Large colon

Rectum
Base of caecum
Small intestine
Kidney
Liver
Anus
Diaphragm
Oesophagus
Small colon
Large colon
Caecum

MUSCULAR SYSTEM OF THE HORSE

Mastoido humeralus
Splenius
Serratus magnus
Gluteus esternus
Trapezius
Latissimus dorsii
Fascia lata
Biceps abductor femoris
Sterno maxillaris
Pectoralis parvus
Antea spinatus
Postea spinatus
Terus externus (long abductor of the arm)
Rectus abdominus
Intercostal muscles
Triceps extensor brachii
Serratus magnus
Obliquus adominus externus

and nutrients are absorbed through the walls into the blood. By the time the food reaches the rectum, only waste is left, which leaves the horse's body as droppings through the anus.

Approximately 65 per cent of the horse's body consists of water. The horse has two kidneys, which filter the blood and send the waste and excess water to the bladder, where it is held until the horse urinates.

The horse also has a complex nervous system, a reproductive system, an endocrine system for releasing hormones and a lymphatic system, which drains excess fluid and helps the body to fight infection.

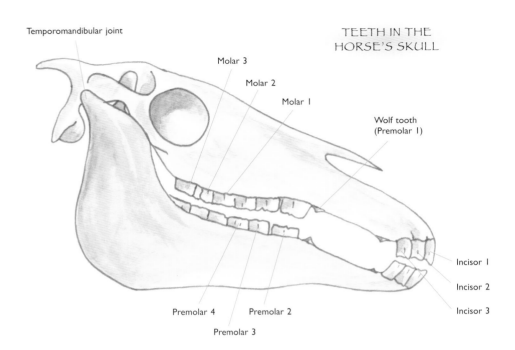

Temporomandibular joint

TEETH IN THE
HORSE'S SKULL

Molar 3

Molar 2

Molar 1

Wolf tooth
(Premolar 1)

Incisor 1

Incisor 2

Incisor 3

Premolar 4       Premolar 2

Premolar 3

*The first of the temporary foal teeth
to erupt are the two central incisors
on the top and bottom jaw, as seen.*

## Teeth and Age

**Milk and Permanent Teeth**
Foals have a full set of milk teeth, some of which may be present at birth. The milk teeth continue to develop until the horse is around a year old. From the age of two and a half, the horse sheds its milk teeth and the permanent teeth replace them.

**How Many Teeth?**
Adult horses usually have 12 incisors, 12 premolars and 12 molars. Incisors are the biting teeth at the front of the mouth, while the premolars and molars are used for chewing and are at the back. In addition, male horses (stallions or geldings, which are castrated males) generally have four canines (or tushes) in the 'interdental space' between the incisors and the premolars. Females (mares) do not usually have canines

and, if they do, they are likely to be small. So most adult geldings and stallions have 40 teeth, while mares have 36.

Some horses also have one or more wolf teeth. These sit in front of the second premolar (the first tooth behind the interdental space) and are the remnants of the old defunct first premolar. Sometimes the wolf teeth cause pain or problems with the bit and are removed.

## Ageing

An experienced person can age younger horses with some accuracy. After the age of eight there are clues, but even an expert can be 5 to 10 years out in their estimation. The development of the incisors is the clearest ageing tool.

The middle two incisors on each jaw are the central incisors. The temporary centrals are the first milk teeth to come out, at two-and-a-half years, and by three the horse will have its full permanent centrals. At three and a half, the next two teeth back on each jaw on each side, the temporary lateral incisors, come out, replaced by the age of four by their permanent equivalents.

At four and a half, the horse sheds the temporary corner

incisors, the furthest back of these front teeth. By the age of five, their permanent replacements are fully grown. Males generally grow their tushes between the ages of four and five.

At seven, a hook appears on the corner incisors of the top jaw, hanging over the top of the lower corner incisors. This will remain for around a year. Another hook can appear later in life, often at around 13, which is generally permanent. As the horse ages, the teeth slope forwards more and appear longer.

**Galvayne's Groove** This develops down the outside of the upper corner incisors. The groove usually appears at around the age of 10, will be halfway down the tooth at 15 and stretches to the bottom at 20. By the age of 25, the groove will have disappeared from the top half of the tooth and at 30 it will have gone altogether.

## Tables

The teeth wear down with

use, and more is pushed up through the gum. The top surface of the lower incisors, the 'tables', can be used to help with ageing, as a different cross-section is exposed.

In the younger horse, a large dark hole shows in the centre of the table, called the 'infundibulum'. This gets smaller with age until it disappears completely. As the infundibulum shrinks, a black mark between it and the front of the teeth grows. This is the 'dental star'.

The central incisors show these changes first, then the laterals, and next the corner incisors. By the time the horse is eight years old, the infundibulum is likely to be nearly gone or have disappeared completely, with the dental star much in evidence. With continuing wear, the dental star becomes a dot in the middle of the tooth.

With increasing age, the tables also become more triangular.

## TEETH IN THE HORSE'S SKULL

3 Years

5 Years

10 Years

15 Years

20 Years

## STRUCTURE OF THE FOOT

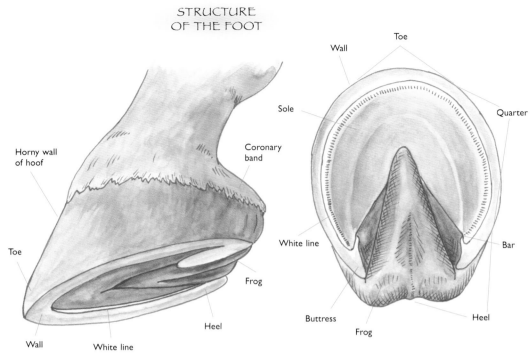

Horny wall of hoof

Toe

Wall

White line

Coronary band

Sole

White line

Frog

Heel

Toe

Wall

Sole

Quarter

White line

Bar

Buttress

Frog

Heel

### Bones

The main bone in the foot is the pedal bone. Above this, the short pastern extends from the lower leg down into the foot. The joint between the pedal bone and the short pastern is the coffin joint. Behind this is a small bone called the 'navicular' bone.

### Other Structures

Inside the hoof wall are the laminae, which are like leaves of tissue attaching the wall to the pedal bone. The insensitive, horny laminae are on the outside, by the wall, with the sensitive laminae inside them.

## Structure of the Foot

### External parts

The outside of the horse's foot, which can be seen when the foot is on the ground, is called the 'hoof wall'. When the foot is lifted, the sole and frog underneath are visible. The wall grows continuously, taking about a year to regenerate from top to bottom. The domesticated horse wears the foot down faster than happens in the wild, which is why most horses wear metal shoes. A farrier will trim the foot and replace the shoes approximately every six weeks.

A large percentage of lamenesses stem from the foot, either following an injury such as a sharp object piercing the sole or due to poor foot shape or internal problems, which can be triggered by bad conformation. Corrective shoeing can sometimes help.

Probably the largest non-bony structure in the foot is the digital or plantar cushion, a piece of tissue at the back of the foot below the bones. Below this and the

RIGHT

*Nuzzling and chewing each other, as seen, is an important part of socializing and bonding for horses, and also helps to remove parasites from hard to reach places.*

## The Senses

The horse evolved as a grazing animal and its natural defence is flight not fight, so its senses are therefore highly developed to detect approaching danger.

### Sight and Hearing

The horse's eyes are on the side of its head, giving it an excellent range of vision. With its head down grazing, the horse can see nearly all around it, although it does have limited vision directly in front and behind it. It is thought that horses may have a more limited colour vision than humans, or see colours differently. They see better in the dark, however, and can probably see further than humans.

Horses have finely tuned hearing. Their two large ears are highly mobile so that they can pick up sound from every direction. The brain analyses incoming sounds from both ears and works out from where the noises originate.

### Taste, Smell and Touch

Anyone who has tried to feed a horse medicine knows that these animals have an acute sense of smell and taste. In the wild, these senses would prevent them from eating poisonous plants, while smell would help them to recognize other members of their herd and to detect predators.

Horses tasting or smelling something unusual will sometimes display the flehmen response, lifting the head and curling back the upper lip. Stallions also do this as part of sexual behaviour.

Horses are also sensitive to touch. They sometimes even have an involuntary reaction to it, such as twitching the skin to remove flies. They also enjoy some touching; horses will often groom each other with their teeth, and many horses relish the feel of being brushed by their rider.

pedal bone are the sensitive sole and frog, which line their equivalent insensitive external structures. At the top of the horse's foot is the coronet band. Inside, the coronet has an excellent blood supply to carry nutrients to the wall. There are also tendons and ligaments in the foot, which allow movement.

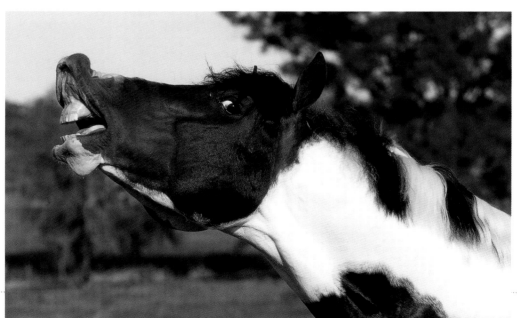

## Fascinating Facts

Horses seem to possess a 'sixth sense', which allows them to tune into human moods and detect danger. There are plenty of stories of horses not wanting to pass places of death or danger, or saving their riders lives by refusing to cross a bridge, which is later found to have collapsed.

---

LEFT

*Curling the top lip back as seen is referred to as the flehmen response, or flehming, and facilitates horses to smell certain scents, particularly pheromones.*

**GOOD CONFORMATION**

*LEFT*

*When assessing conformation the horse must be examined on hard standing and in good light. It is also important to see the horse move on the straight, and in a circle on both reins, to evaluate the way it moves.*

muscled) than that of one which is fit and well. Although some faults can be harder to recognize in the correctly muscled horse, an expert should still be able to pick out serious problems. Equally, an experienced person should be able to spot good conformation in a horse in poor condition.

If the horse's profile is concave, this is known as a 'dish face', and often signifies Arab or Welsh breeding. The opposite, a Roman nose, generally indicates heavy horse blood, but can be a sign of a genuine horse.

Make sure that the head is well set on the neck and that the horse is not 'thick through the gullet'. This will make it difficult for the animal to work in an outline.

The neck should be of good length for a comfortable ride and curve naturally out of the

## Conformation

The horse's conformation describes its shape. Conformation is not just important to make a horse look attractive and move well for the show ring. A horse with good conformation is also likely to stay sound longer, be a more comfortable ride and be able to gallop faster and jump higher.

Although broadly speaking the same conformation traits are desirable whatever sort of horse you are examining, certain points are more

important for different disciplines. For example, a horse with a ewe-neck is never going to make a top dressage horse, but it may be a good jumper. And some horses do break the rules and defy average or poor conformation to stay sound and become excellent performers.

**Assessing Conformation**
Assessing conformation is largely a matter of experience. It is more difficult to assess the conformation of a horse in poor condition (too fat, too thin or wrongly

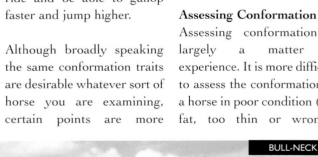

**EWE-NECK**

When assessing a horse's conformation, start by taking an overall look at the animal. Are its different parts in proportion? Does it give an impression of kindness and good character? Next, move on to analyse its different parts.

## Head and Neck
Look for a horse with a kind expression in its eye and an attractive head. Too much white showing in the eye can indicate bad temper, while small 'piggy' eyes can go with an obstinate nature.

shoulder, with the crest well developed. A ewe-neck (well-developed muscle underneath the neck and weak topline, a condition that can sometimes be improved with correct work), bull neck (short and thick) and swan neck (long neck which is dipped in front of the withers, then arched, with the highest point further back than the poll) will all make it hard for the horse to work correctly. If the neck is set too low on the shoulders, the horse will struggle to stay off the forehand and work 'uphill'.

**BULL-NECK**

## Withers, Shoulder and Front Leg

The withers should be higher than the croup in the mature horse or the animal will find it very difficult to work 'uphill'. Young horses' hindquarters are often above the withers. Very high, prominent withers may cause problems with saddle fitting. The horse should have a good angle from the wither to the point of shoulder. This angle dictates the length of its stride and should be the same as the angle of the pastern of the front legs. A horse with an upright shoulder will have a short stride and be less comfortable to ride.

The front legs should be a pair. Viewed from the front, the legs should not turn in or out. The forearms should be well muscled, and the cannon bones should be short because long cannon bones are likely to compromise the horse's soundness. The horse's 'bone' is assessed by measuring the circumference of its leg just below the knee and dictates how much weight it can carry. The amount of bone will vary depending on type, but a horse with too little bone will be weedy and weak.

The knees and fetlocks should be large, flat and well defined, not rounded. The elbow must not be 'tied in', as this will restrict movement. Seen from the side, if the knee appears to be behind the cannon bone, which comes out of it at a forward angle,

HIGH WITHERS

the horse is 'back at the knee'; this is a serious fault that can lead to lameness. In contrast, being mildly 'over at the knee' is not usually a problem.

## Chest, Body and Back

The chest should be broad enough (and the barrel deep enough through the girth) to give adequate room for the heart and lungs. If the chest is too narrow, with 'both front legs out of one hole', the horse is likely to brush (rub or knock its front legs against each other); if it is too wide, the action is likely to be rolling and uncomfortable. 'Well-sprung ribs' means that the ribs come well out from the backbone, giving a comfortable platform for the rider and room for the essential organs.

BACK AT THE KNEE

**HOLLOW BACK**

wide, flat and well muscled. From behind, the hips should be level. A horse with a pronounced croup (buttocks) has a 'jumper's bump', while if the quarters slope sharply from croup to dock (top of the tail) the horse is 'goose-rumped'. Both can indicate a good jumper.

The horse should have good length from the point of hip to the point of buttock and be 'well let down' (good length from stifle to hock). From the side, the point of buttock and point of hock should form a straight line, which then follows down the back of the cannon bone to the fetlocks. If the hocks hang out behind it, the horse will find engagement difficult, and if the fetlocks are in front of the line the hocks will be too bent and weak. These are called 'sickle hocks'.

An excessively long back is likely to be weak, and such a horse will be harder to collect and keep together than one which is 'short-coupled'. A longer back is more common in mares, which need room to carry a foal. A dipped back is called a 'hollow', or 'sway', back and can develop with age, while a 'roach' back curves upwards towards and over the loins.

On a 'herring-gutted' horse, the underside of the body slopes steeply upwards towards the stifle. This is a conformation fault that can be seen whatever condition the horse is in, but many horses will 'run up light' and show this tendency to some extent after hard work.

**Hindquarters and Back Leg**
The hindquarters should be

**POOR HINDLEG CONFORMATION**

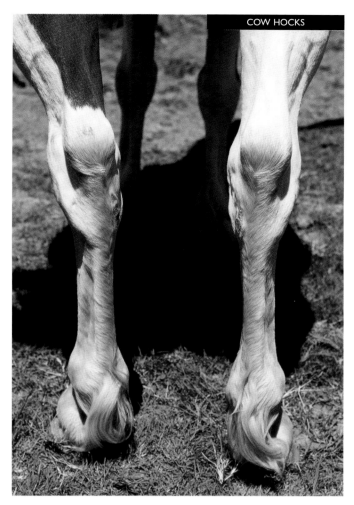

COW HOCKS

The hocks should be large and well defined. Viewed from behind, 'cow hocks' describe those which are turned in, with the toes turned out, while 'bowed hocks' are turned out, with the toes turned in. Both cause strain.

**Feet**

The front feet should be a pair in size, shape and slope, as should the back feet. The front feet will be more upright than the hind, and the slope should follow the angle of the pastern for the best chance of soundness.

Wide heels, a large frog (wedge-shaped pad on the bottom of the foot) and concave sole are desirable. Small, narrow or 'boxy' feet are likely to cause soundness problems. Flat feet, which are often large, too sloping and with low heels, are a trait seen particularly in Thoroughbreds, and due to the lack of concavity in the soles they are prone to bruising. Feet which turn either outwards or inwards (pigeon toes) can both put strain on the limbs.

BELOW

*The term 'flat feet' is used to describe a horse that lacks concavity in its soles. This is most common in the front feet, and is best seen by picking the foot up and looking at the underneath.*

COW HOCKS

BAY

CHESTNUT

## Colours

### Solid Colours

Probably the most common colour of horse is a bay. Bay horses are brown, with black points; the points being the mane, tail, muzzle, tips of the ears and lower legs. Bays can be 'bright', 'light' or 'dark'.

Horses can also be brown or black or grey. No horse is ever correctly described as white, even those that are pure white are known as grey. Dappled grey horses have ring-shaped markings of darker and lighter shades on their coats, while flea-bitten greys have specks of black or brown on their white coat. Iron greys are those with a steely, dark grey appearance.

Chestnut horses have a ginger or orange coat. Chestnuts come in 'light' or 'dark' shades, while 'liver' chestnuts have a deep liver colour. Some chestnuts have a pale mane and tail, known as 'flaxen'.

Dun horses are a yellowy brown colour, and vary in shade; a dun horse might be described as 'mouse', 'yellow', 'silver', 'blue' or 'golden'. Duns have black points, and also have a dorsal, or 'eel' stripe, which is a black line along the backbone. Some duns also have black stripes, known as zebra markings, on their legs. Palomino horses have a yellowy gold coat, with a white mane and tail.

### 'Coloured' horses

Any horse of more than one colour, or which is an unusual colour, can be known as a coloured horse.

---

BELOW

*Dun horses always have black points and may have a dorsal stripe. Buckskin is a similar colour to dun, but the coat has an almost metallic sheen. Buckskins can also have a dorsal stripe.*

GREY

DUN

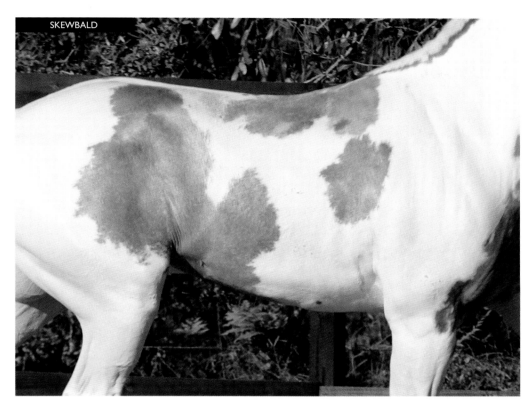

SKEWBALD

the horse is clipped to let it carry out its work more comfortably (more usual in winter, but sometimes carried out in summer, too), the clipped part of its coat may be quite a different shade.

## Breed and Colour

Breed and colour are sometimes linked – for example, Fell ponies are most commonly black, dark brown or bay, although they can also be grey. Many breed societies will not accept coloured horses in their studbooks.

## Colour and Superstition

There are many superstitions and prejudices about horse colours. Traditionally, chestnut mares have been seen as flighty and unreliable, although many owners of such horses will tell you this is not true. In some circles, coloured horses were seen as common or somehow undesirable for many years, but coloured horses are increasingly performing at the top level in many disciplines.

A piebald horse is black and white, while a skewbald is white and any other colour. Roan horses have white hairs and another colour interspersed through their coat. The most common roans are blue roans, where the hairs are white and black or brown, and strawberry roans, where the hairs are white and chestnut.

Spotted horses come in a number of common variations, including 'leopard', with dark spots on a white background; 'snowflake', which is the reverse; and 'blanket', a white rump with dark spots on it.

In the United States, some coloured horses and ponies are registered as pintos. Pintos can be a variety of

*ABOVE*

*Skewbald colouring consists of patches of white coat with any other colour except black. In the United States, skewbald and piebald horses are commonly referred to as Paints.*

breeds, but must meet specific colour requirements, while Paint horses are basically coloured horses with Quarter Horse or Thoroughbred blood. There are many terms and subdivisions, used mostly in the United States, for different coat patterns. In general, however, tobianos have a white coat, white legs and white across the back, with patches of colour. Overos have a coloured coat, with splashes of white that rarely go across the back.

## Changing Colour

Horses can change colour with age. Greys are usually

born dark and become lighter as they get older. This process takes place at a different rate in different breeds and individuals.

Horses can also appear a different colour when sporting their thick winter coats to when they have their sleek summer coats. And if

ROAN

STAR

BLAZE

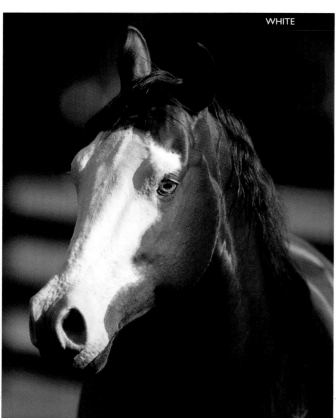

WHITE

## Markings

Many horses have some white on their head and legs. These markings are very useful for identification and will be drawn onto the horse's passport or other documentation, such as a vaccination certification.

**Head**

A blaze is a wide white mark, usually starting above the eyes and running between them down the front of the horse's face, with the white being broad enough to cover the nose bones. If the white covers the eyes, forehead and much of the muzzle, this is known as a 'white face'. A

'stripe' is a narrower white mark down the face. A 'star' is white on the forehead or between the eyes, and a 'snip' is white on the nose, perhaps extending into the nostrils.

A horse can show these markings in combination, so it might have a star, then a gap in the middle of the face with no white markings before a snip. Or it may have a star which extends into a stripe.

BELOW

*The small white nose marking referred to as a snip, has pink skin pigmentation beneath the white hair. Sometimes, as here, the pink skin is clearly visible.*

STRIPE

SNIP

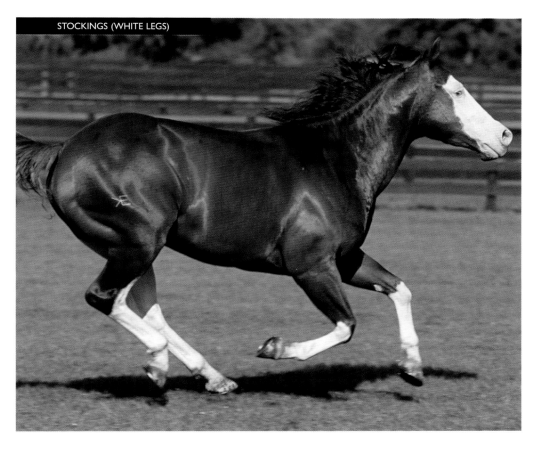

STOCKINGS (WHITE LEGS)

## Legs

A horse can have white markings on any, all or none of its legs. A stocking is when the white extends from the foot to between the fetlock and the knee or hock, while on a sock the white finishes at the fetlock or below. If a horse has patches of colour in the white, most commonly on the coronet band, these are called 'ermine marks'.

## Acquired Markings

As well as markings the animal is born with, horses can have acquired markings. These can be the result of accidental damage. A horse may grow white hair after a cut, for example, and many horses have some white hairs on their withers where they have been rubbed by a saddle or rug.

Acquired markings also include those deliberately put on the horse for identification. Some horses are branded with a hot iron, resulting in a pattern in the coat, which identifies their breed or breeder. These brands are usually on the shoulder, hindquarters or saddle area.

Freeze marking is a popular way of marking horses as a deterrent to thieves and to make the horse easier to identify if it is stolen. Horses are usually freeze-marked under the saddle. Superchilled markers are used, which destroy the pigment so the hair grows back white. Each horse is marked with a unique four-digit number. Grey and light coloured horses are given a bald freeze mark, so the markers are held on longer and the hair follicle is destroyed. This is usually done on the shoulder to prevent the saddle rubbing on a bald mark.

Other methods of identification include microchipping (where the horse has a tiny permanent unique chip inserted under the skin of its neck, which can be read with a special scanner) and stamping the horse's hooves with the owner's postcode (which has to be redone regularly, as it grows out).

## Whorls

Whorls are like a human's hair parting; places where the hair swirls round to grow in a different direction. They are commonly found on the forehead, at the top of the neck and on the chest. Head and neck whorls, and those on other parts of the body on horses with few identifying features, are usually marked with a cross on the horse's passport or other identification document.

STOCKINGS

# BEHAVIOUR AND PSYCHOLOGY

Most horses today are kept for pleasure or competition. They are trained to carry humans and behave in a certain way. Although they live in an environment which is not natural for them, the majority of horses adapt and learn to fit into a society which is human- rather than equine-driven. Some of their natural responses may become muted, but horses do not lose their instincts, and many reactions that humans see as annoyances or faults are simply natural behaviour coming through.

### Herd Instinct

In the wild, horses are herd animals, living in groups for company and protection. The herd leader is usually a mature female, with the group made up of females, foals and immature youngsters. As colts reach maturity, they will leave and form bachelor groups. A mature stallion will live on the edge of the herd, claiming his harem of mares by scent-marking piles of faeces and urination spots. The stallion's harem may incorporate a number of small bands, each under an alpha female, but his position is always vulnerable to challenge by a younger stallion.

Horses are therefore highly sociable animals, and many are unhappy if they have to live alone. They can also become distressed if they are left on their own in the short term. For example, if a horse is left in the field when its companions come in, it may gallop around or jump the fence to join them.

Some horses are naturally leaders in the herd, while others are happy to follow. When a new group of horses are turned out together, there is likely to be some galloping around and squealing, as the horses sort out who is the boss.

BELOW
*Horses in the wild live in small groups (herds) that include several mares and youngsters, as seen, and are watched over by a stallion.*

BELOW
*This piebald is warning the palomino to keep its distance by flattening its ears and kicking out with its hind leg.*

BOTTOM
*Grooming, primarily along the neck, withers, back and flanks is an important part of bonding and socialization within the 'herd'.*

have a routine in their daily lives and work. They are intelligent animals, with long memories of good or frightening experiences. They learn by repetition, and many are willing and even anxious to please. This means that they can be highly trained – for example, to take on narrow jumps on cross-country courses or perform difficult dressage movements.

## Different Temperaments

Horses vary widely in their temperament. This is partly linked to their breed, so a Thoroughbred is likely to be more flighty and 'sharp' than a heavier type. But individuals are also different in their natures, and much is governed by the horse's treatment.

## Communication

Much of equine communication is through physical signals and body language. Some of these signals are easily recognizable by humans, such as laying back the ears as a sign of displeasure or aggression. Horses also use smell, releasing pheromones, which other horses can sense, from the skin glands, and touch, such as mutual grooming. Horses also communicate vocally, such as through squeals and whinnying.

## Flight Instinct

Horses are naturally prey animals, herbivores that evolved to eat grass and run away from predators. Although horses will fight if forced to do so, their first instinct when confronted with danger is flight.

In the domesticated situation, this instinct means horses spook or shy away from unusual sights and sounds.

Horses can often hear or see potential danger earlier than humans and will jump away quickly. As horses are so big and strong, it is easy for humans to be hurt accidentally if they are not alert to this potential unpredictability.

## Learning

Horses are creatures of habit and will be happiest if they

A horse's behaviour will be altered partly by its short-term management – for example, many horses are more relaxed if they spend longer in the field and less time cooped up in a stable. Much of the horse's later behaviour is dictated by how it is treated and trained during its first interaction with humans when it is a youngster.

## Fascinating Facts

The tallest horse ever on record measured 2.2 m (7 ft, 2 in) tall in 1850 and all 1.5 tonnes (3,360 lbs) of him went by the name of Sampson, an English Shire.

ABOVE

*This horse is being held while being groomed to prevent it from spooking or shying away. Both handlers should always be on the same side of the horse.*

# Care, Management & Riding

# CHOOSING AND BUYING A HORSE

Choosing to become a horse owner is a major decision, one which should be carefully thought out, particularly if this is your first venture into owning horses. It is both exciting and easy to rush into buying the first horse you see. Take your time, and consult an expert. Make sure that you see a range of horses so that you develop an idea of what you want and, most importantly, what is suitable. Be prepared to keep looking until you find the right one.

## Points to Consider

First, all prospective horse owners should ask themselves whether they should own a horse. Are you prepared to devote the necessary amount of time to looking after it? Do you have somewhere suitable to keep it? Perhaps most importantly, can you afford to buy one, and sustain the accompanying costs?

Horses are a big responsibility. They require care all year round, in all weathers, regardless of whether you are unwell or busy. Do you have someone you can turn to for advice and support, and who could look after the horse in an emergency?

It is worth taking the time to find the right horse when looking to buy. Once purchased the horse becomes a major part of your life with a strong bond forming between horse and owner.

**Are You
Experienced Enough?**
No one should buy a horse without having the knowledge and experience to look after it. Of course, you will learn a great deal as you go along, but a basic level of riding ability and a

rudimentary understanding of a horse's needs are essential. Although it is lovely to have your horse at home, it is often more sensible to keep your first horse at a good livery yard. This should mean you will have help looking after it and can ask the yard owner for advice. Many people learn to ride in riding schools and, despite having reached quite a sophisticated standard of equitation, are surprised how different it is and how much hard work is involved in owning and caring for your own horse.

> **LEFT**
> *It can be beneficial to keep your horse at a good livery yard, such as this pictured, where there are professionals on hand to help.*

the initial lump sum to purchase the horse is only the start. Make a careful list of what you will need to buy in the way of tack, rugs and grooming kit. Work out how much it will cost to keep it at livery or, if the horse is to live at home with you, what the extra costs will be in terms of electricity and water, as well as hay, hard feed, bedding, stable and fencing maintenance, grass upkeep and tools. Factor in vet's fees, as well as routine expenses such as vaccinations, worming and farriery.

## How Much Do You Want to Spend?

Horses can cost anything from a few hundred dollars or pounds to many millions. It is a good idea to work out your budget, then stick to it. Be realistic; you are not going to find your dream event horse for nothing, but be wary of spending tens of thousands on a first horse. You may decide horse owning is not for you, and it is best to stick a toe in the water before plunging in. Remember that

## What Sort of Horse?

There are so many different sorts of horses that it can be

*RIGHT*
*Cob types such as this are often sensible in nature and quiet to handle. They are also good weight carriers and are suitable for the larger rider.*

difficult to decide which one is suitable for you. Don't be too ambitious; it is often better to be under-horsed than over-horsed. Consult your instructor, who should

have a good idea of what will suit. Consider in what circumstances you will be keeping it: if the horse is to live out in a field all the time, it may be better to get a hardy native breed than a thin-skinned Thoroughbred. What do you wish to do with it? If your ambitions lie in the show ring, you will need to choose very carefully a horse that is true to type with good conformation and good looks. If you are nervous, make sure you are looking for a sane, sensible horse; an ex-racehorse may be tempting and cheap, but would a sturdy half-bred or cob be more suitable?

## Fascinating Facts

The most expensive horse ever sold was a 2-year-old Florida-born colt, reportedly going for $16,000,000 on 28 February 2006. However, as of September 2007 Green Monkey was yet to run his first race…

*LEFT*
*Different breeds have different characteristics, and it is worth considering these before purchasing. Thoroughbreds, such as the one pictured, can be quite sharp in temperament, which is not always beneficial for a novice owner.*

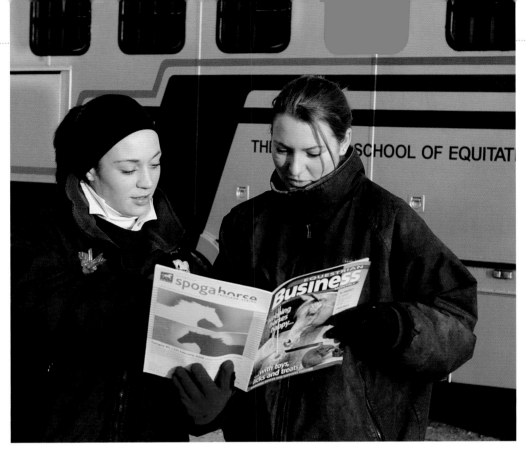

check carefully that the horse you do see is indeed the one advertised.

### Horse Dealers

The advantage of going to a dealer's yard is that often they will have a selection of horses to show you, rather than just one. As long as you check that the dealer has an excellent reputation within the horse world, this can be a good way to buy a first horse, as they are more likely than a private seller to take an unsuitable horse back. Their reputation relies on client satisfaction, and good dealers are experienced at finding the right horse for the right person.

## Where to Look

There are many places to look for a horse to buy. The main ones are:

### Trade Papers and Magazines

The equestrian press is often the best place to look for horses. Remember that all horses sound great in an advertisement; do not take all the seller says at face value. Local papers often have an equine section, and sometimes better value can be found here than in the classified sections of national magazines.

### The Internet

There has been a vast increase in the amount of horses advertised for sale on the Internet in recent years. A quick search will reveal many sites, with horses ranging from top competition animals to small ponies. Many horse dealers now have their own websites, which can be a useful tool, but check how often the ads are posted and updated. It is easy to fall in love with a horse that was sold months ago. Never buy a horse without going to see it, however, and

### Auctions

Some great bargains can be found at auction, but it is a big risk to take and best left to those with a good deal of experience.

LEFT

*When looking at a horse it should be seen trotting up on a hard surface in a straight line. Observe its movement from in front, from the side and from behind to check for soundness and to evaluate the way it travels.*

## What to Ask

Don't be afraid to ask the seller as many questions as you like, and do take a friend, ideally with lots of experience, with you.

• Before you arrive, ask for the horse to be left out in a field so that you can see it being caught and brought in.

• Look carefully at the horse and its conformation. Does it have any lumps, bumps or scars, and what is the explanation for them?

• Has it ever suffered from any serious veterinary problems?

• How old is the horse and how big is it? What sex is it?

• How is it bred?

• What has it done? Does it have a competition record? Has it been hunting?

• Why is it being sold?

• Does it bite, kick, buck, rear, or suffer from a stable vice such as crib-biting, wind-sucking or box-walking?

• Does the horse suffer from any seasonal problems, such as sweet itch in the summer or mud fever in the winter?

• Is it vaccinated, and does it have a passport? (In the United Kingdom and Republic of Ireland, for instance, it is illegal to sell a horse without one.)

• Watch it being tacked up.

## Fascinating Facts

A common nickname for horse racing is The Sport of Kings.

How does it react to the bit being put in its mouth or the girth tightened? Does it stand still when it is being mounted?

• Ask to see it ridden, on the flat and over fences. In its home environment, expect it to go as well as it can.

• Ride it, first in an enclosed environment, then, if you like it, ask if you can take it for a short hack. This should give you a chance to see how it reacts to traffic.

Most importantly, ask yourself whether you like the horse, whether you feel confident around it, is it the sort you are looking for, and is it worth the money the seller is asking.

# FEEDING

When you have bought your horse, check what its previous owner has been feeding it. This is important not only as a guide, but also because abrupt changes in a horse's diet are not advisable. You will also need to know about the principal rules of feeding, how much you should feed your horse and the different types of feed available. It is also important that you understand how different feeds break down into the three main types and ensure that you feed your horse in the correct combination and proportions.

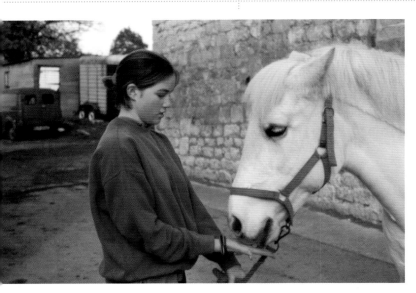

### Principal Rules of Feeding
• Feed small amounts of food regularly.
• Feed the best-quality food that you can afford. Cheap food is a waste of money, as its nutritional values are low.
• Feed according to the type of horse, its temperament, the amount of work it is doing and the condition it is in.
• Make sure that clean, fresh water is always available.
• Introduce changes to a feeding routine gradually, so that the bacteria in the horse's intestine have time to adapt accordingly.
• Feed something succulent every day.
• Horses are creatures of habit and thrive on routine. Feed at approximately the same time every day.
• Don't feed immediately before or after exercise.
• Make sure that all feed and water buckets are cleaned regularly.

### How Much Should You Feed Your Horse?
It is not easy to work out how much your new horse needs feeding, and it can be a case of trial and error. The following calculation should provide a rough guide that you can adapt to your own horse:

Take the horse's weight in kilograms (either weigh it on a weighbridge or use a weight tape), and multiply it by 2.5. Divide the total by 100. The resulting figure is how much total food the horse requires per day. So a 16-hh horse might weigh 600 kg (600 x 2.5 / 100 = 15). This means that the horse should receive 15 kg of food.

Horses are grazing animals, and most of their diet should

be grass or hay. For a horse in medium work, a good rule of thumb is that 70 per cent of its diet should be roughage, and 30 per cent should be made up of concentrates, such as oats, barley, sugar beet, etc.

This is obviously dependent on the horse's age, temperament and size. A Welsh pony will very rarely need concentrates in its diet and will survive well on relatively poor grazing, while a fit Thoroughbred may need quite large amounts of concentrates to supply the energy it needs.

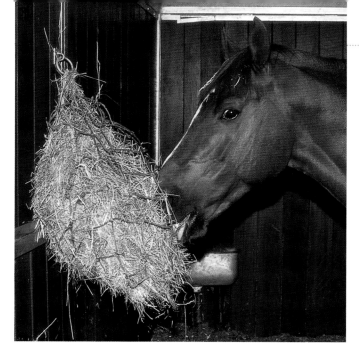

## Feed Types

Feed is split into three main groups: roughage, concentrates, and vitamins and minerals.

*From top clockwise: rolled oats, horse and pony nuts (also called cubes or pellets), and flaked barley.*

### Roughage

For most horses and ponies, roughage means grass, which should almost always provide the main part of a horse's diet. Mature horses in little or no work are unlikely to need anything else, as is the case with small native ponies. Hay is dried baled grass, and is fed in the winter when grass is poor and lacking. Other forms of fibre include haylage, which is richer than hay and may not be suitable for native ponies and horses who suffer from obesity. Chaff is chopped hay or straw, and can be fed to bulk out small feeds and to prevent a horse bolting its food too quickly.

### Concentrates

These are divided into mixes and nuts, and 'straights'. 'Straights' are oats, barley, sugar beet and linseed. Mixes and nuts are these core components mixed together in varying quantities to form a range of pre-balanced feeds for all types of horses.

Barley should be cooked for at least two hours before feeding or bought in a pre-cooked formula, as it swells in a horse's stomach. It is a carbohydrate-rich food that is good at putting on condition and giving slow-releasing energy.

Oats should be fed crushed, rolled or cooked. They are easily digestible and palatable, but are high in energy and unsuitable for many types of horses and ponies.

Sugar beet is a by-product of the sugar industry, and therefore high in energy and very palatable. It is useful for putting on weight and for tempting shy feeders to eat. It comes in cubes, which must be soaked in cold water for 24 hours before feeding, or shreds, which should be soaked for 12 hours. Linseed is poisonous to horses unless is it is cooked until the shiny seeds split and become jelly-like. Fed in small quantities, it is excellent for putting on condition.

Gambling is often synonymous with horse racing and there are three common bets placed on races: bet to win, bet to place, and bet to show.

### Vitamins and Minerals

Many horse owners like to give their animals extra vitamins and minerals, often unnecessarily. Sometimes there is a need to supplement the horse's usual diet, but it is wise to consult an expert first. A salt or mineral lick is often popular. Other supplements such as garlic, for respiration, and various additives to improve hoof quality or aid joint suppleness can be useful. But it is easy to spend a fortune on fashionable products that your horse really does not need.

*The small bowl of pellets shows sugar beet before it has been soaked. Underneath is a large bowl of soaked sugar beet that is now ready for feeding.*

# ENVIRONMENT

There are two main ways to keep a horse: principally outside (in a field) and principally inside (in a stable). Not all horses are suited to either. It is perfectly possible to keep a horse outside, rugged or unrugged, but it is useful to have a stable to bring it in to if necessary, such as for veterinary treatment. Hardy native types cope best with this sort of management. More highly bred horses may also cope, but many prefer to be stabled at night during the winter.

## Grass-kept Horses

The bare minimum amount of land on which a horse can be kept is 0.4 ha (one acre), but it is much easier on a plot of 0.8–1.2 ha (two to three acres). This allows the land to be divided up and rested as necessary.

### Fencing

Make sure that your field is well fenced. The best fencing is solid post-and-rails, with either a tall hedge or trees for shelter. But taut plain wire (*not* barbed wire) or a thick hedge can be used, although the latter must be checked regularly for gaps. The gate should be made of treated wood or metal, and be high enough to stop horses from jumping

out. For your convenience, make sure that it is properly hung and has a secure fastening. If the gate opens on to a road, a chain and padlock are advisable. Check all fencing frequently for damage and weakness.

It is nice for horses to have a field shelter where they can escape the worst of the winter weather, and avoid the flies in the summer. If you are keeping more than one horse together, check that the

shelter has a wide-enough entrance to prevent one horse trapping another in there, and some sort of bedding should be provided so that horses are not standing either in deep mud or on hard concrete. Always leave the cobwebs in the corners to catch the flies.

### Water

Your field must have a clean, fresh supply of water. A tank linked to the water supply with a cock-and-ball system for replenishing it is ideal. A stream is fine, as long as it does not have a sandy bottom which the horse could suck up while drinking. If buckets are used, they will need to be filled up a couple of times a day, and more often in summer.

---

**LEFT**

*Horses must be provided with an adequate shelter to protect them from the elements (hot and cold), and the shelter must be large enough to accommodate the number of horses using it.*

Check your field regularly for poisonous plants. These include ragwort, which has distinctive yellow flowers and, if eaten, is likely to prove lethal. Others include: yew; deadly nightshade; bracken; foxgloves; acorns; laburnum; privet; black and white bryony; ivy; locoweed; Johnson grass; field horsetail; tall fescue; perennial ryegrass; hemlock; common pokeweed; common cocklebur; hemp

Not suitable are ponds without a stream running through them – the water becomes stagnant – or old baths with sharp edges. Remember that, in winter, water may freeze over and will need to have the ice broken up.

## Grass

It can be tricky to provide your horse with enough grass, without it being too little or too much. Grass grows particularly lushly in the spring and autumn, and may need to be restricted at these times. Small areas can be partitioned off with electric fencing. In the winter, the growth and quality may

be insufficient and the horse's diet will need to be supplemented with good-quality hay.

Grass management is important. Investigate whether it needs fertilising, obviously removing all horses while this is done. Particularly long grass may need topping and the clippings removed. Buttercups are a sign that the grass is poor, and may need reseeding with a carefully selected assortment of grasses.

dogbane; white snakeroot; yellow and white sweet clover; common milkweed; and some mustards.

## Management

All horses kept at grass need checking twice a day. They should be groomed less than stable-kept horses in order to preserve the coat's natural oils, which help to keep the horse warm and waterproof. Rugs should be removed and replaced every day, and feet checked for stones.

If you are feeding several horses in the field, space out the feeds or piles of hay to avoid fights, and to ensure each horse gets enough.

### RIGHT

*This is not an ideal way to feed hay as much is wasted, and there is a chance of bullying. It is better to leave a number of small piles of hay that allows each horse its own. Only as much hay should be put out as is eaten – it is preferable to feed smaller amounts of hay more frequently than to provide one large pile as pictured.*

## Stable-kept Horses

### The Stable

A pony stable should be a minimum of 3.6 m x 3 m (12 ft x 10 ft); a horse should not be kept in a stable less than 3.6 m x 3.6 m (12 ft x 12 ft), ideally made of stone, which has the advantage of being cool in the summer and warm in the winter. But there are many modern stable companies who will build you durable, well-designed wooden stables at a reasonable cost.

It is useful to have hard standing outside the stable so that you can tie your horse up outside to be groomed and to be mucked out. Inside, the floor should slope slightly towards a drain at the front of the stable, so that urine does not collect. The stable door should be at least 1.1 m (3 ft 7 in) high, and fastened by bolts at both the top and the bottom.

The stable must be well ventilated. It is better for horses to be well rugged in cold weather than for the stable to get stuffy. Also, all light switches and fittings should be covered and out of the reach of the horse.

### Bedding

There are many types of bedding, and you should consider which suits you and your horse best. Do not be tempted to skimp on bedding; horses like to lie down and should be able to do so in comfort and without damaging their knees and hocks.

Straw is warm, can be banked high at the sides and drains well. It is also the cheapest form of bedding, coming either in small bales or big round ones. But some horses suffer from dust allergies, which can cause respiratory problems. These animals will need a dust-free form of bedding, such as good-quality shavings, woodchip or paper. Hemp is a new, dust-free form of bedding, but can be quite expensive.

Shavings are easy to muck out and warm, but can get very wet and heavy because they do not drain well.

Well-fitted rubber matting on top of the stable floor stops horses having to stand on cold concrete and provides support for their feet and joints. Mats must be taken up and scrubbed from time to time.

## Mucking out

You can either muck your horse out completely every day, removing all droppings and wet patches, or 'deep-litter' the bed. This means picking up the droppings, then putting more bedding on top to absorb the wet. A thick, warm bed can be built up like this, but it will need totally removing about once a month, and it is more difficult to keep horses and rugs clean with this system. Muck heaps should be placed away from the stable, away from any water supply and downwind of the yard to prevent dirty straw being blown back.

## Water

Water can be provided either in buckets, which need filling up and cleaning out, or by way of an automatic drinker which self-fills as the horse drinks. This is obviously less labour-intensive, but some horses do

not like to drink from these, and it is impossible to check how much a horse is drinking daily.

## Hay and Feed

Hay should be fed in a net, which must be tied up high enough to prevent a horse from getting its hoof caught in it, but slightly lower than eye level so that seeds do not fall into the horse's eyes; on a rack; or in piles on the floor. This last method is more wasteful, but is also more natural as the horse feeds with its head down, as it does in the wild. Feed can be placed in a manger, which will need regular cleaning out; in buckets, which may be in danger of being kicked over; or in a trough which can be clipped straight on to a horse's door.

## Tack and Feed Rooms

Tack rooms must be properly secured, with substantial locks and an alarm system. All tack should be marked, as should rugs.

Feed rooms should also be kept locked. Feed bags should be placed in bins or at least on pallets to prevent the bags from becoming soggy. A tap with hot running water will make life easier.

## Fascinating Facts

Horses can be described as hot-blooded and cold-blooded but not in the literal and most commonly used definitions of the words – it describes their temperament. Hot-blooded horses, such as race horses, exhibit more energy and sensitivity, while the cold-blooded horses, such as draught breeds, are quieter and calmer.

LEFT

*Stable-kept horses must be turned out for a period of time daily, or exercised. They cannot be kept in for days at a time, it is detrimental to their physical and mental health – the exception being in the case of illness or injury.*

### Exercise

Horses cannot just be left in their stables all day. If they are not turned out for a few hours, which is the best and most natural way of managing them, they must be properly exercised, either ridden or on the lunge, every day.

### Rugs

If a horse is kept in a stable during the winter, it can actually become colder than its grass-kept counterpart because it is not moving around and keeping warm. It will therefore need rugging, particularly if it has been clipped. Modern stable rugs, made of nylon with padded fillings, come in several weights from light to heavy. It is good practice to use a thin cotton sheet as the bottom layer, which should be washed once a week. This saves the rest of your rugs from getting dirty and keeps the horse cleaner. All rugs should be washed and, if they are outdoor rugs, re-waterproofed, a couple of times a year.

Outdoor rugs are called 'New Zealand rugs', and are both warm and waterproof. If a horse comes in from the field wet, it may be better to leave the rug to dry on the horse if you do not have a system of drying the rug quickly, as it is unpleasant for a horse to have a cold, damp rug put back on in the morning.

## Travelling with a Horse

Everything possible should be done to ensure that a horse has a good travelling experience. Bad travellers have been made that way, usually by bad driving, and it may well be difficult to re-establish their confidence.

### Clothing

Horses should be travelled with adequate leg protection, be it travelling boots or bandages. The former are much easier to put on, particularly for inexperienced

owners, but bandages may be more suitable on very long journeys because, if applied correctly, they provide a degree of leg support.

A tail bandage and tail guard will keep the tail from being rubbed and protect it. Do not, however, put the tail bandage on excessively tightly.

A poll guard, made from foam or a bandage wrapped around the headpiece, is advisable on long journeys and for bad travellers.

Rugs will depend on the weather. In the summer, a sweatsheet or cotton sheet may be enough; in winter, a sweatsheet and thick wool travelling rug with a surcingle (a type of girth or band used

to keep a blanket, saddle or pack secure round the middle) to keep them in place might be needed.

### Transport

Horses travel either in a special lorry (truck) or a horse trailer pulled by a four-wheel drive vehicle. Each should have rubber matting

and a small amount of bedding on the floor, and must be well maintained and frequently checked for safety. Horses often like to spread their legs for balance when travelling, and for this reason it is safer to have partitions that are not solid attached to the floor. Always drive slowly and carefully, and remember that you will have to anticipate braking and turning much sooner than you would in a car.

### Journeys

Plan long journeys carefully, and arrange to have stops every three hours. This rests horses and is an opportunity to give them a drink and replenish their haynets. You might also walk them around

to stretch their legs, but never unbox on the side of the road, and make sure you will be able to get them to load again, otherwise it might be safer to leave them in the box until you get to your destination.

# GROOMING AND MAINTAINING

Regular grooming should be part of your daily routine with your horse. It keeps your horse's skin and coat healthy and clean. Horses that are stable-kept should be groomed more thoroughly than those that are kept on grass, as they have less need of the coat's natural oils and have a tendency to become scurfy underneath their rugs. It is also an opportunity to spend time with your horse and to bond with it outside of a ridden situation.

---
RIGHT

*From left to right starting at the bottom, a plastic curry comb (red), a dandy brush, a water brush, a rubber curry comb (black), a tail comb, a metal curry comb, a hoof pick, a body brush (dark bristles in middle, pale bristles round edge), a small comb and a sponge. The folded material is a stable rubber.*

## Grooming Kit

The term 'grooming kit' is given to the collection of brushes and tools that we use to clean our horses. Here are some of the most useful:

### Dandy Brush

This stiff brush is used to remove mud, and is used on the legs and body. Avoid using on sensitive clipped areas or on the mane or tail.

### Body Brush

A body brush is a soft-bristled brush used to deep-clean scurf from the coat. It is used on the whole body, in conjunction with a metal curry comb. Also use to brush out the tail and on delicate areas such as the head.

### Curry Comb

A plastic or rubber-toothed curry comb can be used in small circular motions on the coat to loosen and remove mud, excess hair (when the

---
LEFT

*The dandy brush has stiff bristles and is useful for removing mud and dirt from the legs in particular. Avoid using on sensitive areas such as the head, or on the mane or tail.*

horse is shedding its coat) and scurf. It can be useful on sensitive horses that object to hard brushing with a dandy brush. Metal curry combs should be used only to

---
BELOW

*The body brush is a soft bristled brush used for removing dirt, dust and dead hair from the coat. It should be used in conjunction with a metal curry comb, which is used to clean the brush, never on the horse.*

clean dirt and scurf out of a body brush, and not on the horse itself.

### Hoof Pick

This is a blunt metal or tough plastic hook which is used to remove dirt and stones from horses' hooves. Take care with the sensitive parts of the hoof, and always pick downwards away from the heel to avoid damaging the frog.

horses love a bath on a hot day to cool down; if you must bathe them on cold days, use warm water and dry them thoroughly.

### Sweat Scraper
This is a tool with a handle and a curved rubber strip with which you scrape off excess water after washing your horse down.

### Hoof Oil
Hoof oil, applied with a small brush, is a bit like nail polish for horses and is a cosmetic touch used to make them look smart on competition and hunting days. It has a drying effect on the hoof, and should be used on special occasions such as high days and holidays.

### Stable Rubber
This is a finishing cloth used to provide gloss to a coat and remove final traces of scurf. It is often used in the show ring to make the horse look its best just before the judge examines it.

### Scissors
Round-ended, blunt scissors can be used to trim unwanted hair around the horse's chin and muzzle, and remove feather from their fetlock joints. They are also used to shorten the tail, but should never be used on the mane.

### Mane Comb
A wide-toothed comb of metal or plastic is used to comb out the mane, and can be used gently on the tail.

### Water Brush
A soft brush with close-set bristles, this brush is used with water to remove stains from the horse's coat and sweat marks. It can be used for cleaning hooves and for laying manes and tails tidily.

### Sponge
Sponges are used for washing horses or for cleaning areas such as the eyes, nose and dock.

### Shampoo
Horses who live outside most of the time shouldn't be washed often because of the loss of the coat's natural oils. When you do wash your horse, such as after strenuous exercise or before a competition, use special horse shampoos which are gentler than the ones we use. Some

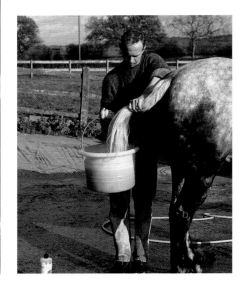

## Grooming Tips

### How to Wash a Tail

Soak the tail in a bucket of lukewarm water to loosen the dirt. If you cannot fit the whole tail in a bucket, wet the top part of the dock with a water brush. Shampoo with a special equine shampoo, and rub vigorously. Rinse thoroughly, changing the water as it becomes soapy. Squeeze out the water with your hands, and swing the tail to help get rid of any remaining water. Comb through the ends gently to prevent tangles. To help the tail remain untangled, spray lightly with a show-sheen product and brush through with a body brush a few strands at a time.

### Turning a Horse out for a Show

Wash the mane a few days before (*see* Helpful Hint). On the morning of the show, thoroughly wash the horse's whole body and tail to remove dirt and stains. Scrub hooves and socks. Make sure you dry the horse thoroughly, particularly if the weather is at all cold. First use a sweat scraper to get rid of surface water, then rub down with a towel. Plait the horse's mane and tail (see section on how to plait), and rug and bandage the horse up until you are nearly ready to go into the ring. Next, carefully apply hoof oil, and use a chalk block to make the horse's socks white. A touch of baby oil can be used to emphasize its eyes and muzzle, which should have been sponged clean first. Run a stable rubber over the coat to remove all final traces of dust, and check that the horse's plaits are still neatly in place.

## Helpful Hints

Don't wash your horse's mane the day before a show. It will be slippery and more difficult to plait. Instead, wash it a couple of days earlier so that some of the natural oils return.

RIGHT

*Always wash the mane thoroughly a few days before the show, taking care to remove all scurf, dust and dirt. Be careful not to get soap into the horse's eyes.*

## Grooming Horses Which Live Outside

If a horse is grass-kept and without rugs, the skin should be in a healthy condition and it is unnecessary to groom it unless it is being ridden. Grooming should be limited to:

• picking out the feet every day and checking the shoes.

• brushing down with the dandy brush to remove mud and sweat marks. (After exercise, do not wash down, but allow the sweat to dry, then brush it off.)

• sponging out the eyes, nose, muzzle and dock.

If the horse is rugged, the skin will become scurfy in the same way as that of a stable-kept horse, and more regular and thorough grooming will be required.

## Strapping

Strapping is a traditional way of improving muscle tone and development by rhythmically 'thumping' the horse's shoulders, quarters and neck with a leather massage pad, followed by 'sliding' the pad over them. It is rarely used these days except by old-fashioned horsemen and women, but done correctly it can be tremendously useful and beneficial. It should be attempted only by people who know what they are doing, otherwise quite a lot of damage could be done. Get someone experienced to show you how to do it.

## Helpful Hints

Sick horses or those on enforced box rest should be groomed regularly. It provides stimulation for their coat and, most importantly, their muscles, which are otherwise not being used, and makes them feel as though they are getting some attention.

them. Always clip against the direction of the hair growth, and use long, sweeping strokes. Pull the skin taut over any 'fiddly' places, such as the elbows and stifle joints. Work quickly and, if the clippers become very hot, allow them to cool down before starting clipping again. Make sure that the blades are sharp and well oiled, and send the blades away to an expert to be resharpened and maintained when they become blunt.

### Trimming

Trimming the excess hair from areas such as the head and legs can improve the horse's appearance. Use a pair of blunt scissors to remove unwanted hair from the coronet band at the top of

## Helpful Hints

Never clip the inside of the ears. The horse needs this hair for protection and warmth. If you wish to neaten up your horse's ears, just trim the most wispy bits of hair carefully with a pair of blunt scissors.

BELOW

*Take care when clipping the horse's head. Some horses do not like the noise and sensation of it and will react, although the horse pictured is very relaxed.*

the hoof and the back of the heels and fetlock joint (known as 'feather').

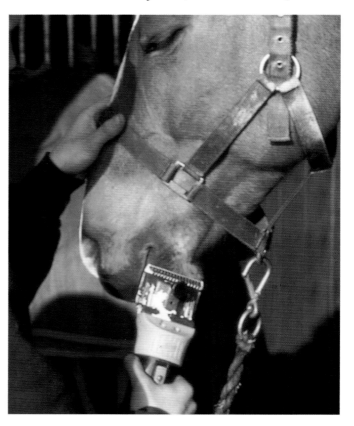

## Trimming and Plaiting

### Clipping

Clipping involves removing part of the horse's winter coat with electronic clippers. It is done so that horses become less sweaty during winter work, makes grooming easier, allows horses to dry faster and means that cuts, grazes and lumps can be spotted more easily.

**How to clip** Introduce horses which have not been clipped before to clippers gradually. Let them become accustomed to the noise of the clippers first, and use a helper to stand at their head to reassure

## Helpful Hints

The hair will stick to your clothes when clipping, so make sure that you wear overalls from which it can easily be brushed off, or a plastic coat or jacket.

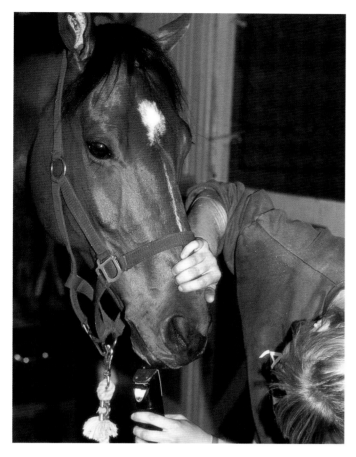

LEFT
Some clippers have smaller heads than others. The smaller the head the easier it is to clip awkward areas such as the whiskers, under the jaw bone and the ears.

To trim the horse's 'beard' underneath its chin, either use scissors or a quiet pair of clippers. Trim close to the jawbone, and gently stretch the loose skin to achieve a neat appearance. Some people remove the horse's chin whiskers with a pair of scissors, but others believe horses need these whiskers as part of their sensory equipment.

Trim the end of a horse's tail to about 12 cm (5 in) below its hocks. This will not prevent the tail being used to whisk away flies, but will keep it out of the wintry mud.

**Mane and tail pulling** Always use a comb to 'pull' tails and manes, not a pair of scissors. This achieves a more natural look. Take a small section of mane, backcomb it and tug the remainder out sharply. Do a little at a time, and it is kindest to the horse to do this after exercise, when the body is warm and the hair comes out more easily.

**Plaiting**

Plaiting manes and tails is done to improve a horse's appearance and make it look smart for competitions, showing and hunting.

**Plaiting a mane** Brush the mane and damp it down so that it lies flat. Divide the short well-pulled mane into small equal sections with rubber bands. Starting at the top, plait each section tightly and secure the bottom either with an elastic band or using needle and thread, depending on which you find easier. Roll up the plait to form a neat 'knot', and either stitch in or secure with another elastic band.

Tradition used to dictate that you made either seven or nine plaits along the neck and one at the forelock, but these days you can choose how many suits your horse – or how many it takes you to reach the end of the neck.

**Improving the appearance of the neck** Thick, chunky plaits will make the neck look shorter and bulkier; lots of small plaits will lengthen the neck and slim it down. Dressage horses often have a great number of small plaits banded with white tape, while show horses usually have bigger, more spaced-out plaits, sewn in for neatness.

BELOW
This style of plaiting is seen more typically amongst the Spanish breeds of horse, and also for some draught breeds. It enhances the look of the topline and can only be done on horses with long manes.

## Shoeing a Horse

There is a growing trend to leave horses unshod and, for certain horses, with careful hoof trimming this may be satisfactory. But for the majority of the horse population, the application of metal shoes allows them to do the work expected of them. The art of shoeing horses is called 'farriery', and the person who shoes your horse is a 'farrier'. Each horse's hooves are different, and it is important to find a farrier who will take time to understand what your horse needs.

**The Structure of the Hoof**
The exterior is made up of three parts: the wall, the sole and the frog (*see also* page 34). All three are non-sensitive and contain neither nerves nor blood, which is why

nails can be driven through the wall and why the frog and wall can be trimmed back without causing pain or bleeding.

**The wall** This is the part of the hoof visible when the foot is on the ground. It grows downwards from the coronet, like a fingernail.

**The sole** This thin structure protects the hoof from injury from underneath, and is slightly concave, to provide grip.

**The frog** This wedge-shaped structure grows downwards from the heel on the underside of the horse's hoof. It is the horse's anti-slipping and anti-concussion pad, and should be flexible and cushion-like.

**How Often Should My Horse Be Shod?**
Most horses will need shoeing every four to six weeks, depending on how quickly their hooves grow and how much work they are doing. Even when the shoes are not badly worn, the hoof will have grown and needs trimming.

**Signs That a Horse Needs Shoeing**
• The foot is long and out of shape.
• The shoe has worn thin.
• The shoe is loose or has come off.
• The 'clenches' (the nail heads that protrude from the hoof wall) have risen and stand out.

## The Farrier's Visit

Before your farrier arrives, make sure that your horse's legs and feet are clean and dry, and that it is standing in a suitably sheltered place, preferably with a flat, clean surface.

To remove a shoe, the farrier cuts all the clenches, using a buffer and driving hammer. He then levers the shoe off with pincers. The overgrowth of hoof wall is removed with a drawing knife, and ragged parts of the sole and frog are trimmed away. A rasp is then used to give the foot a level bearing surface.

The new, hot shoe is then taken to the hoof on a pritchel and seared to the hoof to check that the shoe fits the shape of the foot. After any

adjustments, the shoe is cooled in water and nailed on. The first nail is usually driven into the toe, and outwards from there. The end of the nail, where it penetrates from the wall, is turned over and twisted off, leaving a small 'clench'. The clenches are tidied up with the rasp, and the toe-clip tapped lightly back into position.

### The Newly Shod

**Foot** Check that:
• the shoe has been made to fit the hoof, not the hoof made to fit the shoe.
• the type and weight of the shoe is suitable for the horse.
• the frog has been correctly

trimmed: it should make contact with the ground on soft surfaces, as its role is as a concussion pad.

• no daylight shows between the shoe and the hoof, particularly at the heel region.
• the heels of the shoe are neither too long nor too short.

## Helpful Hints

Metal studs can be fitted into the heel of a shoe to lessen the risk of slipping. It is preferable to use one on the inside and one on the outside of each shoe, to maintain the balance of the hoof. Studs come in various shapes and sizes; as a general rule, small pointed studs are used when the ground is hard, and bigger, squarer ones when the ground is soft and wet.

# HEALTH

Keeping a horse healthy means constant vigilance. The horse cannot tell you if something is wrong, so your perception and assessment of its condition are vital to its wellbeing. You will also need to take certain active steps to maintain your horse's health, such as worming. Learn what is and isn't normal for your horse, and maintain a weather eye for any signs of deterioration or change. Any deviations from the signs of good health listed below should be noted and appropriate action taken as quickly as possible.

## Signs of Good Health

- The horse should be standing and behaving normally.
- It should be alert and confident.
- There should be no signs of sweating at rest, except in very hot weather.
- Its eyes should be bright and wide open.
- The membranes under the eyelids and the linings of the nostrils should be salmon pink in colour.
- It should be eating well and chewing normally.
- Its coat should be sleek and lying flat, not dull and 'stary'.
- Its limbs should be free from heat and swellings.

- It should be standing evenly on all four feet. Resting a hindleg is quite normal; resting a front leg is a cause for concern.
- Its urine and droppings should be normal in colour and passed at the normal rate. Horses fed on hay will pass light-coloured, yellowy-brown droppings, while those at grass will pass dark green droppings.
- The skin should move easily over the horse's ribs, which should neither be too visible nor obscured by excess fat.

ABOVE

*The horse in this picture is a good example of a horse in good health. The coat is shiny, ears pricked and eyes alert.*

- At rest, the horse's temperature should be within the range 37°–38.5°C (99.5°–101.3°F).
- At rest, the horse's respiration (breathing) rate should be 10 to 20 inhalations per minute.
- At rest, the horse's pulse should be 36 to 42 heartbeats per minute.

## Routine Healthcare

### Vaccination

All horses must be vaccinated against tetanus, which is a serious disease, picked up from bacteria in soil, that can result in death. If you do not know the vaccination history of your horse, it must have an initial course of injections, then a booster every year.

Flu vaccinations are optional but recommended, and are compulsory if you wish to compete at affiliated level in any discipline. The course consists of an initial injection, a second one between 21 and 90 days later, a third one between 115 and 210 days after the second, and annual boosters afterwards. These need to be six-monthly if you are competing under International Equestrian Federation (FEI) rules.

Always ensure that your horse's vaccinations are up to date. If they lapse, you will have to start all over again.

harrowed so that the droppings are broken up and spread. Do not graze horses with donkeys, as the latter pass on lungworms.

Wormers usually come in the form of a paste, which can be

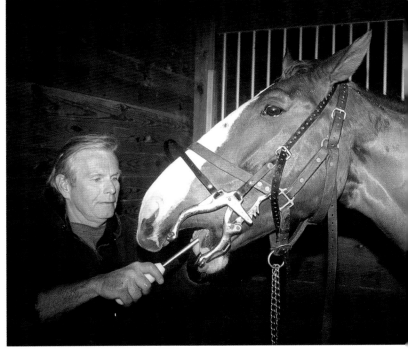

### Worming

All horses and ponies can suffer from worms, caused by ingesting immature larvae while grazing. It is important to control these worms, through pasture management and a worming programme.

Droppings should be picked up from pasture or, if the field is too big to make this practical, have the field

'injected' into the mouth so that the horse eats it. Take advice from your vet about a suitable worming programme; there are different types of wormers to combat different worms. On average, horses should be wormed every six to eight weeks.

### Teeth

It is good practice to have your horse's teeth checked at least once a year, either by your vet or a qualified horse dentist. Some horses will never need anything done to their teeth, while others may need regular treatment and rasping for sharp edges and uneven wear.

water and gently rub the wound, changing the cotton wool frequently.

Do not apply a wound ointment or powder because these make dirt stick and attract infection. If possible, apply a non-stick dressing, then bandage. Keep the horse in a stable, if possible, because it is easier to keep the wound clean. Check the horse's tetanus vaccinations are up to date.

established. Wounds near joints are dangerous because of the risk of joint oil (synovial fluid) leaking out of the joint capsule and serious infection resulting. If a horse falls over on the road and damages its knees, seek veterinary advice, however superficial the injury may look

• if the cut is big enough to need stitching, whether it is jagged-edged or clean-edged
• if the horse has picked up a puncture wound. This is a

## First Aid and Wounds

There are several different types of wound. Some you will be able to manage yourself, but others will need veterinary attention. If in any doubt, call the vet. It is better to be safe than sorry. Keep the vet's phone number to hand to minimize delays.

### Minor Wounds

Superficial grazes, scrapes and small cuts can be managed by clipping away the surrounding hair and cleaning thoroughly. To wash the wound, use a mild antiseptic solution in warm, clean water from a clean bucket. If you do not have antiseptic handy, kitchen salt will suffice. Soak pads of cotton wool in the

### When to Call the Vet

Always call a qualified veterinarian in the following situations:

• if blood is spurting from the wound
• if the wound is to the foot, over a joint or near a tendon, or to the eye. Infection in the foot is difficult to treat once

small, deep wound, perhaps from a nail or sharp pointed object. The danger is that they are easy to miss and, because of their depth, may have damaged the internal structures of the horse or contain foreign bodies and dirt that you cannot see. They are difficult to clean out, and may need poulticing

If you have called the vet in an emergency, there are a few things you can do to help the situation. If blood is spurting, push a clean pad of cotton wool into the wound, and either hold or bandage into place.

With all major wounds, try to prevent the horse from panicking or moving too much, so that further damage is minimized. Make sure that you have warm water and some clean towels ready.

Deep wounds, where the blood is not spurting out, can be liberally hosed with cold water until the vet arrives. This will constrict the blood vessels and help to stop the bleeding.

## Girth Galls and Saddle Sores

If a horse's tack does not fit properly, it will rub and cause a sore patch. Wash the area with a weak antiseptic solution, and, when the skin has healed, harden it up with surgical spirit. Most importantly, discover what is rubbing and take steps to prevent it. A fleece girth-guard should be used until the problem is solved. For saddle sores, do not ride the horse until they are completely healed, and seek the advice of a saddle-fitter.

RIGHT

*Girth galls such as this pictured can quickly become open sores if they are not noticed. They must be allowed to completely heal before the horse is saddled again, and the girth should be changed.*

LEFT

*Cold hosing is an excellent therapy for any type of bruising injury on the legs or feet, and helps to reduce inflammation.*

## Mouth Injuries

Badly fitting bits, or those with sharp or worn edges, can damage the mouth, particularly if combined with rough riding. Cracks to the corners of the mouth are most common, which can become very sore. Check the bit for damage or pinching, and change it accordingly. Applying calendula cream, or haemorrhoid cream formulated for humans, will help to heal the sores. In bad cases, you may have to refrain from using a bit for some days.

## Signs of Ill Health

Common signs of illness include:

- dullness and depression
- failure to eat and sudden weight loss
- a dull and 'stary' coat
- patchy sweating at rest
- box-walking and general unease
- getting up and lying down repeatedly
- ears laid back
- runny, weeping eyes
- a running nose

- abnormal pulse and respiration rates
- a raised temperature
- swelling or heat in a leg
- resting a foreleg, or shifting constantly from one leg to another
- lameness
- drinking more than normal and urinating more than normal
- discoloured droppings and urine, or droppings of an unusual consistency
- patchy hair loss
- coughing
- skin lumps

- aggression towards other horses or humans
- disinclination to socialize with other horses in the field
- poor performance and poor exercise tolerance

It is important to know what is 'normal' for your horse, particularly its respiration and pulse rates and temperature.

### Taking Your Horse's Temperature

Grease the bulb of a thermometer, preferably a digital one, and gently insert it into the horse's rectum. Do not stand directly behind the horse in case it kicks, and hold the tail out of the way. Hold on to the thermometer firmly (plenty of these have been lost inside horses, which necessitates a visit to the vet), and leave for two minutes, or until it bleeps if it is digital. Withdraw the thermometer and read the temperature. Make sure that you wash the thermometer thoroughly.

### Taking the Pulse Rate

The easiest places to feel the pulse are where the facial artery crosses the jawbone and just below the horse's elbow. Make sure that you take the pulse rate with your fingers, not your thumb, which has a pulse of its own. Count the number of pulses in 15 seconds, and multiply by four to get a reading.

### Taking the Respiration Rate

Watch the horse's flanks move in and out, and count for a minute. Breathing should be regular and quiet.

# Fascinating Facts

Horse racing is one of the most widely attended spectator sports in the United States, some say second only to baseball...

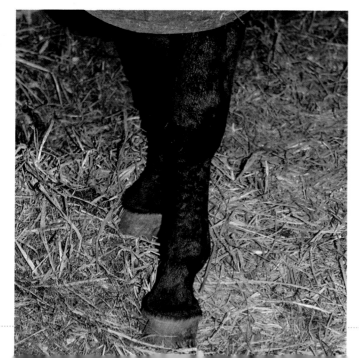

---

LEFT

*Whenever a horse rests or 'points' a front leg, as seen here, it indicates pain in the limb and should be investigated immediately.*

---

ABOVE

*When checking the horse's pulse rate always use your fingers, and not the thumb, this is because the thumb has its own pulse, which confuses the reading.*

# Common Ailments and Treatment

All horse owners should possess a basic first-aid box containing the following:

- cotton wool
- blunt-ended scissors
- a thermometer
- antiseptic solution for cleaning wounds
- a variety of different-sized dressings
- surgical tape
- gamgee tissue
- a selection of bandages
- self-adhesive bandage,

such as Vetwrap
- Animalintex or similar impregnated multi-layered poultice
- Epsom salts
- a clean bowl or small bucket
- Vaseline
- your vet's and farrier's phone numbers

### Lameness

Many horse owners will have to cope with some degree of lameness in their horse at some point. It can range from mild to severe, and be sudden in onset or gradual. If both forelegs or both hindlegs, or all four legs, are affected, it can be difficult to detect because there may not be an obvious limp; the stride

length may just be shorter or the horse may be unwilling to go forwards freely.

Nearly all lameness is a result of foot pain (the most common reason) or damage to the leg's soft structures, such as tendons and ligaments.

### Laminitis

Laminitis is a painful condition of the feet, caused by inflammation of the laminae, which are sensitive membranes on the inside of the hoof wall. It can affect any horse at any time of the year, but is particularly prevalent in small ponies, especially natives, in the

spring. It has many causes, but the most common is carbohydrate overload from too much rich food, particularly grass. Others include insulin resistance, too much work on hard ground, infection, lameness resulting in hoof imbalance, a hormonal disease called Cushing's, or reactions to certain drugs such as corticosteroids.

The hoof wall is hot to the touch, with an increased digital pulse. The horse will stand with its weight tipped back on to its heels, and will be unwilling to move. Horses with a severe case of laminitis may lie down and refuse to get up.

**Treatment** Call the vet. In the meantime, make the horse as comfortable as possible. Do not remove all access to food and water, and do not hose the horse's feet in an effort to reduce the heat.

### Other Sources of Foot Pain

Other forms of lameness in the foot may be the result of abscesses, where infection has built up and can cause the horse to be severely lame. Veterinary treatment will be needed to drain the abscess. Corns or bruises at the heel between the frog and the hoof wall are fairly common and are often the result of ill-fitting shoes. Stones can become lodged in the foot and

will make a horse instantly lame. Thrush is a smelly fungal infection of the underside of the foot, with a black discharge oozing from the frog. Bad stable management or poor foot care is the usual cause.

### Tendon and Ligament Damage

The flexor tendons and check and suspensory ligaments at the back of the horse's lower leg are vulnerable and liable to damage because of the amount of strain they take when a horse moves. Some injuries to these do not initially cause lameness, only some heat and swelling. If you suspect damage, rest the

horse immediately and call the vet. It is very difficult for the layperson to tell how severe these injuries are without expert advice. Early identification and treatment can make all the difference to recovery.

## Skin Diseases

Most skin diseases are not serious and are relatively easy to treat. But they can be infectious and spread to other horses, and even people, so prompt and efficient management is vital.

**Ringworm** This is not caused by a worm at all, but is a fungal infection that affects the roots of the hair. It is identified by small round bare patches, and is highly infectious to other horses and humans. The horse should be isolated, and all tack, rugs and grooming kit must be thoroughly cleaned and kept separate from that belonging to other horses. Wash your hands and exposed skin after attending to the affected horse to minimize the risk of cross-infection.

### Helpful Hints

Properly executed, homeopathic remedies can be very helpful in treating horses with skin conditions, from injuries to allergies.

RIGHT

*Mud fever is a painful condition that is commonly seen on the lower limbs, but can also be present on the underneath of the belly. (See page 76.)*

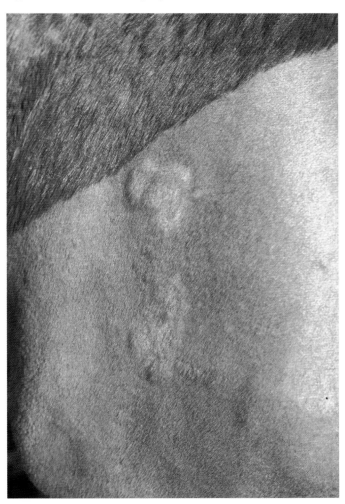

LEFT

*Ringworm manifests as small, round, bare patches, as seen here, although sometimes the lesions will exude a thick serum. It is a highly contagious condition, and can be caught by humans as well as other horses.*

**Sweet itch** This is an unpleasant condition caused by an allergy to midge bites, and causes severe itchiness around the mane and tail. It affects ponies more frequently than horses, and drives them to rub themselves raw. It is incurable, but can be kept under control through careful management. It is helpful to keep the animal in the stable at dawn and dusk, when the midges are at their worst, and fly repellent should be used liberally. There are also some specially designed rugs which have proved highly effective, made of light cloth which tightly covers the horse from nose to tail.

**Mud fever** Many horses suffer from mud fever at one time or another. When the skin surrounding the heels and the lower leg is softened by damp, bacteria enter the skin and infection develops. The skin becomes lumpy and cracked, and may weep yellowy fluid. The horse's legs may swell up, and it can become very painful. Horses get it from standing in wet conditions and mud, and it can be prevented by keeping their legs clean and dry, or covering the legs with grease or baby oil before turning them out. Wash mud off when they are brought in after turn-out or exercise, then dry thoroughly.

To treat, trim the hair back to help keep the legs clean and dry. Your vet will advise you on antibacterial creams to heal the infection.

## Colic

Colic means abdominal pain, and has an almost infinite number of causes and levels of severity, from mild to life-threatening. Always call the vet if you suspect your horse has colic, as early treatment is essential and surgery may be required.

**Symptoms of colic** The horse will look uncomfortable and uneasy, and kick at its belly. There may be patchy sweating, and its heart, temperature and respiration rates may be increased. Other signs are a failure to eat up, not passing droppings as normal, and getting up and down.

**Action** While you are waiting for the vet, try to keep the horse as calm as possible. It may be severely distressed and potentially dangerous; if this is the case, do not interfere. But if it is calm, remove any feed or hay from the stable, and note if any droppings have been passed. If the horse wishes to lie down, let it, but prevent it from rolling if you can. The vet will assess the severity of the problem, identify the type of colic and treat accordingly.

LEFT AND BELOW
*Do not diagnose yourself. Wait for the vet to check your horse thoroughly.*

### Some causes of colic
- Bolting food
- Ingesting sand from a stream or sandy ground
- Working hard too close to a meal time
- Worms
- Sudden changes in diet
- Poor tooth care
- Mouldy hay or hard food
- Drinking too much cold water immediately after exercise

## Fitness Regimes and Training

How fit your horse needs to be will depend on what you wish to do with it, but the fitter the horse is, the easier it will find it to work, and the less risk there is of doing damage to its joints, muscles, tendons and ligaments.

Allow 12 to 14 weeks to get your horse fit enough for hard work, such as horse trials, hunting or any form of exercise that requires considerable exertion.

### Before you start
• Check that the horse's worming and vaccination programmes are up to date.
• Check that its teeth are in

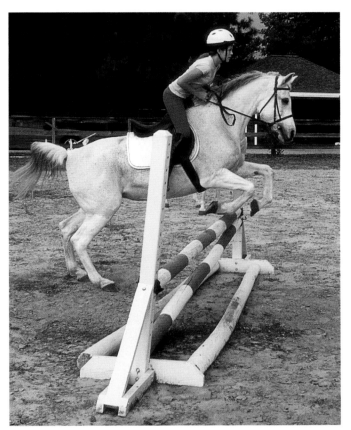

### First stage
• Stay in walk, including road work, for at least three weeks. Start with 30 minutes a day, building up to an hour and a half.
• If the horse is returning from an injury, extend the walking period to six weeks.
• Make sure that the horse walks out in an active manner and in balance; slopping along with the reins swinging will not help to get the animal fit and muscled up.

### Basic Fitness Programme
This plan assumes that you are starting with a totally unfit horse, but one that is in good condition. Horses in poor condition will take longer to get fit and will find it much harder. It would be better to spend some time improving the horse's condition before attempting to work it.

good condition and don't need rasping, and organize for the farrier to visit and shoe the horse if necessary.
• Trim and tidy up the horse's mane, tail and heels.

### Second stage

• Combine walking with slow trotting for another three weeks, building the exercise up to two hours six days a week if possible. Use hillwork to build up muscle.

• Some steady trotting on good roads helps to harden the legs, but do not overdo it, as it can make them jar.

• You can also introduce some schooling on the flat, some slow cantering for

short periods and, towards the end of the six weeks, some simple jumping.

### Third stage

• By this time, the horse should be ready to improve its respiratory fitness as well as its muscular fitness. Find

some open ground with good going, and start with a quarter of a mile of cantering interspersed with trotting. Build up the distance gradually until the horse is cantering for a mile at a

ABOVE
*Trot work, especially on a hill, as seen here is important for building up stamina and strength.*

good, controlled pace, once or twice a week.

• Slow work up a hill is beneficial; hillwork enables you to do shorter, sharper pieces of work with your horse without putting unnecessary strain on its legs by working for long periods of time.

• Hacking, schooling and gymnastic jumping should be done on the other days of the week.

## Interval Training

Interval training is a useful refinement of your basic fitness regime, and can be included in the final two weeks of the programme. It is designed to strengthen the horse's muscles and respiratory system by a gradual increase in 'stress', and consists of repeated spells of canter interspersed with periods of walk in which the horse is allowed almost, but not quite, to recover its pre-work pulse rate before going on to the next interval of fast work. Not allowing the pulse to drop completely strengthens the heart, lungs

There are centres devoted to Equine Assisted Psychotherapy and Equine Assisted Learning, where people with problems and troubles can be helped by both two-legged and four-legged therapists.

and muscles, and helps them to adapt to the stress placed on them. It also develops the capacity of the horse's respiratory and circulatory systems.

As an example, a horse getting fit for a novice-level one-day event would canter for three minutes, walk for three minutes, and canter again for three minutes, increasing the canter periods depending on how much fitter you wish the horse to become.

You must be practical: tailor your horse's fitness programme to suit the time you have available and your facilities. Not everyone has a hill to work up, or good hacking. Cantering the horse in balance round and round the school on each rein can, if done properly, be just as good if it is your only option.

## Rider Fitness

Riders are increasingly aware of the need to be fit to ride. Fitness is important because a lack of fitness for a specific activity results in early fatigue, which leads to a failure of skill and an increase in the risk of injury. If you 'hit the wall' and get very tired halfway round a cross-

*RIGHT*
*It is important for the rider to be fit as well as the horse. If the rider is unfit then it adds to the burden on the horse, especially when jumping.*

*ABOVE*
*Always wash the horse down after work to remove traces of sweat from the coat and to cool him down.*

country course, you effectively become a passenger and cannot help the horse when it needs it. We all want to ride our horses to the best of our abilities, and being unfit makes you a less effective, less balanced rider.

It also increases your risk of injury and your risk of falling off. Even if you don't want to compete, getting fitter can help you stay safe and injury-free.

Fitness can be divided into stamina, strength and suppleness. Stamina strengthens your heart and lungs, strength tones your muscles to allow you to do physical work without injury, and suppleness enhances mobility. For general fitness and non-competitive riding, a balance of all three is best. Depending on your riding discipline and how well schooled your horse is, suppleness and stamina are probably the most important, followed by strength. Stamina becomes more important the longer the duration of your discipline; endurance riding requires higher levels of stamina than dressage. Jockeys riding in races and event riders have to have a far higher amount of strength than endurance riders or dressage competitors.

# GROWTH AND BREEDING

Deciding to breed a foal is a big decision, one that should be thought through from all angles. Is the mare you are breeding from exceptional in terms of conformation, temperament and performance? Can you afford the stud fee of a good stallion and the associated costs with bringing a foal to life? If not, strongly consider buying a foal with proven parentage instead; it will be cheaper in the long run and less of a risk. But breeding a foal is also exciting and, if everything works out, very rewarding.

## The Lifecycle of a Horse

### Young Horses

A horse's life starts after an 11-month gestation period. Foals, whether they are colts (male) or fillies (female), are called so until their first birthdays, when they become yearlings.

• Foals have small bodies with what seem like excessively long limbs and big joints, and a short, fluffy mane and tail.

• Yearlings still look very young, and are ungainly and unfurnished. The limbs still look rather out of proportion to the body, and the mane and tail are still quite fluffy. In the Northern Hemisphere, all horses have

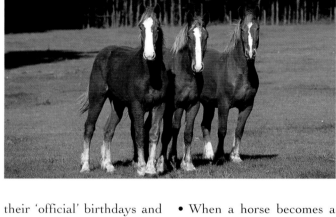

their 'official' birthdays and turn a year older on 1 January; the official horse birthday in the Southern Hemisphere is 1 August. Between 1 January (or 1 August in the Southern Hemisphere) and the actual date of their birthdays, horses are referred to as 'rising' to that age; i.e. 'rising five' means that the horse will be five years old soon.

• When a horse becomes a two-year-old, it begins to look more like an adult horse. The head is defined as much as it will be as an adult, and the limbs are more in proportion. The mane and tail begin to look normal. The body, however, lacks maturity and has very limited muscle. This is not so true of Thoroughbreds, which have been bred for early maturity for centuries and race in their two-year-old year. Remember, though, that they are carrying very light weights and racing in straight lines, not being asked to balance a large human while turning circles or jumping.

• Three-year-olds are distinguishable from fully adult horses only by a lack of muscle and general immaturity, and at four the horse is considered to be an adult. They are still referred to as 'fillies' and 'colts' until they are four, or five in the racing industry, when they become 'mares' and either 'geldings' or 'horses', 'entires' or 'stallions', depending on whether or not they have been castrated.

**Adult Horses**

Although different breeds of horses take different amounts of time to mature, they are considered to be adult at four years of age. This is the age when they can be exhibited in anything apart from youngstock classes, and when most horses apart from Thoroughbreds in the racing industry begin to receive formal education and work. The years from six to 12 are probably the prime of the horse's life and their best competitive years, although many horses, particularly those who mature late, may achieve their best results in their teenage years.

**Older Horses**

A horse is generally considered to be a 'veteran' at the age of 16; however, with modern advances in veterinary care, the science of feeding and understanding of welfare issues concerning the geriatric horse, many people

do not consider their horse to be 'old' until it is in its twenties. Indeed, horses can live into their thirties if well cared for.

Old horses show signs of age: the bone structure on the head looks more pronounced, the neck tends to lose muscle, the back often hollows and the withers stand out, and the limbs and joints may show signs of wear. The amount of work they do may need to be reduced, and the time spent warming up and cooling down should be extended.

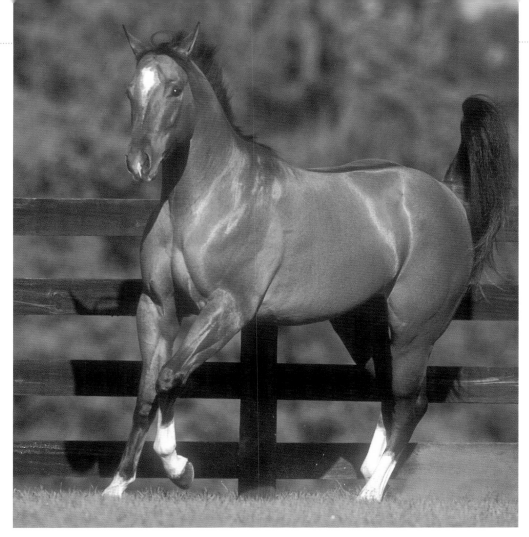

• Does she have good breeding? Horses with good bloodlines are easier to sell.

• Has she been a good performer? Again, the offspring will be more popular if its dam has a proven competition record.

• Has the mare got a good temperament?

• Is she sound? Many people decide to breed a foal from their much-loved mare because she is no longer sound enough to be ridden. This is not good practice; the foal may well inherit the same weaknesses as its mother.

## Choosing a Stallion and Mare

When choosing to breed a foal, you should first think about the mare. Remember that traits are inherited from both parents; it is all very well choosing an outstanding stallion, but if the mare is a poor specimen it is unlikely that you will breed a champion, or even a good, useful all-rounder.

• Does she have any serious conformation faults that she might pass on to the foal?

If you can honestly answer yes to all these questions, you then need to think about the stallion you would like to use. There is a huge range of stallions available at a variety of prices. It is well worth going for the best you can afford; the foal is likely to be a nicer animal and easier to sell should you decide to do so. Even if you plan to breed a horse for your own use, it is

• Is the stallion of a breed likely to cross well with your mare? For obvious physical reasons, it is not a good idea to cross a Shire horse with a Welsh pony, and non-traditional outcrosses, such as a part-heavy horse/part-Arab, are unlikely to inherit the strengths of both and none of the weaknesses, and will be harder to sell.

## Fascinating Facts

Most race horses are bred thoroughbreds who can reach speeds of 65 km/h (40 mph), but the American Quarter Horse, specifically bred for sprinting, has been clocked at speeds over 80 km/h (50 mph).

BELOW AND RIGHT

*The conformation of the stallion should be carefully assessed, as should his temperament, competition record and fertility.*

society? This will ensure that he is true to type and a good example of the breed.

• Is he a well-made horse with good movement, and would his conformation complement that of your mare? Two horses with weak hindlegs are very unlikely to produce one with a good hindleg.

• Is he sound?

• Does he have a good fertility rate?

• Is his stud fee within your price range? Some studs offer reductions to mares with proven competition records, so it is worth investigating this.

• When is the fee due? Often if the mare is not in foal by a certain date, or even does not give birth to a live foal, you may get a free return to the stallion.

• How far away is he? How practical will it be to travel your mare a great distance to be covered?

• Does the stud have a good reputation for getting mares in foal, and for looking after your mare well while she is in residence.

• What job do you want the foal to do? Try not to breed indiscriminately out of sentiment. Pick a stallion that is a dressage sire if you want a dressage horse, or an eventing stallion if you want to produce an eventer.

ABOVE

*Morgan horses, such as this fine stallion, are particularly popular in America, and are often crossed with Arab or Thoroughbred to produce small show horses.*

sensible to think about the future. Your circumstances may change, and a saleable foal will have a much better chance of a decent life.

• Does the stallion have an established breeding record, i.e. has he sired suitable foals before? It is safer to choose a well-recognized sire than one which is just starting out on a career at stud, particularly if you are a first-time breeder.

• What is his performance record? If he has not competed, why is this?

• Is he graded with a breed

# The Breeding Process

### AI or not?

Breeders must decide whether they want to use artificial insemination (AI) or have their mare covered by the stallion. If they choose AI, the semen can either be frozen or chilled. Fertility rates with frozen semen are often lower than with chilled, and it has a short life span once unfrozen.

### Advantages of AI
• You don't have to travel your mare to stud.
• You have a wider range of stallions to choose from, particularly from abroad.
• There is much less risk of sexually transmitted diseases.
• There is risk of the mare being hurt by the stallion while being covered.
• There is better quality control on semen.

### Disadvantages of AI
• It is more expensive than a stallion covering a mare.
• You need good infra-structure to transport the semen, and a vet that specializes in AI to administer it.
• Some semen will not survive the thawing/cooling process.

Mares should have a thorough pre-breeding assessment before under-

going AI, which should take into account any previous breeding history and the age of the mare: fertility declines after the age of 10, although many mares conceive at much higher ages. Accurate prediction of ovulation is important because the best time for AI with chilled semen is in the 24 hours leading up to ovulation. Pregnancy rates will generally fall if insemination is outside this range. This time interval is shorter than if fresh semen or natural mating is used, and the window of opportunity is even shorter with frozen semen.

*RIGHT*

*The mare is artificially inseminated through the use of a long 'insemination pipette', as seen here. The professional, whose arm is in a sterile sleeve, guides the end of the pipette to the cervix and into the opening of the uterus, at which point the semen is deposited from the pipette.*

*LEFT*

*This stallion is having his semen collected so it can be used for artificially inseminating mares. Artificial insemination cuts down on the risk of injury to the stallion and mare that can occur during traditional breeding.*

### In-Hand Breeding

The most commonly used method on studs is in-hand breeding, whereby the mare and stallion are brought together just for mating and are held by handlers. This

should always be carried out by professionals, and all precautions must be taken to minimize damage to the mare or stallion.

### Embryo Transfer

This is a relatively new method of producing a foal, whereby the mare whose egg is fertilized does not carry the foal to term, as this is done by a surrogate mare. It is increasingly used on top competition mares so that their careers are not interrupted and so that several foals can be born at the same time, rather than just one, as in theory there is no limit to the amount of eggs that can be fertilized and transferred to recipient mares.

However, it is very expensive and requires highly specialized veterinary expertise.

### Pregnancy

It is important to establish whether a mare is pregnant as soon as possible, and that she is carrying just one foetus. Twin foetuses are rarely successful, and are often aborted or die shortly after birth. If a mare remains at stud, she will be 'teased' about 12 days after mating to see if she responds to the stallion; if she doesn't, she will be examined by a vet a few days later. This will be done by manual palpation and with an ultrasound scanner. The usual pattern for scanning is 15 to 18 days after covering, again at 21 to 28 days, and once again at 35 to 40 days.

### Care of the Mare

To give a mare the best chance of producing a strong, healthy foal and of recovering quickly from the birth, good care during her pregnancy is important.

• Make sure that she has adequate nutrition. She will not need extra food in the early months, but consult a nutritionist later on to ensure that she is getting the right vitamins and minerals,

• Light exercise is a good idea; she will tell you when she no longer wants to be ridden.

• Keep stress to a minimum.

• Reduce the risk of infection, which could cause abortion or foetal damage, by keeping her away from young stock, horses-in-training and competition horses.

• Make sure that she has regular veterinary examinations, and check that her vaccinations are up to date.

## Fascinating Facts

Hormone-replacement drugs for women have been made with hormones derived from pregnant-horse urine. In recent years, these have been argued to be dangerous to humans.

LEFT

*A pregnant horse.*

BELOW

*The ultrasound probe is inserted into the horse's rectum. The uterus, read through the rectum wall, will show up as a dark fluid-filled mass with the embryo visible within.*

LEFT
*The heavily in-foal mare should be kept quiet and in a stress-free environment. She should be carefully observed for any signs of foaling as she nears her due date.*

## Foaling and the Young Foal

Mares are either foaled at their owner's home or at stud. For first-time breeders, it is advisable to have your mare foaled at stud by experts, just in case something goes wrong. Make sure that you are there, too, so that you can learn what to do next time. Very occasionally, a disaster happens and either the mare or foal is lost during foaling. There are special organizations and charities that can help by finding foster mares or motherless foals (i.e. they help people who need a mare for a motherless foal, or find motherless foals for mares who have lost theirs), which can make the whole business less painful for the horse and the humans involved.

### Foaling

Some mares foal outside in the field, but many are brought inside to a special foaling box. This must be large enough, with a thick bed and high banks of bedding against the walls. Most mares give birth at night or in the early morning, and most prefer to do so alone if possible. Mares 'wax up', where the teats secrete a waxy solution, before giving birth, but this can be misleading and happen quite some time before the foal is ready to be born.

When she is ready, the mare will become restless and pace around, holding her tail to one side. After the allantoic sac is broken and fluid gushes out, the mare will usually lie down. A normal labour will last between only 30 minutes and an hour, and the feet can appear out of the vulva after about 15 to 20 minutes. They should be followed by the nose, then the head, shoulders and chest.

It is usually at this stage that the amniotic sac is broken, and the foal can breathe. The rest of the foal's body should then appear, with the hind feet last. The mare will then lick and nuzzle the foal and

encourage it to its feet. The placenta will probably be expelled some time after this. If the process described above does not happen fairly quickly, the vet should be called at once.

BELOW

*After foaling it is imperative that the foal suckle as quickly as possible to ingest the infinitely important colostrum that is only present for a limited time in the mare's milk.*

### The Young Foal

A normal foal should be attempting to stand within 20 minutes of birth and should be up within one hour, and should suckle within an hour or two. Once on its feet and sucking, it should become increasingly well co-ordinated; after all, in the wild a foal must be able to travel with the herd within a few hours. Any delay in these timings means the vet should be consulted, as a delay in dealing with a weak foal could be serious. A foal's legs are 90 per cent of the length that they will be as an adult.

Like a human infant, the foal receives nourishment and antibodies from the colostrum in milk that is produced within the first few hours or days following birth. The mare needs additional water to help her produce milk for the foal and may benefit from supplementary nutrition.

The mare and foal are usually kept apart from others for a few weeks, then turned out in a group with other mares and foals. At about four weeks, the foal will begin to eat grass and grain alongside its mother, and at 12 weeks the foal needs more nutrition than the mare can supply from milk alone. Foals grow quickly, and can put on 1 kg (3 lb) a day.

Foals are typically weaned at about six months, but some are left on the mare longer. Most foals accept weaning easily, but some will become upset by it, and it is better if they have company of the same age and do not have to live alone at this stage.

### Helpful Hints

It is a good idea if a foal receives some basic training, such as being taught to lead, having a headcollar put on and being groomed, as well as having their feet picked up, inspected and trimmed by the farrier.

ABOVE

*Foals benefit from being turned out with others so they can socialize and play – the herd environment is their natural one.*

# TACK AND EQUIPMENT

It is easy to accumulate large amounts of tack and equipment, such as boots and rugs, for your horse, most of which you will use only once and which can cost you an absolute bomb. Invest in smaller amounts of the best-quality saddlery you can afford, and clean and maintain it carefully to ensure that it lasts. Also, make sure that it is not left lying around where it could easily be stolen: there is a considerable market in second-hand tack of doubtful provenance.

## Saddles, Girths and Stirrups

### Saddles

A good saddle is essential, and should be treated as an investment. It should be

comfortable for both horse and rider, and expert advice from a saddle fitter should be sought. The three most popular types of saddle are:

• **general-purpose saddle** This is designed for all types of riding and general activities. It is sensible to buy this as a first saddle, as it can be used for both dressage and jumping. It will be fairly forward-cut without being as extreme as a jumping saddle, with a knee roll.

• **jumping saddle** This usually has a flatter seat than

ABOVE

*When riding side saddle, the rider positions their seat squarely on the flat seat, the left leg hangs normally, and the right leg hooks over the top pommel. The lower pommel helps to secure the left leg.*

a dressage saddle, and is designed for riding with short stirrups, so has a forward-cut saddle flap and knee and thigh rolls to help keep the rider's leg in place.

• **dressage saddle** This is generally the most deep-seated saddle and often has a high cantle. The stirrup bars are further back than on a saddle predominantly used for jumping. The girth straps are longer than usual, and it is used with a short girth, to prevent the girth buckle lying under the rider's thigh.

LEFT

*The deep seat of the dressage saddle helps to stabilize the rider's position, while the long and straight flaps encourage the leg to lie in the correct position.*

## Girths

Girths secure the saddle on a horse's back, and it is really important that they fit well and are in good repair. Check the stitching regularly. Girth sizes are determined by how long they are from end to end, including the buckle, and are usually measured in inches. There are three main types of leather girth: the three-fold, where a single piece of leather is cut straight and folded over to form three layers; the Balding, which starts straight, with two buckles, but divides into three strips which cross over and are stitched together to reduce the width of the girth behind the horse's elbow where it could rub; and the Atherstone, which is also shaped to provide comfort for the horse, but is one solid strip of leather.

Girths can also be made of webbing, soft nylon or synthetic fabrics, which are easy to wash, but do not last as long as leather girths, string and a variety of synthetic leathers.

## Stirrups

Stirrup leathers and stirrup irons should be of good quality and well maintained; it is not much fun if your stirrup leather breaks halfway around a cross-country course or during a long-distance ride. Irons should be made of stainless steel, not nickel, which has a tendency to wear thin and break. They should be large enough to allow about 1 cm (½ in) at each side of the rider's foot; getting your foot stuck in the iron is very dangerous if you fall off. But don't use stirrup irons which are too big and allow the whole foot to slip through. Rubber treads fitted to the irons are a good idea, as they prevent the foot from slipping.

Stirrup leathers are made of ordinary leather (cowhide), rawhide or buffalo hide. The leathers tend to stretch when new, so check that the holes are still level with one another. It is also a good idea to switch the leathers over from time to time, as the one on the left stretches more because of the additional pressure of the rider mounting and dismounting.

# Fascinating Facts

The fastest horse ever recorded was Secretariat, who holds the world record for finishing a mile and a half in two minutes and twenty-four seconds at the 1973 Belmont Stakes.

at the other to the bit rings.

• **bit** This is the main device for communicating with the horse, and comes in an almost infinite variety of shapes, sizes and materials. The cheekpieces and reins are attached to the bit by buckles, hooked billets or stitching.

• **reins** These are the long strips of leather between the bit and the rider's hands, down which communication signals are passed. Make sure that they are the correct width for the rider's hands, and the right length.

• **noseband** This aid to control fits around the horse's nose and is a separate piece of leather which attaches only to itself, but fits through the browband loops and over the head under the headpiece. It comes in a variety of forms, such as the cavesson, which is the standard simple noseband; the drop, which fits below the bit and is stronger; and the 'flash', which is a combination of the two.

## The Double Bridle

This has two bits, called the 'bridoon' (snaffle) and the 'curb', and an extra headpiece and cheekpiece, called a 'slip-head' is used to secure the bridoon. They are buckled on the right side, whereas all other bridle straps are fastened on the left. The curb bit must have a curb chain attached to it, and a lip strap should be threaded through the 'fly' (extra) link in the centre of the curb chain to hold it in place. As there are two bits, there are also two sets of reins, and it is a good idea to make these slightly different to each other so that it is easy to tell which set controls which bit.

## Bridles and Bits

There are three main types of bridle: snaffles (any bridle used with one bit), double bridles (with two bits) and bitless bridles.

### The Snaffle Bridle

The snaffle bridle is made up of the following parts:

• **headpiece and throatlash** Made from the same piece of leather, the headpiece goes over the top of the horse's head and, in conjunction with the cheekpieces, keeps the bit in the horse's mouth. The throatlash extends down from the headpiece, and fastens around the horse's throat to keep the bridle in place.

• **browband** This attaches to the headpiece and goes around the brow at the front of the horse's head to prevent the headpiece slipping back.

• **cheekpieces** These keep the bit in place by attaching at one end to the headpiece and

*The long metal shanks that form part of this bitless bridle act as levers, so when contact is made pressure is exerted on the front of the nose, at the poll, and behind the jaw by the curb chain.*

### The Bitless Bridle

These are usually used to keep a horse with a sore mouth in work while the damage heals, but can be useful if a horse is particularly fussy or difficult in his mouth. They rely on nose pressure and leverage to control the horse. The most common form is the hackamore.

### Bits

The snaffle is the basic schooling bit and the most commonly used bit. It comes in a range of forms with different mouthpieces and rings or cheeks, each of which have a different action in the horse's mouth. Some popular ones include the eggbutt snaffle, the loose-ring snaffle, the French link, the straight-bar snaffle, the Dr Bristol or

ABOVE

*Pelham bits should preferably be ridden with two reins, though can be ridden with one through the use of a leather coupling, as seen here.*

the hanging-cheek snaffle. Gags are a type of snaffle, but more severe than most and, as well as acting on various parts of the horse's mouth, also apply poll pressure.

Pelhams are a combination of the curb and the bridoon from a double bridle in one bit. Critics say that this blunts the effectiveness of the bits and is a less sensitive aid, but many horses go well in them. They should be worn with a curb chain. Some riders have 'roundings', which enable just one rein to be used. Some pelhams, such as the Kimblewick, are designed to be used with a single rein, but most, such as the Rugby, globe, half-moon or broken, are used with two reins.

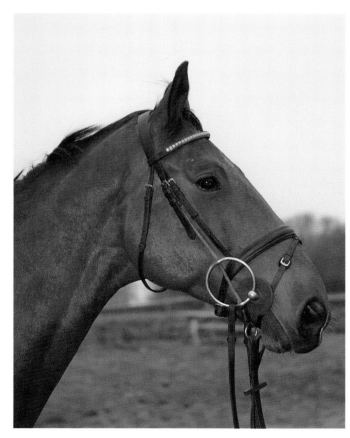

LEFT

*Gags should always be used with two reins, as seen here. They are a severe bit and exert pressure on the poll, while also applying upward pressure to the corner of the mouth that acts to raise the head.*

## Martingales and Reins

There are three types of martingale: standing, running and Irish.

### Standing Martingale

This is used to stop the horse raising its head too high. It consists of a piece of leather, which loops around the girth and passes between the horse's front legs, through a supporting loop on the neck strap, to the cavesson noseband. It should not be fitted too tightly and should not be used to hold the horse's head down.

### Running Martingale

This is a more moderate way of encouraging the horse not to carry its head too high, and takes effect only when the horse raises

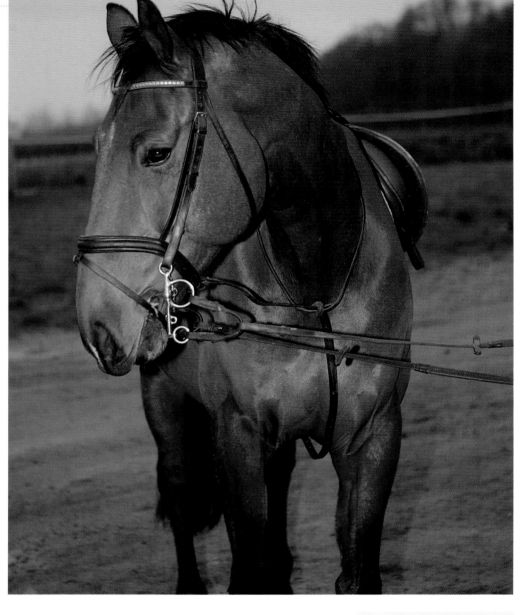

---

RIGHT

*Running martingales should always be used in conjunction with rubber martingale stops. These are positioned on the rein between the bit ring and the martingale ring.*

its head beyond the angle of control. It attaches to the girth between the forelegs; after it passes through the rubber ring on the neck strap that holds it in place, it divides into two. Each of these two ends is fitted with a metal ring, through which the reins are passed. Make sure that it is not too tight or, more commonly, too loose. As a rough guide, when the martingale is attached to the girth and both rings are taken to one side, it should be long enough to reach the horse's withers.

## Helpful Hints

Always use martingale 'stops', which are pieces of leather or rubber that fit on to the reins and stop the martingale rings from getting caught on the bit or the rein fastenings.

---

LEFT

*Standing martingales attach to the back of a cavesson noseband, and prevent the horse from raising its head above a certain level.*

### Irish Martingale

This is simply two metal rings connected by a leather strap approximately 10 cm (4 in) long. The reins are threaded

slippery, but is expensive and can be difficult to clean.
• **rubber** Rubber-covered leather, either on one side of the rein or both, gives the best grip. When a pair of these reins becomes tatty, do not throw them away immediately; often they can be re-covered with rubber by a saddler, as long as the leather underneath is sound.

through it under the horse's neck. It is most commonly seen in racing, and is used to keep the horse's reins in place and stop them flying over its head.

### Reins

Reins are available in several materials:

• **leather** Plain leather is very smart, gives the best feel and is most correct in the show ring, but can become slippery in the rain or on a sweaty horse. Plaited leather is less

• **webbing** These give good grip and, if they have leather 'bars' on them, do not slip.
• **string** These are often suitable for children because they are particularly pliable and should not slip, but may not be smart enough for competing adults.

**Lungeing reins** Lungeing reins are long webbing reins that fix on to a lungeing cavesson (a special type of padded leather headcollar used for lungeing) and allow the horse to move in a large

circle around the lunger. They should be at least 7 m (23 ft) long and have a rotating clip joint.

**Side reins** Side reins are used when lungeing a horse, and run from the bit to the saddle or surcingle to encourage correct carriage and flexion. They are made from webbing or leather, sometimes with added elastic inserts for flexibility. They should be carefully fitted and adjusted by an experienced person, and must be the same length each side. It is advisable to warm the horse

up on the lunge without them, then clip on the side reins when the horse is ready to work.

**Lead reins** Lead reins, made out of webbing and leather, attach via two clips to each bit ring. They are used for leading animals in hand, such as stallions, and in in-hand and leading-rein classes in the show ring.

## Boots

There are many types of boots designed to stop the horse from injuring itself or being injured. The main ones are travelling boots, brushing boots, over-reach boots, knee boots and hock boots.

### Travelling Boots

Worn while travelling, these boots are made of synthetic fibre, either padded or lined with fleece, and fastened with Velcro straps. They cover the whole lower leg from just above or just below the knee or hock to the coronet band. They must fit correctly and not slip down. Modern boots are so good that it is hardly ever necessary to travel horses in bandages now, except on particularly long journeys.

### Brushing Boots

These are worn while the horse is being ridden, and protect the cannon bones and the sensitive structures in that area, such as tendons and ligaments, from damage. They are shaped to fit the contours of the leg, and come in different sizes. The fastenings should be on the

outside of the leg with the strap ends pointing backwards. They are made of leather, Neoprene and synthetic fibres.

### Over-reach Boots

These fit around the lower pastern and hoof, protecting the coronet band and bulb of the heel. Simple over-reach boots are made of a single piece of ridged rubber and are pulled on; more sophisticated designs are made from padded synthetic

materials, are shaped and do up with straps.

### Knee Boots and Hock Boots

These protect the horse while travelling and are made of thick felt or synthetic material. They are also sometimes worn for exercising on the road and for hunting in country where there are walls to be jumped. The top straps must be done up tightly and the bottom strap loosely, so that there is no restriction of leg movement.

## Helpful Hints

Clean your boots thoroughly after use, as mud and sweat will rub the horse and give it sores. Straps should be kept soft and pliable, and should be checked regularly for weaknesses.

# Rugs

Not all horses need to wear rugs, but horses which have been clipped or those with fine coats will need extra protection from the cold and bad weather.

### Turnout Rugs

Called 'New Zealand rugs', these are designed for outdoor use. They should be both warm and waterproof. Old-fashioned canvas lined with wool is satisfactory but heavy, and there are many modern rugs which are light, easy to handle, hardwearing, warm and weather-resistant. They are fastened with cross-surcingles under the horse's stomach, and often have leg straps or fillet strings under the tail. It is important that they fit well, allow for movement and do not rub.

### Stable Rugs

A variety of rugs for indoor use is available. They come in all fabrics, and are padded to different weights. The less bulky ones are machine-washable, and it is a good idea to use a cotton sheet underneath the stable rug to help keep both the rug and the horse clean. In really cold conditions, a cheap duvet or comforter can be used between layers of rugs and held in place with a surcingle.

### Sweat Rugs

These are made of cotton mesh, synthetic 'breathable' fabrics or towelling, and are used on a sweating horse while it cools down to prevent chills, while travelling or to help dry a horse after it has been bathed.

### Summer Sheets

These are made of cotton and are used as an under-rug, for travelling in summer, or to protect the clean, groomed horse from dust and flies.

## Equipment Care

### Tack

Saddles, stirrups, bridles and martingales should all be cleaned regularly. Using a cloth and warm water, remove all the mud, grease and scurf from tack, then rub in glycerine saddle soap with a sponge. The bottoms of saddles and bits should be washed after each ride, and numnahs (saddle pads) and saddle cloths should be washed as soon as they become dirty: this may be after each ride, and certainly if the horse has sweated much. From time to time, take the bridle to pieces and clean each part separately before putting it back together. Girths should be washed to remove sweat and mud and to prevent girth galls.

Give your tack a good inspection every six months, and check for signs or wear and tear. Never compromise on safety, and take anything with loose stitching to the menders. Check your saddle tree by holding the pommel and cantle, and squeezing together gently. If the leather on the seat wrinkles, it may have a broken tree. Check that bits have not developed sharp edges or are not wearing thin.

### Rugs

Stable rugs and sweat rugs, if made from modern synthetic materials, can be washed and dried. Older, heavier rugs, such as those made from jute, will not wash easily, and these should be combined with a washable sheet as an under-rug, they can also be brushed. Some outdoor rugs can be washed, but they will need re-waterproofing afterwards. Generally, scrubbing the worst of the mud and stains off is enough, although there are specialist rug washers who will wash and mend your rugs for you. Check all bindings and straps regularly; horses are good at breaking them.

### Boots and Bandages

These should be washed, either in a machine or, if leather, by hand and soaped, after each wearing. Fastenings should be repaired and replaced as necessary.

# RIDING AND TRAINING

Riding is the reason most of us own a horse. Achieving harmony and understanding between horse and rider may be a long, slow process, but it is the aim of all who ride and worth working hard to reach. Good instruction from a qualified teacher who you find easy to understand and who truly wishes to help you improve is extremely valuable. Don't be afraid to 'try out' a few instructors in an effort to find the one with whom you click best, and be clear about what you want to achieve.

## Riding Gear

The most essential part of your riding gear is a hard hat that complies with the most recent safety standards. It is better to sacrifice elegance for

comfort and safety than to compromise your head, and hats should be fitted with a chin strap. Appropriate boots should be worn; these should have a heel, to prevent the foot from slipping through the stirrup. Short boots are more comfortable if worn with half-chaps to protect the lower leg. Trainers and athletic shoes are *not* suitable. It is a good idea to wear gloves when riding, even in the summer, to help prevent blisters and rubs. Jodhpurs or breeches are the best clothing for your legs, but many people ride happily in jeans or tracksuit trousers if just hacking. Hacking jackets are best kept for competitions and hunting. Make sure that your clothing is light and comfortable, and close-fitting enough to avoid restricting movement or becoming entwined in tack.

## The Paces

The horse has four basic paces: walk, trot, canter and gallop. At all paces, the rider should be in balance and harmony with the horse, and the horse should be going in a balanced, rhythmical manner.

### Walk

This is a four-time gait, and should be purposeful and regular. The sequence of footfalls is: left hind, left fore, right hind, right fore. The horse always has two feet on the ground at the same time.

### Trot

The trot is a diagonal two-time pace, with two beats to a stride. The sequence of footfalls is: left hind and right fore together, then right hind and left fore together, with a moment of suspension, when all four feet are above the ground, in between.

LEFT

*The canter is a three beat gait. A good canter should maintain a steady and even rhythm with the propulsion coming from the hindquarters.*

collection and extension. In collected paces (walk, trot and canter), the rhythm and tempo remain the same, but greater activity is shown. Each step is higher and shorter, covering less ground, and the speed is thus decreased. Extension (extended walk, trot and canter) is the opposite; again, the rhythm and tempo remain consistent, but the horse covers more ground with each stride without hurrying and losing the regularity. Both require more impulsion (controlled energy) than the basic paces.

## Canter

The canter is a three-time pace with three beats to the stride. When the left foreleg is leading, the sequence of footfalls is: right hind, then left hind and right fore together, then left fore. The leading leg is always last. When the right foreleg is leading, the sequence of footfalls is: left hind, then right hind and left fore together, then lastly right fore. There is a moment of suspension after the leading leg touches the ground.

## Gallop

This is the fastest pace of the horse, and a proper gallop (instead of a speedy canter) is a four-time movement. The sequence of legs with the left fore leading is: right hind, left hind, right fore and lastly the leading leg, the left fore, followed by a moment of suspension when all four legs are off the ground. The

sequence of footfalls with the right fore leading is: left hind, right hind, left fore, and lastly the right fore, followed by a moment of suspension.

When a horse is going in the correct way in all four basic paces, it is time to move on to more advanced work. This can include changes within the individual paces:

## The Basics

**Mounting and Dismounting**
Before you can ride your horse, you have to get on it. Check the girth is tight

*BELOW*

*When mounting place your left foot in the nearside stirrup and your right hand to the back of the saddle, jump and land lightly and fluidly in the saddle.*

enough to ensure that the saddle will not slip round. Pull the stirrup irons down, and check the stirrup length is approximately right. To do this, pull the stirrup leathers down, put your hand at the top near the buckle and lift up the stirrup iron. It should approximately reach your armpit.

We generally mount from the 'near side' (the left), but it is important to be able to do so equally well from both sides. Stand with your left shoulder to the horse's left shoulder, and take the reins into the left hand, which should then be placed in front of the withers. Put your left foot into the stirrup iron, and pivot to face the horse. Place your right hand at the back of the saddle, and spring lightly up,

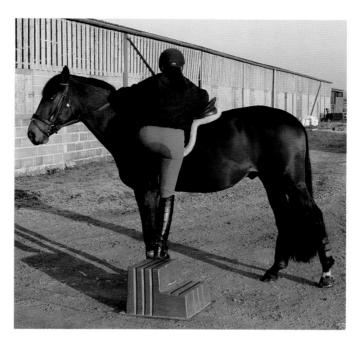

taking care to lower yourself into the saddle and not to land heavily on the horse's back. Put your right foot into the stirrup, and quietly gather up the reins in both hands. Although everybody should be able to mount from the ground, it is in fact often better for the horse's back to use a mounting block.

It is equally important to be able to dismount from both sides, and the horse should be used to you doing this. But usually we dismount from the near side. Remove both feet from the stirrups, and gather the reins in the left hand. Put your left hand on the horse's neck, and lean forwards. Swing your right leg back over the horse's hindquarters, allowing both feet to slip to the ground. Bend your knees and land lightly, clear of the horse.

Do not swing your leg over the front of the saddle and jump off facing outwards. This is dangerous because, if the horse moves while you are getting off, you can fall down and land flat on your back with your head near the horse's front feet.

**Adjusting the girth and stirrups while mounted** It is important to be able to change the length of your stirrups and to tighten or

loosen your girth without getting off. To alter the right stirrup, do not take your feet out of the stirrups, but draw up your leg, hold the reins in the left hand and use the other hand to adjust the stirrup leather. To adjust the girth on the left-hand side, hold the reins in your right hand, and put your leg forward over the knee rolls of the saddle. Lift up the saddle flap and adjust each girth strap as necessary, taking care not to pinch the horse and that the buckle guards are lying flat over the girth buckles. Ideally, the girth buckles should be at the same height on the girth straps on both sides of the saddle.

## The Rider's Position

The rider should sit squarely in the saddle, at the lowest part. You should feel your seatbones are carrying equal amounts of weight on each side, and your back should be straight. Don't be tempted to sit rigidly upright; your whole body should be supple and without tension, with the seat, thighs and knees lying relaxed and straight. The ball of the foot should rest on the bar of the stirrup iron, with

the natural drop of the rider's weight keeping it in place. The rider's ear, shoulder, hip and heel should form a straight line, and another straight line should pass from the rider's elbow through to the hand and along the rein to the horse's mouth.

Fascinating Facts

Anna Sewell's first and only novel, *Black Beauty: The Autobiography of a Horse*, was first published in 1877 and was an instant bestseller with an aim to abolish the mistreatment of horses, which won some success by helping end the use of the checkrein, a strap used to keep horses' heads held high that was damaging to the horses' necks.

ABOVE LEFT

*This rider is holding the reins correctly and is beginning to establish a contact.*

## Holding the reins

To carry the reins correctly, they come from the horse's mouth through the rider's third finger and little finger across the palm and over the index finger, with the thumb on top. It is important that the third finger holds the edges of the rein in the joints nearest the palm and that the fingers are closed securely, but without tension.

When holding two reins – for example, if you are using a double bridle – hold as for the single rein, except that the little finger of each hand should divide the reins. The bridoon rein is usually held on the outside.

## Contact

This refers to the relationship between a rider's hands and the horse's mouth, down the reins. It is important to be able to move your hands independently of the rest of your body, and to keep them still and soft despite other parts of your body being in motion. When you take up the reins, you should feel some weight in your hands. This consistent weight, which should be flexible and soft, but ever present, should stay the same at all times and at all paces. The horse should accept this consistent contact happily, but will do so only if the rider is in harmony with the horse, responsive and can 'go with' the movements of the horse's head and neck without tightening or dropping the contact.

The hands should be carried with the thumbs uppermost and the backs of the hands facing outwards. Wrists should neither be floppy nor too stiff.

## Movement

Riders must learn to position themselves correctly at all paces, and to stay balanced and in harmony with the horse at all times. The more supple and flexible a rider is, the better that person will learn to ride.

### At Walk
The only difference between the rider's position at halt and at walk is that the body moves slightly at the hips and waist in rhythm with the horse's

natural movements, and the elbow and shoulder joints move to allow the rider's hand to follow the movements of the horse's head and neck.

### At Trot
In rising trot, the rider rises from the saddle for one beat and sits in the saddle for the alternate beat (also called 'posting'). The rider's shoulders should lead the movement, in order to stay in balance, without tipping forwards and allowing the weight to come forwards on to the horse's shoulders. The back should remain straight; do not allow your body to collapse at the waist. Keep an even weight in the stirrups,

and keep the stirrups on the ball of your foot. Try to maintain a steady and even contact on the reins. Learning to trot is probably the hardest part of learning to ride; walk and canter are much easier, but practice makes perfect.

### At Canter
At canter, the rider's weight usually stays in the saddle. Supple hips are important to absorb the movement of the three-time beat of the canter, and the upper body should move in rhythm with the horse. If the rider tenses his back, he will bump in the saddle and the experience will be uncomfortable for both horse and rider.

### At Gallop
At gallop, the rider should carry her weight out of the saddle and on to the knees and stirrups. The reins and stirrup leathers will need to be shortened to allow this. The upper body should be inclined forwards, but with the weight posed over the centre of gravity. Balance is essential.

## The Aids

The aids are how the rider communicates with the horse, and are divided into 'natural' aids and 'artificial' aids.

### Natural Aids

**The legs** These are used to encourage the horse, and to ask the horse to change pace and direction. The inside leg asks for impulsion (energy) from the horse, and

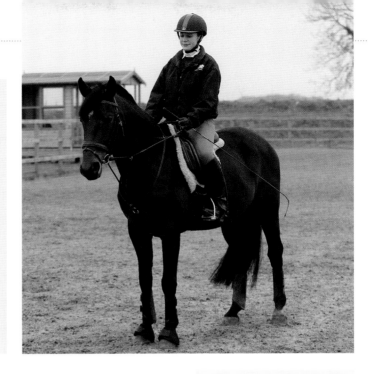

Fascinating Facts

In medieval times to 'earn your spurs' was to gain knighthood. Today the tradition of awarding spurs has continued when bestowing honour upon individuals in certain organisations, such as the British Order of the Garter or the American Order of the Spur.

**The voice** This is a useful aid, particularly in training the young horse and when used in conjunction with the other aids. It is also used to reward the horse, praise it, soothe it or, if necessary, reprimand it.

### Artificial Aids

**The whip** is used to teach respect for the rider's leg aid, or to correct the horse. But take care never to use it in anger. It is almost always because the horse does not understand that it disobeys; this is your fault, not the horse's. It can be useful to reinforce the leg aid if the horse does not respond, and

ABOVE

*This horse is wearing a running martingale, and the rider is carrying a long schooling whip, which should only be used lightly, but is a useful aid for encouraging the horse to move forward.*

to keep its mind on the job, by way of a quick tap behind the leg. Never hit a horse on the head or any other sensitive part of his body.

**Spurs are** made of metal, and fit around the rider's heel. The short shank at the point of the heel can be used to give a more refined leg aid, and should be used only by experienced riders.

to encourage it to bend correctly. The outside leg controls the hindquarters.

**The hands** These should keep an even contact with the horse's mouth at all times. They are the principal methods of communication and should be used carefully. The inside hand is used for direction,

while the outside hand controls and regulates the speed and pace, and controls bend. Used in conjunction with the legs, they are also your 'brakes'. All movements of the hands should be subtle and clear: remember that you are asking a question via a very sensitive part of the body, i.e. the mouth.

## Basic Manoeuvres

### Changing Pace

To change pace up, or increase speed, make sure that the quality of the pace you are in is as good as possible. Sit softly in the saddle, and give a firm nudge with the legs, while avoiding restricting forward movement with the hands. To ask for canter, balance the horse in trot, sit for a few strides, bring the outside leg back behind the girth while keeping the inside leg on the girth, and give the horse a firm nudge with the outside leg. Keep the contact constant and avoid leaning forwards.

BELOW

*This horse is demonstrating
a lovely 'square' halt. Its front legs
and back legs are parallel as seen,
and it is standing balanced and
ready for another command.*

To change down a pace, or decrease speed, maintain a good contact, keep the leg on to ensure impulsion is not lost, and ask the horse to slow down with a light 'pull' on the reins.

### The Halt

The halt should be 'square', i.e. the horse is standing still and straight with its weight balanced equally over all four legs. To ask for halt, repeat the instructions to decrease pace, but make the aid a little firmer and remember to use the leg as well as the hand. Never tug sharply at the horse's mouth or fail to prepare the horse for the transition.

### Turns and Circles

When circling or turning, the rider wants the horse's body to bend equally from poll to tail. Make sure that you resist the temptation to twist your own body; keep the hips and shoulders parallel to those of the horse, and turn your head only to indicate the direction you want to take. Your inside hand controls the direction, so ask the horse to turn with a firm but sympathetic aid. Keep the outside hand back to control the pace and stop the horse's neck from bending too much without its body following. The outside leg stays on the girth, while the inside leg may nudge the horse to encourage the horse to change direction and bend.

BELOW

*The rider is guiding this horse
around a circle. The horse and rider
should remain in balance while
moving round a circle.*

## Jumping

### Rider Position

To jump successfully, riders need to shorten their stirrup leathers by a couple of holes. This closes the angles at the knees and ankles, which should help give you a balanced and secure position over the jump, and allows you to balance over the centre of gravity without putting pressure on the horse's back. Practise the 'jumping position' in walk,

LEFT

*When jumping, the rider's hands should not press downwards on the neck, or be restrictive. Here the horse is jumping a cross pole.*

trot and canter before attempting to jump. Hold your weight out of the saddle (as for galloping), keeping the head up and hands forward. To practise

the position required over the fence itself, halt the horse, and fold forwards from your hip joints with a flat back and chin up. Make sure that your lower legs stay in the correct position, neither too far back nor too far forward. Push your hands forwards slightly along the horse's neck without dropping the contact and without using the neck to balance yourself. Practise again until you can do it smoothly and without overbalancing.

### Phases of the Jump

A horse's jump is divided into five phases:

ABOVE

*The horse should make a nice, rounded and athletic shape over an obstacle when jumping, as seen here over this upright fence.*

- **Approach** The horse must be going forwards in balance, with plenty of impulsion and in a good rhythm. This is the most important phase of the jump, and the one that usually determines how good the jump itself will be.
- **Take-off** The horse lowers its head and stretches its neck before take-off to assess the fence, and as it takes off it shortens its neck, raises its head and lifts off the ground, folding its forelegs beneath it. The horse's hocks come underneath it and, as its hind feet touch the ground, the horse stretches its head and neck, and uses its hindquarters to spring forwards and upwards.
- **Moment of suspension** The horse is stretched to its fullest in the air, with a rounded back.

• **Landing** The horse straightens its front legs, raises its head to balance itself and touches down with first its front, then its back, legs.

• **The getaway** The final phase should see the horse's hocks coming underneath it to rebalance and re-establish a good rhythm.

### Starting to Jump

Start with trotting poles, to get you and the horse used to the idea of negotiating obstacles. These are heavy poles placed approximately 1.3–1.5 m (4 ft 3 in to 5 ft) apart for a horse; for a pony, place them approximately 1–1.35 m (3 ft 3 in to 4 ft 6 in) apart. They teach balance,

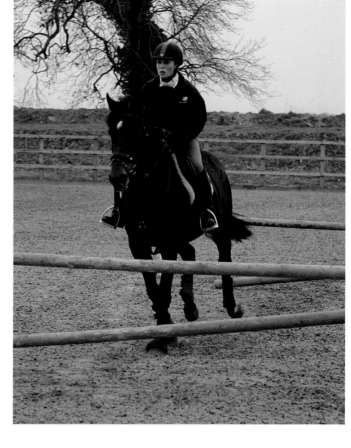

rhythm and engagement, and help the rider to judge distances and 'get their eye in'. Use at least three poles to stop the horse jumping them in one go, and trot over them on each rein and from each direction. Do not canter over them unless you have increased the distances between them to account for the increase in stride length. Add small jumps (cross-poles or uprights) into the grid, starting with two trotting poles and one jump at the end, until you and the horse are jumping a variety of obstacles in a straight line. Next, begin to build small courses, remembering to repeat each exercise on each rein to prevent the horse becoming one-sided.

## Fascinating Facts

### Jumping Distances

Aproached in canter a one-stride double for a pony will be approximately 6.1–7.3 m (20–24 ft) in distance. A two-stride double is about 9.4–10.4 m (31–34 ft). For a horse, the distances will be about 7–7.8 m (23–25½ ft) for a one-stride distance and 10.4–11 m (34–36ft) for a two-stride distance. A bounce (no stride in between; the horse takes off as soon as it lands) will be about 3–3.6 m (10–12 ft) for a pony and 3.3–4.3 m (11–14 ft) for a horse.

## Training a Young Horse

It is important that a horse's early education is done correctly. It is best left to those who know what they are doing; however, if you decide to train your young horse yourself, be sure to progress slowly, and take plenty of advice and help from experts.

Here are four golden rules to follow:

• Always be consistent and patient. Do not rush: horses like routine and need to have their confidence developed.

• Remember that young horses learn all the time. Make use of every opportunity to teach them about something new, and make sure that you never cut corners with their education.

• Try to imagine life as your horse sees it. It will help you to understand when and why it is frightened and will help you to anticipate how your horse will behave in certain situations.

• Remember that all horses need discipline: they will learn to take advantage if they can, and it is essential that they respect, but do not fear, you.

All horses are different, and will take different amounts of time to adjust to new situations and learn new things. You must be prepared to adapt your training regime to your horse, and do not panic if things take longer than you predicted.

**Lungeing and Long-reining** Lungeing can be used throughout a horse's active life as a method of training, or just for exercise. It teaches the horse to listen, to understand voice commands and to trust and obey the trainer. Done correctly, it will also increase concentration, strength and rhythm. It is a good way for a young horse to learn without the added problem of having to balance a rider on its back. Take care to lunge in big circles that do not put unnecessary pressure on its young joints, and do it for short periods of time. Voice commands must be simple and clear, and take time to make sure that your horse understands what you are asking.

**Long-reining** is when a person walks behind the horse, controlling it by the use of two reins attached to the bit, then taken through rings on the side of a roller. It is not easy to do well, but once mastered is an excellent way of getting the young horse to move forward confidently, and of developing the horse's outline, balance and understanding before it begins to be ridden. The horse can be schooled through all movements at all paces in the school, and asked to go out along lanes and tracks. Take care to make all commands clear, and remember that you are directly attached to the young horse's very sensitive mouth.

### Starting to Ride

It is a good idea to work with an assistant in the beginning. Commence by riding in the school or a small area to allow you and your horse to get used to each other, and to the idea of riding. Gently teach the horse, using a light, firm aid, to start, stop, steer and turn. Do not ride tight circles or ask anything too ambitious too quickly.

As soon as it is safe to do so, start to hack out to maintain your horse's interest and forward thoughts. Try to get the horse used to hacking with a companion or on its own. And don't just slop along down the road: hacking is a great way to school the young horse. Introduce hillwork to help balance your horse and improve its fitness.

*ABOVE*

*Long reining is a useful method of training for a young horse and helps the horse to gain in confidence and athleticism.*

Negotiate hazards whenever possible: open and close gates, walk down to the river, inspect that tractor on the side of the road, walk past those cows …

*RIGHT*

*Hacking out gives the horse a break from schoolwork and helps to keep his interest. Hacking out with another horse will give a young horse confidence.*

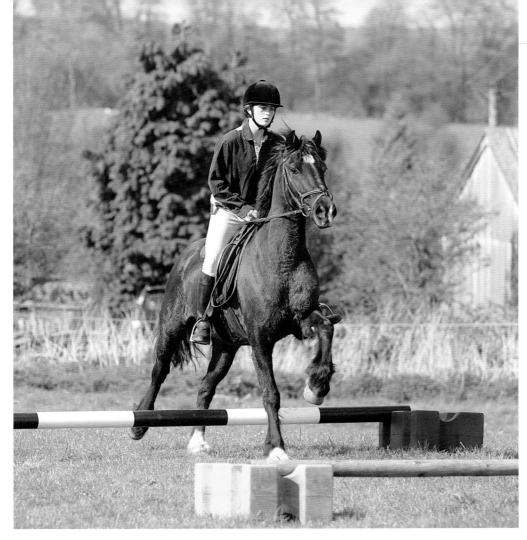

have to cost the earth, and the greater variety the young horses sees the better. Make sure that you give it a chance to jump ditches, water and small combinations before you take it to a small competition. Hunting is an excellent way of introducing young horses to a variety of terrain and types of obstacles in a herd atmosphere.

Use every opportunity to socialize your horse and introduce it to new things and new occasions. Not only will it be fun for both of you, but also it will have the added benefit that, when you take your horse to its first event, it will take it all in its stride. It is important to stay calm and confident; never lose your temper or take it out on the horse. Remember that you are in charge, and be firm but sympathetic. Horses do not think like humans, and it is unfair to expect them to do what we want if we do not give them the correct signals.

Practise 'schooling' (i.e. straight lines, bends and transitions) on tracks and in fields; your horse will learn that schooling is not something that only takes place in the confines of a school or arena.

### Starting to Jump

The best way to teach a young horse to jump is to find small natural obstacles while out hacking. This takes away from the enormity of the occasion and lets the horse know that jumping is a perfectly usual thing to do and no fuss is to be made about it. Keep fences, whether outdoors or in a school environment, small and straightforward,

and praise the horse when its completes the task successfully. Take care to give the horse all the help that you can; present

it correctly and do not overface it.

Use your imagination when building fences; they do not

## Fascinating Facts

A poignantly accurate inscription found at the Horse Park in Kentucky, USA, reads 'History was written on the back of a horse.'

LEFT

*Lots of horses really enjoy jumping. Keep them interested by jumping different sorts of fences including show jumps and cross country fences.*

# COMPETING

Although winning should never be the be-all-and-end-all of why you ride, competing is, for many people, an enjoyable way of socializing with other people and horses, and a good way of checking that their riding and training are progressing in the right way. It is a good idea to try a variety of disciplines before you settle on one or two to do; consider what suits you and your horse, what you like the look of and what is practical.

## Show Jumping

Show jumping, or stadium jumping, is a jumping class in which horses and riders negotiate a course of brightly coloured fences which are easily knocked down.

BELOW

*The jumps in a show jumping course will all be different, some are brightly coloured and others quite creative. Most courses will include at least one combination of either two, or three jumps in a line and on a measured distance.*

Heights range from 'clear round' classes over fences 0.3 m (1 ft) high to the towering fences seen in international Grand Prix classes.

### Equipment

Riders wear breeches, boots, either a shirt and tie or stock shirt and stock, a tweed, black or blue jacket, and a crash helmet that conforms to current safety standards. It is a good idea to wear gloves. Long hair should be neatly tied up or secured in a hairnet.

Horses should be presented looking their best, and usually wear forward-cut saddles specifically designed for show jumping. Most horses wear protective leg boots, often open-fronted tendon boots.

### Rules

The course will include verticals, spreads, double and triple combinations, with turns and changes of direction appropriate to the level of competition. The purpose is to jump cleanly over a set course within an allotted time. Time faults are given for exceeding the time allowance. Jumping faults are incurred for knocking fences down and for refusals. Horses are allowed a limited number of refusals; either one or two, depending on the rules under which the class is judged, before being eliminated. A refusal can also lead to a rider going over the time allowed. Placings are based on the lowest number of faults accumulated. Those who jump clear in the first round of the competition usually have a jump-off over a raised and shortened course, and the course is timed; the fastest clear round over the jump-off course wins.

Competitors should walk the course carefully beforehand. This is a chance for the rider to walk the lines he or she will actually ride, finding the fastest and best possible paths.

*Robert Smith is seen here jumping a large square oxer fence where the front and back of the jump are the same height, with a large spread in between.*

## Types of Jumps

• **Vertical** An upright fence made of poles or planks with no spread.

• **Filler** Not a type of fence, but a solid part below the poles, such as a gate, flower boxes or a roll-top.

• **Oxer** A spread fence, wider than a vertical. In essence, a vertical with a back pole added on a separate set of wings.

• **Square oxer** Both top poles are of an equal height.

• **Ascending oxer** The furthest pole is higher than the first.

• **Swedish oxer** The poles slant in opposite directions, so that they appear to form an X shape when seen head on.

• **Triple bar** A spread fence using three elements of graduating heights.

• **Wall** This type of jump is usually made to look like a brick wall, but the 'bricks' are constructed of a lightweight material and fall easily when knocked, so as not to damage the horse.

• **Hogsback** A type of jump where the tallest pole is in the centre.

• **Combination** Usually two or three jumps in a row, with no more than two strides between each. Two jumps in a row are called a 'double', and three jumps in a row are called a 'treble'. If a horse refuses the second or third element in one of these combinations, they must jump the whole combination again, not just the part they refused.

• **Fan** The rails on one side of the fence are spread out by degree, making the fence take the shape of a fan.

• **Open water** A wide ditch of water which a horse must jump cleanly.

• **Liverpool** A ditch or large tray of water under a vertical or oxer.

## Principal Events

The principal international show-jumping events, held under the rules of the Fédération Equestre Internationale (FEI), are the Olympic Games, held every four years; the World Championships, also held every four years, on the 'even-numbered' years between Olympics; the annual World Cup; and continental championships, run every two years. Nations Cup

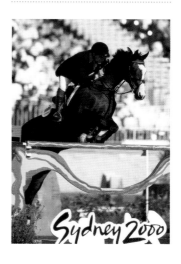

*Water jumps such as this one, which is called a Liverpool, are very wide and must be jumped cleanly. If the horse puts a foot in the water it is given penalty points.*

competitions take place throughout the world several times a year. Each show-jumping nation also has a national championship.

## Cross-Country

Cross-country is when riders and horses tackle a course of solid obstacles laid out in open country. A cross-country fence can be designed into almost any shape, and the higher up the levels a rider progresses, the more imaginative the designs become. Cross-country is the middle, and most influential, element of eventing, which is discussed later on.

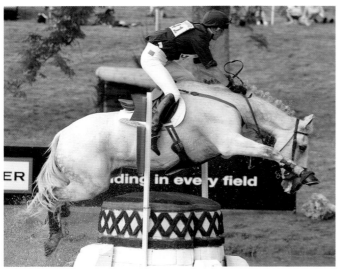

### Cross-Country Fences

These can include:

• **Arrowheads** These are narrow fences, shaped like triangles with the point towards the ground, designed to test accuracy and straightness.

• **Coffins** These are combination fences, consisting of an upright set of rails, with one or two strides to a ditch, then a further one or two strides to another set of rails. The horse must approach the fence in a short, bouncy canter, in balance and in a good rhythm, and the rider must keep his or her riding strong and determined.

• **Corners** These are a V-shaped fence that can have an angle of up to 90 degrees, meant to be jumped on a line perpendicular to an imaginary bisecting line of the angle, as close to the narrowest point as possible. It is a great test of accuracy and requires precise riding, as there is no room for error.

• **Trakehners** The trakehner is a rail hanging over a ditch.

Off-putting to both horse and rider, this is a test of boldness and bravery, and should be approached with energy and confidence.

• **Stone walls** Solid fences such as these are easy to jump, but require bold riding and bravery on the part of the horse.

• **Roll-tops** These are wooden fences with a rounded profile, which are forgiving and easy to jump.

• **Drops** The horse will not know that it is to land lower than its take-off spot, but the rider will, so it is up to

the rider to make sure that the horse is well balanced with its weight on its hocks. The rider should lean back and slip the reins, but be ready to gather the horse up again on landing.

- **Steps and banks** These are tests of a horse's power and agility, and should be approached from a short, bouncy canter.
- **Open ditches** These are more intimidating to the rider

are decided by several methods from those who jump clear, such as using a 'timed section'; this is part of the course, including jumps and perhaps a gate which must be undone and shut

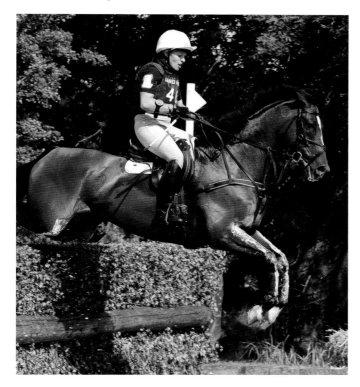

than the horse, and the rider should therefore ride strongly and confidently, maintaining balance and rhythm, and remember to keep his or her head up and not to look down into the bottom of the ditch.

### Hunter Trials

These are solely cross-country competitions, usually organized by riding clubs, Pony Clubs or hunts, and most often held in the spring or autumn. They take place in open fields, and competitors jump a course of wooden jumps usually of fairly basic design. The aim is to jump a clear round, and the winners

## Fascinating Facts

Polo, a sport played on horseback, originated in Persia around 522–486 BC as a training game for the cavalry, the king's guards and troops on horseback. Polo would eventually become the Persian national sport.

RIGHT
*When riding over a cross-country course, it is customary to put protective boots on the horse's legs and over-reach boots on its front feet. The rider will also wear a body protector as seen.*

again, where riders have to go as fast as possible within the limits of safety. Some hunter trials are judged on style or, in the case of pairs classes, on how well each pair keeps together over the fences.

### Equipment

Riders must wear a crash cap of approved standard and a body protector. Generally cross-country colours (a coloured rugby shirt and hat

cover) are worn, but a plain sweatshirt and your standard hat cover are perfectly acceptable. It is a good idea to wear long sleeves to protect your arms, and never jump in anything but the correct footwear. Always remove all jewellery. Most people put protective over-reach and brushing boots on their horses' legs, and the saddle may be secured with an overgirth.

# Dressage

Dressage is simply the correct training of horses. Any horse, from a Welsh Pony to a Thoroughbred, can do well, and dressage training will be of benefit to any horse undertaking any job. Competitive dressage, run internationally under the rules of the FEI but in individual countries by national governing bodies, is a way of testing that you and your horse are training along the right lines. Affiliated dressage starts at preliminary

level and continues through to Grand Prix. Dressage also forms the first part of the three-day event.

## The Arena

There are two sizes of arena: 20 m x 40 m (66 ft x 132 ft)

and 20 m x 60 m (66 ft x 198 ft). The smaller arena is used for the lower levels of both pure and eventing dressage, while the 'long' arena is used at the more advanced competitions.

The letters along the sides of the arena indicate where movements should take place. In the short arena, the letters, commencing clockwise at A, run A-F-B-M-C-H-E-K, with D, X and G on the centre line. The letters in the long arena are A-F-P-B-R-M-C-H-S-E-V-K, with D-L-X-I-G on the centre line. X

always marks the centre of the arena. At the start of the test, the horse enters at A and progresses down the centre line. The judge sits at C; as a rider progresses up the levels, there will also be judges at up to four other letters: B, E, M and H.

## Scales of Training

The training scale is used as a guide for the correct training of the dressage horse. It is not meant to be a rigid format, but a series of 'building blocks' with which to progress. Each element is interconnected. First defined in Germany, their German

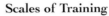

meanings are more encompassing and comprehensive than the words in English. The six scales are:

• relaxation (*Losgelassenheit*)
• rhythm and regularity (*Takt*)
• contact (*Anlehnung*)
• impulsion (*Schwung*)
• straightness (*Geraderichtung*)
• collection (*Versammlung*)

ABOVE

*This elegant combination of horse and rider are competing in a top level competition. The rider is wearing the top hat and tails required for this level of competition.*

## Equipment

At lower levels, riders wear tweed, black or blue coats with a shirt and tie or stock and stock shirt, and either a crash cap or hunting cap, although the former is recommended for safety. At advanced competitions, a tailcoat with a yellow waistcoat and top hat is correct.

Horses are not permitted to wear boots or bandages, or training aids such as martingales. Novice horses wear snaffle bridles, and advanced horses compete in double bridles. Dressage saddles, designed to help the rider to adopt the correct position and with straight flaps to avoid hindering the horse's movement, are used – although beginners would be advised to start in a general-purpose saddle rather than buy an expensive dressage saddle that they may not use again. Horses have plaited manes, but their tails are usually left unplaited. Turnout is very important.

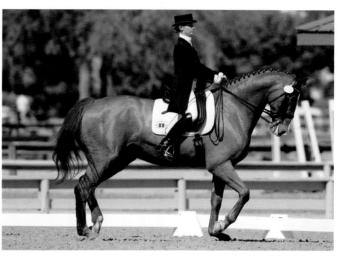

## Principal Events

The Olympics, World Championships and cont-inental championships run in a four-year cycle. At these, team medals are contested first, and all four team members ride the Grand Prix test, which is divided into two parts on consecutive days. The three best scores from each nation are totalled to count for the final team score. From 2008, the Olympic teams will consist of only three riders, so all three scores will count. The scoreboard is then wiped clean, and the top 25 riders from the team competition go on to perform the Grand Prix Special, battling for gold, silver and bronze individual medals. The top 15 from this then go on to a further competition for another set of medals for the Grand Prix Freestyle (*Kür*), which is performed to music of the riders' choice.

LEFT

*Eventing is mentally and physically challenging for horse and rider because it includes dressage, as seen here, show-jumping and cross-country phases, requiring a versatile and well trained horse.*

It is important to leave yourself enough time to walk the show jumping and cross-country courses thoroughly, and work out your approach to each fence.

Between phases, cool your horse down, untack the horse if appropriate, and make sure that it is comfortable. It is unwise to leave your horse tied to the back of the lorry

levels. Many Pony Clubs and riding clubs also run unaffiliated one-day events at novice and open standard, and horse and rider comb-

## Eventing

Eventing is possibly the ultimate test of horse and rider. The competitor is expected to complete a dressage test, cross-country round and show-jumping round, so must be proficient in all three phases and

prove boldness, accuracy, suppleness, trainability and stamina.

### One-Day Events

At affiliated level, each country's national body runs one-day events, where all three elements take place on the same day, at a variety of

ABOVE

*It is important to keep the horse cool between phases at an event. At the top events, and in hot climates, fans such as these, which are blowing a fine mist of cool water might be used to keep the horse cool.*

inations should be proficient at these before attempting affiliated competition.

You will be given set times by the organizers at which you must do each phase; there will usually be an hour or more between each one. The dressage is always performed first, then the show jumping and finally the cross-country, although the last two phases are sometimes swapped around.

(truck) or trailer if you are not in attendance, in case it breaks free. Leave yourself enough time to warm up correctly for each phase; it is no fun to be in a hurry and you will not perform to your best. After the cross-country, dismount after crossing the finishing line, loosen the girth and walk the horse back to the lorry. Wash the horse down thoroughly to cool it and remove sweat, and walk it until its heart rate has returned to normal. Check the horse carefully for any lumps, bumps and cuts that it might have picked up across country, and let it drink – but do not let it drink too much too quickly because it might develop colic.

## Three-Day Events

These are run under the auspices of the FEI, which is the governing body of all horse sports internationally. They start at CCI* level, and the top level is CCI****. There are six CCI**** events in the world each year: Badminton and Burghley in Britain, Kentucky in the United States, Luhmuhlen in Germany, Pau in France and Adelaide in Australia.

Although they are called three-day events, the competitions actually take five days from start to finish. The first veterinary inspection, where the horses are trotted up in front of the ground jury (panel of judges) for soundness, takes place on Wednesday. There are then two days of dressage on Thursday and Friday. The cross-country phase is completed on Saturday, and the show jumping, preceded by a final veterinary inspection and trot-up, finishes the event on Sunday.

completed a short section of 'roads and tracks', to be completed in trot in a certain time, then galloped round a steeplechase course, then underwent a short section of roads and tracks, which led then to the 10-minute box. Here horses were washed and cooled down, and inspected by the vet during a 10-minute interval, then they set out on a tough cross-country track of several miles. Almost all events have now adopted the shortened version of a three-day event, however, which does not include roads and tracks, or steeplechase. Riders must be sure therefore that they have warmed their horses up

A three-day event is very demanding for horse and rider, and both must be in peak physical condition. Until recently, Saturday's cross-country phase was termed the speed and endurance section. Riders and horses first sufficiently to undergo such a demanding test without these elements, which were in effect preparation for cross-country, and be sure that their horses are fit enough to complete the course without distress.

## Showing, Gymkhanas and Other Events

There are a multitude of activities that you can do with your horse, either competitively (such as showing, endurance riding, team-chasing or driving) or non-competitively (such as fun rides and hunting). The only important thing is to find something that both you and your horse enjoy and are suited to, and the best way to do this is to try a range of different options.

Competing is a good way of measuring the progress you are making as a rider and as a trainer of your horse, and it is a good incentive to improve,

ABOVE

*It is important for the horse and rider to practise at home and be prepared physically and mentally for competitions.*

but it should not become all-important and you must be realistic in your expectations.

The key to all success is preparation. Practise at home what must be done in the show ring, and make sure that your tack, horse and clothing are clean and ready the night before. Get there in plenty of time, and check whether things are running to order before you get your horse out of the lorry (truck) or trailer. Leave enough time to dress, warm up and have a final polish before your class; if entering more than one class, ensure that they do not clash.

### Showing

'Showing' is a very broad term, but basically covers classes judged on conformation, way of going, turnout and paces. At the top end, your horse will have to be a beautifully

behaved runway model with exceptional presence, but there are lots of local shows with classes for all sorts. Some are for specific breeds or types, such as native ponies or coloured horses; others are judged on suitability, jumping, turnout or simply the pony the judge would most like to take home. Working hunter classes will require you to jump a round over rustic fences, then those who complete this successfully will be asked to come back into the ring and perform a show.

There are also many in-hand classes where the horses are not ridden, but shown by someone on the ground. These may be a good starting point if you have nerves about riding in front of other people. All young stock and breeding stock are shown in-hand, and there are classes for almost all types of horse in-hand at many shows.

# Helpful Hints

Keep your individual show short and sweet, and design it to show your horse off to its best advantage. Use the ring cleverly, and plan your show in your mind well before starting. The judge may have a great many horses to watch that day, and will appreciate brevity.

RIGHT (TOP & BOTTOM)
*There are many different types of gymkhana games, but for all of them the pony and rider have to be very athletic and quick.*

Usually, all competitors walk, trot and canter around as a group in ridden classes, then are asked to give short individual shows. The judge may then ask to see the horses or ponies without their saddles and trotted up in front of them, and will then pick a winner. Remember that showing is subjective; what one judge likes another will not, and it is best to shrug your shoulders and plan for another day if things do not go to plan.

Turnout is very important, and horses should be as clean and tidy as you can manage. Your appearance is important, too; find out the correct attire for the class you are entering, and make sure that you are spotless and neat. Most classes will require horses and ponies to be plaited; however, classes for native ponies and Arabs do not.

## Gymkhana

Gymkhana games are often offered at local shows and Pony Club events, and consist of a series of races while carrying out different activities. Some popular ones include:

- bending race
- egg-and-spoon race
- walk, trot and canter
- ride and run
- apple bobbing
- sack race

Fast, nippy ponies are best suited to these, but there is no reason why the average horse should not give them a go, provided the rider continues to ride well and not get carried away in the heat of the moment into wrenching the mount's head around, walloping the horse or generally riding badly.

## Endurance

Endurance riding is long-distance riding over various types of terrain. This can be a very rewarding sport for those who do not wish to show or jump their horses, and is known for its friendliness and approachability at the lower levels. Arab horses are particularly well suited to it because of their great stamina, but any type of horse can do well. Rides start at just a few miles in distance, but progress up the grades to international competitions, which can be as much as 160 km (100 miles) in a single day, and many more over several days. Fitness of both horse and rider is crucial, and there are well-regulated veterinary inspections.

## Hunting

Hunting has always been an excellent training ground for horse and rider, and great fun for them both as well. It teaches horses to cross different terrain and jump a variety of obstacles in company, and is a good way of getting young, inexperienced horses socialized and going forwards. It is never compulsory to jump, and there are many hunts who jump little or not at all. Contact your local pack for more details and to ask whether you may come out. Horses should wear clean, well-fitting tack, and riders should be neat and tidy. Remember that you will be in the saddle for a long time, and it is important to be warm and comfortable.

## Fun Rides

These are organized by local hunts, Pony Clubs or riding clubs, and consist of riding in groups or alone round a preset course, which will often include optional jumps. They are an enjoyable, relaxed way of getting used to riding in public and a way to educate your horse about how to behave with other horses without the pressure of competition.

## Competition Checklist

If you go to a competition or other outing with your horse, you will need some of the following items, depending on the type of event in which you are taking part. It is better to take too much than too little, and you will soon know what is necessary and what is not.

### Horse
• Saddle and numnah (saddle pad)

• Stirrups and stirrup leathers
• Girth
• Martingale/breastplate if worn
• Basic first-aid kit, including your vet's telephone number
• Plaiting bands/needle and thread
• Grooming kit: dandy brush, body brush, curry comb, hoof pick, stable rubber, hoof oil and brush, mane comb
• Two buckets: one for washing and one for your horse to drink from
• Sponges and sweat scraper
• Sweat rug and surcingle
• Travelling boots
• Tail bandage
• Headcollar and rope
• Water carrier and lots of water

### For jumping
• Brushing boots, over-reach boots, bandages and gamgee tissue
• Studs and tools to put them in and take them out

• Cross-country surcingle
• Tape for boots, to make sure they will not come off mid-round

### Rider
• Approved standard hat
• Jacket
• Shirt and tie, or stock shirt, stock and stock pins
• Light-coloured breeches or jodhpurs
• Boots, or jodhpur boots and half-chaps
• Hairnet
• Basic human first-aid kit
• Whip/spurs as required
• Gloves
• Body protector
• Cross-country shirt and cap cover
• Waterproof clothing for wet conditions and sunscreen for hot days

# The Breeds

# EVOLUTION AND PRIMITIVE BREEDS

In accordance with Charles Darwin's (1809–82) theory of evolution, horses have evolved just like other animals over the millennia into the types and breeds that we see today. Through studying fossils, scientists can trace the original horse, the *Eohippus*, or dawn horse, back around 60 million years. They can also learn about the horses that followed – *Mesohippus*, *Miohippus*, *Merychippus* and *Pliohippus* – through to the modern horse, *Equus caballus*. The past helps up to understand the story of the horse today.

## Eohippus, the Dawn Horse

The origins of horses seen today can be found in the animal known by scientists as the *Eohippus*, or dawn horse, which existed up to 60 million years ago until around 40 million years ago. Scientists know that the *Eohippus*'s ancestors were part of the Condylarth group, which had five toes on each of their four feet and from which all creatures with hooves evolved. The *Eohippus* had just four toes on its front two feet and only three toes on the back feet. It also had pads on its feet similar to those of

dogs. As distinct from today's horses, it was also only about 35 cm (14 in) tall, although some dawn horses were as small as 25 cm (10 in) and others a little bigger than 45 cm (18 in).

The remains of these animals have been found in and around Wyoming, in the United States, as well as in Europe. In

1867, the most complete remains of a dawn horse were found in rock of the Eocene period in Wyoming.

Dawn horses are thought to have roamed in areas around the world, including Europe, America and Asia. Scientists suggest that these dawn horses lived in jungle habitats, as they were designed to eat

the leaves of shrubs. They also suggest that the horse's coats were dark with lighter spots, which would act as camouflage in wooded areas.

BELOW
*The Konik retains many characteristics of a primitive horse, particularly seen in its dun or grullo coat colouring with a dark dorsal stripe.*

BELOW
*Eohippus, or Dawn Horse, was a tiny animal with four toes on its front feet, and three on its back feet.*

## Fascinating Facts

Though it is hard to trace the origins of the first horseshoe, it is suggested that the Romans appeared to protect their horses' hooves with the predecessor of the horseshoe, the hipposandal.

same time, their muscles developed to allow greater movement and ligaments supported the foot.

## Mesohippus and Miohippus

After *Eohippus* came the *Mesohippus* and *Miohippus*. The *Mesohippus* existed in the Oligocene period about 35 to 40 million years ago. It had only three toes, with the central toe larger and longer than the other two. They were on average 10 cm (4 in) bigger than the *Eohippus*. It is thought that the horse's territory must have changed to firmer footing, and as a result more toes were no longer required. The increase in the horse's size and number of teeth also suggests they may have

begun foraging for a variety of taller foliage.

Scientists believe that at this time the horse's coat also changed to a more solid colour and that their eyes were positioned to allow for more lateral vision. This and the animals' increased size made them more adept at fleeing predators; despite this, *Mesohippus* was extinct by the mid-Oligocene period.

The *Miohippus* was a larger version of the *Mesohippus*, standing at about 60 cm (24 in), and it had an increased number of incisor teeth, again pointing to a change in diet.

The *Miohippus* developed around 30 million years ago and marked the gradual change of horses from browsers to grazing animals.

## Merychippus

The *Merychippus* developed next, during the Miocene period. These animals were about 90 cm (36 in) high and had less rounded backs than their predecessors, being more reminiscent of today's horses. They took even more weight on their central toes, although they still had three toes on each foot. With their bigger frames and longer necks, the *Merychippus* could reach high branches and their teeth were stronger so as to be able to grind grasses. By now, the eyes and head were shaped to allow a greater degree of vision from all around the animal. At the

## Pliohippus

The first single-hoofed horse was *Pliohippus*, which evolved about six million years ago. *Pliohippus* was the archetype for today's modern horse, *Equus caballus*, which was established a million years ago. *Pliohippus* was just over 120 cm (4 ft) in height and had a stiff upright mane. This species' head was also bigger and its neck longer than its predecessors. The ligaments in the legs developed further again for greater speed and agility.

## Equus caballus

The species *Equus caballus* was established about one million years ago. This species moved continents over the land bridges that existed until around 9,000 BC, from America to Europe, Asia and Africa. The animals became extinct in America around 8,000 years ago and were replaced by the Spanish conquistadores only in the sixteenth century.

## Primitive Horses

Scientists generally agreed there were three principal types of primitive horse that formed the basis for today's breeds. These are the Asiatic Wild Horse, the lighter Tarpan previously found in Eastern Europe and the Ukranian steppes, and the Forest Horse.

The primitive Tundra Horse no longer exists, but it is thought to be an ancestor of the Yakut, a tough small horse standing about 12.2 hands (hh) that can cope with the freezing conditions of the Arctic Circle. Although a primitive breed, it is not one thought to have had an effect on modern breeds.

### The Forest Horse

The Forest Horse was thought to stand up to 15 hh and be of stocky frame. They were believed to have inhabited Europe around a million years ago, but no longer exist. They had big wide hooves and a coarse coat, being a hardy type predecessor of today's heavy horses.

### Przewalski's Horse

The Asiatic Wild Horse came from the central Asian steppes and is the only true wild horse still in existence today. It is also known as Przewalski's Horse after the

Russian explorer Nikolai Mikhailovitch Przhevalsky (1839–88), who described the horse in 1881 after one of his expeditions.

### Tarpan

The Tarpan inhabited Russia, Eastern Europe and the Ukranian steppes. The last true wild Tarpan died in 1880, but a semi-wild herd now roams in Poland. The breed is thought to have influenced lighter stock today. The breed has a dark stripe running along its back and generally has a short wide neck. They stand about 13hh.

### The Konik

Those Tarpans that exist today in Poland have been redeveloped using the Konik horse, which bears a strong resemblance to the breed, and Przewalski stallions. The Konik is a Polish breed genetically similar to the extinct Tarpan. It exists in

reserves in areas including the Netherlands, Latvia and the United Kingdom.

### Sorraia

The Sorraia horse is an ancient breed discovered about 1920 that has outlived the Tarpan and other types of wild horse. Some argue that the Sorraia is an original wild horse, but others doubt whether selective breeding has influenced the type.

### Icelandic Horses

Icelandic horses are said to bear a closer resemblance to primitive breeds because they have not been influenced by selective breeding since the Vikings introduced them to Iceland from Scandinavia and Britain.

ABOVE

*The Bosnian pony retains many primitive characteristics especially noticeable through their heavy frame, short legs and thickset neck.*

## Bosnian

The Bosnian pony is an ancient breed originating from the former Yugoslavia. The type resembles the Konik and Huçul breeds. The Bosnian pony is thought to be the product of Tarpan and Przewalski breeding. The breed is used

BELOW

*The Fjord pony (shown here) bears a striking similarity to the Asiatic Wild Horse, or Przewalski, from which it might have descended.*

today for farm work, as well as a pack and riding animal. These ponies are notoriously sure-footed over difficult terrain. They have large heads, short, thick necks and straight backs in keeping with the primitive breeds.

## Fjord

The Norwegian Fjord horse is though to be one of the oldest breeds in the world. Believed to have migrated to Norway about 4,000 years ago, it has been selectively bred for about half that time. The origins of the breed are debated, but it is thought to have come from Przewalski lines. The Fjord is primitive in colour as

ABOVE

*The Tarpan was one of the primitive horse breeds that influenced the development of modern breeds, including the Gotland (shown here).*

well as type, and has a thick coat allowing it to endure tough winters.

## Gotland

The Gotland pony has lived on the wooded moors in Sweden for thousands of years. It is thought that the breed descends from the wild Tarpan.

## Friesian

The Friesian horse is an ancient breed thought to have descended from the primitive Forest Horse. Native to the

## Fascinating Facts

Horses are known to have two blind spots, directly behind them and directly in front of them, but horses have the ability of seeing in two directions as once, which is known as monocular vision.

Netherlands, the breed has influenced some modern British native types, including the Fell pony.

BELOW

*The Friesian may have descended from the primitive Forest Horse, and has itself influenced the development of other breeds.*

# WILD AND FERAL HORSES

**W**ild horses are those whose ancestors were not domesticated, whereas feral animals have domesticated ancestors who were at some point released into the wild. There are several types of feral horses in many different countries, from Mustangs in the United States, to Brumbies in Australia. Canada has Sable Island horses and Namibia the Namib Desert horses.

ABOVE

*The Exmoor is believed to have descended from the primitive Pony Type 1, and shares a similar jaw configuration to its ancient ancestor.*

## Przewalski's Horses

Przewalski's are believed to be the only remaining true wild primitive breed in existence. Only a few hundred of the breed are thought to exist today. They roam parts of Central Asia in small herds of five to twenty. A few can also be seen in captivity. The breed was though to be extinct until

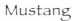
BELOW

*The Przewalski, or Asiatic Wild Horse is the only truly wild horse breed still in existence and is strikingly primitive in appearance.*

rediscovered by Russian explorer Przhevalsky (Przewalski is the Polish spelling of his name) in 1881. They have large heads, long ears, no forelock and lighter coloured muzzles. They are light in colour with a dark dorsal stripe and stripes on their legs, and they stand about 12 to 13 hands (hh).

## Mustang

Mustangs are said to be descendants of Iberian horses with Andalusian or Barb blood that were brought to Mexico and spread throughout North America.

During the nineteenth century, Mustangs escaped and were released into the wild and formed herds. Later, some of these stallions were replaced with different types such as Thoroughbreds in attempts to improve the breed.

Since the 1900s, the number of feral Mustangs in the United States has decreased dramatically as the horses were sold for meat or military uses. The animals came under protective law from

the 1970s, but there are still thought to be fewer than 25,000 in existence, in areas such as Nevada and Montana.

## Exmoor

Exmoor, in the south-west of England, has high moorlands that are home to herds of feral Exmoor ponies. These are the oldest ponies in Great Britain. As well as the original stock,

breeders continually try to improve the breed. The animals roam free until the autumn, when mares and foals are rounded up to be inspected and branded by the breed's society.

There are fewer than 1,000 in the world, but the Exmoor National Park Authority has founded two herds that are protected in their natural environment.

BELOW

*The American Mustang is a feral horse of widely divergent conformation. They generally have an extremely tough constitution.*

The ponies are about 12.3 hh and are generally brown, bay or dun. Their most distinctive marking is their mealy muzzle. They have broad foreheads, thick necks, wide backs and short legs, all characteristics that link them more closely with primitive breeds.

## Fascinating Facts

The first evidence of a nailed-on horseshoe appears around AD 500–600 and is credited to the Celts of Gaul.

ABOVE
*The Australian Brumby lives a feral existence, although they are routinely rounded up and sold, and can make riding horses.*

For centuries, the Exmoor pony existed on the moor with little human interference. In the past 200

RIGHT
*These horses are particularly tough and brave, and are favoured by the French cowboy for herding the dangerous Camargue bulls.*

years, however, changes such as enclosure of parts of the moor and crossbreeding of native ponies has affected the breed.

## Brumby

The Brumby ponies are free-roaming in Australia. The feral breed is found across the country including south-eastern areas, the Northern Territory and Queensland. The breed is thought to have been established from the escaped horses of European settlers. Many horses also arrived in Australia from South Africa, the UK and Indonesia. There is thought to be a fair amount of Thoroughbred influence.

Over the years some of the feral horses have been rounded up and sold.

## Camargue

The free-roaming Camargue horses are found in south-eastern France on the watery plains and salt marshes. The ancient breed is believed to

BELOW
*These diminutive and rare ponies are not always correct in their conformation, but are extremely hardy.*

have been crossbred with other breeds including Arabian blood. They stand from about 13.2 hh to 14hh.

## Misaki

The Misaki is a pony native to Japan and dates back around 2,000 years. There are only about 100 of the breed still in existence, and it is considered an endangered species. The feral horses live in national parks and stand around 12.2 hh to 13.2hh, with most being black or bay in colour.

# THE EQUUS FAMILY

*Pliohippus*, the first single-toed animal related to today's horse, developed during the Pliocene period about six million years ago and stood more than 120 cm (4 ft) in height. Today's horse emerged from the *Pliohippus* in the later part of the Ice Age, being known as *Equus caballus*. Zebras, asses and hemionids also evolved from the *Pliohippus* and are part of the genus *Equus*.

At the end of the Ice Age, horses existed in Europe and Asia, but zebras were prevalent in South Africa, asses in north Africa and hemionids in the Middle East. While horses were being domesticated in Eurasia, on the other side of the world their *Equus* family counterparts were also being put to use.

BELOW

*Each zebra has its own unique pattern of stripes, and a short upstanding mane. The plains zebra is the zebra most commonly seen in captivity.*

## Zebras

There are only three main species of zebra still in existence, the plains, Grevy's and mountain zebras. The quagga, another variety of zebra, became extinct in the nineteenth century.

### Plains Zebra

The plains, or common, zebra is also known as *Equus quagga* or Burchell's zebra, and can be found in parts of eastern and South Africa, as well as in captivity. They are on average 13.3 hh, with males weighing more than females. Like all zebras, they have distinctive black-and-white markings that are vertical on the body and horizontal on the legs. Some coats have an area of brown hair between the black and white hair. For all zebras, these lines serve as camouflage.

In the wild, zebras live in dry habitats and have to migrate to find water and food. They graze on a variety of grasses, as well as plants, leaves and other forage. These animals are hunted in the wild by, for example, lions and crocodiles. They inhabit open plains when possible, to give them the best chance of spotting predators from a distance and therefore being able to flee. They live in herds with one stallion to each few mares and their young.

There are generally agreed to be four types of plains zebra, all with differences in their markings – the Grant's zebra, Chapman's zebra, Selous's zebra and Burchell's zebra (confusingly, a subspecies as well as the alternative overall name).

## Grevy's Zebra

Grevy's zebras live in dry savannah habitats in parts of Kenya, Ethiopia and Somalia. These zebras cope with dry, hot habitats and even survive for periods of time without water. They have large wide ears and particularly distinctive and narrow stripe patterns. Their bellies, however, are usually completely white. They are the largest of the zebras, standing at around 15.3 hh. They, too, live on grasses and foliage. Again, these animals live in small family or bachelor herds.

When born after a gestation period of 13 months, Grevy's zebras are light brown with darker brown stripes, again for camouflage. They were until recently poached widely

for their distinctive skins, causing numbers to diminish and the species to become endangered. Such hunting is now banned in Kenya.

## Mountain Zebra

There are two subspecies of mountain zebra that live in southern parts of Africa, these are Hartmann's zebra and the Cape Mountain zebra, which is an endangered species and so given protection in Kenyan national parks.

They largely inhabit the desert type areas of south-west Africa.

## Donkeys

The common domestic donkey or ass stands around just over a metre (3 ft) high. There are also miniature

breeds, however, that can be nearly half this height, and other breeds that can reach up to 15 hh. Donkeys originate from North Africa and are built to endure hot climates and desert landscapes.

Despite being from the same species, donkeys differ from horses in that their bray is not like a horse's neigh, they have long ears, they do not have forelocks and their manes tend to be short and stiff. They have shorter tails than horses and are often flatter at the withers and across their backs. They can be a variety of colours, including black, brown and grey, and have a dorsal stripe that forms a cross at the withers.

## Mules

Mules are a cross between a horse or pony and a donkey. The offspring of a male donkey and female horse is correctly referred to as a 'mule', whereas a female donkey and a male horse would produce a 'hinny'.

Hinnies and mules differ in stature and temperament, and mules are more common being generally preferred. Broadly speaking, mules are said to have a horse's body with a donkey's limbs, which are straighter than those of a horse. They have longer ears than horses and similarly short manes to donkeys. Again, like donkeys, they have low withers and flat backs.

The hinny, in contrast, tends to have the body of a donkey, but the ears are shorter than those of a mule and the mane and tail longer and fuller. Their legs are stronger and the hooves less upright, the body rounder and deeper, and the head shorter and narrower.

It is possible for a mule to be bigger than both its parents, and mules tend to live longer than either other species, too. Mules are generally stronger and hardier, and have more stamina, than hinnies. Mules are popularly used to transport tourists on riding holidays in areas of difficult terrain as they are sure-footed and reliable, despite their stubborn reputations.

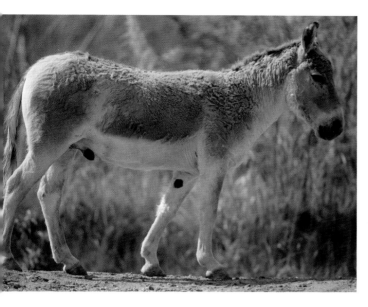

## Hemionids

Hemionids are half-asses, possessing some attributes of horses and donkeys. Also known as Asian wild asses, or onagers, hemionids live in desert habitats in areas such as India, Israel and Syria.

predominantly brown coat. They are recognizable for their particularly long legs. Some onagers are endangered species. They have been used to pull carts, but also have a bad reputation for being difficult to tame.

The Mongolian kulan is a type of hemionid found in desert habitats of Central Asia and standing between 12 hh and 13 hh. Their numbers are declining due in part to poaching. They are

They tend to be slightly bigger than donkeys and have a black dorsal stripe and

grassland areas. They are one of the biggest types of wild ass, standing around 14 hh. Kiangs have large heads and short upright manes like donkeys. Their coats, like other onagers, change colour with the seasons and are more chestnut in the summer and darker in the winter. Their

said to run even faster than a Thoroughbred, reaching speeds of up to 75 km/h (40 mph). They have particularly large nostrils, allowing them to take in large amounts of air per breath and therefore compensate for the thin air of their habitat.

The kiang is another subspecies of hemionid. The kiang is native to Tibet, where they live in wooded and

bellies are all-white, a characteristic of several types of zebra, ass and hemionid. They also have a dark dorsal stripe running from their manes to their tails. Wolves are a threat to these animals, as are human poachers.

## Fascinating Facts

According to superstition the luckiest horseshoe comes from the hind leg of a grey mare, but if you hang any horseshoe upside down the luck runs out.

# EXPLAINING BREEDS

So what is a breed? A breed is a subspecies of an animal – in this case, a horse or pony. Horses and ponies of the same breed will, to a greater or lesser extent, resemble each other physically, in size, shape and sometimes colour. They may also have similar traits in terms of their physical capabilities, such as speed, and their temperament. A true 'breed' is one with a true-breeding population, which reliably passes on the same characteristics to offspring again and again. But many 'breeds' of horse exist which are too recent to be totally true-breeding, as this is a process which takes multiple generations to establish.

ABOVE

*The Arab horse has been influential in the majority of all 'modern' horse breeds, and almost always improves the stock it is crossed with.*

## Arabs and Thoroughbreds

The Arab is the oldest breed of horse, and the only one which is truly pure. With the Barb, from North Africa, and the Spanish horse the Andalusian, it is one of the three breeds which have had the greatest influence on light horses the world over.

The Thoroughbred developed chiefly from Arab blood, but it is a larger, faster specimen. Nowadays, the Thoroughbred is the most influential breed in the world. It is also an example of a breed with a 'closed studbook'. Only animals whose parents are registered in the studbook (or another registry recognized by the studbook) can be admitted into such a studbook.

In the United Kingdom, the Thoroughbred studbook is called the *General Stud Book*, and it has been published every four years since

1793 by Weatherbys, which administers racing in the UK. Thoroughbred studbooks around the world are based on the *General Stud Book*, and all Thoroughbreds can be traced back to the first edition.

ABOVE

*The Thoroughbred is one of the best known, classiest and important breeds of horse in the world.*

## Old and New

Some breeds of horse are old and well recognized, while others are more recent and are still developing. Examples of old breeds include the United Kingdom's native ponies, which developed over hundreds of years of natural

LEFT

*Sadly the numbers of this magnificent breed, the Cleveland Bay, have greatly diminished and efforts are under way to restore it.*

selection to survive in wild regions such as the Welsh mountains and Exmoor.

The Cleveland Bay is another ancient breed in the UK, but one which has been influenced by humans. A bay packhorse was bred in an area of Yorkshire including Cleveland in the Middle Ages. It was known as the Chapman Horse because it carried the wares of chapmen (travelling traders). Andalusian and Barb blood was introduced into the Chapman Horse to create the Cleveland Bay in the latter part of the seventeenth century.

ABOVE
*This American Shetland is finer and longer in the leg than its Scottish counterpart, and has more horse-like proportions.*

Essentially, breeds are created by people taking individuals of different breeds with certain characteristics and trying to fix those characteristics through selective crossbreeding and inbreeding. The breed can come to bear little resemblance to its original foundation stock. For example, the American Shetland is an artificial breed with little in common with its Scottish ancestors. This breed was developed by crossing finer Shetlands with Hackney

ponies, then introducing some Arab and small Thoroughbred blood.

An example of a very new breed is the Wielkopolski, which originated in Poland in the 1960s. It is a cross between two now-extinct Polish breeds, the Poznan and the

BELOW
*The Wielkopolski is a Polish success story. The young breed has proved to be exceptionally talented for producing sports horses.*

Mazury, with Arab and Thoroughbred influences, too. The Pony of the Americas is another recent breed, which is now very popular in the

United States. This breed originated in 1954 when an Appaloosa mare was crossed with a Shetland stallion. Welsh ponies and other breeds including Arabs and Quarter Horses have also contributed to the Pony of the Americas.

## Studbooks

There are many studbooks for different breeds all over

the world, some with more stringent requirements for inclusion than others. There are also organizations, such as Sport Horse Breeding of Great Britain, which

ABOVE
*The distinctive and elegant Pony of the Americas is an athletic and popular breed that has proved its merit in the competitive forum.*

accept horses of different breeds, but have rules for inclusion based on breeding, performance and/or progeny, and which hold gradings (tests to determine suitability for breeding) for stallions and mares.

## Fascinating Facts

The phrase 'That's a horse of a different colour' originated in Shakespeare's *Twelfth Night* in 1601

# TYPES

'Types' of horses are not breeds, but usually a group of breeds that share similar characteristics or are used for a particular activity such as polo or hunting. They do not have a breed registry, and may either be one of a certain number of different registered breeds, or horses of mixed and indifferent breeding that are alike in appearance, behaviour or use. Polo ponies, cobs, hacks, hunters, draught horses, gaited horses – all are examples of 'types' of horse.

## Polo Pony

All horses used to play the sport of polo are referred to as 'ponies', although most of them will be quite a bit bigger than the official maximum height of a pony (14.2 hands (hh), or 147 cm/57 in). Most polo ponies measure between 15 hh and 16 hh, and are usually Thoroughbreds. Many ex-racehorses find a second career in polo, but there are also studs which

purpose-breed polo ponies, particularly in Argentina. There the ponies may be a combination of Thoroughbred blood and the native Criollo breed. Polo ponies need to be fast, agile and quick-thinking – and, due to the rough nature of the sport, brave. They are competed with hogged (shaven) manes.

## Riding Pony

The term 'riding pony' is usually used to refer to show ponies, originally developed in the United Kingdom, but now found worldwide. Ranging in

height from about 12 hh to 14.2 hh, they are fine, elegant creatures that more resemble small horses than traditional ponies. They are usually a mix of either Thoroughbred or Arab blood with Welsh, and developed after the Second World War when small Thoroughbreds and Arabs were turned out on the Welsh

hills to improve the stock. There are three main types: the show pony, which looks like a miniature show hack or Thoroughbred; the show hunter pony, which is just as elegant, but stockier and able to carry a little more weight; and the working hunter pony, which has more substance and is more 'workmanlike' than the other two types.

## Fascinating Facts

The first female jockey, Diane Crump, broke onto the scene in 1969 and became the first woman to ride in a pari-mutuel race in North America.

## Hunter

'Hunters' can either be show hunters, or 'working' hunters, i.e. those whose job it is to go hunting, termed in the United States a 'field hunter'. Show hunters in the United States are usually judged on how well they perform over a course of fences; show hunters in the United Kingdom are usually exhibited on the flat. Turnout, attitude, movement and conformation are important. In the United Kingdom, show hunter classes are divided into lightweight, middleweight and heavyweight sections, and are won by quality animals that demonstrate substance, manners and elegance.

ABOVE

*Hunters vary considerably in stamp and type, but should always have correct conformation and good paces.*

'Field' hunters must have the stamina, manners, jumping ability, boldness and speed to carry their riders over a variety of terrain for several hours at a time. They come in an infinite variety of shapes and sizes, but are united by possessing the characteristics listed above.

BELOW

*Cobs are distinctively heavy through their frame and generally have the most wonderful, calm temperaments.*

ABOVE

*The Hack is one of the most elegant of show horses, and should have impeccable manners as well as superb conformation and movement.*

## Hack

Hacks are most elegant members of the showing community, and should have superb movement, manners and conformation. They are primarily Thoroughbreds, and classes are divided into small hacks (up to 15 hh) and large hacks (up to 15.3 hh). Disobedience and misbehaviour are severely punished in hack classes – they are supposed to perform an advanced show smoothly, calmly and obediently. The type originally developed from the smart riding horses that ladies and gentlemen used to parade around London's Hyde Park in the nineteenth century in order to 'be seen'.

## Cob

'Cobs' are small, stocky horses with compact bodies, short legs and steady dispositions. They are usually of unknown or mixed breeding; perhaps an Irish Draught horse crossed with a hunter mare with a little Thoroughbred blood. They are different from Welsh Cobs, which are a separate breed. It is said that the classic show cob has 'the head of a lady and the backside of a cook'. Show cobs in the United Kingdom are divided into three classes: lightweight cobs, exceeding 148 cm (58 in) and not exceeding 155 cm (61 in), able to carry up to 90 kg (196 lb); heavyweight cobs, exceeding 148 cm (58 in) and not exceeding 155 cm (61 in), able to carry more than 90 kg (196 lb); and maxi-cobs, exceeding 155 cm (61 in). They are shown hogged (manes clipped off).

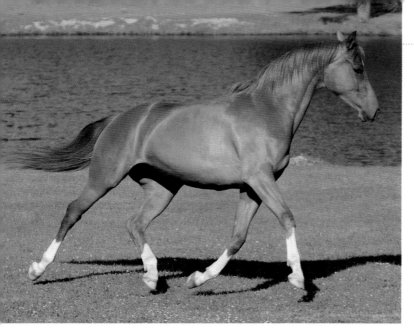

## Warmblood

'Warmblood' is a generic term used to describe a group of sport horses, originally developed in Europe, that resulted from a cross between coldbloods (draught horses) and hotbloods (Arabs and Thoroughbreds). Particularly used in show jumping and dressage due to their good movement and trainable temperaments, there are a number of different types, such as Swedish Warmblood, Dutch Warmblood, Trakehner, Danish Warmblood, Selle Français, Hanoverian and Holsteiner.

Each has slight variations, but are similar types. They have become increasingly popular in the eventing world since more emphasis was placed on the dressage phase, but many event riders still prefer the Thoroughbred's bravery. The warmbloods' studbooks are carefully regulated, and stock are performance-tested, with the emphasis placed on rideability and temperament.

## Draught Horse

These are large, heavy horses originally used for pulling agricultural machinery and for farm work, such as Shires, Clydesdales, Percherons and Suffolk Punches. Although rarely used for their traditional occupations nowadays, the breeds are still preserved, through the show ring and for exhibitions. Often they

are crossed with lighter breeds, such as the Thoroughbred, to produce sport horses and riding animals. They have been developed for strength, docility, patience and stamina, with muscular builds. Their conformation tends to be more upright through the shoulder than most riding horses, to equip them better for pulling carts and machinery.

## Palomino Horses

Palomino is a colour, not strictly a type, but is often seen as one and there are separate showing classes for them. Any breed or type can be registered as palomino providing it has a golden-coloured coat and white mane or tail. Some breeds that have palomino representatives are the American Saddlebred, Tennessee Walking Horse, Morgan and Quarter Horse. The colour is fairly rare in the Thoroughbred, but does in fact occur and is recognized by the Jockey Club (the breed registry for thoroughbred horses in the US, Canada and Puerto Rico).

## Mountain and Moorland

The term 'mountain and moorland' is used to describe the breeds of pony native to the British Isles. Shetlands, Exmoors, Dartmoors, and Welsh Sections A and B ponies are called the small breeds, whereas Highlands, Connemaras, Dales, Fells, New Forests and Welsh Sections C and D ponies are the large breeds. They are shown in their native state, untrimmed with unpulled and unplaited manes. They are hardy and designed to survive in relatively poor grazing areas, and often become fat and 'overtopped' unless their nutritional intake is carefully controlled.

## Gaited Horses

This is the collective term for horses that perform the smooth, four-beat intermediate gaits known as 'ambling'. Ambling is usually faster than a walk, but slower than a canter. There are two basic types: lateral, where the front and hind feet on the same side move in sequence; and diagonal, where the front and hind feet on opposite sides move in sequence. Examples of gaited horses include the American Saddlebred, the Paso Fino, the Tennessee Walking Horse, the Racking, some Saddlebreds and the Icelandic horse. The latter's four-beat gait is known as the 'tolt', and is a surprisingly comfortable way to cover long distances over rocky terrain.

# Ponies

  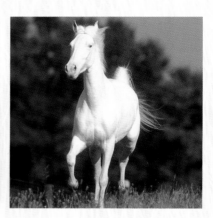

It is hard to believe that the world's vast array of pony breeds – from the Shetland of Scotland to the feral herds of Assateague and Chincoteague, to Indonesia's dancing Sumbawa – derived from just two 'prototypes'.

Pony Type 1 is thought to have lived in north-west Europe and is similar to the Exmoor and the Icelandic. It was usually brown or bay, and stood a little over 12 hh. It probably had the Exmoor's distinctive 'toad eye' and 'snow chute' to protect its tail, as well as the double-layered coat that made it superbly resistant to wet and cold.

Pony Type 2 was considerably larger than Type 1, standing around 14–14.2 hh. It probably looked very similar to the Przewalski, with a convex profile and the dun colour with dark points and dark dorsal stripe. Like Type 1, it was resistant to cold and inhabited northern Eurasia. Its modern counterpart might be considered the Highland Pony.

## A Plethora of Ponies

From these two types, we now have myriad breeds of ponies. Just in England, Scotland and Wales alone, there are the Exmoor and Dartmoor from the south-west of England, the New Forest from the south, the Fell and Dales from the north, the Shetland, Eriskay and Highland from Scotland and the four Welsh Pony and Cob breeds. Even Ireland has her own breed, the beautiful and hardy Connemara.

All over the world, there is virtually no country that does not have its own pony breed. The United States has her own American Shetland, which bears little resemblance now to its Scottish cousin, and the grandly named Pony of the Americas, as well as the American Walking Pony, with its delightfully named 'Merry Walk'. Norway has her Fjord; Africa, the Basuto and Nigerian; China, her Guoxia; and Indonesia, the Java and Sandalwood. And in Spain and Portugal, there is the Sorraia – the unassuming forerunner to the majestic Andalusian and Lusitano.

# AMERICAN SHETLAND

TEMPERAMENT: calm, gentle, intelligent

ORIGINS: United States

SIMILAR BREEDS: Shetland, Hackney Pony

HEIGHT: maximum 117 cm (46 in)

COLOUR: all colours

PERSONALITY TYPE: warm-blooded

USE: child's pony, harness

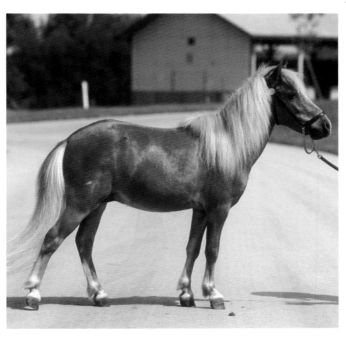

**U**nlike its Scottish ancestors, the American Shetland Pony is a fine-limbed, athletic little animal, elegant as well as sturdy. The ponies were first introduced to the United States in the 1800s, where their strength, stamina and durability were to prove invaluable in pulling the ore carts for America's mining industry. Mechanization ended the Shetland's career in the mines, but the introduction of Welsh Pony, Hackney and other blood refined the breed, and it became a highly sought-after child's pony.

## Hackney Blood

After little more than 100 years, the American Shetland Pony bears scant resemblance to its shaggier Scottish cousin. An altogether more elegant creature, it stands higher than the 107 cm (42 in) upper height limit in the Scottish Shetland Pony Stud Book, with animals being registered up to 117 cm (46 in).

The infusion of Hackney blood has given it a smaller, more delicate head, almost Arabian in profile, as well as the distinctive high-stepping action. The diamond-shaped head is slightly dished, with large eyes and a small muzzle, set on a long, slender neck. Its body is compact and muscular, and comparatively narrow through the shoulders and girth, making it particularly suitable as a child's first pony. It has a good, level topline, long hip and high-set tail, with straight legs.

## In Harness

While its calm nature and gentle disposition make it most suited as a child's pony, the American Shetland is also a superior driving animal.

Intelligent and strong, hardy and trainable, this pony retains the native characteristics of its island heritage. The American Shetland Pony Society recognizes two types: the Classic, as described here, and the Modern Shetland, a far showier animal with a higher proportion of Hackney blood. Both types are immensely popular in the United States and can command high prices.

# CHINCOTEAGUE/ASSATEAGUE

HEIGHT: 12–13 hh

COLOUR: all colours

PERSONALITY TYPE: warm-blooded

TYPICAL USE: children's riding pony

TEMPERAMENT: intelligent, willing

ORIGINS: United States

SIMILAR BREEDS: Mustang, Welsh, Arab

**M**arguerite Henry made these ponies famous in her renowned book *Misty of Chincoteague* (1947). But fact is often stranger than fiction, and it has been suggested that the wild herds of Assateague and Chincoteague islands, off the coast of Maryland and Virginia, swam to the islands from a shipwrecked galleon. It is more likely, though, that the ponies are descended from horses that were brought to Assateague Island in the seventeenth century by mainland owners.

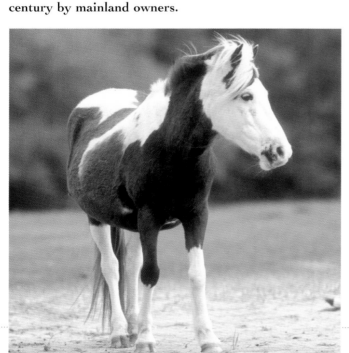

## Charming for Children

Although they are often called wild, the equines on Assateague are actually feral, meaning that they are descendants of domestic animals that have reverted to a wild state. The ponies can be tamed and make charming children's mounts, as they are sturdy, intelligent and willing.

The ponies vary in appearance. Some resemble Welsh or Arabian; others are more like Mustangs. They are usually between 12 and 13 hh, although some are bigger. All common colours are seen, including pinto or paint. They

LEFT

*These ponies live a mostly feral existence, although those that are captured and tamed make excellent children's ponies.*

have expressive heads, with a broad forehead, slightly dished profile and tapered muzzle, with large nostrils. Their eyes are large, and they have small, wide-set tipped-in ears.

## Saltwater Cowboys

Grazing on the islands is poor, and some of the herd are removed from Assateague as foals and fed a high-protein diet to increase their size. Almost 80 per cent of the ponies' diet is saltmarsh grass and, because of the high percentage of salt in their diet, the ponies drink twice as much water as normal equines, giving them a bloated appearance.

To keep the herds to a reasonable level, the Chincoteague Volunteer Fire Company, which manages the herd on the Virginia end of Assateague Island, holds an annual pony penning each July. The ponies are rounded up by the so-called 'saltwater cowboys' and, at low tide, swum across from Assateague to Chincoteague, where they are auctioned off. The remainder are swum back to the island.

# PONY OF THE AMERICAS

TEMPERAMENT: gentle, obedient, intelligent

ORIGIN: Iowa, United States

SIMILAR BREEDS: American Shetland, Shetland, Appaloosa

HEIGHT: 11.2–14 hh

COLOUR: spotted

PERSONALITY TYPE: warm-blooded

TYPICAL USE: child's riding pony, show

America's eponymous pony breed owes its existence to one animal – a black-and-white spotted colt called Black Hand. In 1954, an Iowan Shetland breeder named Les Boomhower was offered an Arab-Appaloosa mare who was in foal to a Shetland stallion. When the foal was born, it was white, with black patches, one of which, on its flank, looked like a handprint – hence the name. Boomhower, a lawyer by profession, set up a new breed registry with his friends , and the Pony of the Americas was born.

## Strict Criteria

The first registered Ponies of the Americas were subject to strict criteria before they could be entered into the new registry. The pony's head had to be small and neat, and slightly dished like that of the Arab, with neat, fine ears and expressive eyes; the body had to be compact and muscular, and the colouring Appaloosa. It had to have clean, straight legs and good feet.

The spots on the pony's coat had to be visible from a distance of 12 m (40 ft), but a variety of coat patterns – blanket spot, leopard spot and roan – were permitted. The ponies were intended for children, so they had to be gentle, obedient and easy to train.

## Delightful Character

Its gentle disposition and small size were to make the Pony of the Americas the perfect mount for a nervous child. The permitted size of the breed increased over the years, and infusions of Welsh, Mustang, Arab and Appaloosa blood were used to refine it. By the twenty-first century, the Pony of the Americas was more of a little horse – a little horse with an attractive appearance and delightful character that make it an enduring success.

### ABOVE

*These fine limbed and well-conformed ponies reflect the Arab and Appaloosa blood of their heritage, as well as the Shetland pony. Roans like this are quite rare for the breed.*

## Fascinating Facts

Black Hand was to found an extremely popular new breed – 15 years after his birth, there were 12,000 registered Ponies of the Americas; by 1996, there were 40,000.

# AMERICAN WALKING PONY

HEIGHT: up to 14 hh

COLOUR: any solid colour

PERSONALITY TYPE: warm-blooded

TYPICAL USE: leisure, riding, show, harness

TEMPERAMENT: intelligent, kind, obedient

ORIGIN: Georgia, United States

SIMILAR BREEDS:
Tennessee Walking Horse, Welsh Pony

How do you like the sound of a Merry Walk? The American Walking Pony, first registered as a breed in 1968, is said to be seven-gaited and, as well as the charmingly named Merry Walk, can perform the Pleasure Walk, Western Walk, jog-trot, trot, lope and canter. The breed was founded using the Tennessee Walking Horse and Welsh Pony to produce an exceptional animal with smooth gaits and elegant appearance.

## Jumping Ability

It is a tall pony, standing up to 14 hh, with exceptionally comfortable gaits and the

arched neck and delicately dished face of the Welsh Pony, from which it also inherited its jumping ability. Intelligent and gentle, it is a versatile breed, with presence and quality, making it highly successful in the show ring. The Welsh blood also means that it makes a good, light hunter pony.

The American Walking Pony has the typically small, refined head of the Welsh Pony, set on a well-muscled neck and sloping shoulders to allow for freedom of movement. Its chest is broad and deep, the back compact and the hindquarters muscular. It can be any solid colour, but bright palominos and liver chestnuts with flaxen manes and tails are highly sought after.

## Unique Gaits

The Pleasure Walk and the Merry Walk are unique to the breed, both being faster than an ordinary walk, with the Merry Walk the quicker of the two, with less head movement. Both gaits are exceptionally light and smooth, and therefore comfortable for the rider. To ensure the American Walking Pony retains these characteristics, only horses that have been registered with both the Walking Horse and the Welsh Pony societies are made available for stud. It continues to be popular, as its reputation gains momentum.

## Fascinating Facts

The American Walking Pony is sometimes called a 'dream walking', a tag it has picked up because of its smooth gaits, including the unusual Merry Walk.

LEFT

*These elegant ponies combine the best characteristics of their ancestors, the Welsh pony and the Tennessee Walking Horse.*

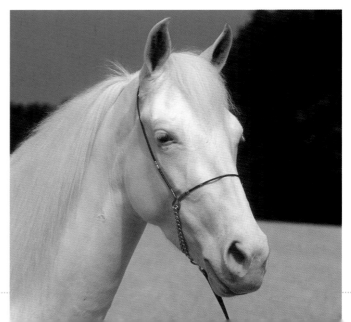

# WELARA

TEMPERAMENT: gentle, calm but lively

ORIGIN: California, United States

SIMILAR BREEDS: Arab, Welsh

HEIGHT: 11.2–14.2 hh

COLOUR: all solid colours

PERSONALITY TYPE: warm-blooded

TYPICAL USE: child's pony, show

An attractive and gentle creature, the Welara was developed as recently as 1981, ultimately the result of a breeding experiment by Lady Wentworth, a British peeress whose influence on Arabian horse breeding has had a deep and lasting effect, and who in the 1920s used the Arabian stallion Skowronek on Welsh Pony mares imported from the Coed Coch Stud in Wales. The Welara exhibits both Arabian and Welsh characteristics, being intelligent and eager, as well as a beautiful animal. It inherits the dished face of both the Arab and the Welsh, and the presence of both breeds.

## Great Beauty

The Welara is a large pony of tremendous quality and exceptional good looks. The mixture of Welsh and Arabian blood can vary – indeed, purebred Arabs that are too small to be registered as Arabians can be accepted into the Welara register – and all colours are accepted, except spotted, which is not permissible in either foundation breed.

RIGHT
*This is a very recent breed developed through crossing Welsh stock with Arabs to produce a quality, intelligent, small pony.*

# CHOCTAW

TEMPERAMENT: intelligent, lively

ORIGIN: Mississippi, United States

SIMILAR BREEDS: Mustang

HEIGHT: 13.2–14.2 hh

COLOUR: all colours

PERSONALITY TYPE: warm-blooded

TYPICAL USE: riding, trekking, pack

For the Native Americans, the arrival of the horse in the sixteenth century with the Spanish transformed their lives. Its speed and endurance were a tremendous boon to the buffalo-hunting Indians, but the Choctaw, a tribe whose homeland centred on Mississippi and who were agriculturalists rather than hunters, also put the horse to good use. They used a small strain of Spanish horse – standing between 13.2 and 14.2 hh – that became known as the Choctaw Pony.

## Cow Sense

The Choctaw was a hardy, spirited, intelligent little horse, with good 'cow sense' (they were also used for herding cattle), considerable stamina and endurance, and noted agility. To the Choctaw, these ponies determined wealth, prestige, glory and honour. They were also used to barter for other goods.

When the Indian tribes were forced to leave their homelands, the Choctaws took with them to Oklahoma their tough little horses. Threatened with extinction due to outcrossing, the Choctaw Pony is now being preserved.

# CAYUSE INDIAN

HEIGHT: 14 hh

COLOUR: all colours

PERSONALITY TYPE: warm-blooded

TYPICAL USE: riding, pack

TEMPERAMENT: spirited, intelligent

ORIGIN: Canada/United States

SIMILAR BREEDS: Mustang, Barb

Although the term 'cayuse' was applied in general to the little horses ridden by the Native Americans, the Cayuse Indian Pony is recognized as a specific breed. It originated in the north-west and is believed to have descended from French-Norman horses imported to Canada in the 1600s, which had a lot of Percheron blood. This influence would have given the breed bone and substance, and the ability to trot for long periods of time.

## Colourful Influence

The French Canadians later brought their horses into what is now the United States, where they bartered them for goods with the Pawnee Indians, who took them further west. They later crossed these sturdy horses with the lighter Spanish Barb to produce an equine with speed and endurance.

The Cayuse Indian Pony became a recognized breed in the 1800s, and its colourful traits – the French influence

bred spots and colour splashes – can still be seen in American Appaloosa and Pinto horses.

# SABLE ISLAND

HEIGHT: 14–15 hh

COLOUR: bay, brown, black

PERSONALITY TYPE: warm-blooded

TYPICAL USE: feral, trekking

TEMPERAMENT: tough, hardy

ORIGIN: Nova Scotia, Canada

SIMILAR BREEDS: Iberian

For more than 500 years, herds of feral ponies have lived on Sable Island, off the coast of Nova Scotia. Little is known about their ancestry, but they do display some characteristics of the Spanish breeds, suggesting that they may trace back to the Spanish who came to the New World in the 1500s.

## Harsh Environment

Sable Island Ponies today rarely stand higher than 14 hh , perhaps as a result of the

harsh conditions of their barren island home. Tough, hardy and enduring, they are sure-footed and 'good doers', thriving on meagre rations.

The feral herds show a wide range of characteristics, but are mostly dark coloured (with the occasional palomino), with straight or slightly convex profiles. They have short, straight necks, thick manes, a straight back and short, clean legs. They also grow thick, woolly coats.

Sable Island's feral ponies can be tamed and broken to ride if caught young. They make good trekking ponies, although their small stature make them more suited to children than adults.

# GALICEÑO

TEMPERAMENT: brave, hardy, tractable

ORIGIN: Mexico

SIMILAR BREEDS: Iberian

HEIGHT: 14 hh

COLOUR: all solid colours

PERSONALITY TYPE: warm-blooded

TYPICAL USE: riding, herding, pack

Despite its short stature, Mexico's native equine is regarded as a horse, rather than a pony. Standing little more than 14 hh, it has few pony characteristics, with a nicely proportioned head, alert ears, short, muscular neck and narrow chest and body. But although it is finely built, the Galiceño has a tough constitution and great stamina. It can travel at a fast running walk, which is smooth and comfortable, but also ground-covering. The Galiceño is still used by Mexican cowboys for herding.

## Considerable Beauty

It is a breed of considerable beauty and substance, with a refined head, large lively eyes and a small muzzle. Its short neck is set on prominent withers and sloping shoulders; its body is smoothly muscled, with a short, straight back, sloped croup and high-set tail. It has clean legs with strong, well-shaped joints, and usually excellent feet. All solid colours are seen, but albino and pinto are not permitted.

## Spanish Influence

Like so many horse breeds of the Americas, the Galiceño probably owes its existence to the Spanish conquistadores who arrived in Mexico in 1519. It has much in common with the Sorraia and Garrano ponies of Portugal and Spain, and takes its name from Galicia, in northern Spain. These animals were taken to the South Americas in the sixteenth century and retain much of their Iberian characteristics. The fast, smooth running walk that the Galiceño still performs was a much-prized gait in Spanish horses.

The Galiceño is quick and agile, alert and quick to learn. While its small size and gentle nature make it an ideal child's pony, it is strong enough

## Fascinating Facts

A horse can produce nine tonnes of manure each year.

to carry an adult. It has considerable stamina and endurance, and is gaining increasing popularity in the United States, where the registry was set up in 1959.

# DARTMOOR

HEIGHT: 12.2 hh

COLOUR: brown, bay, black, chestnut, occasionally grey or roan

PERSONALITY TYPE: warm-blooded

TYPICAL USE: riding, trekking, harness

TEMPERAMENT: gentle, willing, kind

ORIGIN: England

SIMILAR BREEDS: Exmoor

There are references to England's Dartmoor Pony dating back to 1012, and it is known that during the reign of Henry I (1100–35), when Dartmoor was a royal forest, a stallion was taken from the moor to be bred to royal mares. The Dartmoor Pony today is a good-looking, sturdy native breed with a gentle temperament and rugged hardiness that make it a popular child's pony, although it is strong enough to carry an adult.

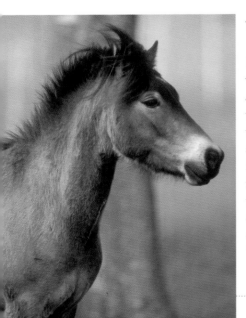

## Wild and Free

Dartmoor itself, in the south-west of England, is an upland area of moorland and granite tors. Rising in places to more than 600 m (2,000 ft) above sea level, it receives the full force of the Atlantic gales. Its indigenous breed had to be tough to survive, and developed a thick, shaggy coat and hardy constitution. They were used in the tin mines and on farms, and later to escort work parties to and from the prison that stands at Princetown – this practice continued into the 1960s. The breed's docility and obedience made it popular with the whole family –

---

LEFT

*The Dartmoor is a rugged and sturdy pony with a calm and equable temperament, making them excellent for children.*

---

Dartmoor Ponies would be used to transport the farmer's wife and children to church in a cart. Once broken to harness, it makes a superb driving pony.

## Rare Breed

There are only about 5,000 Dartmoor ponies left in existence today, and it is listed by the Rare Breeds Survival Trust as 'vulnerable'. Since 1988, positive steps have been taken to restore the more pure-type Dartmoor Pony to its natural habitat. Mares belonging to Moor farmers have been run with a pedigree registered stallion on an enclosed part of the moor for the summer. These mares are then returned to the open moor until they foal. It is hoped that this will encourage the farmers to return to breeding the purebred Dartmoor and give visitors the chance to see the true Dartmoor Pony flourishing in its native environment.

## Fascinating Facts

Bookmakers at racecourses use a sign language called 'tic-tac' to secretly communicate changes in the betting odds of a horse to each other.

# EXMOOR

TEMPERAMENT: kind, biddable, hardy

ORIGIN: England

SIMILAR BREEDS: Dartmoor

HEIGHT: 13.2 hh

COLOUR: dun, bay, brown

PERSONALITY TYPE: warm-blooded

TYPICAL USE: riding, trekking, harness

Evidence suggests that the Exmoor is England's oldest breed of pony. Archeological material dating back some 60,000 years bears an uncanny resemblance to today's breed, and it is thought that they are direct descendants of the first horses to walk to Britain before it became an island. They roam the bleak, open moorland of south-west England and have developed into a tough, resilient little equine able to withstand the most harsh of conditions.

## Unique Features

Battered by wind and rain, Exmoor is cold and wet, and its equines had to survive on meagre rations and with little shelter without human intervention. The breed evolved, and possesses two features that are unique to it: the 'toad eye' and 'ice chute'. The toad eye has a fleshy 'hood' to keep out wind and rain, while the ice chute (or snow chute) is a fan of short, coarse hairs at the top of the tail that funnels off rainwater. The Exmoor also has a double-layered winter coat, a short, fine layer that acts as 'thermal underwear', and a coarser, greasy top layer as a 'raincoat'.

The only permitted colours are dun – usually with a black dorsal stripe – bay or brown, and it is instantly recognizable through its 'mealy' muzzle, a lighter colour around its mouth and nostrils.

## Endangered Breed

Almost wiped out during the Second World War, when troops training on the moor used its native wildlife as target practice, the Exmoor is still rare, listed by the Rare Breeds Survival Trust as 'endangered'. And what a tragedy it would be if the breed were lost; these attractive little ponies, with their distinctive mealy muzzles, make excellent child's ponies, with their sweet nature and tough constitution. They are also

among the purest of equine breeds, with no outcrossing of other blood to 'improve' the stock.

# LUNDY

HEIGHT: 13.2 hh

COLOUR: all solid colours

PERSONALITY TYPE: warm-blooded

TYPICAL USE: riding, competition

TEMPERAMENT: gentle, hardy

ORIGIN: England

SIMILAR BREEDS: Welsh, New Forest

Contrary to popular belief, the ponies of the island of Lundy, situated off the south-west coast of England, are not closely related to the area's Dartmoor and Exmoor ponies. A comparatively new equine breed, the Lundy Pony was developed in 1928 using New Forest and Welsh Section B bloodlines. The island's then owner, Martin Coles Harman, imported 34 New Forest mares and let them run with a Welsh stallion. The stallion died after only a year, having produced just one offspring.

## Height and Substance

Coles Harman's vision was a pony of style and height, a good-looking equine with quality and substance. The one colt the deceased stallion left behind proved his breeder's vision; he was a creamy dun with black points called Pepper, and was to be the foundation of the herd. Allowed to breed unchecked, the herd on the island grew until, in the 1930s, about 50 were rounded up and sent to the

mainland to be sold. During the Second World War, when the shipping lanes were closed, the herd increased to about 100 ponies.

The herd was moved to the mainland in 1980, but the

breed society formed in 1984 returned some of the ponies to the island later in the same decade. Connemara and Welsh Mountain Pony blood have been introduced, but otherwise the breed has had no outside influence.

## Good Doer

Still a rare breed, the Lundy Pony is attractive and hardy, with a wide, deep chest, sloping shoulders and hard, sound legs. It has a neat head and short, muscular neck. Common colours are

### LEFT

*The Lundy, of which there are sadly only a small number, is a well-conformed pony with a natural aptitude for jumping and a quiet temperament.*

dun, roan, palomino, bay and liver chestnut. It is a good doer and strong, but is gentle enough to be a suitable child's mount. It has a natural jumping ability, so would make a good hunting or competition pony.

# HACKNEY PONY

TEMPERAMENT: intelligent, spirited

ORIGIN: England

SIMILAR BREEDS:
Fell, Hackney Horse, Thoroughbred

HEIGHT: 12–14 hh

COLOUR: bay, black, brown, chestnut

PERSONALITY TYPE:
warm-blooded

TYPICAL USE: driving, show

High-stepping, elegant and spirited, the Hackney Pony is a breed in its own right, and not a scaled-down version of the Hackney Horse. It owes its existence to one man, Christopher Wilson, who bred the Hackney Horse St George to a Fell mare in 1866, then interbred the resulting offspring to make a fixed type – for some years, they were known as Wilson Ponies. Left out on the inhospitable Fells with little food or care, the breed became hardy and resilient.

## Exaggerated Action

By 1880, the Hackney Pony was an established breed, and much in demand for its stamina and good looks. The pony has a fine head with tapering muzzle and large eyes, small, neat ears, elegantly arched neck on powerful shoulders, and low withers. Its back is compact, and it has fine legs with good joints. The feet are small and hard, and often allowed to grow long in the toe to accentuate the action. Ponies are usually bay, black or brown, with the occasional chestnut, with some white markings.

## Fascinating Facts

The Hackney Horse takes its name from the French *haquenée*, a language commonly spoken in the country in Medieval times, meaning a riding horse with a particularly comfortable gait.

ABOVE LEFT

*The Hackney is one of the most elegant and refined pony breeds. It has a naturally extravagant, high stepping movement and is athletically built.*

The high-stepping gait is exaggerated in the Hackney Pony – it lifts its knees almost to its chest and brings its hocks right under its body. This action is not just for show; it can move at good speed with the minimum of bounce to a cart or carriage.

## Fluid and Energetic

Its showy good looks make the Hackney Pony popular, and its fluid and energetic gait is spectacular. While the breed has a tendency to pugnaciousness, its spirit and intelligence make it a joy to watch. It is the king of the show ring, exploding across the arena with piston-like speed – head and tail carried high and proud – appearing suspended in the air for a moment at the highest point.

# FELL

HEIGHT: 12–14 hh

COLOUR: Black, bay, brown, grey

PERSONALITY TYPE: warm-blooded

TYPICAL USE: driving, riding, trekking

TEMPERAMENT: docile, brave

ORIGIN: England

SIMILAR BREEDS: Friesian, Dales, Hackney Pony

There were probably small, dark ponies native to England's northern hills – the word 'fell' derives from the Norse word for 'hill' – when the Romans invaded in 55 BC. The Romans brought with them their handsome black Friesian horses and, when they left, they left these horses behind to breed with indigenous stock. The result was the Fell Pony, which retains a striking resemblance to the Friesian Horse. The modern Fell Pony combines strength, agility and style.

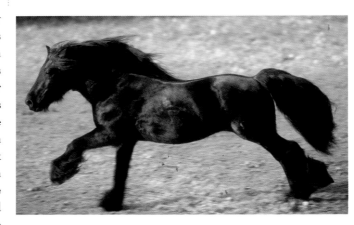

## Sixth Sense

Before mechanization, the Fell Pony was in great demand as a family all-rounder – it would work on the farm, was used for shepherding and also pulled the family carriage. Fell Ponies were used to transport wool across from the Lake District along ancient pack ways to wool merchants, and to carry lead from the mines in England's north-west to the smelting works on the north-east coast. Strong but docile, placid and sure-footed, the Fell was the perfect dual-purpose pony. It seemed to have a 'sixth sense', knowing the safest track through marshy ground or the safest descent on a rocky hillside.

## Royal Endorsement

The Fell Pony suffered, as did many breeds, with the coming of mechanization; however, as riding became a more popular leisure activity, the Fell enjoyed a resurgence. When

## Fascinating Facts

The Duke of Edinburgh, who shaped the sport of carriage driving in the United Kingdom, drove a team of perfectly matched Fell Ponies until he retired from the sport in 2006. He has represented Britain at several European and World championships.

LEFT

*The magnificent Fell pony is a strong limbed and muscular animal that has a majestic bearing and even temperament.*

more and more people took up carriage driving, the Fell's strength and uniformity of type made it an obvious choice.

It has the good looks of the Friesian horses in its ancestry, with a small, chiselled head, bright eye and neat, small ears. Its neck is of medium length, its shoulders sloping and its back long and well muscled. Its legs and feet – which have characteristic blue horn – are good, and it has fine feather at its heels. Its mane and tail are long and fine. It is, indeed, a pony fit for a king, or at the very least a duke.

# NEW FOREST

TEMPERAMENT: intelligent, friendly, willing to please

ORIGIN: England

SIMILAR BREEDS: Lundy Pony

HEIGHT: 14 hh

COLOUR: all solid colours, except blue-eyed cream

PERSONALITY TYPE: warm-blooded

TYPICAL USE: riding

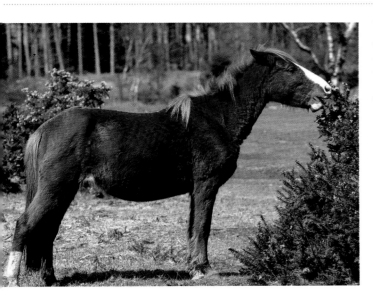

Commoners who lived in the royal hunting ground of the New Forest in southern England, created by William the Conqueror in c. 1079, had been occupying the area since long before then. After a series of struggles, including being thrown off the land and harsh punishments for breaking forest law imposed by the sovereign, the commoners were finally granted grazing rights and, since then, the people of the New Forest have been allowed to graze their ponies in the region. The New Forest Pony – a mixture of Arab, Thoroughbred, Welsh and Hackney – is an attractive, intelligent animal, with little fear of humans and an innate willingness to please.

## Roaming Free

Ponies have roamed free in the New Forest for centuries, and it was not until the end of the nineteenth century that concerted efforts to maintain and improve the stock were made. A polo pony called Field Marshall had considerable influence on the New Forest breed during 1918 and other blood, including Dartmoor, Exmoor and Highland, has also been used. Since 1930, no further outcrosses have been introduced, making the breed more uniform.

The modern New Forest is agile, strong and hardy, able to carry an adult with ease, but narrow across the girth, making it an excellent child's mount. It rarely exceeds 14 hh and there is no lower height limit, although smaller animals tend to be more 'ponyish'. Skewbalds, piebalds and blue-eyed creams are not permitted.

---

### LEFT

*The New Forest pony is a sound and tough animal that is well adapted to its semi-feral existence in the New Forest area of Southern England.*

## Quality and charm

While the ponies freely graze the Forest, every autumn they are rounded up in the annual 'drift' and either kept on as breeding stock or sold at auction. Although the best stock was not always that which was retained – the Commoners naturally wanting the highest prices for those ponies sold – the breed society endeavours to keep this native equine's quality and charm. It makes the perfect all-rounder for a horsey family.

# DALES

HEIGHT: 14.2 hh

COLOUR: black, brown, bay

PERSONALITY TYPE: warm-blooded

TYPICAL USE: driving, riding, trekking

TEMPERAMENT: calm, intelligent

ORIGIN: England

SIMILAR BREEDS: Friesian, Fell

Like its close cousin the Fell, the Dales Pony has its roots in the north-east of England and was used primarily as a pack pony. Both breeds had links to the now defunct Galloway Pony, but the Dales takes its name from the Yorkshire area of the UK. Certainly, the Fell – or Wilson Pony as it was once known – had influence on the breed, as did the Norfolk Trotter and, later, the Clydesdale, which was used to increase the height of the Dales Pony.

## Military Favourite

Due to its hardiness and strength, the Dales was a superlative packhorse and was, for a time, bred specifically to serve the thriving lead-mining industry – they were renowned for their ability to transport heavy loads over rough terrain at speed, sometimes travelling up to 320 km (200 miles) in one week. For the same reasons, they were a valuable asset to the hillside farmer; their speed and endurance made them popular for trotting races, and their agility was prized in the hunting field. Later, they were used widely in the military, their sure-footedness, strength and stamina carving them a niche in both world wars.

## Flashy Gait

The Dales was less affected by mechanization than many native breeds because of its versatility. The pony could work on the farm all day, six days a week, and still be fit enough to transport the farmer and his family to church and take in a day's

hunting. The Yorkshire farmers were also keen on trotting races, but could not afford to keep a horse separately just for racing. So the Dales was increasingly bred to Galloways and Norfolk Trotters, resulting in the fast, flashy gait it shows today. These old bloodlines are reflected in the breed's colouring – although greys and the occasional roan are sometimes seen, most Dales Ponies are black, brown or bay.

# SHETLAND

TEMPERAMENT: intelligent, wilful

ORIGIN: Scotland

SIMILAR BREEDS: Highland, Fell, Dales

HEIGHT: 107 cm (42 in)

COLOUR: all colours

PERSONALITY TYPE: warm-blooded

TYPICAL USE: riding, harness

An ancient law of the Shetland islands states that any man who 'cut any other man's horse-tail' would do so 'under the pain of ten pounds'. This exorbitant fine (for the times) was an indication of how valuable, and how valued, these tiny equines were on the islands off the northern coast of Scotland.

## Ninth-century Evidence

A ninth-century stone carving found on the Shetland island of Bressay depicts a priest mounted on a very small, well-proportioned pony. Certainly, it is believed that the Shetland is Britain's oldest native breed.

On these bleak islands off the northern coast of Scotland, fishing was the main source of income and the Shetland Pony

ABOVE

*These charismatic little ponies are incredibly hardy and intelligent, as well as being extremely strong for their small stature.*

provided raw materials for necessary equipment; their coarse tail hair made excellent fishing nets and lines. Life on the islands was hard for all their inhabitants. The ponies had to cope with a hostile environment, poor grass, hard,

wet ground and continual driving wind. To conserve body heat, the ponies had short limbs, a short back, a thick neck and small ears. Only the hardiest and most intelligent animals survived.

## Island Mystery

How equines arrived on the islands in the first place remains a mystery. The first settlers may have brought them there, and Viking stock mixed with British to create a distinct type. These early hybrids probably combined predecessors to the Fell, Dales and Highlands, and a Scandinavian type with Oriental bloodlines. Or one story has it that animals

from the Spanish Armada flagship, *Gran Grifton*, which foundered off the coast of Fair Isle, were somehow stranded in Shetland – though of course this is many centuries later than the evidence on the stone carving.

Whatever its history, the hardy little Shetland has proved its resilience a thousand times over.

## Fascinating Facts

It may be the smallest of the United Kingdom's breeds, but the Shetland is, pound for pound, believed to be the strongest known equine.

155

# ERISKAY

HEIGHT: 12–13.2 hh

COLOUR: grey, black, bay

PERSONALITY TYPE: warm-blooded

TYPICAL USE: riding, harness, competition

TEMPERAMENT: honest, amenable, intelligent

ORIGINS: Scotland

SIMILAR BREEDS: Highland

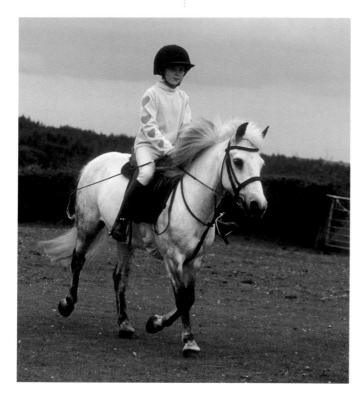

**P**erhaps the most pure of the Scottish breeds, the Eriskay is thought to be a direct descendant of the Celtic Pony, and is the only surviving native pony of the Hebrides Islands, off western Scotland. They are similar to those ponies depicted on ancient Pictish stones found in the north and west of the country. A distinct and separate breed to the Highland and the Shetland, the Eriskay Pony is almost extinct.

## People-friendly

Able to survive on meagre rations, and tough enough to withstand the harsh conditions of the far north-west of Scotland, the Eriskay also developed as a people-friendly, amenable creature – the animals lived closely with their human owners, and bad temperaments were not tolerated.

LEFT

*The Eriskay is a nicely put together small pony that has a particularly good temperament. Sadly there are very few of the breed left.*

And while other breeds in the region were being 'improved' with the introduction of other equine blood, such as Norwegian Fjord, Arabian and Clydesdale, because of the remoteness of the islands, the Eriskay was left to breed pure. But this also led to the decline of the breed, with only about 20 ponies left by the 1970s. Thanks to a dedicated group of people, the Eriskay Pony was saved from extinction and it is thought that there are now about 300 of them.

## Family Pony

The Eriskay makes an excellent family pony and, despite its diminutive size, is well suited to almost any equestrian sport, including driving. It is tough and hardy, able to live out in the harshest of conditions, and is attractive, too. It has a neat head, with a wide forehead, tapered muzzle and a large, bold eye. Its shoulders are sloping and its back strong, with a sloping croup. It has clean, strong limbs and good feet.

Most Eriskays are born brown or black, turning grey with age, although some retain their dark colour into adulthood.

# HIGHLAND

TEMPERAMENT: intelligent, calm, willing

ORIGIN: Scotland

SIMILAR BREEDS: Shetland, Fell, Dales

HEIGHT: 13–14.2 hh
COLOUR: dun, bay, black, grey
PERSONALITY TYPE: warm-blooded
TYPICAL USE: riding, competition, harness, pack, stalking

Native to Scotland's mountain areas, it is thought the Highland spread into the country after the retreat of the glaciers 10,000 years ago. Certainly, there have been horses in

*The robust Highland pony is extremely versatile, making an excellent riding pony as well as being used for driving, trekking, packing and stalking.*

the Highland region and the Western Isles for millennia, and it is sometimes said of the breed that 'it is too old to know how old it is'. The modern pony still has 'primitive' markings of the earliest equines and is the only British native breed still to do so without any conscious selection.

## Versatile and Willing

The Highland was originally a crofter's pony – a vital asset to the crofters, or small-holding farmers, who eked out an existence in this harsh environment. Versatile and strong, the pony could work the land and was strong enough to carry heavy loads for long journeys. It was a farm horse, a packhorse and a carthorse, all rolled into one. The Highland is hard-working and willing, and has an inbred sure-footedness ideal for the treacherous terrain. It is still used on Scottish estates today, and Highland Ponies tend to dislike being stabled, so it is economical to keep.

## Ancient Markings

A good-looking equine, the Highland can be all ranges of dun – mouse, brown, blue, yellow – and has the ancient markings: the eel stripe, shoulder stripes, zebra markings on the legs and dark mane and tail. Greys and the occasional liver chestnut with silver mane and tail are sometimes seen. Its head is alert and well carried, with a broad muzzle and deep jowl. It has a good length of neck and a deep chest, with plenty of heart room. It has powerful quarters with good, strong legs and clean, flat hocks. Its limbs are sturdy with plenty of bone.

Today's Highland is, perhaps more than any other breed, versatile enough to compete in and excel at every equestrian discipline.

# WELSH MOUNTAIN (Section A)

**HEIGHT:** 12 hh

**COLOUR:** all solid colours

**PERSONALITY TYPE:** warm-blooded

**TYPICAL USE:** riding, harness

**TEMPERAMENT:** gentle, spirited, intelligent

**ORIGIN:** Wales

**SIMILAR BREEDS:** Welsh Sections B, C, D

The Welsh Mountain Pony's Arabian heritage is clear in its dished face, but it is far from being just a 'pretty toy'. **The Welsh Mountain Pony – or Section A in the Welsh Pony and Cob Society Studbook – is the foundation of all the Welsh breeds and has roamed the hills and valleys of Wales for centuries. It was certainly there before the Romans, and its Arabian inheritance is possibly due to their abandoning their horses when they withdrew in 410 AD.**

## Semi-Feral

Led by proud stallions, bands of Welsh Mountain Ponies

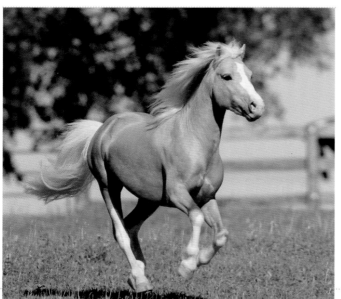

survived and thrived in the harsh environment they inhabited. Galloping across mountains and leaping ravines, they made the most of their inherent sure-footedness and endurance. Nature's rule of 'survival of the fittest' could have been written for the Welsh Mountain Pony – it is a tough, sound and hardy little creature, with a strong streak of native intelligence.

These attributes mean that it has always been in high demand, whether as a strong, sound working pony for riding or for driving. There is evidence it pulled the chariots in ancient sport arenas; it has also worked in the mines. Yet its gentle nature means that it makes an excellent child's mount.

## Most Beautiful

The Welsh Mountain Pony is also, perhaps, the most beautiful of Britain's mountain and moorland breeds. Its small head has neat, pointed ears, big, bold eyes and a wide forehead. Its

## Fascinating Facts

Even an edict of Henry VIII (1509–47), that all horses standing under 15 hh should be destroyed, failed to eliminate the Welsh Mountain Pony. Hidden in desolate areas where its would-be slayers were reluctant or unable to go, it continued to live and reproduce, and to thrive.

LEFT

*The Welsh pony breed is highly attractive and has had a positive influence on many other breeds. The Section A is the smallest of the Welsh ponies.*

jaw is clean-cut and tapers to a small muzzle. The silhouette of its face should be concave – or dished – but never convex nor too straight. Its neck is of good length and its shoulders sloped to well-defined withers. The limbs must be set square, with good, flat bone and round, dense hooves. It carries its tail high and proud.

The Welsh Mountain breeds true, passing on its best qualities and its undeniable beauty to its offspring.

# WELSH PONY (Section B)

TEMPERAMENT: gentle, kind, intelligent

ORIGIN: Wales

SIMILAR BREEDS: Welsh Sections A, C, D

HEIGHT: up to 13.2 hh

COLOUR: all solid colours

PERSONALITY TYPE: warm-blooded

TYPICAL USE: riding, show

good-looking pony, its fine head, well-balanced body and low, smooth action make it a natural for the show ring. It has an innate jumping ability, so makes a good all-rounder for the keen young rider, but retains the Welsh Mountain's sweetness and gentle nature, making it ideal for a nervous youngster.

LEFT

*The Welsh is perhaps the most striking of the British pony breeds, and is renowned for its excellent and extravagant movement.*

As riding became ever more popular, there was a growing demand for a child's pony, an attractive and safe mount standing under 13.2 hh. The idea was to keep the enduring qualities of the Welsh Mountain Pony, but to refine them and breed a taller animal, without losing its charm and essential pony character. The result, which is Section B of the Welsh Pony and Cob Society Studbook, is an elegant creature, with the beauty of the Welsh Mountain Pony, but standing a full hand and a half higher and appearing finer – a true riding pony.

## Darley Descendant

To produce the taller, riding type of pony, a stallion called Merlin – a direct descendant of the Darley Arabian, which founded the Thoroughbred – was used on Welsh Mountain mares. The resulting ponies were sometimes referred to as 'Merlin's'. It is possible that other breeds, perhaps New Forest and Hackney, as well as the larger Welsh Section Cs, were introduced.

Hardy, balanced and fast, these ponies were for generations the primary form of transport for Wales's hill farmers, herding sheep and wild ponies over rough, mountainous country. They had to be tough and strong, and so only the very best were bred from to retain these qualities in future generations.

## Show-Ring Success

The Section B keeps all the desired characteristics of its smaller counterpart, but has more quality; an extremely

The Welsh Section B can hold its own among top-class riding ponies and can turn in a top-level performance in almost any competition arena.

# WELSH PONY (Section C)

HEIGHT: 13.2 hh

COLOUR: all solid colours

PERSONALITY TYPE: warm-blooded

TYPICAL USE: riding, harness, competition

TEMPERAMENT: kind, equable, intelligent

ORIGIN: Wales

SIMILAR BREEDS: Welsh Sections A, B, D

Desire for a bigger animal than the Welsh Mountain and the Section B, but one still possessing the essential pony characteristics, led to the use of Andalusian, the now-extinct Pembroke Carthorse and Norfolk Trotter and, more recently, Hackney bloodlines to create a handsome, versatile all-rounder that was hardy and strong, yet kind and willing. That animal is the Welsh Pony of Cob Type, or Section C of the Studbook.

## True All-Rounder

Spanish blood provides the breed's substance and good looks, and it was further refined using Arabian and Thoroughbred blood. Its head is fine and intelligent, with neat, small ears and a bold eye. It has a good length of neck, strong, sloping shoulders, a muscular body and clean legs with hard, dense hooves. Some silky feather is permitted, and all solid colours are seen (greys are rare). The Section C has good jumping ability. It makes an ideal harness pony or an excellent child's hunting pony, and would not be out of place in the dressage arena.

# WELSH COB

HEIGHT: no upper height limit

COLOUR: all solid colours

PERSONALITY TYPE: warm-blooded

TYPICAL USE: riding, driving, all-rounder

TEMPERAMENT: even-tempered, willing, clever

ORIGIN: Wales

SIMILAR BREEDS: Welsh Sections A, B, C

In silhouette, the Welsh Cob (Section D) should look like a scaled-up model of the Welsh Mountain Pony. An ancient breed, it has been a chariot horse, a knight's charger, a warhorse and an all-round form of transport. Julius Caesar, arriving in Britain in 55 AD, much admired the British chariot horses. The Welsh Cob, also known as a 'rouncy', was used to lead the legendary fighting horses known as 'destriers' in battle. To this day, the Cob's extra-ordinarily powerful and ground-covering trot is its defining feature.

## Arabian Influence

It is known that animals native to Wales date back to 1600 BC, and after the Crusades (1100–1500), Arabian horses left behind were taken into Wales and used on local stock. In the eighteenth and nineteenth centuries, Norfolk Trotter and Yorkshire Coach Horses were used to add height and substance. The Welsh Cob crosses particularly well with the Thoroughbred to produce an excellent hunter or competition horse, but the purebred Cob competes with success in almost every equestrian discipline; its spectacular action is proving popular in the dressage arena.

# CONNEMARA

TEMPERAMENT: kind, intelligent, equable

ORIGIN: Ireland

SIMILAR BREEDS: Irish Hobby (extinct)

HEIGHT: 12.2–14.2 hh

COLOUR: predominantly grey, though all solid colours are permitted

PERSONALITY TYPE: warm-blooded

TYPICAL USE: riding, driving, all-rounder

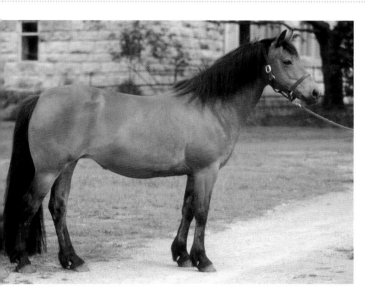

**W**ild and beautiful, Connemara, on Ireland's west coast, has been home to the ponies that bear its name for centuries. It is sometimes thought that the Spanish horses of the conquistadores, perhaps shipwrecked off Ireland's treacherous coastline, were the basis for this sturdy and rugged mountain and moorland breed. It is likely, though, that small equines inhabited this craggy, lunar-like landscape millennia before, to evolve into Ireland's only native breed.

## True Survivors

Most probably, Celtic warriors brought their dun-coloured ponies to the country and used them to draw war chariots and carts along the beaches and plains of their new home. It is known that the tribes of western Ireland were mounted, and it may in fact be that when some of the Spanish Armada was shipwrecked off the Connemara coast in the sixteenth century, horses swam to the shore and bred with the native stock.

Whatever their origins, Connemara ponies are true survivors, able to thrive in the harsh environment and hazardous, rocky coastal terrain, where one misstep could send them crashing to their deaths.

## Farmer's Friend

Connemara farmers caught and tamed these wild ponies, and they were to prove invaluable. Hardy and thrifty to keep, the ponies could easily carry heavy loads, whether clearing rocks from the land, carrying seaweed for fertilizer or turf cut from the bogs which served as fuel for cooking and heating. The pony would then pull the cart to carry the farmer and his family to church on Sundays. The farmers would usually choose to own a mare, so they could breed a foal to supplement their sparse income.

Arabian and Thoroughbred blood has latterly been used to refine the breed, but the Connemara remains hardy, versatile and equable, with quality and jumping ability – in all, a great family pony.

BELOW

*The rugged and beautiful Connemara is Ireland's only native pony breed, and is noted for its surefooted movement and athleticism.*

# LANDAIS

HEIGHT: 11.3–13.1 hh

COLOUR: bay, brown, chestnut, black

PERSONALITY TYPE: warm-blooded

TYPICAL USE: riding

TEMPERAMENT: intelligent, lively, gentle

ORIGIN: France

SIMILAR BREEDS: Welsh Section B

S aid to resemble a miniature Arab, the Landais – one of just three pony breeds native to France – is a good-looking, gentle creature with origins tracing back to the early eighth century, when it lived wild in the forests of the region. Since then, it has been heavily influenced by foreign blood, most notably Arabian, first introduced around the time of the Battle of Tours (also known as the Battle of Poitiers) in AD 732, and again in the early twentieth century.

## Mostly Amenable

The Landais is sometimes referred to as the Barthais, which was once a separate breed, although slightly bigger and heavier. It is not known when the two breeds merged, and little is known about the Landais itself. What is certain is that it

---
LEFT

*The attractive and small Landais pony reflects the Arab influence in its ancestry through its quality appearance and good action.*

---

originated in the Landes region of south-west France, and is an amenable riding pony with athletic paces and innate jumping ability. It is friendly and easily trained, although it can be a little wilful.

Ponies are usually dark colours – bay, brown, chestnut and black – with a neat, ponyish head, thickset neck, prominent withers, straight back, strong, muscled legs, thick mane and high-set tail.

## Endangered Breed

In the early 1900s, there were about 2,000 Landais ponies, but by the Second World War numbers were in serious decline, with only about 150 remaining. To avoid too much inbreeding, some Welsh Section B blood was introduced to keep the Landais' pony qualities. There is also evidence of some Spanish influence, but since 1981 the breed's studbook has been closed to less than pure animals to prevent further outcrossing. The breed is officially recognized as being endangered, with fewer than 100 purebreds still remaining.

The modern Landais shows clearly its Arabian heritage and makes an excellent child's pony – it would be a tragedy if it were allowed to die out altogether.

# POTTOK (Basque)

**TEMPERAMENT:** quiet, calm, willing

**ORIGIN:** France

**SIMILAR BREEDS:** Welsh Section B, Landais

**HEIGHT:** 11.2–14 hh

**COLOUR:** all colours, except grey

**PERSONALITY TYPE:** warm-blooded

**TYPICAL USE:** riding, harness, competition, pack

Prehistoric engravings found in caves in the Pyrenees Mountains of the Basque region of France show the existence of a pony, or small horse, more than 10,000 years ago. Whether the Pottoks are ponies or small horses – their name, pronounced 'pot-ee-ok', comes from the Basque word *pottoka*, which means 'small horse' — is open to debate, but they are thought to descend from the Magdalenian Horses of 14,000–7,000 BC. This, in turn, is thought to be related to the ancient Tarpan.

ABOVE

*The elegance of these ponies' appearance belies their toughness and stamina. They are popular riding ponies and are also used for packing.*

## Rounded up

Although only about 150 Pottoks remain in the region, they were once integral to Basque life. They were used primarily as pack animals – it is said partly to smuggle goods between France and Spain, their dark colour acting as perfect camouflage for night journeys – or in the mines, from France to Italy.

Sturdy and sure-footed, the Pottok was uncomplaining and enduring, able to work for long hours and cover great distances.

Now, all the ponies in the Basque region are in ownership and no longer wild, although they still run free in the mountains. They are traditionally rounded up on the last Wednesday in January, branded for identification and either sold or returned to the mountains as breeding stock.

## French Champion

The Pottok is a tough little creature of considerable endurance. It is sturdy and robust, with a comparatively large head for its size, small ears, short neck, long back and shaggy mane. It has small but sturdy hooves for mountain walking, which is what made it such a good pack pony. Since the late 1970s, however, there has been increasing demand for the Pottok as a riding animal, particularly as a child's mount because of its calm disposition. Today, it is also finding growing acceptance as a dressage mount.

## Fascinating Facts

In 1983, a purebred Pottok named Kuzko was French national champion in a discipline combining dressage and show jumping.

# ARIÈGEOIS

HEIGHT: 13.1–14.3 hh
COLOUR: black
PERSONALITY TYPE: warm-blooded
TYPICAL USE: pack, harness, riding

TEMPERAMENT: calm, quiet, equable

ORIGIN: France

SIMILAR BREEDS: Dales, Fell

## Fascinating Facts

An Ariègeois pony was gifted to the then British Prime Minister Tony Blair in 1997.

RIGHT
*The Ariègeois is a particularly striking breed, often used for driving, that is renowned for its calm, even and forgiving temperament.*

Stocky, sturdy and hardy, the Ariègeois, named for the Ariège River between Roussillon and Catalonia, bears a strong resemblance to the Fell and Dales pony breeds of Britain, and to the cave drawings found in its native home. Some of the carvings and wall pictures at Niaux in the Ariège, made by Cro-Magnon man, are recognizably the Camargue horse; others, just as surely, show the Ariègeois in its winter coat with its characteristic 'beard'.

## Mental Balance

In Ariège, most of the breeders raise the ponies in the open air all year round. The foals are born in the spring snow, and there are rarely any problems. In June, the herd is led up to the summer pastures to spend several months in total freedom in the high mountains. This life with the herd gives the Ariègeois the mental balance for which it is known.

The Ariègeois is always solid black in colour, its coat taking on a rusty sheen in the winter – white markings are rare. Its mane and tail are thick and long, and, vital to a mountain breed, it has good, hard feet.

## Ancient Breed

The Ariègeois is sometimes referred to as the Merens Pony and almost certainly has

Eastern blood, perhaps crossed with the heavy pack mares of the Roman legions to add substance and bone. It is certainly an ancient breed – Julius Caesar describes it accurately in his commentaries on the Gallic Wars of 58–51 BC.

Perhaps because of the remoteness of its mountain home, the Ariègeois was almost unknown until the twentieth century, when its reputation as a superlative pack pony began to spread. Because of its dark colour, it was valued by the smugglers who worked along the Spanish border, and was crucial to hill farmers in the region, for whom the tractor was virtually useless because of the terrain, and in the mines.

# ASTURCÓN (Asturian)

TEMPERAMENT: hardy, placid

ORIGIN: Spain

SIMILAR BREEDS: Galician, Galiceño, Sorraia

HEIGHT: 12.2 hh
COLOUR: black
PERSONALITY TYPE: warm-blooded
TYPICAL USE: riding, pack

Also known as the Asturian, this breed originated in northern Spain and is known to be at least 3,000 years old. While its ancestry is not well documented, it is thought to be a hybrid of Garrano, Sorraia and Celtic Pony. The Romans referred to these equines as Asturcóns and apparently thought well of them; Pliny the Elder (AD 23–79) described them as a small horse that did not trot, but moved its legs on each side together. They were also popular in France in the Middle Ages.

## Ladies' Mount

The Asturcón's unusual gait, a sort of amble, was peculiar to the breed and made for an extremely comfortable ride, so the ponies were popular as ladies' mounts. Known as 'palfreys' in England, they were called *haubini* in France, the word later becoming 'hobbye' and thence 'hobby horse'. Some Asturcón blood was introduced into Ireland, where the Irish Hobby was to be greatly admired. The amble is an inherited rather than learned gait, and there have been ambling horses in China, Turkey, Mongolia and Siberia. Neither the Garrano nor the Sorraia, thought to be the Asturcóns close relatives, have this gait.

## In Decline

The Asturcón is also closely related to, and sometimes referred to as, the Galician, after the region of north-west Spain, and both have had some influence on the Galiceño Pony of Mexico. It has a small though rather heavy head with a straight

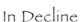

ABOVE

*This ancient breed has a natural gait, best described as an amble, which is particularly smooth, even and comfortable to ride.*

profile, small ears and large eyes. Its neck is long and thin, with a flowing mane, and it has high-set withers, a long, straight back and a low-set tail. Although not particularly good-looking, it is well shaped and very hardy.

As recently as the 1970s, there were thought to be some 20,000 of these ponies living semi-feral in the hills of north-west Spain, but their numbers have since been in decline.

# SORRAIA

HEIGHT: 14 hh

COLOUR: dun

PERSONALITY TYPE: warm-blooded

TYPICAL USE: stockhorse, riding

TEMPERAMENT: gentle

ORIGIN: Portugal and Spain

SIMILAR BREEDS: Garrano, Asturcón, Mustang

**T**he Sorraia's distinctive grey-dun colouring (also known as 'grullo') with black mane and tail betray its genetic links with the extinct ancient Tarpan, and this breed is indeed an ancient one, sometimes also having the primitive dorsal stripe. It originates in the area between the Sor and Raia rivers – from which it takes its name – that run through Portugal and Spain. It is also sometimes known as the *marismeño*, or the 'horse of the swamp'.

Sorraia was used to herd the fighting bulls of the region and other livestock.

The breed was discovered in Portugal in the 1920s by Portuguese scientist Ruy d'Andrade, who coined its name, and who, by selecting

LEFT

*Surprisingly, the slightly unprepossessing looking Sorraia horse is an ancient breed that gave rise to the magnificent Iberian horses, the Andalusian, Lusitano and Alter Real.*

## Foundation of Glory

The tough little Sorraia is thought to form the basis of the mighty Iberian horses, the Andalusian and the Lusitano, as well as the less influential Alter-Real. It is hard to believe that such an unassuming creature could have been the foundation of such glory. DNA from the breed has also been discovered in the Mustangs of North America, and it is thought that the indigenous Iberian breed was taken to the New World with the conquistadores, where it bred with other equines. The grullo colouring still occurs in the Mustang.

The modern Sorraia is always grullo or dun, with no white markings, and sometimes has stripes across its neck, shoulders and back. Foals are born with the zebra-striped markings all over, which acts as superb camouflage in the wild.

## Saved from Extinction

While the Sorraia is nothing much to look at, it is renowned for its ability to withstand extremes of climate, particularly dry, hot conditions, and to survive on short rations. Its

hardiness and agility made the Sorraia highly valuable to local stockmen. Once captured and tamed, the

30 of the little equines to run as a protected herd, saved it from almost certain extinction.

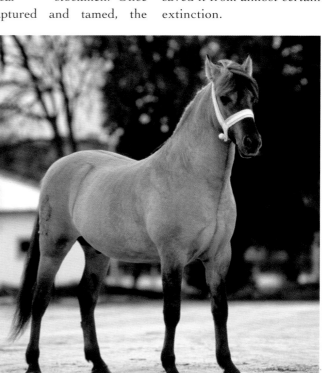

# GARRANO

TEMPERAMENT: quiet, willing

ORIGIN: Portugal

SIMILAR BREEDS: Sorraia

HEIGHT: 12–13 hh

COLOUR: bay, chestnut, brown

PERSONALITY TYPE: warm-blooded

Use: pack, harness, riding

The Garrano, or Minho, is closely related to the Sorraia. Some ponies have distinct Arabian dished faces, the result of infusions of Arab blood implemented by the Portuguese Ministry of Agriculture. The modern Garrano is a slightly more refined pony than its ancient ancestors (which played a role in the development of the influential Iberian breeds), although some still bear a resemblance to the extinct Tarpan. It has a pretty head, small ears and large, lively eyes. Good-looking, with both speed and stamina, it resembles a scaled-down version of the mighty Andalusian and Lusitano.

## Influential Breed

It has a comparatively long neck, straight shoulders, a deep, wide chest and a short, compact back, with sloping quarters, a low-set tail, short, strong legs and very hard feet. Inherently sure-footed, the Garrano travels easily over the steep, densely wooded terrain of its homeland in the Minho and Tras os Mentos regions. A popular military pack pony, it is also competed in the region's trotting races and makes a good harness pony.

# PENEIA

TEMPERAMENT: amenable, quiet

ORIGIN: Greece

SIMILAR BREEDS: Pindos

HEIGHT: 10–14 hh

COLOUR: roan, chestnut, black

PERSONALITY TYPE: warm-blooded

TYPICAL USE: agriculture, harness, pack, riding

The Peneia, or Pinia, is found in the Ilia and Achaia regions of Greece's Pelopponese. This rare pony breed is probably closely related to the Pindos, with outcrosses to Anglo-Arab, Anglo-Norman and Nonius. The breed's studbook was started only in 1995, but the Peneia is thought to be an ancient breed.

As of 2002 there were only 231 breeding mares and 69 stallions.

### Stamina and Endurance

The Peneia is extremely tough and hardy, with sound constitution and great stamina. Used for all forms of work, it has a very amenable temperament and is sure-footed across rough terrain. It tends to be heavily framed, with a coarse head, muscular neck, broad, strong back and very sound legs, but is often cow- or sickle-hocked with weak underdeveloped hind-quarters. It has a rather stilted, uneven stride, but does have an innate jumping ability. Peneia stallions are often used to breed mules.

LEFT

*As with most of the Greek breeds of pony, the Peneia is renowned for its hardiness and stamina.*

# SKYROS

HEIGHT: 11 hh

COLOUR: bay, brown, grey, dun

PERSONALITY TYPE: warm-blooded

TYPICAL USE: harness, pack, agricultural

TEMPERAMENT: gentle, docile

ORIGIN: Greece

SIMILAR BREEDS: Exmoor

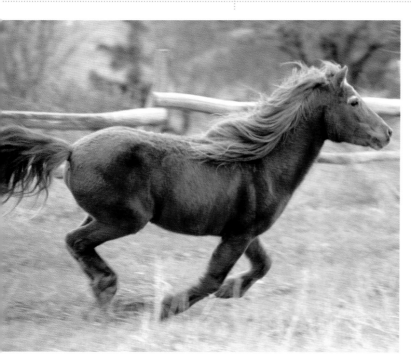

**T**his tiny pony, which takes its name from the Greek island it inhabits, is facing extinction and the race is on to save it from dying out completely. As of 2001, there were just 93 breeding mares and 52 studs. There are now believed to be fewer than 150 ponies on the island, and not all of these may be purebred. They resemble a smaller version of England's Exmoor Pony and are thought to be at least as ancient as their more northerly cousin.

## Parthenon Connection

It is thought that the ponies were introduced to Skyros by Athenian colonists in the fifth to eighth centuries – some believe they are the little equines seen on the frieze at the Parthenon – and they made the most of their island habitat. They are fairly unprepossessing, with a small head (which often has the same mealy muzzle and prominent eye of the Exmoor), straight shoulders, narrow body and short legs with small feet.

Skyros is an island of contrasting halves, the north side being lush and fertile, while the southern side is less hospitable and more mountainous. During the winter months, when food and water are plentiful, the ponies live in the southern mountainous part of the island commonly referred to as the *vouno*. At the onset of summer, they migrate north in search of water and food.

## Semi-Feral

The ponies continue to live a semi-feral existence on Skyros. Farmers on the island round them up at harvest time for threshing grain, although increasing mechanization has reduced this practice. They are also used to breed mules, and the existence of some of these progeny left on Skyros threatens further the breed's ability to procreate. While it is illegal to export the ponies, donkeys or mules may be exported and sold, which makes it more economic to breed them.

RIGHT

*This is a small and tough breed of pony that lives a semi-feral existence on the Greek island of Skyros.*

# PINDOS

HEIGHT: 13 hh

COLOUR: bay, brown, black, occasional roan

PERSONALITY TYPE: warm-blooded

TYPICAL USE: agriculture, riding, harness, pack

TEMPERAMENT: stubborn, wilful

ORIGIN: Greece

SIMILAR BREEDS: Peneia

Sometimes known as the Thessalonian Pony, the Pindos is an ancient breed, raised in the Thessaly and Epirus regions of Greece – it is thought to be a descendant of the now-extinct Thessalonian Horse, which was developed by the Greeks and renowned for its courage and beauty. Greece, however, is not an ideal place for breeding horses – it has harsh weather conditions and poor, infertile soil. These conditions, and the mountainous region the Pindos inhabits, have produced a pony noted more for its endurance than its good looks.

## Climbing Ability

The Pindos, while not much to look at, is an inordinately hardy and enduring pony with functional abilities that more than make up for a lack of aesthetic beauty. It has all the qualities that accompany a mountain breed, which include remarkable climbing abilities. It is also agile and sure-footed, with hard feet and sound constitution. It is a good doer and able to withstand blistering heat and punishing winters, with temperatures still as low as –13°C (9°F) in the early spring. The Pindos pony is also long-lived, with animals of 40 years old or more recorded.

It is used by the local people of the region for agricultural work, ploughing, harness, pack and riding – despite its small stature, the Pindos is strong enough to carry an adult.

## Wilful

The Pindos has a rather unattractive, coarse head with a small eye, a medium-length neck and back, and a narrow frame. The hindquarters are poor and the high-set tail indicates Eastern influence, as do their fine legs and tough hooves. They are usually dark in colour with no white markings, although the occasional animal will have a light-coloured mane and tail, perhaps the result of an unsuccessful attempt to introduce Haflinger blood. The pony does have a reputation for being wilful and stubborn.

## Fascinating Facts

A subspecies of the Pindos exists as an endangered wild herd on the island of Kefalonia, off the coast of western Greece. They are known as the Ainos Horses, named after the island's Mount Ainos, the third highest mountain in Greece. It is thought there about 20 of these ponies left.

BELOW

*The Pindos is a very old breed thought to be a descendent of the Thessalonian horses of ancient Greece.*

# BARDIGIANO

HEIGHT: 13 hh

COLOUR: bay, black, brown

PERSONALITY TYPE: warm-blooded

TYPICAL USE: riding, pack, agriculture

TEMPERAMENT: quiet, kind

ORIGIN: Italy

SIMILAR BREEDS: Avelignese, Haflinger

Although it is native to the northern Appenine region of Italy, the Bardigiano bears a striking resemblance to Britain's Exmoor Pony, as well as southern Italy's Avelignese, Austria's Haflinger and the Spanish Asturcón (Asturian). Both the Haflinger and the Avelignese have a common ancestor in the Arab stallion El Bedavi, and the Bardigiano is noticeably Eastern in appearance, with a neat head, broad forehead, tapered muzzle and slightly dished face, with not even the merest suggestion of coarseness.

## Producing Mules

During the First and Second World Wars, Bardigiano mares were used to produce mules for the military, the effect being a sharp decline in the number of good breeding stock. The introduction of outside stallions almost proved disastrous, as the breed began to lose its distinctive

*BELOW*

*The Bardigiano breed are noted for their fine heads, seen here, which reflect the influence of Arab blood in the breed.*

sure-footed and robust. It has a quiet, kind temperament, which makes it an excellent child's pony, as well as being suitable for farm work, light draught and as a pack animal.

## Roman Ancestors

The Bardigiano is undoubtedly related to an ancient breed of horse, named the Abellinium by the Romans, but has adapted to its rough mountain habitat and is a small, attractive creature. It retains pony characteristics, such its pretty head, with a deep chest, strongly built body and short, sturdy legs with hard joints and plenty of bone.

It has the thick, full mane and tail of many pony breeds, and the mealy muzzle so distinctive in the Exmoor sometimes occurs, suggesting again the closeness of the ancestry of both breeds. Like the Exmoor, it is little affected by the cold and wet.

characteristics. In 1972, a committee was formed to re-establish and protect the breed.

Today's Bardigiano is a useful and attractive equine, tough and enduring as most mountain breeds, as well as

## Fascinating Facts

A foal usually inherits its father's (sire's) looks, but its mother's (dam's) constitution and personality.

# AVELIGNESE

TEMPERAMENT: placid, hardy

ORIGIN: Italy

SIMILAR BREEDS: Haflinger

HEIGHT: 13.3–14.3 hh

COLOUR: chestnut with flaxen mane and tail

PERSONALITY TYPE: warm-blooded

TYPICAL USE: trekking, pack

Italy's version of the Haflinger is a strong, robust little animal that takes its name from Avelengo, an area of the Alto Adige, which has been an Italian region since 1918, and is used mostly for pack and draught. It bears a striking resemblance to the Haflinger – both breeds contain bloodlines that can be traced back to the Arabian stallion El Bedavi – but stands slightly bigger than its Tyrolean cousin, reaching about 14.3 hh. It is widely bred in Tuscany, Emilia and central southern Italy, although it is also found throughout the country and is believed to be the most prolific Italian breed.

## Oriental Influences

Although the Avelignese is considered a coldblood, and exhibits many coldblood characteristics, it almost certainly has Oriental influences. It is undeniably attractive, with a small head of considerable quality, a broad forehead tapering to a fine muzzle and a fairly short, crested and muscular neck. Its powerful shoulders are ideal for carrying a harness collar, and it has a broad, deep chest and wide, compact back.

Its hindquarters are muscular and well rounded, and its shoulders are quite upright, so its stride is fairly short. It has generally good legs with hard, dense bone, well-formed joints and some feathering around the fetlocks. Its feet are exceptionally hard and well formed.

### ABOVE

*The resemblance of the Italian Avelignese to the Austrian Haflinger is striking – both breeds share similar bloodlines that trace to the Arab stallion El Bedavi.*

## Unflappable Nature

The breed is always a bright chestnut, with flaxen mane and tail – a pleasing combination – and is very versatile. The stocky Avelignese has the typically placid coldblood temperament, which makes it an ideal mount for children, novices or nervous riders, and has sufficient stamina to be used for endurance riding. But it is also used extensively for working the land in its mountainous homeland, where motorized vehicles are impractical. It is sure-footed and strong, and virtually unflappable.

# DÜLMEN

HEIGHT: 12.3 hh

COLOUR: dun, black, brown

PERSONALITY TYPE:
warm-blooded

TYPICAL USE: riding, driving

TEMPERAMENT: tough, trainable

ORIGIN: Germany

SIMILAR BREEDS: Senner (extinct)

As a country most famous for its warmblood breeds, it is perhaps strange that Germany possesses only one native breed of pony – there used to be a breed called the Senner that existed in the Teutoburg Forest, but this is now extinct. The Dülmen is an ancient breed found near the town of the same name, in the Merfelder Bruch. Ponies have been documented as being in this area since the early 1300s. The Dülmen's exact origins are unknown, but it is thought to have developed from primitive equines.

The ponies are left largely to their own devices, foraging for food and seeking shelter, with little outside assistance. The ones that survive are invariably the strongest and, as a breed, they are exceptionally tough and resistant to disease.

## Tameable and Trainable

The Dülmen is easily tamed and trained, and makes an excellent child's pony. It is also used as a driving pony and for working the land. Although not particularly

attractive – they tend to coarseness and their hindquarters are poor – they are highly valued for their hardiness and adaptability. Many still retain the primitive dun colouring – the browns,

## Fascinating Facts

Each year, on the last Saturday in May, the Dülmen are rounded up in the traditional Wildpferdefang, and the colts separated. The colts are sold at public auctions, and the mares returned to the Merfelder Bruch with one or two stallions.

chestnuts and blacks seen suggest infusions of foreign blood at some point in the breed's past.

## The Last Wild Herd

The Dülmen used to live in large wild herds throughout Westphalia, but during the nineteenth century, when land was divided and parcelled separately, they began to lose their natural habitat. There is only one remaining wild herd. This is owned by the Duke of Croÿ and roams about 350 ha (860 acres) of the Merfelder Bruch. This area combines a wide diversity of small habitats, ranging from woodland to heath and open moorland.

# HAFLINGER

TEMPERAMENT: happy, willing

ORIGIN: Austria

SIMILAR BREEDS: Avelignese

HEIGHT: 13.2–15 hh

COLOUR: all shades of chestnut, with flaxen mane and tail

PERSONALITY TYPE: warm-blooded

TYPICAL USE: light draught, harness, pack, riding, competition

**A**ll modern Haflingers must be able to trace back to the breed's foundation stallion, 249 Folie, a descendant of the influential stallion El Bedavi. Folie was bred to a Tyrolean mare and the breed's name comes from the village of Hafling, high in the southern Tyrolean Mountains in what are now Austria and Italy. The Austrian Haflinger bears the famous Edelweiss brand mark – a flower with an 'H' in the centre – and the breed is sometimes referred to as the 'Edelweiss Pony'.

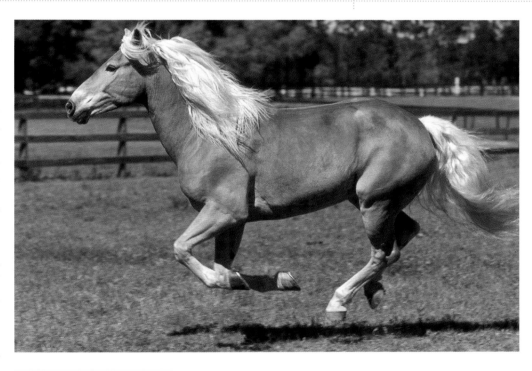

## Golden Pony

The Haflinger is instantly recognizable by its glorious colour – its coat ranges from pale, shimmering gold to rich, glowing chestnut, and every shade in between – and flaxen mane and tail. Most Haflingers stand around 13 hh, although bigger animals are sometimes seen. In the Second World War, the military demanded stockier, sturdier equines, and the Haflinger breeders obliged, but thereafter emphasis was placed once more on elegance and increased height.

*The Haflinger is a popular and versatile pony breed whose elegant appearance reflects the influence of Arab blood early in the breed history.*

And the Haflinger is, indeed, an elegant creature. It has a lean, refined head with a large, lively eye, a medium-length neck with well-defined withers, and good, sloping shoulders. Its deep, broad chest and muscular back make it a powerful equine, and it has excellent legs and hard feet. Haflingers often live beyond 40 years old.

## Happy Nature

Tyrolean artwork from the early 1800s shows a small but noble equine carrying packs and riders across the steep alpine trails, and the modern Haflinger retains this sure-footedness. Many of the mountain villages are accessible only by these narrow, rocky paths, and the agile Haflinger was invaluable to the villagers. But its happy nature makes it an ideal family horse, too, and there is little to which it cannot turn a hoof – it can be used for light draught, harness or pack work, and competes successfully in a wide range of equestrian disciplines.

# KONIK

HEIGHT: 12–13 hh

COLOUR: dun with black dorsal stripe

PERSONALITY TYPE: warm-blooded

TYPICAL USE: agriculture, harness

TEMPERAMENT: gentle, hard-working, eager to please

ORIGIN: Poland

SIMILAR BREEDS: Tarpan (extinct), Hucul

**K**onik translates as 'little horse' – it is a Polish diminutive that actually means 'horsie' – and Poland's native breed is perhaps more horse than pony, although it stands barely 13 hh. It bears a strong resemblance to the Tarpan, a now-extinct European breed, and it is thought that farmers captured the remaining wild Tarpans and bred them to their domestic horses. The Konik certainly has many features of the Tarpan, including the primitive colouring of dun with dark dorsal stripe and dark points.

## Valuable Commodity

The modern Konik has the gentle nature and eagerness to oblige that made it so popular with Polish farmers – this is a horse that works

ABOVE
*The ancient Konik breed is close in appearance to the Tarpan, and retains primitive physical characteristics in its colouring and conformation.*

hard to please and is thus a valuable commodity. It is also used under harness and for light draught work, for which it is well suited, being hardy, robust and self-reliant.

It has a quiet temperament and is easily managed. It is a stocky equine, with a large head, short, strong neck set on low withers, upright shoulders, broad body, deep girth and strong, sound legs.

Some Arab blood has been introduced for refinement, so occasionally other colours than its distinctive dun do occur. Today, the Konik is mostly bred at the Polish state stud of Jezewice and at Popielno, where careful selection ensures the breed continues.

## Breeding Programme

In the twentieth century, several attempts were made to breed back a Tarpan-like horse, using Koniks,

Przewalski's Horse, Icelandic horses and Gotlands. Semi-wild herds of Koniks now exist in nature reserves in the Netherlands, Latvia and the United Kingdom, where it can be seen in Kent and Cambridgeshire. While the attempts to re-create the Tarpan may not have been entirely successful, it can only be good to try to preserve the reliable and sturdy 'little horse' of Poland.

## Fascinating Facts

7.1 million Americans are involved in the industry as horse owners, service providers, employees and volunteers.

# HUCUL

TEMPERAMENT: hardy, placid

ORIGIN: Poland

SIMILAR BREEDS: Tarpan (extinct), Konik

HEIGHT: 12.1–13.1 hh

COLOUR: bay, black, chestnut, dun

PERSONALITY TYPE: warm-blooded

TYPICAL USE: riding, pack, light draught

Hroby, Ouşor, Pietrousu and Prislop – and the horses were carefully bred to preserve the purity of these bloodlines. In 1922, 33 ponies were sent to the then Czechoslovakia to establish a herd there that would become known as the Gurgul line. The studbook for the breed was opened in 1982.

LEFT

*The Hucul with its sturdy build is very strong and this, combined with its tractable temperament, makes it popular in its home country for riding, packing and light draught work.*

The Hucul, one of the oldest breeds of native pony in Europe, perhaps more than any other resembles the extinct Tarpan. It dates back to the thirteenth century and is believed to be the result of crossing Mongolian Horses with the wild Tarpan. It originated in the Carpathian Mountains in Eastern Europe – it is sometimes called the Carpathian Pony, or the Mountain Tarpan. Borders have changed many times throughout history along this mountain range, and both Romania and Poland could lay claim to being the Hucul's country of origin.

## Foundation Stallions

The Hucul's isolated mountain home is in the Eastern Carpathians, a region called Huzulland, which has a harsh, unforgiving climate. With no other equine influence, a distinct breed evolved of a robust and enduring little equine. It is compact and muscular, with a deep, broad chest and exceptionally strong neck and back. It has an attractive head with large, expressive eyes and small, mobile ears. Its legs are strong and sound, and it has excellent feet – the Hucul rarely needs to be shod.

## Different Versions

The first stud farm was established at Roaduti, in Romania, using five foundation stallions – Goral,

As the Hucul was used and bred by a variety of people in a variety of places, slightly different types emerged – the Hucul of Romania was different to the Czech and Polish versions. Today, Huculs are bred mainly in the Bucovina region of Romania, as well as Hungary, regions of the Czech and Slovak republics, Poland and the Ukraine.

# KLEPPER (Torijski)

HEIGHT: 14.3–15 hh

COLOUR: chestnut, bay, dun, grey

PERSONALITY TYPE: warm-blooded

TYPICAL USE: agriculture, riding, pack, tourism

TEMPERAMENT: willing, obedient

ORIGIN: Estonia

SIMILAR BREEDS: Vyatka

Estonia's native breed is one of the few that has been little influenced by outside blood. In its turn, it played an important role in the development of the now-extinct Obva breed and the Vyatka. It has also been used with, variously, Hackney and Ardennais blood to create the Toric (*see* page 337). The original Klepper first arrived in Russia via Novgorod as early as the fourteenth century, when it was in demand for its willing temperament, **good working qualities and adaptability.**

## Foundation Mares

As agriculture developed and demand for good working horses increased, the Klepper was crossed with larger breeds to give it more size and strength. The Tori Stud was established in 1856 with 47 mares and seven young stallions. As well as breeding pure Kleppers, the stud also crossed them with light harness and saddle breeds; the best mares resulting from the cross were used to develop the Toric. The purebred stallion Vansikasa, a horse of great strength and endurance, won many championships and its daughters were foundation mares of the Toric.

As with so many equines, mechanization was to have a devastating effect on the Klepper, and it is no longer bred on mainland Estonia, surviving only on the islands of Saaremaa, Hiiumaa and Muhu. It is thought there are only about 1,000 purebreds left.

## Long-lived

The Klepper today is also known as the Torijski. It is an attractive and amenable equine. Standing up to 15 hh, it has a well-proportioned head with a wide forehead, although there is a tendency to coarseness; the neck can be on the short side, and the withers are set low. The chest is very wide and deep, and the Klepper has short, clean legs and extremely solid hooves. The breed is long-lived, with some horses reaching 40 years old.

ABOVE

*There are very few pure bred Kleppers left, their numbers having dropped dramatically through the advent of mechanization.*

# ZEMAITUKA

**TEMPERAMENT:** quiet, biddable

**ORIGIN:** Lithuania

**SIMILAR BREEDS:** Konik

**HEIGHT:** 13.2–14.2 hh

**COLOUR:** dun, black, brown, bay, palomino

**PERSONALITY TYPE:** warm-blooded

**TYPICAL USE:** riding, light draught, agriculture

**A** lso called the Zhumd, this is an ancient breed originally from Lithuania, on the Baltic Sea, and closely related to the Konik and therefore the ancient Tarpan. Little is known about the breed, except that very few are left in existence. Its natural habitat is harsh and unforgiving, with poor forage and freezing temperatures. The Zemaituka has developed into a tough little equine, able to survive on meagre rations.

*ABOVE*

*The Zemaituka is closely related to, and bears a resemblance to, the Konik, pictured, with both breeds displaying primitive coat colours and characteristics.*

## Sport Horses

Over the years, other breeds have had influence on the Zemaituka, including native Russian blood and light horse breeds from Poland. More recently, Arabian blood has been introduced, which can be seen in the animal's surprisingly fine head. There were, at one point, two distinct types of Zemaituka: a finer quality riding type and a heavier light draught type. This distinction has been blurred as, after the Second World War, conscious effort

## W ise ords

'If you want a kitten, start out by asking for a horse' — Anon

has been made to increase the breed's size and bulk, making it suitable for both riding and light draught.

Today's Zemaituka is an attractive, sturdy creature with a gentle, biddable nature and an endearing eagerness to please. Despite its rather solid and massive frame, it is generally agile and athletic. When crossed with a lighter breed, such as a Thoroughbred, it produces excellent sport horses.

## A Good Doer

The Zemaituka is a good doer with considerable stamina and endurance, and is seemingly unaffected by fatigue. It has an attractive head with large, kind eyes and small, mobile ears. It has a well-muscled neck, broad, deep chest, rather straight shoulders, a compact, straight back and a sloping croup with low-set tail. Its legs are short and muscular (although the breed has a tendency towards poor hocks), and its feet are well formed and hard. The most common colour is dun or mouse dun, with a dark dorsal stripe and black points – indication of its ancient origins. Blacks, browns, bays and palominos also occur.

*BELOW*

*The Polish Wielpolski, pictured, and Arab blood was used to refine the Zemaituka, lending it greater elegance and making it suitable for riding and light draught work.*

# BOSNIAN

HEIGHT: 13–14.2 hh

COLOUR: bay, black, brown, grey, palomino

PERSONALITY TYPE: warm-blooded

TYPICAL USE: riding, pack, agriculture, light draught

TEMPERAMENT: quiet, docile

ORIGIN: Bosnia

SIMILAR BREEDS: Hucul, Konik

**T**he Bosnian is the third of the three Balkan breeds, together with the Hucul and the Konik. They are all ancient breeds, and the Bosnian is thought to be the result of a cross between the Tarpan and Przewalski's Horse, also known as the Asiatic Wild Horse. Since the 1900s, it has been selectively bred, to ensure the endurance of the breed, which suffered serious decline following infusions of Oriental blood.

## State Control

Oriental blood was introduced by the Turks during the Ottoman Empire, and the resulting deterioration of the breed was rectified by infusions of more Tarpan blood. Selective breeding in the twentieth century has saved the breed, which is highly prized, and for many years, when Bosnia was part of the former Yugoslavia, the principal centre for breeding the Bosnian was the Borike Stud in Bosnia. Stallions were strictly controlled by the state, but the mares were under private ownership.

_____
LEFT

*The Bosnian pony is a small and tough breed, which has much in common with the ancient Hucul and Konik breeds.*

During the 1940s, three stallions – Agan, Barat and Misco – had an important influence on the breed, generally improving it. Agan and Barat were probably pure or almost pure Przewalski, while Misco was of a lighter, finer type.

## Useful and Functional

The modern Bosnian retains the primitive appearance, but also possesses quality and refinement. It has a heavy head with a straight profile, full forelock and small ears. A short, muscular neck joins long, sloping shoulders, a deep, wide chest and a straight back with sloping hindquarters. The primitive dorsal stripe and black points are sometimes seen, although most solid colours occur.

It is an extremely useful and functional little animal, suited to riding, light farm work or draught and pack, as it is sure-footed enough to cross rough terrain inaccessible to motorized vehicles. Hardy and tough, its docile temperament makes it easy to handle and safe to ride.

_____
RIGHT

*The Hucul, pictured, Konik and Bosnian are the three Balkan breeds and share many similarities, particularly in their stocky conformation.*

# KAZAKH

TEMPERAMENT: placid, docile

ORIGIN: Kazakhstan

SIMILAR BREEDS: Mongolian Pony

HEIGHT: 14 hh

COLOUR: grullo, bay, brown, chestnut, palomino

PERSONALITY TYPE: warm-blooded

TYPICAL USE: riding, pack, meat

Originating in Kazakhstan and primitive in origin, the Kazakh is one of the breeds with its roots in Przewalski's Horse. A true working breed, it is sturdy, hardy and strong, with great stamina and a thick waterproof coat. Its short, rather choppy stride can make it uncomfortable for riding, but it is a good pack animal.

## Sub-Types

Over the years the Kazakh has been subject to infusions of outside blood, not all of them successful. There are two known sub-types, the Dzhabe and the Adaev, with the latter being of lighter frame and generally more lively. The Dzhabe has a rather plain, coarse head and short, muscular neck leading to

straight shoulders and back, and is commonly bay or liver chestnut. The Adaev type has a much more refined head, slightly longer neck, pronounced withers and compact body. It is usually bay, grey, palomino or chestnut. Both types have strong legs and good hard feet. The Adaev is more suited to riding, with a smoother stride.

# VYATKA

TEMPERAMENT: willing, docile, hardy

ORIGIN: Russia

SIMILAR BREEDS: Konik, Klepper

HEIGHT: 14.2 hh

COLOUR: roan, dun, bay, brown, chestnut

PERSONALITY TYPE: warm-blooded

TYPICAL USE: pack, harness, light draught

The rare Vyatka, or Vyatskata, originated in the region around Russia's Vyatka and Obva rivers. The pony probably descended from the Tarpan, with Konik and Estonian/Klepper influences. It was affected by edicts from state breeders during the reign of Peter the Great (1672–1725); and Estonian horses imported to the Urals for use in the mining industry in the eighteenth century were likely crossed with the native Vyatka breed.

## Sharply Declining Numbers

The result was a sturdy equine of speed and extraordinary endurance, able to thrive on meagre rations. It made an excellent light draught horse. With increasing mechanization and more intensified agriculture, however, numbers fell sharply.

The Vyatka's ancient roots are clearly seen in its most common chestnut or bay roan colouring, with a black dorsal stripe along its back and zebra stripes on its forelegs. Some also have a wing-shaped marking over the shoulders. Brown, bay and chestnut are also seen, as well as the much less common

black. It has a small, clean-cut head, a strong, thick neck, a deep girth and powerful shoulders and hindquarters.

# PONEY MOUSSEYE

HEIGHT: 12 hh

COLOUR: grey, chestnut

PERSONALITY TYPE: warm-blooded

TYPICAL USE: riding, pack, light draught

TEMPERAMENT: quiet, easygoing

ORIGIN: Cameroon

SIMILAR BREEDS: Nigerian

Little is known about the Poney Mousseye, which comes from Cameroon, a country on the west central coast of Africa. The tiny equine – it stands barely 12 hh – probably has common roots with the Nigerian, which in turn probably dates back to the Barb, which, taken to Nigeria by the nomads, mated with the local ponies. Although this is the received wisdom, it is entirely possible it was the other way around, with the Nigerian descending from the Poney Mousseye.

## Disease-resistant

A rare breed, the Poney Mousseye is found mainly in areas around the Logone River. This particular region is notorious for the tsetse fly, the bite of which carries sleeping sickness, also known as African trypanosomiasis, which can cause brain damage and, if untreated, death. The Poney Mousseye, however, appears resistant to the disease, while other equine breeds are not.

## Easygoing

The Poney Mousseye has remained largely uninfluenced by other breeds because of its geographic isolation and, whatever its origins, the modern Mousseye certainly shows little of its supposed Barb roots. It has a plain head with straight profile, which tends to be on the heavy side; a short, thick neck; and a long back. It has a sloping croup – which perhaps betrays its Barb origins – a compact body and short but strong legs. The only defect is occasionally underdeveloped hindquarters. Versatile and easygoing, the Poney Mousseye makes a good,

LEFT

*The purity of the Poney Mousseye breed has remained relatively intact due to their geographic isolation.*

ABOVE

*The precise origin of the Poney Mousseye is unclear, but they often show a striking similarity to the Barb, pictured.*

willing child's riding pony, and is strong and hardy enough for light pack work because of its great stamina and endurance.

The Nigerian, while similar in appearance to the Poney Mousseye, is larger, standing up to 14.2 hh. It has the same sweet nature and stamina, and is equally resistant to heat.

# BASUTO

TEMPERAMENT: brave, affectionate

ORIGIN: Lesotho, Southern Africa

SIMILAR BREEDS: Cape Horse

HEIGHT: 14.2 hh

COLOUR: chestnut, bay, brown, grey, white markings

PERSONALITY TYPE: warm-blooded

TYPICAL USE: riding, trekking, polo

**T**his tough, brave pony was developed in Lesotho (formerly Basuto-land), a country landlocked by South Africa, in the eighteenth and nineteenth centuries from the region's Cape Horse. Both breeds descended from the first horses introduced to South Africa by the Dutch East India Trading Company, which brought four equines to the Cape area in 1653. These horses were probably Arabian and Persian, and founded the Cape Horse, a large, quality creature that was a popular warhorse.

## Stamina and Bravery

The Basuto was smaller and stockier, but tough and sure-footed, traits it almost certainly developed to cope with the rocky and hilly terrain over which it was ridden, sometimes at considerable speed. Possessing incredible

### Fascinating Facts

It is possible today to appreciate horses in South Africa by going on a safari horse trail in the Western Cape area.

BELOW LEFT

*The Basuto pony is renowned for its stamina and speed, over the most treacherous terrain. They are plucky and affable in temperament.*

stamina and bravery, the Basuto grew in popularity, and this was almost its undoing – in high demand, hundreds of thousands of them were exported and many of the best were killed in action during the Boer War at the end of the nineteenth century. With so many spread to the winds, and some of the best breeding stock cut down in its prime, the Basuto was almost wiped out.

## Polo Pony

An attractive little equine, the Basuto has a rather large but neat head, set on a long neck, with straight shoulders and long, straight back, ending with a muscular, sloping croup. It has good, tough legs and sound, hard feet. Although technically a pony – the Basuto rarely stands taller than 14.2 hh – it does have horse-like qualities, including an exceptionally long stride.

Today, the Basuto is often used for racing – making good use of that long stride – or polo, where its speed and agility are great assets. Its friendly, amenable nature makes it a suitable mount for a child, and its stamina means that it is an excellent pack pony. There is in progress a concerted effort to save the Basuto breed.

# BURMESE

HEIGHT: 13 hh

COLOUR: brown, bay, black, chestnut, grey

PERSONALITY TYPE: warm-blooded

TYPICAL USE: pack, trekking

TEMPERAMENT: quiet, willing

ORIGIN: Burma

SIMILAR BREEDS: Manipuri, Bhutia, Spiti

The Burmese, bred by the hill tribes of Burma's Shan, is sometimes called the Shan Pony. Superbly adapted to its mountain environment, this ancient breed is resistant to the harsh climate and sure-footed enough to traverse the steep, rocky terrain at

RIGHT

*These small, tough ponies are ideal for packing and trekking over mountainous terrain and are particularly surefooted.*

speed. **Its short, rather choppy stride is well suited to the rugged topography.**

## Function Not Beauty

The Burmese probably developed from the Mongolian, with Oriental influences. It is neither particularly speedy nor athletic, and is rather unprepossessing to look at, with emphasis on function

rather than beauty. It does have a fine head, with a straight profile and a pleasingly wide forehead. Its long, muscular neck is in proportion to its body, but its back tends to be too long. The withers are not pronounced,

and its shoulders are rather straight. It has a deep, wide chest, fine but strong legs and small, hard hooves. Quiet and willing, it is an ideal mount for children or novices.

## Fascinating Facts

The Burmese's stamina is renowned. In 1887, an equestrian explorer called George Younghusband travelled 2,900 km (1,800 miles) on a Burmese called Joe, which the adventurer described as a 'loveable scamp'.

# MANIPURI

HEIGHT: 13 hh

COLOUR: most solid colours, pinto

PERSONALITY TYPE: warm-blooded

TYPICAL USE: polo, racing, military

TEMPERAMENT: intelligent, alert

ORIGIN: Burma/India

SIMILAR BREEDS: Bhutia, Spiti, Burmese

The Manipur Cavalry was respected and feared throughout upper Burma during the seventeenth century. Part of the credit for this must go to the agile, tough and athletic Manipuri. A cross between the ancient Mongolian Wild Horse and the Arabian, it was later used in the Second World War and as a

transport animal. **Before it was a warhorse, however, the Manipuri was the original polo pony.**

## Polo by Torchlight

The King of Manipur introduced polo in the seventh century. Later, Akbar the Great (1542–1605), a

polo aficionado, played the game at night by torchlight and kept his own huge stables, which can still be seen today at Agra.

The intelligent Manipuri, with its speed and stamina, was a natural for the game, but its small stature counted against it. As polo's popularity spread, over the

years the upper height limit for polo ponies was increased, then abolished altogether. Still, the Manipuri remains popular. Undeniably attractive, it has a muscular neck, broad chest, well-sprung ribs and compact body, with sloping shoulders, muscular hindquarters, a sloping croup, strong legs and good feet.

# BHUTIA AND SPITI

TEMPERAMENT: willing and quiet, though can be bad-tempered

ORIGIN: India

SIMILAR BREEDS: Tibetan, Manipuri, Burmese

HEIGHT: 12–13.2 hh

COLOUR: grey, chestnut, roan, bay

PERSONALITY TYPE: warm-blooded

TYPICAL USE: pack

High in the Himalayan region were three distinct types of pony, the Bhutia, Spiti and Tibetan. Probably descended from ancient Mongolian strains, over centuries they have interbred to the extent that many of their individual characteristics have long been lost. They are now categorized as the 'Indian Country Bred', although the Tibetan Pony retains some of its purity. The Bhutia is found today in Nepal, Bhutan and the Sikkim and Darjeeling regions of India, while the Spiti is found in the Kangra Valley, north-eastern Punjab.

## Self-sufficient

Bhutia and Spiti are frugal feeders and thus economical to keep. They are also incredibly tough and self-sufficient. Both are rather plain and thickset, with a comparatively large head with a pronounced jaw, short neck, low withers, sloping quarters and deep chest. The shoulders are a little upright and straight. The legs tend to be short but very strong, with exceptionally hard feet. Excellent pack ponies, they can make good riding ponies, as they have great stamina and endurance.

BELOW

*Bhutia and Spiti, like these rugged ponies seen here in the wetlands of Mongolia, are very self-sufficient.*

# MONGOLIAN

TEMPERAMENT: quiet, biddable

ORIGIN: Mongolia

SIMILAR BREEDS: Przewalski's Horse

HEIGHT: 12.1 hh

COLOUR: dun, bay, brown, black

PERSONALITY TYPE: warm-blooded

TYPICAL USE: riding, racing

Purported to be largely unchanged since the time of Genghis Khan (1206–27), the Mongolian is an ancient breed that resembles Przewalski's Horse, of which it is believed to be a direct descendant. There are thought to be about three million Mongolian Ponies. Able to survive on minimal rations, it is used for riding and racing, which play a big part in the Mongol lifestyle.

## Prized Attributes

Even today, the ponies live out on a plateau 1,820 m (6,000 ft) above sea level, in punishing winds and a winter temperature down to –40°C (–40°F). Breeders believe that, when stall-fed, the pony loses its great speed and exceptional hardiness, both highly prized.

The ponies retain many of the primitive characteristics, though not all have dun colouring and black points. Small and stocky, they have a large head, short legs and very long manes and tails – and considerable stamina. Racing ponies with a child in the saddle will run at full gallop over a distance of 35 km (22 miles) and are trained to keep running even if the rider falls.

# CHINESE GUOXIA

**HEIGHT:** 11 hh

**COLOUR:** bay, roan, grey

**PERSONALITY TYPE:** warm-blooded

**TYPICAL USE:** riding, harness

**TEMPERAMENT:** calm, willing

**ORIGIN:** south-west China

**SIMILAR BREEDS:** Mongolian

A bronze statue of a pony recovered in south-west China is thought to be of a Guoxia, and is dated at 2,000 years old. The word Guoxia translates as 'under fruit tree horse', so it may have been that the pony, which is small in stature, worked in orchards collecting the fruit. Little is known about the Guoxia, and it was thought to be extinct before it was rediscovered in 1981.

## Marauding Tribes

Not particularly horse-orientated, the Chinese were forced to deploy mounted warriors and even breed their own horses in defence against the marauding nomadic tribes who continually attacked the nation's borders. The tough, hardy Guoxia is probably a descendant of the Mongolian and, through it, Przewalski's Horse.

It has a comparatively large head, with small, alert ears, a short neck, rather straight shoulders, a short, straight back, strong legs and very hard feet. Its generally gentle, friendly nature makes it an excellent child's first pony. Very strong with considerable stamina, it is also used in harness, despite its small size.

RIGHT
*The gentle Chinese Guoxia makes a good child's pony.*

# TIBETAN

**HEIGHT:** 12.2 hh

**COLOUR:** usually bay or grey

**PERSONALITY TYPE:** warm-blooded

**TYPICAL USE:** riding, trekking, pack, light draught, racing

**TEMPERAMENT:** energetic, willing

**ORIGIN:** Tibet

**SIMILAR BREEDS:** Mongolian

Although Tibet's native pony breed is undoubtedly descended from the Mongolian, it has remained largely pure for many years and is revered for its incredible strength and endurance. The Dalai Lama historically keeps Tibetan Ponies, and a Tibetan Pony was often sent as a gift to the Chinese emperor, particularly during the Tang and Ming dynasties.

## A Versatile Friend

An excellent worker, resilient and energetic, the Tibetan is used for light draught, riding and packing. Extremely sure-footed, in some parts of Tibet it is the only form of transport. It is also used for trekking, which is becoming increasingly popular. Despite its small size, the Tibetan is ridden in racing as well, as it has a swift turn of foot.

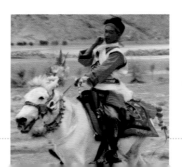

It has a straight head, pronounced jawline and small ears and eyes. Its short, muscular neck is set on flat withers and straight shoulders. It has a straight back, broad, powerful hindquarters, strong, straight legs with solid joints, and hard feet. It is usually bay or grey, but most solid colours are seen.

# TOKARA

TEMPERAMENT: gentle, placid

ORIGIN: Japan

SIMILAR BREEDS: Misaki, Hokkaido, Kiso

HEIGHT: 12 hh

COLOUR: bay, brown, chestnut, roan

PERSONALITY TYPE: warm-blooded

TYPICAL USE: riding, light draught

Once numerous, these little ponies are now rare, although a preservation project is under way. They were discovered in 1950, when a Dr Shigeyuki Hayashida found a group of small equines living in the south side of the Tokara Islands and gave them their name. They were believed to be the descendants of horses taken to the island in the 1800s, and the island people used them for farming, transport and for processing the sugar cane grown in the area.

## National Treasure

The Tokara suffered a severe decline after the Second World War. In an attempt to preserve the breed in a near original form, a number of animals were taken to Nakanoshima on Tokara Island, where

they range freely during the year and are rounded up for pest extermination, inoculation and veterinary treatment every 12 months. The breed has been designated a Japanese national treasure.

# MISAKI

TEMPERAMENT: wild

ORIGIN: Japan

SIMILAR BREEDS: Tokara, Hokkaido, Kiso

HEIGHT: 13.2 hh

COLOUR: bay, black, chestnut, cremello

PERSONALITY TYPE: warm-blooded

TYPICAL USE: tourism

The wildest of all Japanese breeds, the Misaki originates in the Miyazaki Prefecture on the island of Kyushu, and lives in the meadows of the Cape Toi, or Toimisake — the word *misaki* means 'cape'. It has been rarely handled by humans and, like the Tokara, has been declared a national treasure in Japan.

The first known record of the Misaki is in 1697, when the Akizuki family of the Takanabe Clan took the wild horses under its protection and created a stud farm.

## Tourist Attraction

The ponies were still left to run wild, but were rounded up once a year to select animals for taming and domesticating, and probably

to castrate any males deemed unsuitable for breeding. The same system is used today – the ponies are rounded up, inoculated and treated for parasites and checked over for their general health. A rare breed, there are thought to be around 100 left. The region is popular with tourists, and the wild ponies are a great attraction.

# HOKKAIDO

HEIGHT: 13 hh

COLOUR: most solid colours

PERSONALITY TYPE: warm-blooded

TYPICAL USE: riding, draught

TEMPERAMENT: placid, willing

ORIGIN: Japan

SIMILAR BREEDS: Mongolian, Kiso

Also known as the Dosanko or the Hokkaido Washu, the Hokkaido lives on Hokkaido's Pacific coast. Originally taken to the island by Japanese herring fisherman, they were left there when the fishermen returned home in the autumn. Those that survived the cold and bears were rounded up when the fishermen returned.

## Nanbu Descendants

The Hokkaido is considered a descendant of the Nanbu, which was used primarily as a military animal. Those taken to Hokkaido were probably inferior specimens. Left to forage in the harsh, mountainous terrain, only the hardiest survived, developing the enduring strength for which the breed is known. Even-tempered, docile and a strong, willing worker, it is bigger than most of the Japanese breeds. Its slightly primitive appearance suggests a relationship with the Mongolian. It has a large, rather plain head, a short neck, thickset body, slender legs and exceptionally hard feet. It rarely has any white markings, and dun colouring with dorsal stripe is common. Many Hokkaidos are natural pacers.

# KISO

HEIGHT: 13 hh

COLOUR: most solid colours

PERSONALITY TYPE: warm-blooded

TYPICAL USE: riding, harness, light draught

TEMPERAMENT: gentle, tractable

ORIGIN: Japan

SIMILAR BREEDS: Mongolian, Hokkaido

Were it not for the Japanese custom of keeping a sacred white horse at certain shrines, the Kiso would have died out completely, as the breed's diminutive size meant that breeding pure was discouraged. Then, during the Second World War, a government edict demanded that all Kiso stallions be castrated, but one was discovered at a Shinto shrine that had been deemed a holy horse and was therefore not gelded.

## Last Purebred

This horse, called Shinmei, was put to a mare called Kayama, and in 1951 bred a colt called Dai-san Haruyama – the last of the purebred Kiso. The breed has been saved from extinction by back-breeding, but there are thought to be only about 100 left. Records exist of horses being bred in the Kiso region as early as the sixth century. According to legend, during the thirteenth century, some 10,000 were produced as cavalry mounts for the famous warrior Kiso Yoshinaka's army. The Kiso undoubtedly owes much to the Mongolian, and dun colouring with black points and dorsal stripe is common.

# NORDLAND

TEMPERAMENT: energetic, even-tempered, willing

ORIGIN: Norway

SIMILAR BREEDS: Icelandic

HEIGHT: 12–13 hh

COLOUR: chestnut, bay, brown, grey

PERSONALITY TYPE: warm-blooded

TYPICAL USE: riding, harness, pack

The Nordland's resemblance to Przewalski's Horse and the Tarpan suggests that Norway's native pony is an ancient breed – well-preserved finds from Viking graves indicate an equine presence in the country that dates back centuries. It is thought to have arrived in Norway from the east, which supports this theory, and perhaps in search for food then concentrated – and developed – in the northern part of the country. It is called, variously, Nordland, Northlands, Lyngen and Lyngshest, and at one time there were two very distinct types of this pony.

## Almost Extinct

The two variations were the Lyngen type from the district in northern Troms of the same name, and the smaller Norland type which was essentially based on examples from the Lofoten district. The Lyngen version was bigger and heavier, and almost always chestnut in colour, while the Norland type was much finer, resembling closely the now-extinct Lofoten Pony. The two types have, however, interbred, and the modern Nordland is basically of one type – although there are still some individuals that are clearly one or the other – with all solid colours occurring except the primitive dun.

The breed was at the brink of extinction after the Second World War, due to a poor economy, sparse food and a general shortage of animals, but a breeding programme fortunately saved it for future generations.

## Fascinating Facts

Horses have been put through their paces in Norway every October since 1991 at the Oslo Horse Show, part of the Western European League in show jumping.

## Equable Temper

The modern Nordland has a plain head with thick mane, medium-length back, sloping croup and sturdy legs, and is generally sound and free of health problems. It is long-lived, surviving into its thirties, and also retains its fertility to advanced age. Easily trainable and willing to work, it has an equable temperament and makes a good child's mount. It is also used for pack and harness.

# FJORD

HEIGHT: 13.2–14.1 hh

COLOUR: all shades of dun

PERSONALITY TYPE: warm-blooded

TYPICAL USE: riding, harness, pack

TEMPERAMENT: calm, gentle

ORIGIN: Norway

SIMILAR BREEDS: Przewalski's Horse, Icelandic, Exmoor

Approximately 90 per cent of Fjord Ponies are brown dun, the other 10 per cent being red dun, grey dun (grullo), gold or yellow dun, although this last is very rare. The occasion bay or brown Fjord is also seen. It is an attractive equine, with a pretty head that is far less heavy than that of Przewalski's Horse and is sometimes slightly dished. It has large eyes, small, mobile ears, a short, crested neck, a powerful body with a deep girth, and excellent legs and feet.

Ice Age cave paintings of ponies of 30,000 years ago bear a strong resemblance to today's Fjord Pony, a Norwegian breed that takes its name from the country's famous waterways. It is thought to have migrated to Norway about 4,000 years ago, perhaps part of the vast herds that came to the Scandinavian peninsula. It has the distinctive primitive colouring of dun with black points, black dorsal stripe and zebra striping on its legs, and shares several similarities with Przewalski's Horse.

## Unique Trait

A unique characteristic of the Fjord is its striking mane – the centre hair of the mane is black, while the outer hair is white. The mane is traditionally cut short so that it stands erect, trimmed into a crescent shape to enhance the graceful curve of the neck. The white outer hair is then trimmed slightly shorter to display the dark line down the centre. In all, the Fjord is a pleasing picture of equine excellence.

The Vikings used the Fjord as a warhorse, then a farm animal – the Vikings were thought to be the first Western Europeans to use horses for agricultural purposes – for which the Fjord's sure-footedness, strength, soundness and exceptional stamina have made it invaluable. It also has an extremely equable temperament and is easily trained.

LEFT

*The heavy-set and thick-framed Fjord pony reflects the primitive characteristics of its ancient history.*

# GOTLAND

TEMPERAMENT: intelligent, lively, gentle

ORIGIN: Sweden

SIMILAR BREEDS: Przewalski's Horse

HEIGHT: 11.2–13 hh

COLOUR: dun, bay

PERSONALITY TYPE: warm-blooded

TYPICAL USE: riding, harness

It has been called a 'living relic of the past', and it is known that the Gotland pony of Sweden is an ancient breed. There have been wild ponies on the Lojsta Moor, on the Swedish island of Gotland, since the Stone Age. It is known in Sweden as the Russ, a word derived from the Norse word for 'horse', and in Gotland itself as the Skosbagga, which means 'forest ram'. The ponies have inhabited the island for about 5,000 years, although it is not known how they first got there, nor whether those early equines were the same as today's Gotland.

## Roaming Free

Discoveries made at an Iron Age village called Vallhagar (220 BC – AD 500), a few kilometres from Lojsta Moor, show that horses became increasingly common as domestic animals during that period, but the Gotland lived in semi-wild freedom in the forests. Farmers kept the ponies to work the land and often had a herd of them roaming free to be captured when they needed new stock. The free ponies would forage for themselves, only returning to the farms if food were short.

It was these farmers who were to save the breed from extinction. By the early twentieth century, there were only about 150 Gotlands left, as agricultural policies had changed and the 'forest rams' were damaging crops. Food shortages and meat rationing during the First World War meant that the Gotland was also hunted for meat.

BELOW
*The attractive and versatile Gotland pony is used for riding and light draught purposes, and has a particularly equable temperament.*

## Saved from Extinction

The Gotland farmers fenced off an area of about 80 ha (200 acres) and introduced to it eight Gotlands, and this tiny herd formed the beginning of a breeding programme to save the equine. It was successful – today there are around 9,000 Gotlands in Sweden, and more elsewhere, the breed proving popular for its equable nature and attractive appearance.

# Fascinating Facts

Gotlands are still watched over on the Lojsta Moor. Each season is marked by an annual Gotland activity: releasing the stallion to the herd each June, judging in July and weaning the foals from the mares in November.

# JAVA/TIMOR

HEIGHT: 12.2 hh

COLOUR: all colours

PERSONALITY TYPE: warm-blooded

TYPICAL USE: tourism, harness

TEMPERAMENT: willing, quiet

ORIGIN: Indonesia

SIMILAR BREEDS: Sumba/Sambawa, Sandalwood

Indonesia's little pony may lack the beauty of the Arabian, but the breed is certainly unique in its heritage. It is thought to be related to the Chinese horses and date back to the fifth century BC. When the Dutch settled in Indonesia and her islands in the late 1500s, the Arabs they traded with brought over Arabian and Barb horses, which were to influence the islands' native stock. The Java and the Timor take the name of the islands on which they originate.

## LEFT

*The Java pony is not known for its good conformation, but looks can deceive, and it is one of the toughest and strongest breeds for its diminutive size.*

Peninsula, is equally important to the islanders – it is used for everything from riding and driving, to light farm work and working with cows. A frugal feeder, like the Java, it is also quick and

agile. It tends to be smaller than the Java, standing between 10 and 12 hh, but is equally unprepossessing, with a large head carried almost horizontally on a short neck, prominent withers, short back and sloping croup, with good legs and hard feet. Large numbers of the Timor were exported to Australia, where they have played a part in the development of the local pony breeds.

## Great Stamina

The desert breeds' influence is apparent in the Java's hardiness; it is extremely tough and very strong – despite its small stature it can carry an adult. It can survive on little feed and has great stamina, although it is also known for its occasionally uncertain temper.

On the island of Java, the ponies are used to pull *sados*, two-wheeled carts that are used to transport whole families and their combined possessions, which they do with ease. They are popular with tourists, who marvel at the sight of the tiny equines pulling such huge loads.

## Australian Pony

The Timor, found on the island of the same name off the southern end of the Malay

# SUMBA/SUMBAWA

TEMPERAMENT: willing, co-operative

ORIGIN: Indonesia

SIMILAR BREEDS: Java, Timor, Sandalwood

HEIGHT: 12 hh

COLOUR: predominantly dun

PERSONALITY TYPE: warm-blooded

TYPICAL USE: riding, pack, tourism

Named for the two islands they inhabit, the Sumba and Sumbawa are essentially the same, developed from Chinese and Mongolian breeds. Possessing all the admirable traits of Indonesia's native breeds, they are famed for an unusual reason – they dance.

Bells are attached to the pony's knees and it dances, with surprising elegance and grace, to the beat of tom-tom drums. The breed may not be particularly beautiful, but to see it dance is a joy to behold.

## Primitive Roots

The Sumba/Sumbawa is primitive in looks, being predominantly dun with dorsal stripe, black points and zebra stripes on its legs. It is found in the Nusa Tenggara province, the west of which is formed of two main islands, Lombok and Sumbawa; the east of more than 500, the biggest ones being Flores, Sumba and Timor.

These islands have poor grazing, yet the ponies thrive. Agile and fast, like the Java and Timor, they are able to carry or pull weights far out of proportion to their tiny stature.

# BATAK

TEMPERAMENT: willing, easy to manage

ORIGIN: Indonesia

SIMILAR BREEDS: Java, Timor, Sumba/Sumbawa, Sandalwood

HEIGHT: 13 hh

COLOUR: all colours

PERSONALITY TYPE: warm-blooded

TYPICAL USE: riding, pack, harness, light draught

Once used primarily as a sacrifice to the gods, today the Batak of Indonesia fulfils a less gruesome role. It still plays a central part in the lives of the people of Sumatra, where it is found, and is highly regarded. Like other Indonesian equines, it is probably Mongolian in origin, but has been improved by Arabian blood and selectively bred. It is probably the next best quality Indonesian breed to the Sandalwood and is used to improve the ponies of the other islands.

## Easy Keeper

Arabian blood is apparent in the Batak's good looks – it has the fine, chiselled head and high-set tail also seen in the Sandalwood. It is an easy keeper, obliging and gentle, and economic to

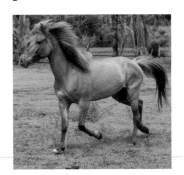

keep. It is lightly built, with a slender frame and narrow chest. Its legs are sometimes rather poor, but it has good, hard feet.

Another Indonesian breed, the Gayoe, also found in central Sumatra, is thought to be a sub-strain of the Batak, but is a stockier, more sturdy creature.

# SANDALWOOD

HEIGHT: 13 hh

COLOUR: all colours

PERSONALITY TYPE: warm-blooded

TYPICAL USE: riding, harness, agriculture, light draught, racing

TEMPERAMENT: quiet, biddable

ORIGIN: Indonesia

SIMILAR BREEDS: Java, Timor, Sumba/Sumbawa

Named for the sweet-smelling wood that is one of the islands' main exports, the Sandalwood is the best of Indonesia's pony breeds, having considerably more quality than the others. This is largely due to greater infusion of Arabian blood. It is known that the Dutch settlers imported Arabian stallions to Sumatra, the biggest of the islands that make up Indonesia, and used them on selected mares to produce a quality equine, which in turn was exported to the other islands to improve their stock.

## Beauty and Grace

The Sandalwood breed still retains a high percentage of Arabian blood, and has inherited that breed's beauty and grace. It is a very versatile pony, with great stamina and endurance, as well as speed and agility. But it also has a quiet, biddable nature, which makes it an excellent child's pony.

ABOVE

*These ponies are elegant and refined, as seen, and have a high percentage of Arabian blood in them.*

The Sandalwood has a nicely proportioned head – sometimes with the slightly dished face of its Arab ancestors – small, alert ears and intelligent eyes. It has a short, muscular neck (on which it carries its head slightly higher than the other Indonesian breeds), a deep chest, long, straight back and sloping croup. It carries its tail high and has slender legs, with the good, hard feet that typify the islands' ponies.

## Three-Mile Races

The breed has also been used to improve Australia's ponies, but it has another role in its homeland. Racing is hugely popular in Indonesia, and the swift little Sandalwood, with speed part of its Arabian heritage, is raced over distances of two and a half to three miles. In Malaysia, where it is frequently exported, the Sandalwood is crossed with Thoroughbreds to produce bigger, faster racehorses.

It has also inherited the Arabian's immunity to heat – the Sandalwood rarely breaks a sweat.

# BALI

TEMPERAMENT: quiet, biddable

ORIGIN: Indonesia

SIMILAR BREEDS: Java, Timor, Sumba/Sumbawa, Sandalwood, Batak

HEIGHT: 12–13 hh

COLOUR: predominantly dun

PERSONALITY TYPE: warm-blooded

TYPICAL USE: riding, pack, harness, light draught

## Minimal Rations

Indonesia's island jewel has its own breed of pony, the eponymous Bali. The pony's ancient origins are apparent in its rather primitive appearance – it is often dun with black dorsal stripes and black points – although there is evidence of Oriental influence. It is probably Mongolian in origin, with infusions of Eastern blood from horses imported by the Dutch in the 1700s.

The Bali is not selectively or consistently bred, so it does have conformation faults, but it is noted for its strength (in comparison to its size) and for its hardiness. It is used to transport stones and coral from the beaches for building, as well as for riding, trekking and sightseeing by tourists. The breed can exist on minimal rations and needs little in the way of care and, as with all of Indonesia's ponies breeds, it has exceptionally good, hard feet.

BELOW
*The Bali's appearance reflects the influence of the ancient Przewalski, pictured, and the Mongolian pony's upright mane and dun colouring.*

# AUSTRALIAN

TEMPERAMENT: intelligent, lively

ORIGIN: Australia

SIMILAR BREEDS: Indonesian breeds

HEIGHT: 12–14 hh

COLOUR: all solid colours

PERSONALITY TYPE: warm-blooded

TYPICAL USE: riding, show

## Founding Sire

With its fine head, arched neck and sloping shoulder, the Australian Pony oozes quality. Its good looks and presence are perhaps surprising, considering Indonesia's rather unprepossessing little Timor formed the foundation of the breed, but later infusions of outside blood refined Australia's pony to make it the equine supermodel it is today. The Timor was taken to Australia in 1803 – the country had no indigenous horses or ponies, so horses did not appear until the British First Fleet arrived in 1788, bringing with it equines.

Later, several stallions exported to Australia were to have a profound effect: two Exmoors, Sir Thomas and Dennington Court, imported in the mid-nineteenth century; a Hungarian stallion called Bonnie Charlie; and Dyoll Greylight, a Welsh Mountain which arrived in 1911. This last is considered a founding sire.

The influence of the Welsh Mountain Pony and earlier infusions of Arabian blood are clear in the Australian Pony's concave profile and high-set, gaily carried tail.

# Light Horses

The term 'light horse' is used to describe any equine over 15 hh that is not one of the heavy draught breeds. A light horse should be well proportioned, with a narrow body and sloping shoulders, and a greater distance from wither to ground than the length of the body. Like a golden thread running through a bolt of silk, the blood of the Arabian runs through the world's horse breeds. The Arabian's prototype was Horse Type 4, a refined creature standing around 14 hh with a concave profile and high-set tail. It came from Western Asia and was resistant to heat, particularly the dry heat of the desert. Today's Caspian Horse is its nearest modern equivalent.

Horse Type 3 stood about 14.3 hh and was long and narrow in the body, goose-rumped with a long neck and long ears. It inhabited Central Asia and was, like Type 4, able to tolerate heat. Its nearest equivalent today is the Akhal-Teke.

## A Pervasive Influence

The influence of the Arabian on the world's horse breeds cannot be underestimated. Without the Arabian, we would not have the Thoroughbred, with all its fire and might. The Arabian influence also extends to the Welsh Mountain Pony, which has its charming dished face, and plays a part in the world's mighty warmbloods, the success story of the twentieth century.

Perhaps the only modern horses largely uninfluenced by the Arabian are the Iberian kings, the Andalucian and the Lusitano. But the Barb, an ancient breed similar to the Arabian that also played a part in the development of the Thoroughbred, was probably the ancestor of the Spanish horses. It, in turn, gave us the Lipizzaner, Vienna's dancing white horse.

Arabian blood has been used in the development of so many breeds, such as Russia's splendid Orlov Trotter and India's distinctive Kathiawari and Marwari. And as horses evolved, they changed the lives of humans across the entire planet. This is summed up beautifully by an anonymous poet:

*Look back at our struggle for freedom,*
*Trace our present day's strength to its source,*
*And you'll find that man's pathway to glory*
*Is strewn with the bones of a horse.*

# BANKER (Shackleford)

TEMPERAMENT: calm, friendly

ORIGIN: North Carolina, United States

SIMILAR BREEDS: Mustang

HEIGHT: 13–14.3 hh

COLOUR: bay, brown, chestnut, dun

PERSONALITY TYPE: warm-blooded

TYPICAL USE: feral

These feral horses eke out an existence on the wild and barren islands off North Carolina's Outer Banks, of which one is called Shackleford – the breed is also sometimes known as the Shackleford Horse. It is most probably Spanish in origin. Although the British colonized these islands, Bankers display many characteristics of the Mustang. The isolated environment, however, means that they have developed into a distinctive breed and remained pure.

## Heat and Hurricanes

The Banker has adapted to be able to survive on meagre rations of marsh grass and scratching through sand to get to water supplies. It is exceptionally tough and hardy, with a good turn of speed and, unlike many feral breeds, is calm and friendly. They regularly experience – and survive – extreme heat, hurricanes, swarms of insects and winter storms, but the breed is increasingly rare and there are very few left.

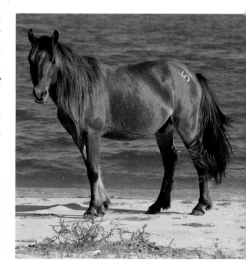

RIGHT

*These feral horses are very hardy and have adapted to their environment exceptionally well, tolerating the extreme heat and cold of the climate.*

# FLORIDA CRACKER

TEMPERAMENT: willing, intelligent, spirited

ORIGIN: Florida, United States

SIMILAR BREEDS: Mustang

HEIGHT: up to 15.2 hh

COLOUR: all solid colours

PERSONALITY TYPE: warm-blooded

TYPICAL USE: ranching, Western riding

Florida's cowboys were nicknamed 'crackers' because of the noise their whips made when they flicked them into the air, and the name was extended to the region's small, tough cattle and the agile little horses the cowboys used to work them. They trace back to the Spanish horses brought to the Americas in the 1500s; however, because of the isolation of the part of the country, they developed into a distinct and separate breed.

## Lost Demand

The breed suffered a downturn in the 1930s. Cattle were moved from the Dust Bowl of the United States' drought-stricken Great Plains into Florida during the Great Depression, and brought with them a parasite called screwworm. Instead of herding and driving the cattle, the cowboys now had to rope them and treat them for the worm. Demand for the Cracker was lost as the cowboys turned instead to the bigger, stronger Quarter Horses. It was saved by a handful of ranchers who continued to breed and preserve the Florida Cracker for future generations.

# MUSTANG

HEIGHT: 13–16 hh

COLOUR: all colours

PERSONALITY TYPE: warm-blooded

TYPICAL USE: ranching, rodeo, Western

TEMPERAMENT: brave, spirited, independent

ORIGIN: United States

SIMILAR BREEDS: Florida Cracker

North America's wild horse takes its name from the Spanish word *mesteño*, or *monstenco*, meaning 'wild' or 'stray', and today's Mustang still roams free across the western United States in huge numbers. The Mustang is Spanish in heritage – descending from the horses brought to the New World in the sixteenth century by the conquistadores. Over the past 500 years, many other bloodlines have been introduced, including Arabian, French and the German East Friesian, but the Spanish blood is still evident.

The East Friesian was introduced in the late 1800s, when the United States government bought the heavy horse from the Germans to pull artillery wagons. It is almost certain that some of these horses escaped and mated with the wild Mustang.

## Captives to Freedom

The arrival of the horse changed the lives of the Native Americans and, as European settlers pushed farther and farther west, they brought more horses with them. These horses either escaped or were freed in Indian raids, and the Indian tribes themselves bartered with or captured horses, adding further to the mix. Wild stallions would also tear down fencing to reach mares. The Indians learned to ride and passed on their newfound skill.

In 1680, the Native Americans rebelled against Spanish rule, and the Europeans left behind thousands of their horses as they beat a hasty retreat. Rather than round the horses up, the Indians left them to roam free.

## Poor Conformation

Although the occasional dun with dorsal stripe gives away the Mustang's Spanish origins – tracing back to the little Sorraia, which in turn was to found the mighty Iberian horses – most of today's Mustangs have little or no Spanish blood. The lack of a monitored and selective breeding programme means that the horse comes in a wide variety of colours, including all solid colours, as well as pintos and paints. Appaloosa markings, palominos, buckskins and blacks have largely been bred out, although some do still occur. Sorrel and bay are the most common colours.

RIGHT

*The American Mustangs live in large feral herds, and are descended from the original Spanish horses introduced by the conquistadores in the sixteenth century.*

Some Mustangs may stand only 13 hh; others up to 16 hh. One of a staggering 18 hh has been recorded. Most are about 14.2 hh. They often have poor conformation, with a rather plain head, short neck, upright shoulder and poor legs. They are, however, very tough and hardy, with innate intelligence and courage.

## Living Symbol

By the year 1900, there were an estimated two million

Mustangs in the United States. Previously, large numbers of feral horses had posed no problems. As the Western states became increasingly settled, however, the herds of Mustang were encroaching on grazing land for cattle, and the ranchers began to regard them as a pest.

A haphazard and indiscriminate form of culling began and, by 1926, the Mustang population had been halved – by 1970, only about 17,000 remained. To protect the horse, Congress labelled the Mustang a 'living symbol of the historic and pioneer spirit of the West', and passed the Wild Free-Roaming Horse and Burro Act in 1971, putting it under federal protection. There are now an estimated 40,000 wild Mustangs, the welfare of which is overseen by the Bureau of Land Management.

## The Kiger Herd

In 1977, a small herd of Mustangs was discovered in the remote area of Beatty's Butte, Oregon, which were strikingly similar in colour and conformation, and which bore the primitive markings. Testing by the Kentucky University found Spanish markers in their blood, suggesting that they carry the original Spanish genes. They are almost all dun, or one of its variations, and have markedly better conformation than the more common Mustangs. They are called Kiger Mustangs, and have their own breed registry.

# AMERICAN BASHKIR CURLY

HEIGHT: 13.3–16 hh

COLOUR: all colours

PERSONALITY TYPE: warm-blooded

TYPICAL USE: riding, competition, Western, trail

TEMPERAMENT: calm, gentle, friendly

ORIGIN: United States

SIMILAR BREEDS: Morgan

**T**he United States' popular 'horse with a permanent wave', the Bashkir Curly is something of an enigma. It was first discovered in 1898, when a young man called Peter Damele and his father were riding in a mountain range near the town of Austin, in the remote high country of central Nevada, when they came across three horses with coats formed of tight ringlets, all over their bodies. From that day, there have always been curly-coated horses on the Damele range, and many Bashkir Curly Horses in the United States can be traced back to the Damele herd.

## Russian Mystery

But how did the horses get there in the first place? For some time, it was thought that the Curlies traced back to the Russian breed called the Bashkir, which was perhaps taken to North America by Russian settlers in the 1700s and 1800s. But horses were not widely used by the Russians, and they were likely to be the more hardy Yakut, rather than Bashkir or its close relative, the Lokai, from Taijikistan, which also had a curly coat.

### RIGHT

*The origins of the American Bashkir Curly are unclear. The smaller Russian Bashkir Curly developed in the harsh Ural Mountains of Russia is an ancient breed.*

Horses with curly coats are nothing new – similar equines were depicted in art and statuary in early China as far back as AD 161. The origins of those in the United States may never be fully explained, but they have been embraced with great enthusiasm.

## 'Marcel' Wave

The American Bashkir Curly is intelligent, gentle, curious, calm and affectionate. Its curly coats can be of three distinctive types: ringlets of several inches in length; the deep marcel wave; or crushed velvet, a soft, dense pile of curls. The preferred mane is kinky, and can also be split, hanging on both sides of the neck. The tail may be ringlets or wavy. The breed sheds its coat in the summer, although sometimes retains curls in its short, broad ears, and has curly eyelashes. It is naturally gaited, moving at a smooth, running walk.

## Fascinating Facts

American Bashkir Curly foals are born with thick, crinkly coats that are reminiscent of astrakhan, and are very friendly and affectionate, characteristics the breed retains into full adulthood. People who are allergic to horses are often unaffected by the Bashkir Curly.

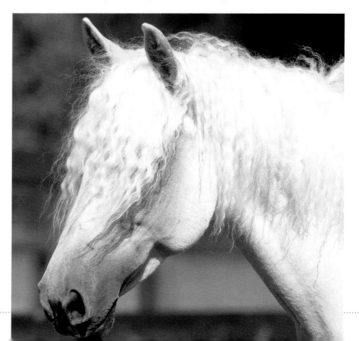

# NOKOTA

TEMPERAMENT: intelligent, calm, reliable

ORIGIN: United States

SIMILAR BREEDS: Mustang

HEIGHT: 14.2–17 hh

COLOUR: roan, grey, black, overo

PERSONALITY TYPE: warm-blooded

TYPICAL USE: competition, riding

Although it is received wisdom that all horses in the United States are Spanish in origin, having arrived with the conquistadores, the Sioux and Lakota Indians claimed to have horses before the Europeans arrived. Certainly, the horses of the Northern Plains, which includes the vast grasslands of North Dakota, were Native American horses, and it is known that the tribes bred selectively, choosing only the best horses to continue the line – tribal chiefs were rightly proud of their equines.

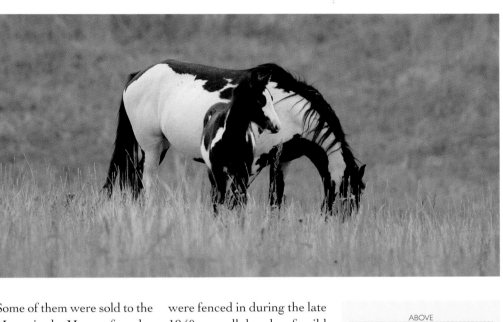

## Evaded Capture

When Chief Sitting Bull surrendered to the US Army in 1881 at Fort Buford, North Dakota, his horses were confiscated and sold on. Some of them were sold to the Marquis de Mores, founder of the town of Medora, gateway to what is now the Theodore Roosevelt National Park in North Dakota. The Marquis allowed his horses to roam free and, although on his death in 1896 they were rounded up and sold, some of them evaded capture. When the national park boundaries were fenced in during the late 1940s, small bands of wild horses were inadvertently enclosed within.

These came to be called the Nokota – a distinctive, separate breed with an exceptional bone structure, gentle disposition and considerable athletic ability.

## 'All-Terrain Vehicle'

The Nokota is generally blue roan (a rare colour, but dominant in this breed), red roan, grey or black, often with a bald (white) face and blue eyes. It has a straight or slightly concave profile, broad forehead, large, kind

ABOVE

*The Nokota horse is a finely built, elegant animal of exceptional athletic ability, which with its tractable nature, makes it a popular riding horse.*

eye, and long, thick mane and tail. It stands between 14.2 and 17 hh, and is large-boned and rangy.

The modern Nokota is sometimes referred to as the 'equine all-terrain vehicle', reflecting its stamina, durability and athleticism. Exceptionally sound, with good legs and solid feet, it is low-maintenance and requires the minimum of care. Nokota owners rarely go back to any other breed.

# AMERICAN CREME AND AMERICAN WHITE

HEIGHT: 14–16.2 hh

COLOUR: white or cream

PERSONALITY TYPE: warm-blooded

TYPICAL USE: all uses

TEMPERAMENT: generally good

ORIGIN: United States

SIMILAR BREEDS: varying breeds are used; colour most important

A horse called Old King, foaled in 1908, was to found a new breed, now known as the American Creme or American White. Old King was true white with pink skin; he had dark brown eyes, which he passed on to 90 per cent of his progeny. He also passed on his colour – when bred to a coloured mare, he achieved 50 per cent white and 50 per cent coloured, and up to 80 per cent of his descendants throw white stock.

## Breeding Legacy

Caleb and Hudson Thompson purchased Old King to found

a new breed then called the American Albino. Caleb and his wife, Ruth, promoted the horse through the White Horse Troupe, which performed such spectacular feats as a six-horse tandem ride, team jumping with the rider standing rather than sitting, high and broad jumping over cars or human 'hurdles', and movements of the High School.

## Fascinating Facts

China not only has the most people in the world, but also has the most horses with 10,000,000.

LEFT
*The American White must have pink skin pigment, and they generally have pale blue or amber eyes.*

In 1937, the American Albino Horse Club was formed to record the descendants of Old King, who died of swamp fever in 1924. The first horse registered was Old King's grandson, Snow Chief 2nd, who left a breeding legacy in his son, White Wings, who sired 108 foals, all but three being white.

## Amber Eyes

Old King and his descendants are not albino, and the American White and American Creme have none of the 'weaknesses' associated with albinos such as deafness or blindness, although they are sensitive to sunlight. The American White may have no slight pigmentation of hair and must have pink skin; all eye colours, including amber and very pale blue, are acceptable.

The Creme must have pink skin, which may take on a deeper tan colour known as 'pumpkin'. Its coat may vary

from a very pale ivory to a deeper rich cream. Its mane and tail can range from pure white, through shades of cream, to a cinnamon; its eyes are usually pale blue or pale amber.

# APPALOOSA

TEMPERAMENT: docile, quiet, energetic

ORIGIN: North-Western United States

SIMILAR BREEDS: Quarter Horse

HEIGHT: 14–15.2 hh

COLOUR: variations of spotted

PERSONALITY TYPE: warm-blooded

TYPICAL USE: riding

The Nez Perce tribe of the American North-West was long famed for its superb horses and for their mastery of them. The explorer Meriwether Lewis noted in a diary entry from 15 February 1806: 'Their horses appear to be of an excellent race; they are lofty, elegantly formed, active and durable … some of these horses are pied with large spots of white irregularly scattered and intermixed with black, brown, bay or some other dark color.' The Nez Perce were the only Indians to breed selectively, and the Appaloosa was the result.

ABOVE

*The distinctive spotted coat patterning of the Appaloosa make them particularly attractive. There are a number of different spot configurations in the breed.*

## Spotted Coat

Known as a 'Palousie horse' – a reference to the Palouse River that flows through the region of north central Idaho and eastern Washington whence the breed originated – the name was soon shortened to Appalousey, then Appaloosa, which was officially adopted in 1938. The Appaloosa is noted for its speed, stamina and endurance – and for its striking coat patterns. There are 13 recognized coat base colours and six acceptable patterns – snowflake, leopard, spotted blanket, white blanket, marble and frost – although the horses can exhibit myriad combinations of base colours and patterns.

## Good-looking

Spots aside, the Appaloosa is a good-looking creature. It has a small, neat head with a straight profile, set on a long muscular neck and deep chest, with good, sloping shoulders. It has a short, compact back with rounded, muscular quarters. It has good, strong legs and hard feet. Its mane and tail are rather thin and sparse.

Its gentle temperament and kind nature makes it an excellent riding horse and it has considerable speed and stamina. The Appaloosa also makes a genuine all-round family horse and is a suitable mount for the most nervous of novice riders. The breed's delightful disposition wins hearts as easily as its striking coat turns heads.

# MORGAN

HEIGHT: 14.1–15.2 hh

COLOUR: all solid colours

PERSONALITY TYPE: warm-blooded

TYPICAL USE: all uses

TEMPERAMENT: gentle, kind, intelligent, spirited

ORIGIN: United States

SIMILAR BREEDS: Standardbred, Quarter Horse, Tennessee Walking Horse

A Vermont schoolteacher and businessman called Justin Morgan acquired a colt foaled in 1789 and named him Figure. The colt's breeding is not clear – and is the subject of much speculation – but it was thought to be by a stallion called True Briton, a much-admired sire of the times. Figure was a handsome bay, with spectacular paces and gentle disposition. He was also athletic, fast and clever, with so much stamina, endurance and ability that tales soon spread of the great 'Justin Morgan horse'.

## President's Mount

The Morgan Horse, as Figure was increasingly known, could outwalk, outrun, outtrot and outpull any other equine. Although he was not particularly big, standing just over 14 hh, his beauty, presence and good manners were deemed suitable for the President of the United States – in 1817, he carried President James Monroe on a muster-day parade ground in Montpelier, Vermont.

Figure was also prepotent, passing on his good looks and his abilities to his offspring. He lived to be 32 and served numerous mares during his long lifetime – and founded the United States' first light horse breed.

## Gold Rush

Figure's legacy was carried by three of his sons, Sherman, Bulrush and Woodbury, back to which all modern Morgans can be traced. And the breed grew with the emerging American nation. Morgans worked alongside their owners clearing fields and forests; they provided transport to the market and to church on Sundays. Figure's descendants pulled stagecoaches throughout New England. Young men from Vermont answered the call of the Gold Rush on the Morgan's back; the First Vermont Cavalry fought the Civil War mounted on Morgans; and Union General Sheridan rode a Morgan into battle. The cavalryman was only ever as good as his horse, and the Morgan was in high demand as a cavalry mount and artillery horse.

By the 1840s, breeders in Vermont and New Hampshire were making a concerted effort to concentrate Morgan lines and, by locating second-, third- and fourth-generation descendants of little Figure, they established the foundations of the new breed. By the mid 1850s, Morgans were selling for high prices and were gaining a fine reputation across the United States for their beauty, speed, agility and temperament.

## Foundation Breed

Morgans are exceptionally good-looking, with a refined, neat head with a slightly concave profile, broad

forehead tapering to a fine muzzle, large, kind eye and small ears. Their neck is elegantly arched and set on well-angled shoulders, with a broad chest, short back, sloping croup and deep, compact body. They have strong legs with flat, dense bone and round, hard hooves. Their proud bearing gives them presence as well as beauty.

But the Morgan was never merely a case of 'Handsome is …' – the breed is athletic and enduring, with both speed and stamina, making it one of the world's most versatile equines. It can be used for almost any equestrian discipline, in either a Western or an English saddle, and is highly successful in driving, show jumping and dressage.

It has also contributed to the formation of other American breeds, including the Quarter Horse and the Tennessee Walking Horse, to which it has passed on some of its spirit, its abilities and its good looks.

## Family Member

The Morgan remains popular today, with about 150,000 listed on the registry (first established in 1894) in all 50 American states and around the world. A calm and sensible ride, it makes a superb all-rounder, and its charming nature and gentle disposition mean that its popularity is unlikely to wane. Indeed, those who have bought a Morgan say that they have not only purchased a horse, but also welcomed a new family member.

## Fascinating Facts

Justin Morgan was a multi-faceted man; from yeoman, musician, stallioneer, and tavern keeper to Town Clerk, Lister and Grand Juryman, in addition to teaching choral singing and music composition, he had many achievements under his belt, but of course was overshadowed by the success of his horse.

# MORAB

HEIGHT: 14.3–16.1 hh

COLOUR: all solid colours

PERSONALITY TYPE: warm-blooded

TYPICAL USE: competition, riding, show

TEMPERAMENT: intelligent, kind, spirited

ORIGIN: United States

SIMILAR BREEDS: Morgan, Arabian

As its name suggests, the Morab is a mixture of two of the most beautiful horse breeds: the ancient Arabian and the more recent Morgan. The coining of the name 'Morab' is accredited to the newspaper tycoon William Randolph Hearst (1863–1951), who crossed his Morgan mares with the Arabian stallions Tsar and Ghazi specifically to create versatile horses for his California ranch. With the mix of the 'desert' type horse, the Arabian, and the athletic ability of the Morgan, these horses were perfectly suited to the rough terrain.

## Unequalled Beauty

The Morab proved both incredibly versatile and hardy. The early remount horses used by the United States military were generally thought to be Morgans crossed with either Thoroughbreds – a breed which, of course, was founded by Arab stallions – or Arabians, and were renowned for their extreme endurance.

Considered to be one of the founding sires of the Morab breed is a registered Morgan stallion called Golddust, a palomino foaled in 1885 renowned for his golden colour, his outstanding trotting record and his unequalled beauty. He was by a registered Morgan stallion called Vermont Morgan and out of a daughter of an imported Arabian stallion Zilcaddie. Golddust sired 302 foals.

## Bona Fide Breed

When William Randolph Hearst died in 1951, much of his breeding programme – and, indeed, almost the Morab – was lost. But American breeders were still producing Morab horses, and their cause was taken up by a woman called Martha Doyle Fuller, who produced Morabs for the show circuit, on which they excelled. Her daughter, Irene Miller, dubbed 'Mrs Morab', started the first breed register in 1973.

While some consider Morabs to be 'half-Arabs' or 'half-Morgans', they are a bona fide breed, as they pass on their distinguishing characteristics to their progeny. The accepted breed standard for today's Morab is 25/75, although the most common is 50/50 – one Morgan parent and one Arabian, with the endurance, ability and abiding beauty of both.

ABOVE

*The Morab was developed through crossing Morgan horses with Arabs, the result generally displaying the best of both, as pictured.*

# PINTO

TEMPERAMENT: varied

ORIGIN: United States

SIMILAR BREEDS: Mustang

HEIGHT: all heights
COLOUR: dual-coloured
PERSONALITY TYPE: warm-blooded
TYPICAL USE: all uses

## Fascinating Facts

A coloured horse descended from two solid-coloured parents of a usually solid-coloured pure breed is called a 'crop out', and is usually overo.

LEFT
*Part coloured horses, called Pintos (or Paints) are further described by the configuration of their markings. This horse is a 'tobiano'.*

Pictures of horses with broken coats – skewbald or piebald or tricoloured – have appeared in art for centuries, suggesting that the 'coloured' horse is nothing new. There is evidence of coloured coats in the wild horses of the Russian Steppes, which suggests the introduction of 'pintos' or paints in Europe possibly as early as during the Roman Empire. The Europeans brought horses to North America, some of which escaped or were set free to form the wild herds, among them those with broken coats.

## Magical Powers

These horses were in turn captured and domesticated by the Native Americans, whose tribal chiefs prized the flashy skewbald or piebald above all others, believing them to have magical powers that would protect the chief in battle. The settlers, too, realized the value of the horse, and they were to use the coloured horses in festivals and parades for extra flashiness.

While other breeds were later used on the little feral American horses to improve and refine the stock and to produce larger animals, the broken coat continued to appear.

## Colour Patterns

There are two recognized Pinto colour patterns: tobiano (the most common) and overo. A tobiano appears to be white with large spots or splashes of colour, originating from the head, chest, flank and rump, often including the tail. Legs are generally white, and the white crosses the centre of the back or topline, although the coloured areas are greater than the white areas. Overo is a coloured horse with jagged patches of white markings, usually around the side or belly and spreading toward the neck, tail, legs and back. Its face is often white – the term 'bald' was applied to a horse with a white face.

205

# STANDARDBRED

HEIGHT: 15–16 hh

COLOUR: bay, brown, black

PERSONALITY TYPE: warm-blooded

TYPICAL USE: racing, riding, show

TEMPERAMENT: docile, willing

ORIGIN: United States

SIMILAR BREEDS: Morgan

A new breed of only about 200 years old, all Standardbreds can be traced back to a horse called Hambletonian 10, foaled in 1849, and were required to be able to trot a mile in 2 minutes 30 seconds – hence the name. A mile is still the standard distance of harness races. The first races were contested along roads, with men betting with each other about who had the swifter horse. The streets were cleared specially to hold these races – many American cities still have a Race Street.

## Amazing Turn of Foot

Hambletonian's great-grandsire was an English Thoroughbred called Messenger, foaled in 1780 and exported to the newly formed United States just after the American Revolution. The Standardbred still has much in common with the Thoroughbred, and not simply its amazing turn of foot. It is not a big horse, standing around 15.2 hh, but has a longer body than the average Thoroughbred. But perhaps its biggest claim to fame is that it toppled the mighty Morgan as the American's favourite horse.

Trotting races – pacing was to come later – were a major sport in the United States in the 1800s, and the Morgan was the undisputed

The Standardbred is a trotting horse used primarily for harness racing, and is one of the world's fastest trotting animals.

king of the racetrack. But it was to be a Standardbred that still holds the record – trotting the mile in 1 minute 55 seconds.

## Two-Minute Mile

Although neither Messenger nor Hambletonian ever raced, they left behind a legacy of swift, agile horses that race-mad Americans took to their hearts. Hambletonian left some 1,355 offspring, and his son, Dexter, set a new record for the time of 2 minutes 17 seconds.

Many Standardbreds 'pace' when they trot; this is when they move their legs on the same side of their body together, rather than in conventional diagonal pairs.

Standardbred champions became household names – Flora Temple, the 'bob-tail nag' of Stephen Foster's much-loved song 'Camptown Races' (1850); Goldsmith Maid, who won 350 heats in her career; world champions Maud S and Nancy Hanks.

Pacers – horses that move laterally, rather than diagonally, as in the trot – began to gain acceptance, and the sport's first two-minute mile was recorded in 1897 by the pacer Star Pointer. One of the most popular Standardbreds ever was a pacer called Dan Patch, which was also one of the fastest, recording the first sub-two-minute mile on 8 September 1906.

Standardbreds can be either pacers or trotters – pacers are often referred to as 'sidewheelers' and tend to be faster than trotters because of the smoothness of the action. A third gait, running, often manifests itself in harness racing, but the horse must return to its natural gait or face disqualification.

## Competitive Nature

The Standardbred possesses the inherent good looks of the Thoroughbred, but is generally more muscular. The head is refined – the occasional suggestion of a Roman nose is sometimes seen, but infusions of Morgan and Arabian blood have made this increasingly rare – and set on a medium-length neck and sloping shoulders. The back is quite long; the hindquarters muscular but sleek. The Standardbred has good, strong legs and hard feet.

It is competitive, which makes it so successful on the racetrack, but willing and calm, with a kind nature. Bay, brown and black are the most dominant colours, although most solid colours do occur.

## Million-Dollar Purse

Although Standardbreds are used for riding (both Western and English) and show, harness racing continues to be the breed's primary occupation. There is even a race named the Hambletonian, a prestigious annual event for three-year-old Standardbreds which is the most coveted North American trotting race. The Hambletonian purse is a cool US$1.2 million. Two races for pacers, the Meadowlands Pace, held at Meadowlands,

New Jersey, and the North America Cup at Woodbine, Ontario, Canada, both carry a $1 million prize pot. In each event, the winning owner receives half the pot; the rest is divided between the next four finishers.

# RACKING HORSE

**HEIGHT:** 15.2 hh

**COLOUR:** all colours, including spotted

**PERSONALITY TYPE:** warm-blooded

**TYPICAL USE:** riding, showing

**TEMPERAMENT:** docile, kind, friendly

**ORIGIN:** United States

**SIMILAR BREEDS:** Tennessee Walking Horse

Neither a pace nor a trot, the 'rack' is an exceptionally comfortable bi-lateral four-beat gait – sometimes known as the 'single-foot' because only one foot strikes the ground at any time. The Racking Horse became popular on the vast plantations of the South before the American Civil War, when it was realized that the horse could be ridden comfortably for several hours because of this smooth, natural gait. The fact that the horse was also very beautiful did nothing to harm its reputation.

## State Horse

The Racking Horse's unique gait is natural – that is, it is inherited, rather than learned. The horse moves quite swiftly, appearing to jump from one foot to another, while its head remains still, but its shoulders and quarters are very active. It is an easy gait to sit into for beginners, while veterans appreciate its smoothness and athleticism.

Determined to preserve and promote the Racking Horse as a distinctive breed, an Alabama businessman

named Joe Bright was instrumental in forming the Racking Horse Breeders' Association of America

### ABOVE
*These beautiful horses have a very fast, very smooth natural gait called the 'rack', which makes them extremely comfortable to ride.*

(RHBAA), established in 1971; in 1975, the Racking Horse was declared Alabama's state horse.

## Enchanting Breed

The breed is thought to have its roots in the Tennessee

Walking Horse, to which it bears a resemblance. It is noble and elegant, with a refined head, long, graceful neck, sloping shoulders, full flanks and muscular quarters. It has fine legs and round, hard feet. As well as being undeniably beautiful, with a graceful and noble bearing, the Racking Horse has an enchanting nature, being kind, calm and very people-friendly – all further traits that make it the ideal mount for the most nervous of beginners.

To be accepted into the RHBAA registry, the horse must first demonstrate the unique natural gaits that give the breed its name.

# PALOMINO

TEMPERAMENT: varied

ORIGIN: United States

SIMILAR BREEDS: Morgan, Quarter Horse, Saddlebred, Tennessee Walking Horse

HEIGHT: 14–17 hh

COLOUR: all shades of gold, with white mane and tail

PERSONALITY TYPE: warm-blooded

TYPICAL USE: varied

The colour of a newly minted gold coin, the Palomino has been prized by emperors, kings and queens, and was the subject of Greek mythology and great art alike. Queen Isabella of Spain (1451–1504) was a great fan of the Palomino – the colour is still sometimes called 'Isabella' – and pale golden horses feature in Sandro Botticelli's celebrated painting *The Adoration of the Magi* (c. 1478–82). During the Crusades, the Emir Saladin presented Richard the Lionheart with a Palomino horse.

## Royal Choice

The history of the palomino colour will probably never be known. Horses of an iridescent gold occur in the Barb, although palomino Arabians and Thoroughbreds are not accepted by their respective registries. The gold horse with ivory-colored mane and tail appears in ancient tapestries and paintings of Europe and Asia, as well as in Japanese and Chinese art of past centuries. Isabella I kept a full 100 of these glorious creatures, and only members of the royal family and nobles of the household were permitted to own one. It is well documented that Isabella sent a Palomino stallion and five mares to New Spain, which was to become Mexico; from there, the golden horse spread into Texas and California.

## Shades of Gold

The ideal colour of a Palomino is that of a new 14-carat gold coin, but shades can range from light, through medium to dark gold. The mane and tail should be pure white, ivory or silver, although up to 15 per cent dark or sorrel hair is permitted. The skin is usually grey, black,

brown or mottled, without underlying pink skin or spots, except on the face or legs. The eyes are usually black, brown or hazel.

There are three basic divisions of Palomino (which is a 'colour' breed, rather than a true breed). The stock type is Western horses, predominantly represented by Quarter Horses, while the Golden American Saddlebred is, of course, typically represented by Saddlebreds, and the pleasure type is exemplified by Morgan, Arabian and Tennessee Walking Horses.

## Fascinating Facts

Cowboy actor and entertainer Roy Rogers's horse Trigger was a Palomino, and as famed as his owner as a star of television and silver screen. Another well-known Hollywood Palomino was Mr Ed, the 'talking' horse of the 1960s television series of the same name.

ABOVE

*Palomino horses, with their beautiful gold colouring and pale mane and tail, are highly sought after.*

# QUARTER HORSE

HEIGHT: 14–15.3 hh

COLOUR: all solid colours

PERSONALITY TYPE: warm-blooded

TYPICAL USE: Western, riding, rodeo, ranching

TEMPERAMENT: gentle, brave, intelligent

ORIGIN: United States

SIMILAR BREEDS: Mustang

Said to be the United States' oldest horse breed, the Quarter Horse is thought to have its roots in the Chickasaw ponies acquired from the Indians, short, blocky little equines of Spanish descent, containing Arab, Barb and Andalusian blood. It is a common misconception that the 'quarter' part of the breed's name denotes the proportion of Thoroughbred blood – although it was certainly used later to improve and refine the Quarter Horse. In fact, the name refers to the distance, a quarter of a mile, over which the horse can sprint.

## Heavy Wagers

Horse racing, sprinting over a short distance, was very popular in the 1600s, and the fastest competitors became known as Celebrated American Running Horses by the British colonists. The original blocky little horse, when crossed with the English Thoroughbred, was unsurpassed. Compact but heavily muscled, the chunky little equine could sprint a short distance from a standstill, outrunning any other breed.

These first races were held in Enrico County, Virginia, with two horses racing against each other down town streets and country lanes, and across flat pasture. Sizeable prize purses were on offer, and there was extensive heavy wagering – disagreements between both owners and punters were common. Some of the grander Southern plantations are said to have changed hands as a result of these head-to-head matches.

## Cow Sense

As more Thoroughbreds were brought to North America, and the breed became more popular, the little Quarter Horse fell out of favour. Distance racing – at which the Thoroughbred excelled — overtook the

ABOVE

*Quarter Horses are one of the world's most popular breeds, in great part due to their huge versatility and intelligent, calm natures.*

shorter sprint races, and oval racecourses were built specifically for the new sport. But the Quarter Horse had other talents. As a stockhorse, it was superb – it could gallop from a standstill, was easy to stop and could turn on the proverbial dime. The Quarter Horse also possessed an innate 'cow sense', an ability to second-guess and outmanoeuvre cattle. As vast cattle ranches spread across the plains in the 1800s, as settlers and pioneers moved westwards, the Quarter Horses went with them.

## Breeding Lines Lost

Despite its widespread and increasing popularity, the Quarter Horse had no registry or breed standard until 1940, when the American Quarter Horse Association (AQHA) was established in Texas. Until then, there was little or no effort made to preserve the Quarter Horse as a breed; no records were kept and, as the custom of the day was to name the horse after its owner, valuable breeding lines were lost as stallions were sold on and their names changed. A horse called Steel Dust, however, foaled in 1843, was to have a profound effect on the breed, with his progeny being called Steel Dust Horses.

## Versatile Performers

Today's Quarter Horse is still the butty little creature of old, heavily muscled and compact, with a neat, attractive head set on a muscular neck and sloping shoulders, and short-coupled with powerful hindquarters and fine, strong legs. It is intelligent but kind and easy to handle, and very versatile. Quarter Horses are still raced and

## Fascinating Facts

As they are highly trainable, Quarter Horses are also used in film-making – the Robert Redford movie *The Horse Whisperer* (1998) featured 17 of them.

used for ranching, but they are also good show jumpers, dressage performers and rodeo horses.

There are 16 recognized colours of American Quarter Horse, including the most prominent colour of sorrel (brownish red). The others are bay, black, brown, buckskin, chestnut, dun, red dun, grey, grullo, palomino, red roan, blue roan, bay roan, perlino (cream coat, darker mane and tail and blue eyes) and cremello.

There are now thought to be around 4.4 million Quarter Horses in the world, and the breed continues to grow in popularity.

### BELOW
*Quarter Horses generally have excellent conformation, being muscular through their frame with strong legs and feet. They tend not to be very tall.*

# COLORADO RANGER

HEIGHT: 14–16 hh-plus

COLOUR: spotted and solid

PERSONALITY TYPE: warm-blooded

TYPICAL USE: ranching, riding

TEMPERAMENT: intelligent, calm

ORIGIN: United States

SIMILAR BREEDS: Mustang

During a world tour in 1878 following his presidency, General Ulysses S. Grant visited Sultan Abdul Hamid of Turkey, who presented him with two stallions on the day of his departure. One was an Arabian named Leopard; the other a Barb called Linden Tree. Both are listed in the studbooks of the Arabian Horse Club and the American Jockey Club, and were to be the foundation sires of the Colorado Ranger, a breed that is far more than just a colour or coat pattern.

which he proposed to call the Americo Arab. He was partly successful – using the two desert stallions, over a period of 14 years he did, indeed, produce a strain of 'Huntingdon horses', more than 100 in all.

Leopard and Linden Tree, although aged, had one more breeding season with another friend of General Grant's, Colonel Colby, and they left an indelible impression on his native mares – a new breed of cow horse that came to be known as the Colorado Ranger.

ABOVE

*These attractive and useful horses are generally, though not always, spotted, and make excellent riding horses.*

Although many Rangers are spotted – some 90 per cent are also registered with the Appaloosa Horse Club – solid colours are acceptable. The

## Two Founding Sires

These two horses reached Virginia in 1879, where a friend of General Grant's, a respected horseman called Randolph Huntingdon, saw the stallions as the ideal opportunity to perfect a new breed of light harness horse,

## Appaloosa Links

Today's Colorado Ranger must be able to trace back to two stallions, Patches (a direct descendant of Leopard and Linden Tree) and Max (a spotted son of the renowned Waldron Leopard). They were both acquired by a

horse breeder called Mike Ruby in the early 1930s, and he kept meticulous records of which sires he put to which mares, their offspring and their colouring. He formed the Colorado Ranger Horse Association in 1935.

horse has an attractive head with alert, mobile ears, a good length of neck, deep, wide chest, compact back and powerful hindquarters. The overall impression of the breed is solid, muscular and strong.

# ROCKY MOUNTAIN

TEMPERAMENT: docile, gentle, intelligent

ORIGIN: United States

SIMILAR BREEDS: Mustang

HEIGHT: 14.2–16 hh

COLOUR: all solid colours; little or no white markings

PERSONALITY TYPE: warm-blooded

TYPICAL USE: trail, pack, riding, endurance, competition

Legend has it that, one day in the 1890s, a handsome horse with striking chocolate-coloured coat and flaxen mane and tail stepped out of the Appalachian Mountains in eastern Kentucky. This may be myth or romanticism, but this horse, a gaited colt, came to be called the Rocky Mountain horse and was the foundation sire of a popular and enduring breed. For some years, the people of the region used this colt on their own saddle mares to produce a special strain of utility horse – the region's best-kept secret.

the field, herd cattle, travel across the steep and rugged trails, and drive the buggy to church on Sundays. In short, it had to earn its keep.

The emerging breed, the Rocky Mountain, answered every call.

## Fascinating Facts

Jumping is not a natural activity for horses and left to their own devices – like most creatures – they are more likely to go around obstructions.

## Family Horse

For the rural inhabitants of eastern Kentucky, the horse was essential, not a luxury. Doctors, postmen, travelling preachers and hundreds of others relied on horses as their means of transport, and the 'Rocky Mountain' horse was ideal. Sure-footed and easygoing, the horse also had an exceptionally smooth and comfortable gait and, even more importantly, stamina. For the one-horse family, the equine had to be versatile and strong; it was used to plough

## Longevity

A horse breeder called Sam Tuttle is credited with preserving and continuing the Rocky Mountain Horse for the first three-quarters of the twentieth century. Gaited horses were becoming less popular with the advent of good roads and better means

RIGHT

*The Rocky Mountain Horse is a relatively young breed that reflects Spanish characteristics, especially in the shape of its head, as seen in this picture.*

of travel, but horses were still used in the more remote areas. Even when times were hard, Sam Tuttle kept a herd of Rocky Mountain Horses and continued to produce them, most famously from a sire called Tobe. This stallion

and his offspring were in great demand.

Tobe continued to breed until the age of 34 and died at 37 – he passed his longevity to his progeny, as well as his sweet nature and easy gaits.

# TENNESSEE WALKING HORSE

HEIGHT: 15.2 hh

COLOUR: all solid colours

PERSONALITY TYPE: warm-blooded

TYPICAL USE: pleasure, trail, show

TEMPERAMENT: gentle, calm, easygoing

ORIGIN: Tennessee, United States

SIMILAR BREEDS: Morgan

That the Morgan played a huge part in the development of the Tennessee Walking Horse is beyond doubt, but several other breeds also influenced it, including the now-extinct Narragansett Pacer, Thoroughbred, Standardbred and Saddlebred. These horses were taken to what was known as the Middle Basin of Tennessee by settlers from neighbouring states such as Virginia and the Carolinas. The breed that was developed possessed an exceptional gait – the swift and smooth 'running walk', for which it was to become renowned.

## Fascinating Facts

If a patient with a back problem does not want to give up their riding, doctors with some horse knowledge will refer them to gaited horses – especially the Tennessee Walking Horse.

## Gliding Motion

The running walk is inherited, rather than learned – indeed, it cannot be taught to a horse that does not possess it naturally. It is a square four-beat gait with a gliding motion, with the head bobbing in time. Some Walkers are known to snap their teeth in time, too, which is not considered a fault.

The horse overstrides, placing its back hoof ahead of the print of its fore hoof. It can travel at speeds of up to 19 km (12 miles) an hour, and sustain them for long distances. The Tennessee Walking Horse is suited to beginners and experienced riders alike, as this gait is supremely comfortable. The Walker also has two other notable gaits: the flat-foot walk, which is slow and even, and the canter, a refined gallop with a slow, comfortable rolling motion (this is sometimes known as the 'rocking-chair gait'). All three gaits are very easy on the rider.

## Gentle Nature

The greatest contributor to the Tennessee Walking Horse was a black stallion called Allan, with both Morgan and Standardbred lines – there was certainly some Hambletonian blood in him, from the foundation sire of the Standardbred. He passed on his considerable good looks, gentle nature and easy gaits.

The registry was formed in 1935, and the Tennessee Walking Horse remains popular to this day because of its beauty and grace.

RIGHT
*The magnificent Tennessee Walker is most famous for its smooth running walk, a fast, comfortable gait that is inherited rather than learned.*

# SADDLEBRED

TEMPERAMENT: calm, gentle, kind

ORIGIN: United States

SIMILAR BREEDS: Mustang, Morgan, Standardbred

HEIGHT: 15–17 hh

COLOUR: most solid colours

PERSONALITY TYPE: warm-blooded

TYPICAL USE: riding, showing

When Paul Revere made his famous 'Midnight Ride' from Boston to Lexington in 1775 at the start of the American Revolution, to warn of the advance of the British Army, he is thought to have been astride a Narragansett Pacer, a horse that had great importance in the development of the Saddlebred. In those early years, horses were vital to the pioneers who settled in Kentucky, and good saddle horses were highly valued. Denmark, the sire who would form the foundation of the Saddlebred, was foaled in 1839.

## Warhorse

By the time of the Mexican War in 1846, the Saddlebred was well established as a breed. Prized for its beauty and utility – like the Narragansett, it was a pacer, rather than a trotter – the Saddlebred also found fame in the show ring. The first 'national' horse show was held in 1885 as part of the St Louis Fair, Missouri, and Saddlebreds were prominent.

---
LEFT

*The American Saddlebred is a particularly flashy show horse that moves with an extravagant action and is amongst the most exciting horses to watch.*

---

The American Civil War saw the Saddlebred become the cavalry mount of choice for the Confederates, as the horses' extreme endurance meant that they could be marched for hours and their bravery kept them calm under enemy fire. Generals on both sides were mounted on Saddlebreds; Stonewall Jackson rode a Saddlebred, while, on the Union side, Ulysses S. Grant also had a Saddlebred as a mount. Confederate General Robert E. Lee's Traveller, perhaps the most famous horse of the war, had Saddlebred lines, his sire being the Thoroughbred Gray Eagle and his dam a mare of mixed breeding.

## Worldwide Fame

Lee's Traveller possessed a smooth rack and, after the Civil War, as the soldiers disbanded, they took their Saddlebreds with them to all parts of the nation. Today, the United States' superb horse breed is found in all 50 states, as well as Canada, Europe, Scandinavia, Australia and Japan. After the Thoroughbred, it is the most popular horse breed in South Africa.

The first American Saddlebred Horse Association was established in Louisville, Kentucky, in 1891, to ensure this beautiful gaited horse continues to grow and improve.

# MISSOURI FOX TROTTER

HEIGHT: 14–16 hh

COLOUR: most solid colours

PERSONALITY TYPE: warm-blooded

TYPICAL USE: riding, pleasure, trail, endurance, showing

TEMPERAMENT: kind, quiet, gentle

ORIGIN: Missouri and Arkansas, United States

SIMILAR BREEDS: Mustang, Saddlebred, Standardbred

A pleasure and utility horse, the Missouri Fox Trotter was developed in the Ozarks of Missouri and Arkansas as a breed that could carry a heavy load for long hours at a swift, ground-covering gait that was comfortable for the rider and sustainable for the horse. Neither a pacer nor a trotter, the horse uses its legs diagonally, walking with its front feet and trotting with its hind, the back foot overstepping the print of the front. This shuffling gait is sure-footed, and the rear feet slide rather than jolt, so it is extremely comfortable.

for racing, but became a utility breed, the broken gait being easy on both horse and rider.

The Alsup family, who settled in the Ozarks before the Civil War, were noted

---
LEFT

*The Missouri Fox Trotter is another of the gaited American breeds, and produces an even, balanced gait making it comfortable when riding over distance.*

---

horse breeders and had a sire called Bremmer, known not only for his good looks and racing prowess, but also for his ability to pass both qualities to his offspring. From the Kissee family came a great sire called Diamond; from the Dunns a prolific stallion called Old Skip.

## Sweet Nature

These horses all played a part in developing the Missouri Fox Trotter. A line from the stallion Denmark, so influential in the Saddlebred, bred some outstanding fox-trotting horses through a sire named Chief, who left a great many superb progeny. The Missouri Fox Trotter gained a reputation for its ground-covering gait, its beauty and its sweet disposition.

The Missouri Fox Trotting Horse Breeders' Association was formed in 1948, but all its records were wiped out in a fire. Re-established in 1955, the MFTHBA has since made great progress – by the beginning of 2005, some 83,000 horses had been registered.

## Morgan Blood

As early settlers moved into the Ozarks across the Mississippi River from Kentucky, Virginia and Tennessee, they brought with them their own horses, a mix of Morgan, Thoroughbred and Arabian, with some other bloodlines. The horses were primarily

# CANADIAN

TEMPERAMENT: kind, sensible, sociable

ORIGIN: Canada

SIMILAR BREEDS: Arab, Saddlebred

HEIGHT: 14–16 hh

COLOUR: black, dark brown, bay, chestnut

PERSONALITY TYPE: warm-blooded

TYPICAL USE: riding, harness, competition

Canada's little-known national treasure is based on French horses (such as Bretons) sent to the New World in the 1600s by France's 'Sun King', Louis XIV (1638–1715). These horses were probably a mixture of Arabian, Andalusian and Barb, the heritage of which can still be seen in today's Canadian breed. With little outside influence, the Canadian, or Cheval Canadien, evolved into a distinct breed, having to endure adverse weather, scarce food and hard work, and became strong and tough, impervious to harsh weather and easy keepers.

## Fascinating Facts

The Canadian Horse was adopted as a national symbol on 30 April 2002.

### RIGHT AND BELOW

*These horses are renowned for their excellent conformation and natural athleticism which, combined with a sensible brain, makes them good competition horses.*

## Iron Horse

These attributes earned the breed the nickname 'Canada's little iron horse'; it spread into the United States and, by the mid 1800s, numbered around 150,000. It was used to improve the strength and hardiness of some of the American breeds and was exported out of Canada for working the sugar plantations in the West Indies; to the United States for the Civil War; and to South Africa for the Second Boer War (1899–1902).

Almost ironically, the number of Canada's 'national treasure' actually in Canada dwindled rapidly. By the 1870s, there were fewer than 400 Canadians left; with the advent of mechanization, the breed almost became extinct.

1895. A new studbook, with improved information, was started in 1907. In 1913, a breeding project was set up at Cap Rouge in Quebec. There are now thought to be almost 3,000 Canadian Horses.

The Canadian is a good-looking all-rounder, with chiselled head, arched neck and the rippling mane and tail reminiscent of its Spanish

## All-Rounder

Realizing the plight of the Canadian, enthusiasts banded together – the first studbook was produced in 1886, and the Canadian Horse Breeders Association was formed in

ancestry. It has strong legs with plenty of bone and exceptionally good feet. It is generally long-lived, and the mares are fertile into their twenties or older. In short, it is entitled to its moniker – the little iron horse.

# AZTECA

HEIGHT: 14.2–15.3 hh

COLOUR: all solid colours

PERSONALITY TYPE: warm-blooded

TYPICAL USE: rodeo, bullfighting, competition

TEMPERAMENT: lively, cheerful, obedient

ORIGIN: Mexico

SIMILAR BREEDS: Quarter Horse, Andalusian

Mexico's national breed was developed only in the 1970s, but it is safe to say that it has an enduring appeal. Developed using Andalusian stallions on Quarter Horses and Criollos, the aim was to produce a breed with speed, athleticism, stamina and power. Designed to be the ultimate all-rounder, it had also to be handsome, obedient, trainable and brave. The ideal was reached in the Azteca — the first 'full' Azteca stallion was called Casarejo, born in Texcoco in 1972.

be the foundation sire of a breed with intelligence, agility and versatility.

To watch an Azteca at work or play is to see equine poetry in motion – its natural balance and ability to collect under itself enables it to leap sideways in the blink of an eye to avoid the horns of a bull. The Azteca excels in the bullring under the Mexican *rejonero* (a type of bullfighter) or in the *charreria* (rodeo), and naturally displays the 'airs above the ground', or *haute école*, of its distant cousin the Lipizzaner.

## Natural Athlete

Casarejo was the offspring of a Spanish stallion, Ocultado, and a Quarter Horse mare named Americana. He was to

## Third Generation

The Azteca has all the exceptional beauty of both the Quarter Horse and the Andalusian. Its head is lean

ABOVE

*This beautiful Mexican breed is still in its infancy, but already the horses are establishing type, displaying the best combination of Quarter Horse and Spanish influences.*

and refined, straight or slightly convex in profile; its eye lively and expressive; its nostrils full and mobile. Its neck is gracefully arched, with well-developed shoulders and deep, wide chest. It has a short, straight back, with muscular hindquarters. Its tail is medium-set and, like its mane, full and abundant. It has long, slender legs with strong joints and well-proportioned feet.

The studbook was formed in 1992, and the third generation is the pure Azteca – five-eighths Andalusian and three-eighths Quarter Horse, or vice versa. Some cutting-horse enthusiasts think that this will be a better cross – time will tell.

# MANGALARGA MARCHADOR

HEIGHT: 14.2–16 hh

TEMPERAMENT: intelligent

COLOUR: predominantly grey, bay, chestnut; other solid colours

ORIGIN: Brazil

PERSONALITY TYPE: warm-blooded

SIMILAR BREEDS: Peruvian Paso, Paso Fino

TYPICAL USE: riding, competition, endurance

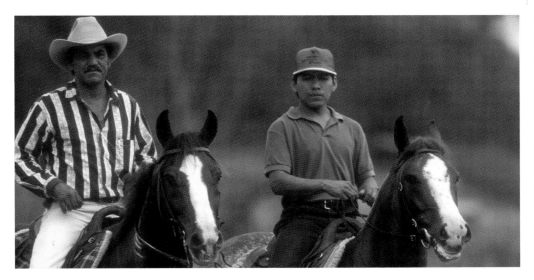

Its name is enchanting; the breed sublime. Indeed, Brazil's national equine is founded on an Alter-Real stallion named Sublime, gifted by the Emperor of Brazil, Pedro I (1798–1834), to his friend Gabriel Francisco Junqueira, an established horse breeder and owner of Campo Alegre, in 1812. By putting him to mares of Spanish and Barb descent, the Mangalarga Marchador was produced – the first part of the name comes from the stud, Hacienda Mangalarga, which subsequently bought and promoted the 'Sublimes', and the second from the horse's gait, the *marcha*.

## Performance Testing

Many of those first mares possessed a fast, smooth ambling gait, which they passed on to their offspring. The Mangalarga Marchador's natural gaits are walk, *marcha* and canter. There are two *marchas*. The Marcha Picada is a lateral four-beat gait with moments of triple hoof support, as also found in two of the Paso Fino's gaits, the Paso Corto and Paso Largo. The Marcha Batida is a diagonal four-beat gait also showing moments of triple hoof support.

The first registry for the Mangalarga Marchador was established in 1949 to promote and continue the breed. To be accepted, horses must pass rigorous performance testing.

## World Record

The Mangalarga Marchador's Spanish origins are clear – it is a horse of considerable beauty, and possesses the agility, endurance and stamina of its ancient ancestry. Indeed, there is little to which the Mangalarga Marchador cannot turn its hoof. Its agility makes it an excellent cow horse; its athleticism is suited to rodeo; its stamina to endurance riding and cross-country; and it possesses a natural jumping ability. It excels in the show ring, where its flying gaits, innate presence and natural *brio* make it the horse to watch.

### Fascinating Facts

The Mangalarga Marchador features in the *Guinness Book of Records* for an endurance ride of 13,992 km (8,694 miles), undertaken by two Brazilian men, which took one and a half years and was completed in 1994

LEFT

*This Spanish-influenced breed is beautiful, intelligent, athletic and has natural flashy gaits, making it a winner in the show ring and on the ranch..*

# CAMPOLINA

HEIGHT: from 14 hh; no upper height limit

COLOUR: all colours

PERSONALITY TYPE: warm-blooded

TYPICAL USE: riding, competition, harness

TEMPERAMENT: lively, kind, trainable

ORIGIN: Brazil

SIMILAR BREEDS: Mangalarga Marchador, Peruvian Paso

A beautiful dark grey colt called Monarca is considered the foundation sire of the Campolina, Brazil's other equine breed (alongside the Mangalarga Marchador). It is named for its developer, Cassiano Antonio de Silva Campolina, who started the breed at his stud, Fazenda Tanque, in 1857. It was not until 1870, however, when Campolina was given a black mare called Medéia, that his eponymous breed really began. Medéia was bred to a pure Andalusian stallion, and Monarca was the result, serving 25 years in the herd of the Fazenda Tanque.

## Elegant and Active

Cassiano Campolina bred Monarca to mainly Criollo mares, but was determined to produce a horse with beauty, presence and smooth, natural gaits. He used several other stallions, including an Anglo-French sire called Menelike;

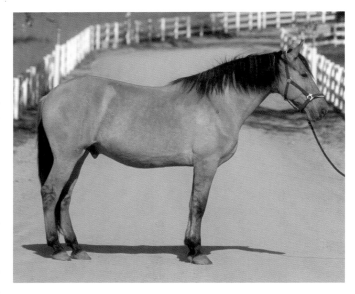

a quarter-Clydesdale named Golias; Teffer, a Holsteiner; Yanke Prince, an American Saddlebred; and Rio Verde, a Mangalarga Marchador. The studbook for the Campolina Horse was closed in 1934, and no other outside breeds were permitted to be used.

Like the Mangalarga Marchador, the Campolina gaits include the *marcha picada* (lateral) and the *marcha batida* (diagonal). The breed standard for the gaits demand that they are natural, with triple support (that is, three hooves hitting the ground at the same time), comfortable, elegant, regular and active.

## Regal Bearing

But the Campolina also possesses a four-beat gait known as the *marcha verdadair* – the true march. At this powerful gait, it can maintain speeds of 9.6–12.8 km/h (6–8 mph). The Campolina combines the stirring flashy gaits of the Mangalarga Marchador with the nobility and grace of the Andalusian, as well as the natural exuberance of the Peruvian Paso. It has the noble head and regal bearing of its Spanish ancestors, as well as the flash and fire of the more recent South American equine kings.

# PASO FINO

TEMPERAMENT: lively, responsive

ORIGIN: Central and South America

SIMILAR BREEDS: Mangalarga Marchador,
Peruvian Paso

HEIGHT: 13–15 hh

COLOUR: all solid colours

PERSONALITY TYPE:
warm-blooded

TYPICAL USE: riding, harness,
showing

## Selective Breeding

These are the horses with the 'fine walk' – *los caballos de paso fino* – and never has a name been more fitting. The Paso Fino is a descendant of the horses brought to the Americas by the conquistadores; finding a continent with no horses, on their second journey to the New World, they brought with them their own, a mixture of Barb, Andalusian and Spanish Jennet. The Jennet had a smooth, comfortable gait, which it passed on to its progeny. Today's Paso Fino has the proud carriage, grace and elegance of its forebears.

Centuries of selective breeding by those who colonized the Caribbean and Latin America produced the Paso Fino, which flourished initially in Puerto Rico and Colombia, and later in other Latin American countries. Awareness of the breed did not reach North America until after the Second World War, when servicemen stationed in Puerto Rico began exporting the horses home, where they were prized for their beauty and supremely comfortable gaits. The Paso Fino gait is performed at three forward speeds – at each, the rider

should appear virtually motionless in the saddle, and there should be no perceptible up-and-down motion of the horse's croup.

ABOVE

*These are amongst the most elegant of the gaited horses and are much sought after due to their comfortable stride and obliging character.*

## Natural Cadence

The Classic Fino is a gait with full collection, with very slow forward speed. The footfall is extremely rapid, while the steps and extension are exceedingly short. The Paso Corto is of moderate speed, with ground-covering but unhurried steps, executed with medium extension and stride. The Paso Largo is the fastest speed, executed with a longer extension and stride, but without losing any natural cadence.

With its lively but controlled spirit, natural gait and

responsive attitude, coupled with the beauty and presence of its Spanish heritage, the Paso Fino is indeed a rare and desirable equine partner. It seems to delight in the company of people and thrives not only in the show ring, but also on trail and endurance rides, in dressage, rodeo, gymkhana, and as a working stockhorse.

## Fascinating Facts

The Paso Fino is the oldest true native breed of horse in the Western Hemisphere.

# FALABELLA

**HEIGHT:** 76 cm (30 in)

**COLOUR:** all colours

**PERSONALITY TYPE:** warm-blooded

**TYPICAL USE:** show

**TEMPERAMENT:** gregarious, gentle, docile

**ORIGIN:** Argentina

**SIMILAR BREEDS:** Thoroughbred, Arabian

Argentina's most famous equine is extremely rare – there are only 900 registered – and its origins are open to debate. One thing is beyond doubt: the Falabella is a miniature horse, not a pony. It should look like a scaled-down model of a Thoroughbred or Arabian, with no pony characteristics at all. Although they tend to grow thick coats in the winter, in the summer they should have the sleek coat of their larger counterparts, and stand no higher than 76 cm (30 in).

## Horse of the Pampas

It is thought that miniature horses, perhaps by a mutation, wandered the Argentinaian pampas for centuries. Perhaps in order to survive their harsh environment – the pampas was unprotected, and battered by fierce winds called El Pampero – and due to continual inbreeding, these horses underwent genetic changes to produce the tough little equine we know today.

The breed was developed by the Falabella family, who first saw the miniature horses in the herds run by the Mupache Indians around Buenos Aires in the mid-nineteenth century. Enchanted by the little creatures, they sought to improve the breed and further refine the shape of the animal, producing an equine that stood less than 102 cm (40 in) at the shoulder.

## Harmonious Form

Thanks to Señor Falabella and his descendants, the breed that takes their name retains its unique charm. They used carefully selected infusions of Thoroughbred, Shetland, Welsh and Criollo blood to ensure the little horses kept their harmonious form, and reduced the upper height limit to 76 cm (30 in) from the previous 86 cm (34 in).

Gregarious and docile, gentle and intelligent, the Falabella breeds true, passing these characteristics to its offspring. It is a good-looking equine, with clean, straight legs and good feet; an attactive, intelligent head; and fine, silky hair. It is also long-lived, often reaching 40–45 years old.

> **LEFT**
>
> *The Falabella has the conformation of a scaled-down horse, rather than a pony, and is typically fine limbed.*

# CRIOLLO

TEMPERAMENT: fearless, independent, affectionate

ORIGIN: Argentina

SIMILAR BREEDS: Mustang

HEIGHT: 13.3–15 hh

COLOUR: predominantly dun, chestnut, bay, grey, roan, black

PERSONALITY TYPE: warm-blooded

TYPICAL USE: riding, herding, polo

**A**rgentina's king of the pampas, the Criollo, was originally feral, the result of Spanish horses of Andalusian and Barb descent that were left to roam free by the conquistadores for about four centuries, adapting to their new world and way of life. Life in the pampas – the grassland area around the delta of the Rio de la Plata – was tough, and only the hardiest of these feral horses survived. They, in turn, bred with equines brought by travellers from Brazil, Chile and Uruguay, with Portuguese and Dutch blood later introduced via Brazil.

## One-Man Horse

The Criollo, or Creole, was the natural partner to the gaucho, Argentina's cowboy. It is said that a gaucho without a horse is like a man without legs. The tough little Criollo was the perfect cow horse – agile, clever, fearless and strong. It also had considerable stamina and was rarely tired. Said to be a 'one-man horse', the Criollo is independent; however, once it gives its trust, it is affectionate and loyal.

When the British came to the South Americas, they brought English Thoroughbreds, which were mated to Criollos to refine and improve the existing stock. With the French came the Percheron, used to add bone and substance. Both almost spelt disaster for Argentina's king of the pampas, as people began to ignore the breed's unique characteristics and natural toughness in favour of larger horses.

## World's Stage

In 1910, Dr Emilio Solanet, professor at the School of Veterinary Medicine and Agriculture in Buenos Aires, brought about 2,000 Criollos into his estancia, El Cardal. From these, he selected 15 mares that would become the breeding stock of the Argentinian Criollo.

To prove the stamina and endurance of the Criollo, and reignite waning interest and faith in the breed, Dr Solanet offered two of his horses to a Swiss schoolteacher who wanted to travel from Buenos Aires to New York. On the trip, which lasted from 1925 to 1928, Aimé-Felix Tschiffely made Mancha and Gato famous in Argentina, and wrote the names of the two horses on the world's stage.

## Fascinating Facts

Not only were Mancha and Gato fairly advanced in age when they made their famous trek (about 15 years), but they also each went on to live until around 40 years of age – definitive proof of the toughness of Argentina's king of the pampas.

BELOW
*These are incredibly tough little horses with enormous stamina and a good brain, making them the favoured mount of the gaucho, the Argentinian cowboy.*

# PERUVIAN PASO

HEIGHT: 14.2–15.3 hh

COLOUR: all solid colours

PERSONALITY TYPE: warm-blooded

TYPICAL USE: riding, harness, showing

TEMPERAMENT: docile, willing, intelligent

ORIGIN: Peru

SIMILAR BREEDS: Paso Fino

**P**eru's national horse breed, the Peruvian Paso or Peruvian Stepping Horse, is the product of a judicious fusion of several Old World breeds – the Spanish Jennet gave its even temperament and smooth ambling gait, the African Barb contributed great energy, strength and stamina, while the Andalusian imparted its excellent conformation, action, proud carriage and beauty to the new breed. This mix of equines, introduced to Peru by the Spanish settlers, was then left in more or less isolation to evolve into a horse of great beauty and presence.

## Pacers and Trotters

As the Peruvian Paso was developing, the outside world was changing. Up to the beginning of the seventeenth century, most horse breeds were pacers (lateral), rather than trotters (diagonal). As an ever-increasing network of roads was created, more people travelled by carriage, rather than on horseback, and the trotter was better suited to pulling a carriage. At the beginning of that century, it was unusual to find a horse that trotted; by the end, it was rare to find one that did not.

But the Peruvian Paso, kept pure by the Peruvian people, continued to pace – of all gaited horses, it is thought to be the only one that is guaranteed to pass on its natural gaits to 100 per cent of its offspring.

## 'Con Brío'

The Peruvian Paso has the *paso llano*, a broken four-beat lateral gait; the *sobreandando*, a faster gait; and the unique *termino*, a graceful, flowing movement in which the horse's forelegs roll outwards from the shoulders, like the arm motion of a swimmer in front crawl, or freestyle. All gaits are smooth and extremely comfortable.

Although it is a different breed from the Paso Fino, there are similarities. Both horses have the presence and beauty of their Spanish ancestry, as well as the abundant flowing mane and tail. And both also have *brio*, that engaging mixture of arrogance and exuberance that makes them such a joy to watch.

## Fascinating Facts

A widely perpetuated and popular myth: if a statue in the park of a person on a horse has both front legs in the air, the person died in battle; if the horse has one front leg in the air, the person died as a result of wounds received in battle; if the horse has all four legs on the ground, the person died of natural causes.

BELOW

*The Peruvian Paso is one of the gaited horse breeds that always passes its gait on to its offspring.*

# HACKNEY HORSE

TEMPERAMENT: spirited, intelligent

ORIGIN: England

SIMILAR BREEDS: Hackney Pony, Shales

HEIGHT: 15 hh

COLOUR: bay, brown, chestnut, black

PERSONALITY TYPE: warm-blooded

TYPICAL USE: harness, riding

It is called the 'Ballerina of the Show Ring', and England's Hackney Horse takes its name from the French *haquenée* (French was commonly spoken in the country in medieval times), meaning a riding horse with a particularly comfortable gait. Over the years, it became 'Hackney', a word synonymous with a general-purpose equine with legendary stamina and soundness, and flashy trot that was greatly admired. These horses were highly valued by commoners and kings alike.

qualities. As roads improved, demand grew for coach horses and, as carriages became more sophisticated, flashier, showier horses were increasingly popular. The Hackney, with its high knee action and regal bearing, fit the bill perfectly. In the flamboyant Regency period, the carriage horse became a status symbol.

Hackney blood has been used in the development of other horse breeds, notably the Holstein, Gelderlander, Dutch Warmblood, Saddlebred and Morgan. It is also used as an outcross to produce exceptional sport horses, passing on its athleticism, speed and stamina, as well as its good looks.

The modern Hackney has a noble outlook, with a straight or slightly convex profile, elegant head carried high on an arched neck and sloping shoulders. It has good feet and its legs are strong, with plenty of good, flat bone and long pasterns that give it its light, springy step.

## Status Symbol

In fact, three monarchs, Henry VII (1457–1509), Henry VIII (1491–1547) and Elizabeth I (1533–1603), all passed Acts concerning horse breeding and the value of the Hackney; Henry VIII went so far as to penalize anyone exporting a horse without authority.

Later, in the early 1700s, imported Arabian blood was added to the Hackney to refine the breed, without detracting from its inherent

## Springy Step

The Hackney, when crossed with other breeds, appears to be dominant – influencing, rather than being influenced.

# SHALES

HEIGHT: 15 hh

COLOUR: grey, chestnut

PERSONALITY TYPE:
warm-blooded

TYPICAL USE: harness, riding

TEMPERAMENT: good-tempered, intelligent

ORIGIN: England

SIMILAR BREEDS: Hackney

Although it is no longer a recognized breed in the United Kingdom, the Shales, a direct descendant of and the modern equivalent to the Norfolk Trotter or Roadster, does still exist. The foundation sire of the American Standardbred was the Thoroughbred stallion Messenger, which descended from Blaze; Blaze's son, Original Shales, founded the Norfolk Roadster and is responsible for the modern Shales, as well as the high-stepping Hackney. The Roadster had similar origins to the Thoroughbred.

*The well-conformed Shales horse was instrumental in the development of the Hackney breed, and remains a useful driving and riding animal.*

BELOW

*It was from the Shales horse that the Norfolk (and Yorkshire) trotters developed, and they in turn influenced the French Trotter, pictured.*

## Social Change

During the seventeenth and eighteenth centuries, the Roadster and the Thoroughbred developed in an almost parallel way; the subsequent differences were due to social rather than evolutionary change. The Thoroughbred was the plaything of landed gentry, who wanted it for hunting and racing. The Roadster or Trotter, however, was much more utilitarian, to be ridden or driven. The trot was far more suited to the carriage horse.

While the carriage horse was increasingly popular – hence the development of the Hackney – people still wanted hunters and riding horses, and these were mostly the Shales strain, which were generally grey or chestnut.

## Polo Pony

The modern Shales has been bred by the Colquhoun family since 1922, when Elizabeth Colquhoun bought a two-year-old colt by Findon Grey Shales, which stood at the Duchy of Cornwall's Tor Stud. The colt, bred by the Prince of Wales, later the Duke of Windsor, was called Royal Shales.

A granddaughter of Royal Shales called Silver Shales – the female line of which traced to the renowned Thoroughbred sire The Tetrarch – was hunted as well as driven, and was also used as a polo pony, proving the breed's versatility. The Shales has the good looks of the Hackney as well as its flash and fire, and it is to be hoped that the breed will continue.

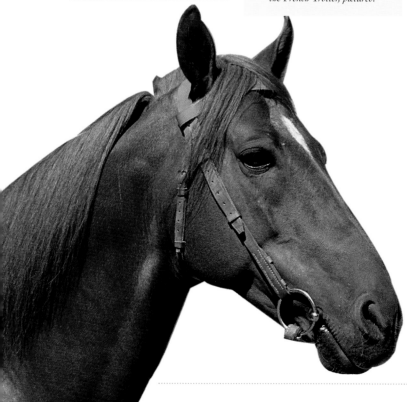

# CLEVELAND BAY

TEMPERAMENT: sensible, intelligent, honest

ORIGIN: England

SIMILAR BREEDS: Yorkshire Coach Horse (extinct)

HEIGHT: 16–16.2 hh

COLOUR: bay, few or no white markings

PERSONALITY TYPE: warm-blooded

TYPICAL USE: harness, riding, hunting, competition

## Fascinating Facts

Around 1869, Fanny Drape, a Cleveland Bay-cross mare, gave a solo exhibition of jumping in hand, clearing a bar estimated to be 2.3 m (7 1/2 ft) high under which her leader ran.

LEFT

*These wonderful, athletic horses were originally used primarily as coach horses although they also make excellent riding horses.*

**T**he United Kingdom's oldest indigenous horse breed originates from Cleveland in north-east England. They were traditionally used to transport goods and materials between monasteries and abbeys in the Yorkshire Dales, and these early pack animals were called 'Chapman Horses', after the name given to itinerant packmen and pedlars. When North African Barbs were imported into the area, they were used on the local Chapman mares to produce a powerful pack and harness horse.

## Police Horse

The Cleveland Bay was almost wiped out with the advent of the motor vehicle, but a few dedicated breeders kept it going, with the society being formed in 1884. As its name suggests, it is always bay in colour, with few, if any, white markings. It is hardy, long-lived and possesses tremendous stamina. Although generally sensible, it has a strong character which, if mishandled, can become spoiled. It is a dominant outcross, and has influenced several European warmblood breeds, including the Gelderlander, Holstein, Oldenburg and Hanoverian. Muscular and strong, it is also good-looking, with a 'hawk-like' profile, well-balanced frame, good legs and joints and sound feet. But most of all it is versatile – bred to be a packhorse or harness horse, it makes a good heavyweight hunter, and its sensible temperament means that it is also a good police horse, working well in crowds and noisy situations.

## Popular Export

As the demand for carriage horses grew, the Cleveland Bay was crossed with the Thoroughbred to produce a taller, more elegant creature, known as the Yorkshire Coach Horse. In the golden age of coaching, in the late eighteenth century, these horses were hugely popular and exported all over the world as matched pairs and teams. To this day, there are still two discernible types of Cleveland Bay: the smaller Chapman type and the larger version that resembles the Yorkshire Coach Horse.

# THOROUGHBRED

HEIGHT: 16 hh

COLOUR: bay, chestnut, black, brown, grey

PERSONALITY TYPE: warm-blooded

TYPICAL USE: racing, competition

TEMPERAMENT: intelligent, spirited

ORIGIN: England

SIMILAR BREEDS: Arabian

If ever there were an example of equine excellence, it must surely be the Thoroughbred. The word is synonymous with speed, grace, beauty and athleticism, and is the given name of the most successful horse breed in the world. The English Thoroughbred – the word comes from the Arabic *keheilan*, meaning 'pure blood' – is based on three foundation sires, the Darley Arabian, the Godolphin Arabian and the Byerley Turk, each brought to England from the Middle East and named after their respective owners.

## Middle Eastern Blood

In the custom of the day, horses were known by the men that owned them, thus the Darley Arabian was owned by Thomas Darley, the Godolphin Arabian by Lord Godolphin and the Byerley Turk by Captain Robert Byerley. They were brought to England from the Middle East around the turn of the seventeenth century.

The Byerley Turk is thought to be the first to be brought back, having been captured from the Turks at the siege of Buda (1686), when the Hungarian capital was part of the Ottoman Empire, and was brought to Britain in 1690. Despite the horse's

moniker, it is likely it was also an Arabian, or possibly an Akhal-Teké.

## Flying Childers

The Darley Arabian was purchased in Aleppo, Syria, by Thomas Darley in 1704 and was shipped to Yorkshire, where he was bred to numerous mares. The most successful matings were with a mare called Betty Leeds, resulting in two influential colts, Flying Childers and Bartlet's Childers. Through the Childers line, the Darley Arabian was the great-great-grandsire of Eclipse, of whom it was said, 'Eclipse first, the rest nowhere.'

The Godolphin Arabian was to be of equal importance, although he was originally

used as a 'teaser', to test if mares were ready to be mated. It is said he fought another stallion for the mare Roxana, on whom he sired Cade, the father of Matchem, who was to prove particularly influential on the American Thoroughbred.

## American Pedigree

All this might still have been lost, were it not for one James Weatherby, who published the first *General Stud Book* of the English Thoroughbred in 1791, listing the pedigrees of 387 mares, each of which could be traced back to Eclipse, Matchem or Herod, whose great-great-grandsire was the Byerley Turk. The *General Stud Book* is still published in England by Weatherbys.

The Thoroughbred found favour in North America, too, the first export to the United States being Bulle Rock, a son of the Darley Arabian, who arrived in what was then the British colony of Virginia in 1730, at the age of 21. By the 1800s, he had been followed by more than 300 others. The first volume of the *American Stud Book* was published in 1873.

## Equine Powerhouse

The modern Thoroughbred retains all the beauty of its Arabian ancestry and the precocious speed of its founding sires. Its refined, chiselled head has a straight profile, rather than a dished or concave one, set on a long neck and high withers. Its

---

RIGHT

*The Thoroughbred is noted for its elegance, beauty and natural athleticism and is a breed that almost always improves the stock it is crossed with.*

shoulders are deep, well muscled and sloping; its girth deep and its hindquarters powerful. It has strong, slender but well-muscled, clean legs and good feet.

It is an equine powerhouse that is proof positive of four centuries of careful, selective breeding. Its names – Diomed, a descendant of Herod and the first winner of the Epsom Derby;

Hyperion, Derby and St Leger winner and hugely successful sire; Sir Archie, one of the best 'American' Thoroughbreds – resonate through history.

Today, 93 per cent of all modern Thoroughbreds can be traced back to one of those three foundation sires – the Darley Arabian, the Godolphin Arabian and the Byerley Turk.

# ANGLO-ARAB

HEIGHT: 15.2–16.3 hh

COLOUR: mostly bay, brown, chestnut

PERSONALITY TYPE: warm-blooded

TYPICAL USE: competition, riding

TEMPERAMENT: sensible, calm, intelligent

ORIGIN: Europe

SIMILAR BREEDS: Arabian Thoroughbred

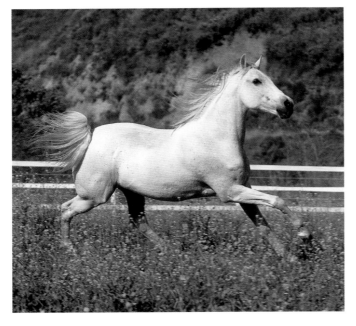

T his harmonious fusion between Arabian and Thoroughbred lines makes a superb sport horse, the most popular cross being an Arabian stallion to a Thoroughbred mare, as this produces larger offspring than would a Thoroughbred stallion to an Arabian mare. Experiments with the two breeds began in the eighteenth or nineteenth century, and are quite a science – selective breeding used to combine the best features of two superlative equine breeds, without obviously favouring either, but to produce a superb all-rounder.

## Best of Both

The aim was to produce a horse with speed and class – the two essential attributes of the Thoroughbred – and the stamina and toughness of the Arabian, with the beauty of both. The Anglo-Arab is a natural athlete with innate jumping ability; add the Thoroughbred's speed and you get an excellent event horse.

The ideal Anglo-Arab should have no more than 75 per cent Arabian blood, and no less than 25 per cent.

## Competition Horse

The Anglo-Arab has a finely shaped head, with the slightly concave profile of the Arabian, but should not be too dished. It has a similar outline to the Thoroughbred, but generally more substance. Its neck should be of good length and gracefully arching from the withers to the poll. Its shoulders are

LEFT

*The Anglo-Arab combines the best of both Thoroughbred and Arab breeds, resulting in a horse with great speed, tenacity, stamina and beauty.*

very powerful and should slope to allow for speed and free movement. It is deep in the chest and compact through the body. It has powerful hindquarters, well-formed legs with plenty of bone and tough joints, and good, hard feet.

A naturally good mover, with a free-flowing and long-striding action, the Anglo-Arab makes an excellent saddle or competition horse. The experiment to cross two of the best equine breeds – the Thoroughbred and the Arabian – must be counted as a resounding success.

# IRISH DRAUGHT

TEMPERAMENT: sensible, gentle, docile

ORIGIN: Ireland

SIMILAR BREEDS: none

HEIGHT: 15.2–17 hh

COLOUR: all solid colours

PERSONALITY TYPE: warm-blooded

TYPICAL USE: riding, harness, competition

Despite its name, the Irish Draught is actually a lighter, free-moving equine, rather than a heavy draught breed. It did start out as an all-rounder, however, working the small Irish farms and doubling up as a hunter, as well as a harness horse to pull the trap or dogcart into town or to church. Today, the breed is perhaps best known as an excellent outcross – mated with Thoroughbreds, it produces superb hunters and competition horses.

## Strong and Handsome

It is thought the Irish Draught has been in existence for at least a century, although it has come worryingly close to extinction on several occasions. To the

ABOVE

*The Irish Draught is a wonderful versatile animal with a natural affinity for jumping. It is renowned for its honest, forgiving and amenable temperament.*

small Irish farmer, his horse had to be docile, tough and economical to keep – its traditional winter feed was young gorse put through a chaff-cutter, boiled turnips and bran or something similar that could be spared from the cows. The breed developed into a strong, handsome equine, standing between 15.2 and 16.2 hh for mares and up to 17 hh for stallions.

## Valuable Outcross

During the periods of poverty and famine in Irish history, breeders stopped registering their animals – breed enthusiasts and the Irish Horse Board endeavoured to get a new studbook started. They found that hundreds of horses were going to the slaughterhouses each week, and there were very few left.

Luckily, the breed was saved and has thrived, as a purebred and as a valuable outcross. In the UK, the broodmare is acknowledged as an excellent dam of hunters when put to a Thoroughbred stallion. The Irish Draught stallion is now being used more and more to get extra bone and substance in the progeny of the lighter type mare.

The breed's excellent feet are those of a hunter rather than a draught horse, and the reason why the Irish Draught produces such wonderful competition stock.

# CAMARGUE

HEIGHT: 13–14 hh

COLOUR: grey

PERSONALITY TYPE: warm-blooded

TYPICAL USE: herding, riding

TEMPERAMENT: lively, good-tempered

ORIGIN: France

SIMILAR BREEDS: Solutre (extinct)

The history of the Camargue Horse is inexorably entwined with that of the tough little bulls that live in the same region – both exist in a semi-feral state in the Camargue region of the Rhone delta. The Camargue Horse is thought to have descended from the Solutre Horse, which lived on the marshland at the edge of the Quaternary Sea during the Paleolithic period, some 17,000 years ago – the musculature and skeleton of the Camargue is the same as that of the Solutre.

## Fascinating Facts

Camargue horses are born dark brown or black, often with a white blaze on the forehead, but turn grey when they reach full maturity, between the ages of five and seven. Their coat lightens to white as they get older.

## Horse of the Sea

Known as 'the horse of the sea', the Camargue thrives in the marshy land it inhabits; it eats leafy grasses, herbs and other ground vegetation. In the spring, it grazes on samphire, as well as the tender shoots of tall reeds. In winter, it survives on dried grass and on goosefoot, a tough plant that most other grazing animals cannot eat. When food is scarce, the horse may graze for 22 hours a day. When food is plentiful, it grazes only at dawn and dusk.

It is thought that Arabian and Saracen horses may have had some influence on the

### LEFT
*This ancient breed of horse is particularly tough and brave, and was traditionally used by French cowboys for working the dangerous Camargue bulls.*

that roars across the delta in the winter, and the fierce heat of the summer sun.

## French Cowboys

The Camargue is brave, agile and lively, but is generally good-tempered and makes an excellent riding horse. Although it rarely stands much higher than 14 hh, it is considered a horse, rather than a pony. It is traditionally used by the *gardians*, the French cowboys who round up the black Camargue bulls,

Camargue, but its natural environment has also shaped it into the rugged little horse it is today. It has to be tough to endure the biting cold wind which have a reputation for being tough and aggressive. The Camargue's delta home was designated a national park in 1928.

# FRENCH TROTTER

TEMPERAMENT: quiet, biddable

ORIGIN: France

SIMILAR BREEDS: Selle Français

HEIGHT: 16.2 hh

COLOUR: chestnut, bay, brown

PERSONALITY TYPE: warm-blooded

TYPICAL USE: racing, harness

Also known as the Norman Trotter, France's native breed is an intelligent but quiet equine, known for its speed and stamina. It was bred as a trotting horse at the beginning of the nineteenth century in the Normandy region on the northern coast of France, by crossing the strong Norman mares with imported English Thoroughbreds, half-breds and Norfolk Trotters and Norfolk Roadsters. These crosses resulted in two distinct types of horse, the French Trotter and the Anglo-Norman saddle horse.

## Ridden Trotting Races

The first trotting races were held in 1806 on the Champ de Mars in Paris – these were ridden races, not harness. As interest and enthusiasm for the sport grew, purpose-built racetracks were opened, the first at Cherbourg in the 1830s. The new sport received official support in 1861 with an Imperial decree, leading to the formation of its first governing body.

Five important bloodlines of the French Trotter were established: Conquérant, Normand, Lavater, Phaeton and Fuchsia, with Fuchsia being the most influential of the early stallions. He was foaled in 1883 and sired almost 400 trotters – more than 100 of his sons produced winners.

## A Great Trotting Tradition

Some Standardbred blood was introduced later, to add more speed, but the Trotteur Français Stud Book closed its register to non-French-bred horses in 1937. It is only in recent years that a limited number of carefully selected French Standardbred crosses have been admitted to the studbook. In its turn, the French Trotter has played an important role in the development of the Selle Français.

France has the greatest tradition of trotting racing outside the United States, and still holds both ridden and driven contests. The Prix d'Amérique is the premier trotting race, and the Prix de Cornulier is the ridden equivalent.

# SELLE FRANÇAIS

HEIGHT: 16–17 hh

COLOUR: bay, chestnut, most solid colours

PERSONALITY TYPE: warm-blooded

TYPICAL USE: riding, competition

TEMPERAMENT: willing, friendly, kind

ORIGIN: France

SIMILAR BREEDS: French Trotter, Thoroughbred, French Anglo-Arab

LEFT

*The Selle Français is an athletic sports horse that excels at competition. Unlike most warmblood breeds they have a high percentage of trotter blood in their history.*

Naturally athletic, kind, willing, strong and good-looking, the Selle Français, France's saddle horse breed, is everything anyone could want from an equine. Like all warmbloods, it is a mixture of breeds, but what makes it unique is the influence of outcrosses to trotters. The Selle Français was developed in the government stud farms of Saint-Lô and Le Pin in Normandy in the nineteenth century, by putting imported Thoroughbred stallions and Norfolk Trotters to native French stock.

## French Influences

The results of these experiments were two types of horse: the French Trotter, a fast harness horse, and the Anglo-Norman, with both a saddle and heavier draught type. The saddle type of the Anglo-Norman could be considered the prototype for the modern Selle Français and is certainly the most recognized foundation stock; however, many of the local French breeds that were bred as saddle horses – such as the Vendeen, Corlais, Angevin, Angonin and Charentais – played an important role in the breed's development.

After the Second World War, the emphasis was put firmly on the production of a riding horse combining speed, stamina, ability and quality. As the Anglo-Norman began to be crossed with the regional breeds, the resulting stock became less diverse and, because of this growing similarity among the equines, in 1958 they were merged together under one name – *le cheval de Selle Français*, or the French Saddle Horse.

## Sport Horse

In less than 50 years, the Selle Français has become widely recognized as one of the world's best competition horses – athletic and strong with good conformation and an intelligent and tractable disposition. The Selle Français has excelled internationally in show jumping, but is also successful in eventing and in the dressage arena. It is bred to race as 'AQPSA' (an acronym for *autres que pur sang association*, meaning 'other than Thoroughbred'), and there seems little at which the Selle Français does not excel.

In 2002, at the World Equestrian Games at Jerez in

Spain, the French show-jumping squad took team gold, all mounted on Selle Français stallions. In 2006, Nicolas Touzaint claimed the eventing World Cup on the classy grey Galan de Sauvagère, a Selle Français; in 2007, he was European Champion.

## Affinity with People

The ideal conformation of the Selle Français is that of a large-boned Thoroughbred, combining both strength and elegance. It has an attractive, expressive head set on a long

neck, sloping shoulders, strong back and good legs with plenty of hard bone. Selle Français horses are seen in many colours, but bays and chestnuts are predominant.

A huge part of their abiding charm is their willingness to please and their almost dog-like affinity with people. They also have that extra spark that separates the superstars from the masses, yet they remain kind and easy to handle.

While the Thoroughbred has made a huge impact on France's saddle horse, Selle Français stallions have also played a role in the development of other breeds. Notably, Furioso II, Zeus and Inschallah were important in the Oldenburg breed; Cor De

BELOW

*This is one of the most versatile of warmblood breeds and has excelled in dressage, show jumping, eventing and even racing.*

La Bryère is often seen in Holstein pedigrees; Le Mexico made a contribution to the Dutch Warmblood, and Alme can be found in pedigrees of most European sport horse breeds.

The Selle Français is also finding favour in the United States as a hunter, for which its elegance, fluid movement and athletic jumping ability make it supremely well suited.

# FRENCH ANGLO-ARAB

HEIGHT: 16.2 hh

COLOUR: all solid colours

PERSONALITY TYPE: warm-blooded

TYPICAL USE: riding, competition

TEMPERAMENT: intelligent, willing

ORIGIN: France

SIMILAR BREEDS: Anglo-Arab, Thoroughbred, Selle Français

Madame de Pompadour (1721–64) founded the Pompadour National Anglo-Arab Stud, which is credited with finding one of the founding sires of the French Anglo-Arab, in 1751. It was an extraordinary success story of horse breeding that was to lead to the development of the French saddle horse, the Selle Français. The stud farm, which established the first Arab breeding programme in France in the late 1700s and was at the forefront of expeditions to Arabia for bloodlines, imported an Arabian stallion called Massoud from Egypt in 1820 to improve the stock.

## National Studs

The other stallion was called Aslan, who came from Turkey in the early nineteenth century. Both stallions were bred to three Thoroughbred mares, Daer, the Cornus Mare and the Selim Mare. They, in turn, produced the three fillies that were to be the foundation mares of the French Anglo-Arab: Delphine, Clovis and Danae.

The stud farm's purpose was to produce exceptional high-class European sport horses. Château Pompadour became a royal stud following Madame de Pompadour's death, then was re-established by Napoleon following the

### ABOVE
*The French Anglo-Arab generally has excellent conformation and disposition, and it is noted for its jumping ability.*

French Revolution. The Pompadour is now one of France's 23 national studs

(*haras nationaux*) that stand Anglo-Arab stallions. The stallions standing at these studs, all over France, are the result of centuries of selective breeding and refinement, and are much in demand to produce international competition horses.

## Correct Action

The French tradition is to breed Anglo-Arab to Anglo-Arab, rather than Arab to Thoroughbred, which produces horses of varying levels of Thoroughbred and Arab blood, usually expressed as a percentage of Arab blood. For example, a French Anglo-Arab would be registered as '41%', meaning its lineage is 41 per cent Arabian and 59 per cent Thoroughbred.

The French Anglo-Arab may be a trifle less elegant than its British counterpart, but it is tough, hard, enormously versatile and athletic. The ones bred at Pompadour are, in general, larger and more muscular, but all the French stock are athletic types with pronounced jumping ability and notable correctness of action.

# BELGIAN WARMBLOOD

TEMPERAMENT: willing, good-natured

ORIGIN: Belgium

SIMILAR BREEDS: all warmbloods

HEIGHT: 16.2 hh

COLOUR: all solid colours

PERSONALITY TYPE: warm-blooded

TYPICAL USE: riding, harness, competition

Belgium is primarily known for its heavy draught breed, the Brabant, but its own warmblood horse is a resounding success – particularly as it was developed only around 50 years ago. The Belgian Warmblood was developed

RIGHT

*This is a relatively young, but very successful breed. Originally bred for the show ring, they now also excel at dressage, show jumping and eventing.*

principally as a show horse, using Arabian, Thorough-bred, Anglo-Arab and Selle Français on the country's lighter agricultural animals. These horses had already been mixed with some

Gelderlander blood to add size; the Arabian and Thoroughbred lines were to add quality.

## Quality and Power

Since then, about 5,000 Belgian Warmblood foals have been born every year, and the demand for this elegant equine seems unlikely to wane. The horse has a head full of quality, well-placed

withers and good, sloping shoulders. Its body is compact, with a well-proportioned back and powerful quarters, and it has good legs and sound feet. Although it was bred primarily for the show ring, the Belgian Warmblood has really found its niche in the competition arena. It excels at dressage, show jumping and three-day eventing, and has become popular all over Europe and North America.

# HISPANO/HISPANO-ARABE

TEMPERAMENT: lively, spirited

ORIGIN: Spain

SIMILAR BREEDS: Andalusian, Arabian

HEIGHT: 14.3–16 hh

COLOUR: chestnut, black, grey, bay

PERSONALITY TYPE: warm-blooded

TYPICAL USE: riding, competition

Two of the world's most ancient and influential horse breeds have been brought together to form the Hispano, a cross between the Andalusian and the Thoroughbred, which is sometimes also known as the Spanish Anglo-Arab. When Arabian blood is added to the mix, it is known as the Hispano-Arabe, and also *tres*

*sangres*, meaning 'three bloods'. The Hispano-Arabe is a cross between a purebred registered Arabian and a purebred registered Andalusian.

## Arched Neck

The Hispano-Arabe usually stands between 15 and 16 hh,

and has the refinement of the Arabian, particularly in its elegant head, and the long, muscular and well-arched neck of the Andalusian. The

shapely withers ensure good saddle placement, and its body is full and strong, with a large chest, deep and muscled with plenty of heart room. The Hispano-Arabe exhibits a solid foundation of ample, extremely dense bone, and extremely strong well-shaped hooves, traits also inherited from the Andalusian.

# ANDALUSIAN

HEIGHT: 15.2 hh

COLOUR: grey, bay, black, roan

PERSONALITY TYPE: warm-blooded

TYPICAL USE: riding, competition, harness

TEMPERAMENT: intelligent, willing, brave

ORIGIN: Spain

SIMILAR BREEDS: Lusitano, Alter-Real

**W**riting in the sixteenth century, King Henry IV's riding master Salomon de la Broue (*c.* 1530–1610) declared: 'I class the true Spanish horse as the greatest, the most handsome, the most noble, the bravest and most worthy of kings.' And there are few today who would dispute that statement. The purebred Spanish horse, or *pura raza española*, is the collective term for these Iberian kings, the Andalusian (also sometimes called the Carthusian), the Lusitano and the Alter-Real.

## Pure Strain

The name 'Andalusian' is taken from the sun-drenched region of southern Spain around Seville, Jerez, Cordoba and Granada, and it is largely thanks to an order of Carthusian monks – hence its alternative moniker – that it remains so pure. The Monastery of Carthuja, founded in 1476 at Jerez de la Frontera, kept a small herd of Spanish horses and preserved the purest strains. The breed developed with hard, sound feet and fine body hair to counteract the rocky, dry ground and hot climate.

But the purebred Spanish horse's history begins way before the fifteenth century. Cave drawings dating back some 20,000 years show horses were in the region that is now Spain, Portugal and southern France during that period.

## Moorish Influences

The most significant event in the Andalusian's history occurred in AD 710–711, when the Moors invaded Spain as the allies of Spanish lords who were at odds with their king. Within seven years they had taken possession of most of the Iberian Peninsula and named it Al-Andalus. It is known that the cavalry were mostly Berbers mounted on Barb Horses – the Arab people who also fought in Spain were infantry, so it was the Barb and not the Arabian that was to have most influence on the Iberian stock. But it is believed that the Andalusian had just as much influence on the Barb breed as vice versa.

### Fascinating Facts

The Andalusian's purity was threatened in the 1800s when Napoleon's army invaded Spain and stole many horses. It was thanks to the small herd hidden at Carthuja that the breed was able to be kept pure.

LEFT

*The Andalusian, like the Arab and Thoroughbred, has had a significant effect on the development of other horse breeds.*

## Noble Appearance

The Andalusian's striking beauty and superb athleticism make it just as popular today, although it is more likely to do battle in the bullring – those same traits of speed, agility and courage are just as essential here – or the dressage arena.

It has a noble, distinguished appearance, and is most often grey, although occasionally bay, black and roan are also seen. It is a compact horse with excellent proportions, standing around 15.2 hh. Its head is attractive, with a slightly Roman (convex) profile, a large, expressive eye and small, neat ears. It has an abundant, slightly rippled mane and tail. Its chest is quite massive and its quarters lean. Its legs are clean, and its feet generally good and hard; its action is quite energetic. The Andalusian is renowned for its ability to learn and for its superb temperament.

Certainly, the Barb and the Andalusian have many characteristics in common. Both tend to have low-set tails and rounded croups, with short to medium-length backs. Both have well-crested medium-length necks. The head of the Barb does show some Oriental influence, but is not dished like that of the Arabian.

## Weapons of Generals

Xenophon (*c.* 431–355 BC), the Greek cavalryman considered by most to be the founder of classical equitation, was hugely impressed by the horses he saw on the Iberian Peninsula, and appreciated their ability to 'collect' – that is, gather their hind legs beneath the fore and fall back on their hocks. This ability, which today is valued in the dressage arena, made the Spanish warhorse swift and agile, able to turn quickly in any direction.

The Andalusian and the Lusitano, its Portuguese cousin, were the chosen weapons of generals from Hannibal to Julius Caesar; their speed, agility and courage were unequalled and lent themselves to the mastery of mounted battle.

RIGHT

*This is possibly one of the most beautiful breeds of horse, as well as possessing great athleticism and a wonderful temperament.*

# LUSITANO

HEIGHT: 15–16 hh

COLOUR: grey, black, bay

PERSONALITY TYPE: warm-blooded

TYPICAL USE: riding, bullfighting, competition

TEMPERAMENT: intelligent, willing, brave

ORIGIN: Portugal

SIMILAR BREEDS: Andalusian, Alter-Real

The Lusitano's name is derived from Lusitania, the Latin name for Portugal, and it has been recognized as a separate breed to the Andalusian only since 1966. There are considerable similarities between the two breeds, as they are both developed from Barb and Sorraia blood, but they do have some conformational differences. The Lusitano has a more pronounced Roman nose than the Andalusian, and a wider forehead, and the Lusitano is considered the purer breed because it has no Arabian blood.

## Majestic

The Lusitano has a more sloping croup and lower set tail than its Spanish cousin, and is often straighter through the shoulder. Dressage expert Sylvia Loch, who founded the Lusitano Breed Society of Great Britain, wrote of the Lusitano: 'To look at, it is noble rather than pretty, with aristocracy written all over its fine, slightly hawked, long face. It develops a powerful neck and shoulder, which makes it look extremely majestic in front.

'The quarters are not large, but the loins are wide and strong, and the hocks long and wiry, giving it the power to bounce forcefully forwards with masterful impulsion. Deep flexion is obtained from the developed second thigh and the longer than usual cannons and pasterns.'

## Bullring Star

In Portugal, the Lusitano is highly prized and particularly valued as the mount of the *rejoneador*, or Portuguese bullfighter. Bulls are not killed in the Portuguese bullring; the aim is to demonstrate the training and schooling of the horse, its agility and balance. It is considered a great disgrace if a *rejoneador* allows his horse to be injured during the fight.

The same characteristics that are essential in the bullring also make the Lusitano extremely efficient at other equestrian disciplines, particularly dressage, or as a working and pleasure riding horse. Its excellent temperament and willingness to learn make it the perfect equine partner.

# Fascinating Facts

Horses produce approximately 10 gallons of saliva a day.

BELOW

*Lusitanos share many similarities with the Andalusian, although they differ notably in the shape of their head.*

# ALTER-REAL

**TEMPERAMENT:** intelligent, highly strung

**ORIGIN:** Portugal

**SIMILAR BREEDS:** Andalusian, Lusitano

**HEIGHT:** 15–16.1 hh

**COLOUR:** bay, brown, grey, chestnut

**PERSONALITY TYPE:** warm-blooded

**TYPICAL USE:** riding, dressage

The Alter-Real was established by the Braganza family in Portugal in 1748, who imported 300 selected Andalusian mares from Jerez in Spain, to form a national stud at Villa de Portel to produce suitable riding and carriage horses for the Portuguese royal family. The word *real* means 'royal'; the first half of the name comes from the national stud, which moved to Alter do Chão eight years later. The energetic Alter-Real was well suited to the movements of the *haute école*, or High School.

## Almost Lost

The stud was sacked by Napoleon's troops in the early 1800s, and the best of the stock was taken for warhorses. Infusions of English Thoroughbred, Arabian and Hanoverian blood were introduced to the remaining horses, with dire consequences, and the breed was also lost, until further Andalusian blood was added to restore the Alter-Real to its former glory.

The breed suffered a further setback in the early twentieth century with the dissolution

of the Portuguese monarchy – the Alter-Real stud was shut down and most of its records destroyed. It is thanks to Portugal's expert Dr Ruy d'Andrade, who salvaged two stallions and some mares to re-establish the Alter-Real, that the breed still exists.

## Highly Strung

The Alter-Real is supremely suited to the movements of the High School. It has a small, neat head, with a pronounced jaw and a

straight or convex profile. Its short, muscular neck is nicely arched with pronounced withers and good sloping shoulders, and it has a compact frame, with a short back, muscular hindquarters and a well-set tail. Its legs are strong with slender but sturdy cannon bones and pasterns. It is generally bay, but can also be chestnut, grey or brown. It is highly strung but intelligent, and is quick to learn, so is perhaps best suited to experienced horsepeople.

**BELOW**

*This Portugese breed had all but died out by the twentieth century, although it has been restored through Andalusian influence.*

# SARDINIAN

HEIGHT: 15.2 hh

COLOUR: bay, brown

PERSONALITY TYPE: warm-blooded

TYPICAL USE: riding, competition, police

TEMPERAMENT: trainable, sensible, calm

ORIGIN: Sardinia

SIMILAR BREEDS: Barb, Anglo-Arab, Salerno

Anglo-Arabs – with which the Sardinian was thought to have particular affinity – were imported, the most notable being Mongarry, Fanon II and Fort Chabrol. Thirty years later, more Oriental blood was introduced, which produced a military horse that was both sturdy and agile.

good turn of foot and plenty of stamina, making it an excellent competition horse.

The modern Sardinian is strikingly similar to the Anglo-Arab. It is used in Sardinia and in Italy as a

> **RIGHT**
>
> *These exceptionally attractive horses are appreciated for their inherent soundness and their particularly amenable temperaments.*

Sardinia's only native equine breed is something of an enigma. Geographically, Sardinia, an island off the west coast of Italy, is well situated for trade with North Africa and is known to have imported North African Barb and Arabian horses for centuries, which would be crossed with the local stock. But what this local stock was, its origins and how it came to this island in the first place are not known. The Sardinian breed was established as a fixed type in the fifteenth century.

When a racecourse was built at Chilivani in 1921, it sparked a national interest and Thoroughbred blood was introduced to give the Sardinian more speed.

## Trainable

Four Thoroughbreds – Rigolo, Zenith, Sambor and Abimelecco – were introduced and resulted in a good-looking, all-round athlete. The Sardinian has a neat, intelligent head with a straight profile, elegant, well-arched neck, well-proportioned body and good sound legs and feet. It is hardy and athletic, with a

## Sturdy and Agile

The Sardinian, like Italy's sport horse, the Salerno, made an excellent military mount, being tough and trainable. In 1874, a stud was formed at Ozieri, in the north-west of the island, to promote and unify the breed. In 1883, several French

police horse, to which its sensible and calm temperament, as well as its inherent trainability, is well suited.

# MAREMMANA

TEMPERAMENT: steady, gentle

ORIGIN: Italy

SIMILAR BREEDS: Salerno

HEIGHT: 15–15.3 hh
COLOUR: all solid colours
PERSONALITY TYPE: warm-blooded
TYPICAL USE: riding, herding, trekking

The Barb probably forms the basis for the Maremmana, bred in Tuscany but almost certainly deriving from horses from North Africa, as well as Spanish, Neapolitan and Arabian blood. During the nineteenth century, Thoroughbred and Norfolk Roadster blood were also introduced. The breed's name comes from the Maremma coast, a region of low marshland in the south-west corner of Tuscany. It is likely that the horse was originally bred to work the land and in harness.

## Semi-Wild

The Maremmana is mainly bred in the northern region of Maremma and was established at the stud at Grosseto, although there are still herds of Maremmana running semi-wild in some local areas.

As well as being utilized as an agricultural animal, it was used by the cavalry as a troop horse and by the police force. But the Maremmana excels at working cattle, and it is frequently used by Italian ranch hands and cowboys, known as *butteri*, and demonstrates an enormous amount of 'cow sense', similar to that seen in the American Quarter Horse. ('Cow sense' is probably best described as the horse's natural instinct to follow and herd cows.)

## Sound Constitution

The Maremmana is not much to look at; it has a plain and rather coarse head (despite the Arabian, Barb and Thoroughbred influences), short neck, weak shoulders, prominent withers and short back. But despite its conformational short-comings, it tends to be tough and hardy, economical to keep and generally very sound. It is also even-tempered, sensible, honest and hard-working, so it is still much in demand as a police mount. And as Tuscany has become an increasingly popular holiday destination, the Tuscan breed has been brought into use as a trekking horse. Crossed with the Thoroughbred, the Maremmana also produces a good jumping horse, with the Italian breed's resistance to fatigue and its sound constitution.

### Fascinating Facts

In the state of Arizona, it is illegal for cowboys to walk through a hotel lobby wearing their spurs.

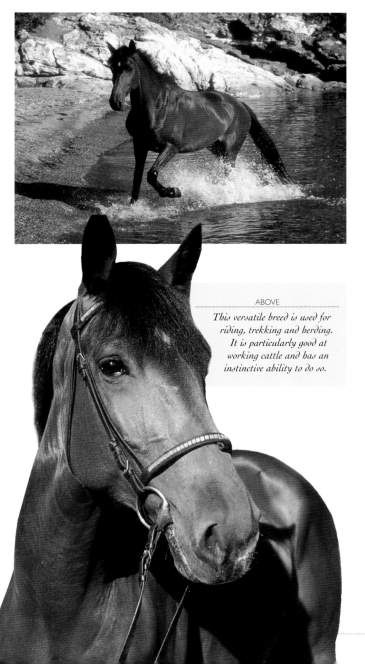

ABOVE

*This versatile breed is used for riding, trekking and herding. It is particularly good at working cattle and has an instinctive ability to do so.*

# SAN FRATELLANO

HEIGHT: 15.2–16 hh

COLOUR: black, bay, brown

PERSONALITY TYPE: warm-blooded

TYPICAL USE: riding, competition

TEMPERAMENT: robust, sensible, hardy

ORIGIN: Sicily

SIMILAR BREEDS: Sardinian, Murgese

**N**amed for the town of San Fratello, at the foot of the Nebrodi Mountains in eastern Sicily, the San Fratellano is the closest thing the island has to a wild horse, with a number roaming free in the Nebrodi Park, in what is now the province of Messina. It is thought to be very similar to the other local Italian breeds – Sicily lies off the 'toe' of the boot-shaped country – such as the Sardinian, Murgese and Sicilian, as well as the French Camargue and, more distantly, the Andalusian.

## Strong Warhorse

It is possible the San Fratellano is related to the Old Sicilian Horse, which was highly regarded by the Greeks, and to the Salerno, Italy's sport horse breed. During its long history, it has been a warhorse, a workhorse and even butchered for its meat. It was popular with the Norman nobility, having been preferred by the Saracens who ruled Sicily until the eleventh century. It was strong and high-spirited, and could bear the weight of a knight in full armour. In the mountainous regions of Italy and Spain, strength was often an advantage over speed.

It is thought the Norman knights who fought at the Battle of Hastings in England in 1066 were mounted on Sicilian horses.

## Natural Jumping Ability

Since then, English and Oriental blood have been introduced to refine the breed and improve on its rather heavy head, although most San Fratellanos still retain this characteristic. It is naturally athletic and sound, and a 'good doer', and is certainly not unattractive; it has a rather convex profile, balanced by a short, muscular neck, sloping shoulders and a broad, deep chest. Its back is strong and its hindquarters muscular and well formed. It has strong legs and good feet. It makes a good competition horse, as it has natural jumping ability.

Today, there are thought to be only about 800 San Fratellanos left in Sicily.

# MURGESE

TEMPERAMENT: amenable, willing

ORIGIN: Italy

SIMILAR BREEDS: Sardinian,
San Fratellano, Friesian

HEIGHT: 15–16 hh

COLOUR: black, grey, chestnut

PERSONALITY TYPE:
warm-blooded

TYPICAL USE: agriculture,
riding, police

A nother rare breed, the Murgese is found in the Murge region of Apulia in southern Italy and is thought to be at least 600 years old. Its natural habitat is dry limestone hills and, much like the harsh Slovenian Karst, the heartland of the old Lipizzaner, this environment invariably produces horses with good, dense bone, hard feet and a sound constitution. The breed resembles the Friesian and is usually black in colour, although chestnut and grey – a suggestion of Oriental influence – both occur.

was saved, but the modern Murgese probably bears little resemblance to the older stock.

It is now a light draught horse, lacking the quality of the Irish Draught, and there is a lack of uniformity of type. The studbook was opened in 1926, and efforts have been made to improve and unify it.

## Good Breeders

There are certain conformational faults, such as flat withers overloaded with muscle and upright shoulders, and these inhibit

free movement. But despite the limitations of its structure, the Murgese is fairly active and energetic, and is amenable, even-tempered and economical to keep. It can be used as a light agricultural horse or as a leisure animal, and is still used by the Italian police force. Crossed with a Thoroughbred or warmblood stallion, a Murgese mare will produce a better riding horse with more quality, good paces and a willing nature.

Murgese mares are good breeders, being well built and roomy, and also produce the strong mules that are still used in the Murge region.

RIGHT

*The Murgese is a rare Italian breed that is similar in appearance to the more prolific Friesian horse.*

## Draught Type

During the late fifteenth and early sixteenth centuries, the governor of Monopoly, in the Puglia region of Italy, kept Murgese stallions and several hundred broodmares to provide remounts for the cavalry, but about 200 years ago interest in the Murgese diminished and the breed almost died out. It

# SALERNO

HEIGHT: 16–17 hh

COLOUR: bay, chestnut, black, grey

PERSONALITY TYPE: warm-blooded

TYPICAL USE: riding, competition

TEMPERAMENT: kind, sensible, spirited

ORIGIN: Italy

SIMILAR BREEDS: Andalusian, San Fratellano

The result of crossing the Andalusian with Neapolitan stock, the Salerno was developed in the region of the same name near Naples in Italy in the sixteenth century as a cavalry horse – it was the official horse of the Italian Army until 1947. Charles III (1716–88), Don Carlos of Naples, who would later become king of Spain, founded the first recorded stud for the breed at Persano, south of Salerno in Campania, in 1763; the breed is sometimes called the Salernitano-Persano.

## Military Choice

As the Italian Army encouraged competitive equestrianism, it made the cavalry mounts available to its soldiers, an act which increased the Salerno's popularity as a sport horse. The Italian military had an equestrian jumping team, mounted primarily on Salernos, which was considered one of the best teams in the world from the end of the Second World War until the 1970s. The breed is naturally athletic, with excellent paces and natural jumping ability. It is also kind and easygoing, while being spirited and energetic, as well as easy to train.

*The Salerno is a popular Italian sports horse breed, and was used extensively by the Italian military equestrian teams for show jumping.*

## Best Jumper

It is thought to be Sicilian in origin, a mixture of Neapolitan, Spanish and Oriental blood. Thoroughbred blood was introduced in the early twentieth century, which greatly increased the quality of the breed. The modern Salerno is a large, upstanding horse with a handsome head with straight profile and square forehead. Its eyes are expressive, and its neck is long and muscular. It has a well-proportioned back, good shoulders, muscular croup and excellent well-formed legs.

It has the reputation of being one of the best show jumpers in the world, but is also beginning to make its presence felt in the dressage arena, where it may well shine because of its excellent temperament and trainability. Its kind nature makes it an amenable riding horse.

# EINSIEDLER

TEMPERAMENT: sensible, calm, intelligent

ORIGIN: Switzerland

SIMILAR BREEDS: all warmbloods

HEIGHT: 16.2 hh

COLOUR: all solid colours

PERSONALITY TYPE: warm-blooded

TYPICAL USE: riding, competition, harness

Switzerland's warmblood has been bred since the tenth century, founded on local Schwyer stock, and takes its name from the Benedictine Abbey of Einsiedeln in the centre of the country – so many of today's modern breeds have the world's monasteries to thank for their very existence. It is also known as the Swiss Warmblood, the Swiss Half-Blood or Schweizer Halbblut. The first studbook was opened in 1655; a more comprehensive version was compiled in 1784 by a Father Isidor Moser.

stallions, three of the most important being Ivoire, Que d'Espair and Orinate de Messil, and a Yorkshire Coach Horse named Bracken. The Swedish Warmblood Aladin also played an important role in the breed's development, as did two Holsteins, Astral and Chevalier.

In the 1960s, Swedish and Irish mares were imported to Avenches, where the stud was located. Avenches continues to be discriminating in its choice of stallions, and as well as the modern Einsiedler it stands Thoroughbreds, Hanoverians, Selle Français and Trakehners. As a result of the breeding programme, the number of imports is waning.

sloping croup. Its legs are strong with well-defined tendons and good joints.

Before an Einsiedler can be used for breeding, it has to pass rigorous tests, with stallions being tested at three and a half and again at five, and mares at three. The tests include jumping, dressage, cross-country and driving.

## Fascinating Facts

New Jersey's state animal is the horse, so designated in Chapter 173 of the Laws of 1977.

### BELOW

*The Swiss Warmblood or Einsiedler has to pass a stringent series of tests – conformation, temperament and ability – before being allowed to breed.*

## Unwise Outcrosses

The Einsiedler has had a somewhat chequered history. During the late seventeenth century and early eighteenth century, some unwise outcrossing to Spanish, Italian, Friesian and Turkish stallions proved detrimental. Later, the breed was improved by Anglo-Norman

## Performance Testing

The Einsiedler is now a superlative competition horse with strength, stamina, agility and good looks. It has a handsome head with straight or slightly convex profile; medium-length, well-proportioned neck; sloping shoulders; prominent withers; straight back and a slightly

# EAST FRIESIAN

HEIGHT: 16–17.2 hh

COLOUR: bay, chestnut, brown, black

PERSONALITY TYPE: warm-blooded

TYPICAL USE: riding, competition

TEMPERAMENT: docile, placid

ORIGIN: The Netherlands

SIMILAR BREEDS: Hanoverian, Oldenburg

In its original form, the 'old' East Friesian is now extinct. It was a heavy type of horse, somewhere between a draught and a warmblood, with warmblood gaits and characteristics. It was used mostly as a carriage or agricultural horse, and was similar to the modern Oldenburg. Its homeland in the Federal Republic of Germany neighboured the Oldenburg region, spreading from the estuary of the River Weser to the borders of the Netherlands; it was bred on similar lines until Germany divided.

## Hanoverian Influence

The East Friesian descended from a mix of Spanish, Neapolitan, Anglo-Arab and Thoroughbred blood. Oldenburg horses were registered in the East Friesian studbook, but this was not permitted the

other way round. The East Friesian has now been absorbed into the Hanoverian – Hanoverian blood was introduced to increase the size and substance of the breed, and the East Friesian registry has joined the Hanoverian's.

# WÜRTTEMBERG

HEIGHT: 16–17.2 hh

COLOUR: bay, chestnut, brown, black

PERSONALITY TYPE: warm-blooded

TYPICAL USE: riding, competition

TEMPERAMENT: sensible, trainable, calm

ORIGIN: Germany

SIMILAR BREEDS: all warmbloods

Germany's oldest state stud, the Marbach Stud at Württemberg, produced this impressive warmblood, a sturdy, handsome horse standing up to about 17.2 hh, but it was not recognized as an established breed until the end of the nineteenth century, when the breed society was founded in 1895 in Stuttgart. The original Württemberg, which dates back to the sixteenth century, was probably the result of Arab stallions put to the country's heavy draught mares.

## Lighter Version

The Marbach Stud was dispersed during the Thirty Years War (1618–48), and it was not until the end of the seventeenth century that the horse-breeding enterprise fully recovered. At that time, Barb and Spanish mares were introduced to Marbach, as well as East Friesian stallions. Later, Anglo-Norman and Trakehner blood was brought in. As equestrian sports became more popular, the lighter modern Württemberg took over from its heavier ancestors. In 1960, the Trakehner stallion Julmond arrived at Marbach, and is considered the breed's foundation sire.

# RHINELANDER

TEMPERAMENT: kind, sensible, trainable

ORIGIN: Germany

SIMILAR BREEDS: all warmbloods

HEIGHT: 16.2 hh

COLOUR: all solid colours, but chestnut most common

PERSONALITY TYPE: warm-blooded

TYPICAL USE: competition

Like all warmbloods, the Rhinelander is descended from the heavy draught breeds, in this case the Rheinish, which was widely considered to be one of the best German coldbloods. As mechanization increased, the need for this heavy horse for farm work diminished, and the old draught breed is no longer recognized in its native land. The Rhinelander, however, although it has only been in existence for some 50 years, has already made its mark in the competition arenas of all equestrian disciplines.

## New Breed

In the late 1950s and early 1960s, breeders began producing a riding-type warmblood to cater for the increasing demand for leisure and competition horses. Mares by Trakehner, Hanoverian and Thoroughbred stallions out of dams with Rheinish ancestry were crossed with stallions of the Hanover/Westphalia area. Stallions resulting from these crosses were then chosen to develop the Rhinelander breed. By 2003, 133 stallions and 3,056 breeding mares were registered with the studbook.

**BELOW**

*The Rhinelander is a relatively new breed and has been successfully developed to produce top competition and sporting horses.*

# WESTPHALIAN

TEMPERAMENT: calm, brave, intelligent

ORIGIN: Germany

SIMILAR BREEDS: all warmbloods

HEIGHT: 15.2–16.2 hh

COLOUR: all solid colours

PERSONALITY TYPE: warm-blooded

TYPICAL USE: competition, harness, riding

Westphalia's coat of arms depicts a jumping horse and, like its neighbour, Hanover, the state has a long tradition of horse breeding. In 1826, the state stud Landgestuet was founded at Warendorf, and in March 1904 the Westphalian Breed Registry was opened in Münster. The first Westphalians were bred based on Oldenburg blood, as well as Anglo-Norman. Since 1920, Westphalian warmblood breeding has been based on Hanoverian lines.

## Dressage Star

The Westphalian first came to the attention of the competition horse world in the late 1970s, when Roman won the World Show Jumping Championship in 1978. In 1982, Fire, another Westphalian, won the jumping in the World Championships, and Ahlerich claimed the dressage equivalent. The Westphalian has a courageous, spirited temperament, but is very willing and docile. Today, the breed is used for general riding and harness work, including carriage driving. It is most talented, however, in show jumping and dressage, and some also excel in three-day eventing.

# HANOVERIAN

HEIGHT: 17 hh

COLOUR: all solid colours

PERSONALITY TYPE: warm-blooded

TYPICAL USE: competition

TEMPERAMENT: level-headed, kind, intelligent

ORIGIN: Germany

SIMILAR BREEDS: all warmbloods

**P**erhaps the best known of all the warmblood breeds – as well as the most successful – the Hanoverian originates from what was the kingdom of Hanover in the state of Lower Saxony in northern Germany. George Louis, Elector of Hanover and later King George II of Great Britain and Ireland, established the first stud in 1735 at Celle. The aim was to produce a quality horse for carriages, riding and agriculture. It was selectively bred from local stock, Thoroughbreds and 14 black Holstein stallions.

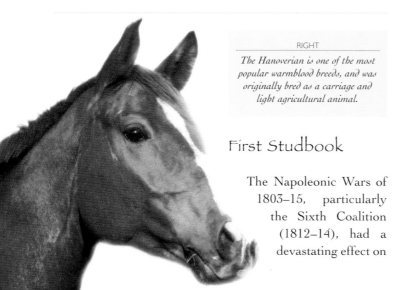

### RIGHT

*The Hanoverian is one of the most popular warmblood breeds, and was originally bred as a carriage and light agricultural animal.*

## First Studbook

The Napoleonic Wars of 1803–15, particularly the Sixth Coalition (1812–14), had a devastating effect on the breeding programme of the Hanoverian; by 1816, there were only 30 stallions remaining – at one time there had been 100. Large numbers of Thoroughbreds were imported to Celle, until 35 per cent of the stock was Thoroughbred, and this had the effect of greatly lightening the breed. The Hanoverian soon became too light to perform the agricultural tasks required, and an effort was made to increase its overall frame using more Holstein blood. The studbook, Verband Hannoverscher Warmblut-zuchter, was opened in 1888.

## Trakehner Influence

By 1924, the numbers of Hanoverians were rapidly increasing, and there were some 500 stallions standing at Celle. Due to the growing demand, another stud was opened at Osnabruck-Eversburg, with 100 stallions. After the Second World War, there was a move towards creating a

lighter type more suitable for riding – Hanoverians had been used extensively by the military – using infusions of Trakehner and Thorough-bred blood.

Today's Hanoverian is an excellent competition horse, both in dressage and jumping, and it is frequently used to improve other breeds. It probably bears little resemblance to the original model first produced in the eighteenth century.

## Elastic Paces

The modern Hanoverian is a noble, correctly proportioned warmblood with natural balance, impulsion and elegant, elastic paces, characterized by a floating trot, a round rhythmic canter and a ground-covering walk. Breeding stock is carefully inspected and selected for correct conformation, athletic ability and inner qualities such as disposition and trainability – the Hanoverian is renowned for its level-headedness, willingness and calm, kind temperament. It is athletic and strong, and shines in all equestrian disciplines.

## Substantial Equine

The Hanoverian has a rather straight head that is in no way coarse. Its neck is strong and well proportioned; it has pronounced withers that extend well into its back, and sloping shoulders. It has a powerful body with deep girth and plenty of heart room, well-sprung ribs and strong hindquarters with sloping croup. Its hocks are broad, clear and well defined, its legs are strong with plenty of bone and it has well-shaped strong sound feet. A substantial creature, the Hanoverian can stand up to 17 hh.

## Breeding Eligibility

Breeding of this excellent warmblood is closely monitored, with only approved and graded

stallions permitted to stand at stud. All stallions must be presented for physical inspection annually to verify their eligibility for breeding. They are granted only a temporary breeding licence, if they score sufficiently highly on conformation, movement and jumping ability.

Within two years, stallions must complete and pass the 100-day stallion performance test that evaluates paces, trainability and athletic ability in dressage, show jumping and cross-country. Mares are also tested, from the age of two and a half, when they are evaluated on type, conformation and movement. A distinctly masculine bearing is desirable in stallions, and mares should have a marked feminine expression.

*RIGHT*

*The modern Hanoverian is much lighter in build than its ancestors, and is recognized as one of the top show jumping breeds in the world.*

# TRAKEHNER

HEIGHT: 16–17 hh

COLOUR: all solid colours

PERSONALITY TYPE: warm-blooded

TYPICAL USE: competition, riding

TEMPERAMENT: alert, intelligent, anxious to please

ORIGIN: Germany

SIMILAR BREEDS: all warmbloods

One of the oldest of all the warmblood breeds, this horse takes its name from the royal stud farm established at Trakehnen, East Prussia, in what is now Poland. Friedrich Wilhelm I of Prussia (1688–1740) realized that a new type of cavalry mount was needed because war tactics had changed, demanding a faster, lighter horse that also possessed power and endurance. In 1732, he moved the best of his cavalry horses to the new royal stud farm and began systematically breeding a horse that would meet these criteria.

## Spirit and Stability

The new cavalry mounts had to be attractive enough to be a representative horse for his officers, but additionally had to be tough enough to survive

**LEFT**

*The Trakehner is one of the oldest and also most popular of the warmblood breeds, and has excelled in the competitive field.*

harsh situations and come out sound. Through his efforts, the Trakehner breed (also known as the East Prussian) evolved.

The foundation stock was the small, native mares called *Schwaike*, which possessed great speed and stamina. When mated to Thoroughbred stallions, these sturdy little mares produced a fast and willing warhorse that could also be used to work the East Prussian farms during times of peace. The object, ultimately, was to add the size, nerve, spirit and endurance of the Thoroughbred to the bulk, stability and nobility of the native breed. Further refinement came with the addition of Arabian blood.

## Floating Trot

Today's Trakehner is characterized by great substance and bone, yet it also displays surprising

refinement, perhaps more so than any other European warmblood breed. It is a superb performance horse with natural elegance and balance. It excels in dressage because of its elegant way of moving – the light, springy floating trot and soft, balanced canter – and the breed also produces excellent jumpers. Perhaps the most outstanding attribute of the Trakehner, however, is its temperament – keen, alert and intelligent, it is also sensible and accepting, and anxious to please.

## Olympic Glory

In 1787, the Trakehnen Stud was taken over by Count Lindenau who, as part of a programme to improve the breed, eliminated a third of the broodmares and two-thirds of the existing stallions. The first studbook was opened in 1877, since when further Thoroughbred and Arabian blood has been introduced only when deemed strictly necessary.

The breed was soon in high demand – good-looking and athletic, Trakehners won every medal for the German Olympic Team at the 1936 Olympics in Berlin. With the Thoroughbred's speed, the Trakehner also excelled in racing, representatives of the breed winning the fearsome Pardubice Steeplechase in the old Czechoslovakia nine times in 15 years.

## The Trek

Although affected by the First World War, the breed quickly recovered – it was

## Fascinating Facts

The trakehner cross-country fence is so-named because, when draining the wetlands area of Trakehnen, East Prussia, in the seventeenth and eighteenth centuries, such fencelines were built in drainage ditches. These fences were also used as a test for the young Trakehner horses of the area.

RIGHT

*Typically Trakehners are beautifully conformed horses and have a natural, free flowing stride, combined with great intelligence and trainability.*

the Second World War that was to bring it to its knees. The defeat of Germany in 1945 led to a retreat from East Prussia, and 1,200 of the 25,000 Trakehners embarked on a three-month march, loaded with their owners' meagre possessions, to the west – this incredible journey is known simply as 'the Trek'. Many were mares in foal, and a considerable

number could not endure the rigorous journey. It is thought that only about 100 horses survived, but those that did are testament to the endurance and hardiness of the modern Trakehner.

The new studbook, the West German Trakehner Verband, was opened in 1947, as the breed was re-established, with remaining Trakehners being painstakingly tracked down and the bloodlines revived without being compromised.

## Thoroughbred Influences

The Trakehner's Thoroughbred influences are clear. It has the refined head, long, arching neck and regal bearing of its ancestry, with the deep sloping shoulders and moderately long back, powerful hindquarters and

strong joints and muscles. These attributes, as well as the Trakehner's kind, honest temperament, have been used to improve other warmblood breeds.

# OLDENBURG

HEIGHT: 16.2–17.2 hh

COLOUR: black, bay, brown, grey

PERSONALITY TYPE: warm-blooded

TYPICAL USE: competition, harness, riding

TEMPERAMENT: kind, calm, intelligent

ORIGIN: Germany

SIMILAR BREEDS: all warmbloods

First bred as a carriage horse, the Oldenburg breed has changed considerably since its development in Germany in the seventeenth century. The 'old' Oldenburg achieved fame throughout Europe under Count Anton Günther von Oldenburg (1603–67), who was renowned as a great horseman and enthusiast of the breed. His aim was to produce a large quality carriage horse that was also able to work as an agricultural horse, and he built the royal stables and riding school at Rastede.

## Eclipse Line

He began to import Spanish and Neapolitan horses, and used these to cross with the East Friesian. One important stallion influential in the early development of the breed was the grey Kranich, who descended from good Spanish lines.

These early Oldenburgs would have been quite heavy-framed and rather coarse in appearance – they are documented as having a pronounced Roman nose. In

the late eighteenth century, Barb, Thoroughbred and Norfolk Roadster blood were introduced to add refinement. In 1897, a Thoroughbred line was introduced that is believed to trace back to the famous Eclipse.

Also around this time, Cleveland Bay stallions were used. The Cleveland Bay was a notable carriage horse of the time, as well as being extremely useful as a riding horse with a good natural jump. There were also infusions of Hanoverian and Anglo-Norman blood.

RIGHT

*The Oldenburg was originally bred as a carriage horse, and is still often used in competitive driving classes.*

## War Losses

The Oldenburg was used during the First World War by the cavalry, but the breed suffered great losses in battle. Afterwards, the Oldenburg was once again chiefly employed for harness and agricultural purposes, and it was not until after the Second World War that there were further efforts to lighten and improve the breed.

With the advent of mechanization and motor vehicles, the breed again fell into decline, and it was realized by Oldenburg enthusiasts that it was necessary to focus breeding on the production of a versatile riding horse. To this end, there were further infusions of Thoroughbred blood, most notably from the stallion Lupus, and more Norman stock, especially from the stallion Condor, who had a high percentage of Thoroughbred blood.

In order to prevent the Thoroughbred characteristics, particularly the 'hot' temperament, from dominating, there was the continued use of Hanoverian blood, which helped to maintain the excellent Oldenburg nature.

## French Sires

The successes with Condor meant that Oldenburg breeders once more turned to French stallions to use on Oldenburg mares. One of the most successful was Furioso II, a highly regarded sire, and the Anglo-Arab Inschallah AA. These influences have shaped the modern Oldenburg into the supreme sport horse it is today. The Thoroughbred blood has added speed, and the high knee action of the original Oldenburg coach-horse type has been mostly eradicated.

The vestiges of this high action has done the Oldenburg no harm, however, in the dressage arena. The Oldenburg Bonfire was ridden to multiple World Cup dressage titles by Anky van Grunsven, and individual dressage gold at the Olympic Games in Sydney in 2000.

## Robust Frame

Like all warmbloods, the modern Oldenburg has the Thoroughbred's good looks, although on a more robust frame. Its head is fine and noble, sometimes with a slightly convex profile, and it has large, kind eyes. A good length of muscular neck is balanced by powerful sloping shoulders and a broad, deep chest. Deep through the girth, it has a long back, muscular quarters and a well-set tail. The horse carries itself proudly, pushing from its hocks and powerful hindquarters for energetic, forward-going paces with active long strides.

The breed now shines in all competitive equestrian disciplines, including carriage driving, for which the Oldenburg was originally formed some four centuries ago.

# HOLSTEIN

HEIGHT: 16–16.3 hh

COLOUR: mostly bay

PERSONALITY TYPE: warm-blooded

TYPICAL USE: competition, harness, riding

TEMPERAMENT: honest, willing, kind

ORIGIN: Germany

SIMILAR BREEDS: all warmbloods

While it might have one of the smallest equine studbooks, there can be no doubting the Holstein warmblood breed is a resounding success. At the 1976 Olympics in Montreal, Canada, Holsteins dominated the proceedings – Granat won the individual dressage gold medal and Madrigal the silver; Albrant won the silver medal in the three-day event; and Torphy earned a silver in show jumping. The same year, Emil Jung won the world four-in-hand driving championship with a team of Holsteins.

## Regal bearing

The Holstein is similar to the Hanoverian and was developed in the state of Schleswig-Holstein, tracing back to a heavy warhorse of the fourteenth century. It was crossed with Andalusian and Arabian stock to lighten the breed then, in the sixteenth and seventeenth centuries, more Spanish and some Neapolitan blood were added. These lines dominated the appearance of the Holstein, which had become an impressive large horse with a Roman nose and regal bearing.

It was well suited to both farm and military work, but, as with so many horse breeds, mechanization made it largely redundant in the nineteenth century. Thoroughbred blood was then added to create a more elegant horse for riding and, latterly, competition.

## Performance

The modern Holstein resembles its warmblood cousins, with its robust good looks, athletic versatility and kind, honest temperament. Its noble head still has the impression of a slight Roman nose, but this in no way detracts from its beauty. It has the long neck, sloping shoulders and powerful hindquarters that promise excellent performance.

And when the Holstein begins to move, its reputation as one of the world's finest sport horses is assured. With its strong haunches providing impulsion, it moves forwards with elevation and suspension, creating an impression of strength, balance and elasticity. This

BELOW
*The Holstein is another of the premium warmblood breeds, and makes an excellent competition horse, being particularly notable for its free flowing action.*

fluid movement, coupled with renowned intelligence, willingness to work and kind temperament, makes the Holstein the ideal sport horse.

# FRIESIAN

TEMPERAMENT: equable, willing, kind

ORIGIN: The Netherlands

SIMILAR BREEDS: East Friesian, Dales, Fell, warmbloods

HEIGHT: 14.3–15.3 hh

COLOUR: black

PERSONALITY TYPE: warm-blooded

TYPICAL USE: riding, driving

A mere century ago, the Friesian was almost extinct. It was originally a heavy draught type, like the East Friesian, probably based on the primitive Forest Horse, a huge coldblood that is now extinct, and crossed with lighter types to produce a heavy but elegant equine with a coal-black coat. It is thought to be one of the oldest domesticated breeds in Europe, native to the province of Friesland in the northern Netherlands – there are references to the Friesian throughout history.

popular. During the Spanish occupation of the Netherlands (1568–1648), infusions of Spanish blood

LEFT

*These magnificent horses with their noble bearing and extravagant action were used to carry the medieval knight into battle.*

were probably added, but not to its detriment. The Friesian is a horse of great beauty, with the abundant, rippling mane and tail that betray those Spanish ancestors.

## Matched Black

During the First World War, the Friesian was almost lost, but Oldenburg blood was used successfully to reestablish the breed. Indeed,

the Friesian contributed to the development of the Oldenburg, and has influenced other equines, notably the American Morgan, the English Fell and Dales ponies and the Shire.

Its Spanish heritage can also be seen in its rather long, fine head, with an elegant, expressive face. It has a powerful neck set on excellent shoulders, a compact body and short, strong legs with hard feet. It also has abundant feather (fine, long hair around its fetlocks) and is always black, with only a small white star permitted. It retains its high-stepping action, which makes it particularly successful as a driving horse – a team of Friesians, in perfectly matched black, is a magnificent spectacle.

## Old Masters

Often painted by the Dutch Old Masters carrying knights into battle, the Friesian made a superb warhorse. What it lacked in height it more than made up for in strength – it was easily capable of carrying a knight in full armour – and its extravagant knee action and proud bearing made it

# GRONINGEN

HEIGHT: 15.2–16 hh

COLOUR: bay, brown, black

PERSONALITY TYPE: warm-blooded

TYPICAL USE: riding, driving

TEMPERAMENT: kind, willing

ORIGIN: The Netherlands

SIMILAR BREEDS: Oldenburg, Gelderlander, warmbloods

The Oldenburg also played a part in the development of the Groningen, along with East Friesian and Friesian. It is somewhere between a draught horse type and a warmblood, being heavier and plainer than its more attractive cousins. What it lacks in looks it more than makes up for in stamina, endurance and versatility. Originally bred as an all-purpose agricultural horse, it also made a good heavyweight riding horse and was useful in harness. It was reliable and could go all day.

**BELOW**

*These useful and versatile horses fall between being a light draught animal and a heavyweight riding horse, and excel in both capacities.*

## One Stallion

From about 1945, numbers of the Groningen have dwindled as the demand for powerful workhorses decreased. By the 1970s, they were virtually extinct, with only one purebred stallion remaining, named Baldewijn. Since then,

there have been efforts by enthusiasts to preserve the breed with recent infusions of Oldenburg blood. The Groningen now has improved conformation and is more compact, with better, more sloping shoulders, mainly due to this outcross. Later, Thoroughbred and Trakehner blood were introduced, to keep the Groningen breed going without compromising it.

## Sloping Shoulders

Today's Groningen is a medium-weight horse with quite plain features, although it does have natural presence and carriage. Its head has a tendency to be quite long and

plain, with a straight profile and long ears. Its neck is very muscular, and its withers are reasonably prominent and long. The shoulders have

## Fascinating Facts

Miniature horses are sometimes used as 'guide horses' in the same way that dogs are used to help the blind.

become more sloping in recent years – probably thanks to the Thoroughbred influences – having originally been quite upright, which gave the breed a short stride. The back can be quite long and the croup flat. The quarters are very muscular, and the tail is set and carried high. The legs are short but strong, and it has good feet. Typically, the Groningen has an excellent temperament, being willing and kind, and it is also an economical feeder.

# GELDERLANDER

TEMPERAMENT: docile, co-operative, honest

ORIGIN: The Netherlands

SIMILAR BREEDS: all warmbloods

HEIGHT: 15.2–16.2 hh

COLOUR: mostly chestnut, bay, grey, black

PERSONALITY TYPE: warm-blooded

TYPICAL USE: harness, riding

A far more handsome creature than the Groningen is the Gelderlander, developed originally as an agricultural horse that had enough quality to be a suitable riding horse too. The people of the Gelderland province of the Netherlands crossed their native mares to Andalusian, Norfolk Roadster, Neapolitan and Norman stallions; later, infusions of Arabian, Anglo-Arab, Furioso, Holstein and Orlov blood were added. In the nineteenth century, English Thoroughbred, Hackney and Oldenburg blood were introduced.

## Fixed Type

Given the diversity of influences, it is extraordinary that a horse of such fixed type should have evolved, but the Gelderlander is widely regarded as being one of the best all-round sport horses of modern times.

It is an extremely versatile horse, with an excellent quiet temperament. The infusions of Thoroughbred have given the breed a certain amount of class, and it makes an eye-catching medium-weight carriage horse. It is increasingly being used for competitive driving, to which it is well suited, being both strong and agile, with plenty of stamina.

It also makes a good middleweight riding horse and possesses a natural jumping ability – although, despite the Thoroughbred influence, it does tend to lack speed. It has great presence and elegance, with a free-flowing action and a particularly stylish high-stepping trot.

## Muscular and Strong

The Gelderlander generally has good conformation, with a long, sometimes plain head and straight profile. Its neck is muscular and gently curves from broad withers to the poll; it is broad and deep

ABOVE

*The Gelderlander horse is athletically built with a willing temperament, and is sought after as a sports horse, and for driving.*

through the chest and has strong shoulders. Its back is straight and long, with muscular quarters, and its tail is set and carried high. Its legs are well-muscled and quite short, with good, strong joints and very hard hooves.

Numbers of the Gelderlander have decreased in recent years, although the breed is used to produce Dutch Warmbloods, which are a much higher calibre of competition horse.

# DUTCH WARMBLOOD

HEIGHT: 16–16.3 hh

COLOUR: bay, grey, chestnut, black

PERSONALITY TYPE: warm-blooded

TYPICAL USE: competition, harness

TEMPERAMENT: sensible, intelligent, trainable

ORIGIN: The Netherlands

SIMILAR BREEDS: all warmbloods

A relatively new breed, the Dutch Warmblood was developed as a versatile riding horse, rather than an agricultural working animal. It combines the finest elements of the Groningen and the Gelderlander with Thoroughbred, Trakehner and Oldenburg blood. The Thoroughbred blood added quality, refinement, speed and courage, while keeping the fundamental level-headedness and calm, sensible nature of the warmblood type. The result is an extremely athletic horse, with good looks and good temper.

## Sophisticated Testing

Although Dutch Warmblood stallions are owned by individuals, the breeding of the horse is monitored by the state-aided Warmbloed Paardenstamboek Nederland. Stallions may be used for breeding only if they pass the

### LEFT
*The Dutch Warmblood is possibly one of the most successful young warmblood breeds, and is a world leader in dressage and show jumping.*

rigorous testing process. All aspects of the stallion are judged, from temperament to athletic ability and intelligence, but their conformation and movement are equally important. The stallions have their lower legs and feet X-rayed to make sure that any conformation faults are eliminated.

Mares are also tested, and the resulting offspring are closely monitored to track their success or failure as a breed standard. This process of testing is one of the most sophisticated approaches used in the world and, as a result, has led to the quick growth and success of this relatively new breed.

## Natural Agility

The Dutch Warmblood is an attractive, athletic horse, with a free-flowing, extravagant movement that has brought it worldwide fame in the dressage arena, but its natural

agility also makes it a good show jumper. Like many warmbloods, it is not the fastest horse, but further infusions of Thoroughbred blood can add speed. It has a handsome, noble head with a wide forehead, a muscular neck, sloping shoulders, deep chest, straight back and powerful hindquarters.

The Dutch studbook is divided into three: the Rijpaardtype, or riding horse; the Tuigpaardtype, or harness horse; and the Basistype, or basic type, most similar to the traditional Gelderlander.

# KNABSTRUP

**TEMPERAMENT:** sensible, alert, intelligent

**ORIGIN:** Denmark

**SIMILAR BREEDS:** Frederiksborg

HEIGHT: 15.1–16.1 hh

COLOUR: spotted

PERSONALITY TYPE: warm-blooded

TYPICAL USE: riding, harness, show

Spotted horses have existed in Denmark at least since the 1600s, when there was a popular strain of 'Tiger Horses' – highly regarded, they were almost solely used by royalty and nobility; those with few spots or plain coats were used as carriage horses, as the spotted equines were hard to match up. The royal line of spotted horses died out, however, probably because of the introduction of the grey gene. The spotted horses of Denmark were resurrected through a mare called Flaebe.

## Great Quality

In 1812, Villars Lunn, owner of a manor called Knabstrupgaard, bought a mare from a butcher called

Flaebe – the mare was named after her owner, as was the custom of the times. It is believed she was of Spanish origin, left behind by a cavalry officer stationed in Denmark during the Napoleonic Wars. Flaebe was dark red – or *zobelfuchs*, in Danish – in colour, with white mane and tail, and her body was covered with tiny white snowflakes. Most

importantly, she was a horse of great quality.

## Glorious Colouring

Flaebe showed her value when she was one of two horses harnessed to take an injured man to a doctor, a journey of around 30 km (18 miles) completed in less than two hours. The first horse never fully recovered, but

Flaebe was back working the fields the following day. Covered by a chestnut Frederiksborg stallion, Flaebe foaled a colt, named the Flaebestallion, which was to be the foundation of the Knabstrup breed. Another colt out of Flaebe was Mikkel, famed for his speed on the racetrack.

The modern Knabstrup is just as striking, with the foundation mare's glorious colouring, the speed of her second offspring and the robust good looks she passed on to the new breed. Sadly, today it is considered quite rare.

## Fascinating Facts

One reason for the tradition of mounting on the near side of a horse is that, historically, men's scabbards would be worn on the left hip and so would get in the way if a horse was mounted from the off side.

LEFT

*Sadly the numbers of this beautiful breed with its spotted coat colouring have become greatly reduced, although efforts are being made to preserve it. The horse pictured has a rare white coat, with very subtle spotting*

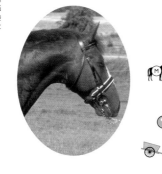

# FREDERIKSBORG

HEIGHT: 15.2–16 hh

COLOUR: chestnut

PERSONALITY TYPE: warm-blooded

TYPICAL USE: riding, harness

TEMPERAMENT: docile, steady

ORIGIN: Denmark

SIMILAR BREEDS: Knabstrup

**N**amed for Frederik II (1534–88), Denmark's oldest breed is literally the horse of kings. It was first bred at the royal stud at Frederiksborg and, during the eighteenth century, was one of the world's most famous equine breeds. It was highly prized as a reliable and elegant riding horse, well suited to the movements of the *haute école*, a high-class carriage horse and a superb military charger. King Frederik imported horses from Italy and Spain to lighten and refine the native stock.

The Frederiksborg passed on its smooth, supple action and its strength and stamina, and this was almost to prove the breed's undoing. So many had been exported because of its popularity that there were few left. Efforts to re-establish the Frederiksborg

LEFT
*Two strains of Frederiksborg were bred, a lighter type for riding and a heavy type used as carriage horses.*

began in the early twentieth century and, although the breed is still fairly rare, could be deemed successful.

## Strong and Attractive

The Frederiksborg is a strong, attractive horse, always chestnut with a flaxen mane and tail, often with white markings on the face and/or legs. Its head is well proportioned, with a

## Fascinating Facts

According to superstition in Lincolnshire, England, if you see a white dog, you should stay silent until you see a white horse.

straight or sometimes convex profile, pointed, mobile ears and large, expressive eyes. Its neck is of medium length, slightly arched and muscular; its shoulders tend to be rather straight, and the withers are pronounced. Its back is short and straight, with a rounded croup. It has excellent legs, well muscled and strong, with broad joints, good bone and small but tough feet.

Latterly, breeding has concentrated on breeding the riding type, rather than the carriage type.

## Two Types

Two distinct types were bred, the riding horse and the carriage horse – for the latter, uniformity of colour and markings was paramount, as the royal carriages were pulled by six or eight perfectly matched horses. The Frederiksborg was also used to found or improve other horse breeds during the seventeenth, eighteenth and nineteenth centuries.

# DANISH WARMBLOOD

TEMPERAMENT: amiable, tough, bold

ORIGIN: Denmark

SIMILAR BREEDS: all warmbloods

HEIGHT: 16.2 hh

COLOUR: mostly bay, but any solid colour

PERSONALITY TYPE: warm-blooded

TYPICAL USE: competition, riding

In 1999, a horse called Marzog, ridden by Anne Grethe Tornblad, was described by an international jury as the 'best dressage horse of the century'. Marzog was a Danish Warmblood. Denmark has a long history of horse breeding that dates back to the fourteenth century, and the monastic stud at Holstein and the royal stud of Frederiksborg both made a contribution to the Danish Warmblood. Also known as the Danish Sport Horse, it is the product of careful and selective breeding.

## No Hanoverian

The Danish Warmblood studbook was opened in the 1960s, and the new breed was based on several different bloodlines. The Frederiksborg, when crossed with the Thoroughbred, produced a quality middle- to heavyweight riding horse; when Trakehner, Selle Français and Wielkopolski blood, plus a little more Thoroughbred, were added, it improved the animal considerably and a distinct type emerged – the Danish Warmblood. Unlike many of today's warmbloods, the Danish version contains no Hanoverian.

## Stringent Examination

Danish Warmblood stallions have to undergo rigorous 100-day testing, but even this stringent examination does not necessarily guarantee approval. This helps to maintain the extraordinarily high standards of the breed. The Danish Warmblood is a horse of great quality with a Thoroughbred look, but with more weight and substance. It has excellent stamina, speed and jumping ability, as well as superb natural elevation through the paces. It has a refined, attractive head set on a muscular neck with good length of rein and a deep, broad chest. Its shoulders should be sloping and its back compact and strong. Its legs are muscular and clean, with particularly well-made hock joints and perfectly formed feet. Like all warmbloods, the Danish has an exceptionally amiable temperament and is both tough and bold, with a beautiful, free-flowing movement.

Marzog is, as will no doubt be seen, one of many successful Danish Warmbloods

BELOW

*The excellent, athletic conformation and intelligence of this breed has seen it rapidly grow in popularity, and become one of the leading sports horse breeds.*

# SWEDISH WARMBLOOD

HEIGHT: 15.2–16.3 hh

COLOUR: all solid colours

PERSONALITY TYPE: warm-blooded

TYPICAL USE: competition

TEMPERAMENT: calm, even-tempered

ORIGIN: Sweden

SIMILAR BREEDS: all warmbloods

Archeological evidence has been found for the existence of horses in what is now Sweden dating to 4,000 BC, and the history of the Swedish horse closely follows that of humans in the region. The original Scandinavian horse was probably quite small, standing no more than 14 hh, high-spirited and having good endurance. In the sixteenth century, a programme was begun to improve the quality of these native horses. Friesians were imported from the Netherlands to increase the size of the native stock.

## Divided Breeding

Following the peace treaty with Denmark at Roskilde, Sweden, in 1658, the Swedish king Carl X Gustav (1622–60) ordered a royal stud to be established at Flyinge. The horses from Flyinge and the national stud farms, which included those at Kungsör and Strömsholm, were often used in the royal stables. Other importations of various saddle breeds were made, but the larger draught breeds were excluded.

The army and the farmers of Sweden had different equine requirements, which meant that the programme was divided. Thoroughbred, Anglo-Norman, Hanoverian and Trakehner stallions were imported to improve the military horse. To direct the breeding efforts and to consolidate the different breeds, the Swedish government began an examination system in 1874, which was to result in the production of the Swedish Warmblood. The Swedish Warmblood Association (SWA) was formed in 1928.

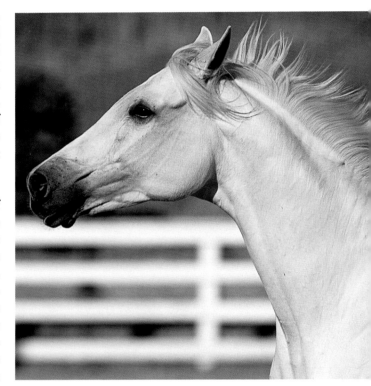

## Olympic Medals

At the Olympic Games in 1912, Swedish Warmbloods won all three dressage medals. At the Rome Olympics in 1960, the Swedish Warmblood sire Drabant had six sons participating. At Seoul in 1988, 13 Swedish Warmbloods competed and six won medals.

Today, the Swedish Warmblood continues to be a superior riding horse with tremendous rideability and intelligence. It is, like most warmblood breeds, pleasing to the eye, with a small, neat head, straight neck, compact body, straight back, rounded quarters and strong legs with short cannons and good feet. It is suitable for both the professional and the amateur rider.

LEFT

*The Swedish Warmblood is another success story in the recent development of warmblood breeds, and particularly excels at dressage.*

# FINNISH UNIVERSAL

TEMPERAMENT: alert, reliable, easygoing

ORIGIN: Finland

SIMILAR BREEDS: light draught horses

HEIGHT: 15.2 hh

COLOUR: chestnut, bay, brown, black

PERSONALITY TYPE: warm-blooded

TYPICAL USE: harness, riding

Its name describes it perfectly. The Finnish Universal, or Finnhorse, is so called because it is said to be able to fulfil all needs for horses in Finland, from draught types to speedy trotters to leisure. In Finnish, it is Suomenhevonen, or Suokki – a sort of pet name. It is thought to be about 1,000 years old and in Finland has been universal indeed, being used as a warhorse by the military, then as a mode of transport and more recently as a trotter. But it is becoming increasingly popular as a sport and leisure animal.

## Mostly Trotters

The Finnish Universal is a sturdy creature standing about 15.2 hh and is of medium build. It is probably based on local stock – it is known there were horses in Finland from around the Bronze Age (3500–1100 BC) – crossed with native ponies from countries along the Baltic coastland and imported foreign breeds. So it is, essentially, a warmblood, although it does exhibit some coldblood characteristics, having an easygoing and docile nature. It is also kind and willing, with a fast-stepping, naturally active stride.

## Coldblood Attributes

Although it has attributes of cold-blooded horses, the Finnish Universal is not unattractive. It has a well-shaped head that is not too large, a strong neck, and powerful shoulders and quarters. Its legs are clean and well muscled, without much feather. It is most often chestnut, although bay, black, brown and the occasional grey do occur. White markings are acceptable.

## Fascinating Facts

Trotting is very popular in Finland, and most of the Finnhorse population is used as trotters – there are an estimated 19,000 Finnish Universals, of which about 2,000 are used as riding horses and about 1,000 as agricultural animals; the rest are trotters.

BELOW
*Although not striking in appearance, the Finnish Universal is an extremely versatile breed and makes an excellent riding horse and light draught animal.*

The Finnish Universal studbook was opened in 1907, and horses have to undergo quite stringent performance testing, which is designed to keep the breed clean.

# ICELANDIC

HEIGHT: 12.3–13.2 hh

COLOUR: all solid colours

PERSONALITY TYPE: warm-blooded

TYPICAL USE: riding, show, all-rounder

TEMPERAMENT: docile, gentle, lively

ORIGIN: Iceland

SIMILAR BREEDS: Exmoor

There is no word in Icelandic for 'pony', so the country's little equine is always known as the Icelandic Horse. Its history dates back to the first settlers of Iceland in the late ninth century, when the Vikings brought with them horses of various origins – claimed by some to be a breed called *Equus scandinavicus* that was in the peninsula and northern Europe at the time. Due to the isolation of Iceland, this stock remained pure, while it was crossbred elsewhere and the original equine type was lost.

## Norse Mythology

The Icelandic bears some resemblance to England's

little Exmoor – it has similar characteristics to the 'toad eye', double-layered coat and 'snow chute' tail, attributes that would be almost essential to survival in the 'land of fire and ice'.

The Icelandic has played a vital role in its home country from the beginning. In heathen times, the horse was highly regarded and renowned in Norse mythology – it played a big part in Norse mythological stories, as several Norse gods and their enemies, the giants, owned them. The most famous of all these mythological horses was Sleipnir, the eight-footed pacer. The influence of the Norse myths is still visible, as many riding clubs bear names of mythical horses, as do

herds of horses in modern Iceland.

## Useful Servant

More prosaically, to the people of Iceland, the horse was the 'most useful servant'. It literally followed humans from birth to death, from fetching the doctor and midwife to pulling the coffin to the cemetery.

The first automobile arrived in Iceland in the year 1904, and almost immediately the horse became redundant.

## Fascinating Facts

The Icelandic is one of the five-gaited breeds, possessing the lateral *tölt* – a one-two-three-four beat gait that is fast and enormously comfortable for the rider. At shows, Icelandic Horses are often ridden at the *tölt* while the rider holds a full glass of beer in one hand and the reins in the other, without spilling a drop.

ABOVE LEFT

*The ancient Icelandic horse breed is particularly tough and willing, and has a fast, smooth, running gait called the 'tölt'.*

Enthusiastic individuals, however, kept breeding good horses, and Iceland's first horse breeding association was formed the same year the automobile arrived. Today, there are about 80,000 horses in Iceland, no small number for a country with just 270,000 human inhabitants.

# KLADRUBER

TEMPERAMENT: calm, kind, energetic

ORIGIN: former Czechoslovakia

SIMILAR BREEDS: Lipizzaner

HEIGHT: 16.2–17.2 hh

COLOUR: grey, black

PERSONALITY TYPE: warm-blooded

TYPICAL USE: harness, riding

Emperors and kings were patrons of the old Kladruby stud, founded in 1579 by Rudolf II, Holy Roman Emperor (and King of Bohemia, now the Czech Republic), and located at the Perlstein stables, where Maximilian II (1527–76) had bred horses for the previous 20 years. The horses were based mainly on imported Spanish and Italian horses, crossed with Neapolitan, Danish, Holstein, Irish, heavier Czech and Oldenburgs. All of the bloodlines used had some Andalusian breeding in their pedigree, and the breed was sometimes called *Equus bohemicus*.

## Grey and Black

The Kladruber has many similarities to the Lipizzaner, which was bred along much the same lines. It was

ABOVE

*The Kladruber is an attractive breed that is always either black or grey. They make excellent driving horses, and are popular as riding horses.*

originally intended as a top-class carriage horse for the Imperial Court. The horse appeared in all coat colours, but, from the mid-eighteenth century, was based on three stallions – the grey Peopoli and two black stallions, both called Sacromoso – and was thereafter always grey or black.

The grey Kladrubers are still bred at the Kladruby Stud in the Czech Republic, but the black herd was destroyed in the 1930s. A few of the black mares were rescued, and there have since been stringent efforts to re-establish the line.

## World-Class

An attractive breed, the Kladruber has a long head with a convex profile and a sensible, kind eye. Its mane and tail hair are abundant and beautiful; its neck muscular and well set with a nice arch from the withers to poll. It has sloping shoulders, a wide, deep chest and quite a long back. Its hindquarters are muscular and strong, and the legs are clean and strong with good joints.

The Kladruber is a strong, long-lived, kind horse with a calm, energetic temperament. It makes an excellent competitive driving horse, possessing both speed and endurance, and is frequently seen at world-class carriage trials. Crossed with lighter breeds, it also makes a superb riding and competition horse.

# WIELKOPOLSKI

HEIGHT: 15.3–16.2 hh

COLOUR: all solid colours

PERSONALITY TYPE: warm-blooded

TYPICAL USE: competition, harness, riding

TEMPERAMENT: willing, even-tempered, kind

ORIGIN: Poland

SIMILAR BREEDS: all warmbloods

Perhaps the least known of all the warmbloods, Poland's version, the Wielkopolski was developed in Central and Western Poland in 1964. It was based on two now extinct Polish breeds, the Pozan and the Masuren, or Marzury, so it is also referred to as the Mazursko-Poznanski. The Pozan, which was a mix of Arabian, Thoroughbred, Trakehner and Hanoverian blood, was a versatile middleweight, useful for riding and agricultural chores. The Masuren was a quality riding horse, chiefly Trakehner in origin.

## Affinity for Dressage

Thoroughbred, Arabian and Anglo-Arab blood were added to refine the breed. And the result is one of the best – if the least publicized – European warmbloods, with the good looks, natural agility and superb temperament of them all. The breed is versatile and talented. It is a natural athlete and quite swift, probably due to the Thoroughbred blood, which makes it a superlative show jumper or event horse. Its natural balance and good movement also gives it an affinity for dressage. It is noted for its equable and willing nature and comfortable long, free paces.

## Presence

Today's Wielkopolski is bred along two lines: one lighter, for leisure and competitive riding; and one heavier, to make an excellent harness horse or middleweight riding horse. Most solid colours are seen, and it stands between 15.3 and 16.2 hh. Both have the Wielkopolski's quality and presence. It has a fine

head with a straight profile and an intelligent eye – the Thoroughbred influence and, to a lesser degree, the Arabian's, are particularly noticeable in its head and in its long, elegant neck. It has the sloping shoulders necessary for a long, flowing stride, and its chest is deep and wide, with plenty of heart room. Its legs are long and slender, but with good joints and well-defined tendons. It has a compact body and the muscular quarters of the equine powerhouse that it is.

LEFT

*The Wielkopolski is perhaps Poland's best-kept secret. It is amongst the most talented warmblood breeds, and also the least publicized.*

# SHAGYA ARABIAN

TEMPERAMENT: intelligent, good-natured, willing

ORIGIN: Hungary

SIMILAR BREEDS: Arabian, Anglo-Arab

HEIGHT: 15–16 hh

COLOUR: mostly grey, bay, chestnut, black

PERSONALITY TYPE: warm-blooded

TYPICAL USE: riding, harness, competition

If the Arabian is the 'diamond' of all horse breeds, the Shagya Arabian is that diamond, cut and polished to equine perfection. It was created on the famous Austro-Hungarian military stud farms in the 1780s, primarily in Hungary at Babolna, Radautz and Piber. Later, stud farms in Topolcianky (Czechoslovakia), Mangalia (Romania) and Kabijuk (Bulgaria) also bred Shagyas. The purpose was to develop a breed of superior cavalry and carriage horses, as well as prepotent sires to be used to improve other breeds.

## More Substance

The Shagya combines the best components of the desert

Arabian – elegance, toughness, endurance and an inborn affinity with humans – with the desirable qualities of a riding horse – substance, trainability, athleticism and excellent movement. It served as a cavalry mount and was displayed in parades for Europe's royalty.

It is bigger than the purebred Arabian, with a larger frame and more substance, although the Arab influence is clear in its concave profile. Most Shagya Arabians are grey, although bay, chestnut and black also appear.

## Outstanding Sire

The oldest damline recorded is that of Moldvai, foaled in 1781; another famous line is that of Tine, born in 1810. The breed was

further developed by carefully breeding back time and again to desert-bred and purebred Arabians, combined with rigorous culling and selection. This long-term process can be traced in an unbroken line from the Shagyas of today all the way back to the beginning of the breed. Many Shagyas have pedigrees more than 20 generations long.

The most important stallion is the dapple grey Shagya, born in 1810. He was bred by the Bani Saher tribe of Bedouins and came to the stud at Babotna, about 58 km (36 miles) from Budapest, in 1836. He was such an outstanding sire that he appears in nearly all Shagya pedigrees. He not only pressed his stamp on the breed, but also gave it his name.

# Fascinating Facts

A horse's heart weighs 4 kg (9 lb).

RIGHT

*The Shagya Arabian is generally noticeably bigger and more substantial in frame than the purebred Arab, and is renowned for its equable temperament.*

# GIDRAN ARABIAN

HEIGHT: 16–17 hh

COLOUR: chestnut

PERSONALITY TYPE: warm-blooded

TYPICAL USE: riding, harness

TEMPERAMENT: intelligent, unpredictable

ORIGIN: Hungary

SIMILAR BREEDS: Arabian

A rare breed, the Gidran Arabian, or the Hungarian Anglo-Arab, originated at the Hungarian stud at Mezohegyes, founded in 1785. The breed can be traced back to the stallion Siglavy Gidran (from which it takes its name), which was imported from Arabia in 1816. Gidran was from the noted Siglavy Arab strain and was an imposing chestnut. Put to a Spanish mare called Arrogante, he produced a colt foal called Gidran II, which was the foundation sire of the Gidran Arabian.

## Upstanding

The Gidran Arabian is a large, upstanding horse, solidly built and exhibiting quality and class. It is almost always chestnut, with the refined head of the Arab, but not quite so delicate. Its neck is well-proportioned in relation to its body and is muscular and well set. It has a nice slope to its shoulders, which allows for freedom of movement, and its chest is deep and wide. Deep through the barrel, it has a strong, sometimes long back. Its quarters are also muscular, and the legs are strong with short dense, cannon bones and well-formed feet. It generally stands between 16 and 16.2 hh, although it can be as big as 17 hh.

## Fascinating Facts

It is thought there are only about 200 Gidran Arabians in existence.

BELOW

*The Gidran Arabian is now, sadly, a rare breed that was originally developed from Arab, Spanish and Thoroughbred influences.*

## Cavalry Horse

During the nineteenth century, the breed was developed further, primarily for use as cavalry horses. A number of mares were used, some local and some Spanish; later, infusions of Thoroughbred and further Arabian blood were added. The Gidran Arab developed along two basic lines: a heavier type more suited to light farm and draught work, and a lighter, faster saddle horse.

The breed sustained substantial losses during the First World War, and afterwards further Arab blood and some Kisber blood were introduced. Later, two Bulgarian stallions were introduced to bring in fresh blood.

# FURIOSO

TEMPERAMENT: calm, energetic, honest

ORIGIN: Hungary

SIMILAR BREEDS: Thoroughbred, Nonius

HEIGHT: 15.3–16.2 hh

COLOUR: brown, bay, chestnut, black

PERSONALITY TYPE: warm-blooded

TYPICAL USE: riding, competition, harness

ABOVE

*The Furioso is an attractive and versatile breed with quality that still reflects the early influence of Thoroughbred blood.*

An English Thoroughbred gave its name to this Hungarian breed, based on the local Nonius mares at the Mezohegyes Stud, which had a formidable reputation as a horse-breeding centre. Furioso was imported in 1841 and sired 95 stallions that were to form the basis of the breed. Another line was based on North Star, imported in 1844, which had some Norfolk Roadster blood. He was the grandson of Touchstone, winner of the 1834 St Leger, and was related to Eclipse.

## Dominant Characteristics

The Furioso and North Star were originally developed along entirely separate lines; however, by the end of the nineteenth century, the progeny were crossbred and the Furioso characteristics began to dominate. For a period, the breed was known as the Furioso-North Star. Today's Furioso bears little resemblance to its Nonius roots and is now bred at Apajpuszta in Hungary and also widely across Central Europe. A versatile riding horse, it is capable of competing in all major disciplines. It is strong and tough, and has a calm but energetic temperament.

## Steeplechaser

The Furioso has a correctly proportioned, refined head – more Thoroughbred-looking than that of the Nonius. Its neck is in proportion to the body and is muscular with a prolific mane. It is often described as having basic workmanlike conformation, for which it owes a debt to the Nonius. It tends to be a little long through the back, but with a compact body, muscular quarters, strong legs and well let-down hocks. Its feet are generally good. It is wide through the chest with sloping shoulders and deep through the girth. Conformational faults that may occur are pigeon toes in front and cow hocks behind.

Hardy and enduring, the Furioso also makes a good steeplechaser — a testament to its Thoroughbred forefathers.

# NONIUS

HEIGHT: 14.3–16.2 hh

COLOUR: bay, brown

PERSONALITY TYPE: warm-blooded

TYPICAL USE: competition, riding

TEMPERAMENT: easygoing, calm

ORIGIN: Hungary

SIMILAR BREEDS: all warmbloods

Like the Furioso, the Nonius has its roots in the Mezohegyes Stud in Hungary and is based on one sire, Nonius Senior. He was foaled in Normandy in 1810, and was taken by the Hungarian cavalry in 1813 after the defeat of Napoleon at Leipzig. He stood at stud for 22 years, during which time the breed that took his name was established. Nonius Senior was by a stallion called Orion, an English half-bred with some Norfolk Roadster blood, and out of a Norman mare.

## Conformational Faults

Records show that Nonius was a light bay five-year-old, standing just under 17 hh. He had a large and heavy head with small eyes and long ears, short neck, high prominent withers, a long back, narrow and low hindquarters and low-set tail. He had short and steep shoulder blades. He was narrow at the knees in the front and at the hocks behind. His conformational faults meant that initially Nonius was little used for breeding in Mezohegyes. It was only when it was noticed that his offspring did not inherit his looks and that they had excellent endurance and more correct conformation that he began to be bred.

## Useful All-Rounder

He was then put to mostly Spanish, Lipizzaner and Kladruber mares. When he died in 1838, he left behind 79 stallions and 137 mares. His son, Nonius IX, was also used to fix the breed type. Thoroughbred blood was later added for refinement.

The Nonius is strong and tough, with an amenable temperament. It makes a useful all-round riding horse, and is generally well built and sound, with good solid legs. It is almost always bay or brown. Recently, Nonius mares have been put to English Thoroughbred stallions to produce first-rate competition and sport horses.

# Fascinating Facts

It is documented that Nonius Senior was not particularly well conformed or attractive, although fortunately he did not pass on these traits to his progeny. It does seem strange, however, that such a poor stallion was used as a primary sire at Mezohegyes.

LEFT

*The Nonius, with its muscular frame and good proportions, makes a top riding horse and an excellent driving horse.*

# KISBER FELVER

TEMPERAMENT: alert, willing, docile

ORIGIN: Hungary

SIMILAR BREEDS: all warmbloods

HEIGHT: 15.2–17 hh

COLOUR: any solid colour

PERSONALITY TYPE: warm-blooded

TYPICAL USE: competition, riding, harness

A relatively young breed, the Kisber Felver was developed at the Kisber Stud in Hungary, which was founded in 1853 primarily to breed Thoroughbreds. The stud produced such racing talents as Kisber, winner of the Epsom Derby, and Kincsem, which made its way into the *Guinness Book of Records* for an unbeaten 54 races. The Kisber Stud not only made its mark on Thoroughbred racing history, but also developed a half-bred that was regarded as the world's most beautiful sport horse.

## Quality Warmblood

The Kisber Felver evolved from crosses of Thoroughbred, Furioso, Trakehner, Arabian, Anglo-Arab and Selle Français. It was originally developed to be a useful sport horse, with more substance than the Thoroughbred, and as a harness horse. Once the Kisber Felver had developed its fixed characteristics, it was commonly used on local stock to improve the progeny.

Those fixed characteristics add up to an attractive, quality warmblood, with a distinctly Thoroughbred look. It has a refined head with alert ears, well-proportioned neck that curves gently from the withers to the poll, sloping shoulders, a deep chest and well-sprung ribs. Its back tends to be quite long, and its legs are muscular.

## Little Known

The Kisber Felver has a tough, sound constitution and is energetic and lively, qualities that made it suitable for military purposes. Breed numbers were dramatically reduced during the First and Second World Wars and, in

1945, more than half of the breeding stock was taken as war damages. In 1961, the remaining breeding stock was moved to the Dalmand Stud Farm, where the Kisber Felver is still bred today.

The Kisber Felver is little known, which belies its merits and worth as a competition horse. It is naturally athletic, and makes a good jumping and eventing prospect.

RIGHT

*The Kisber Felver is a tough and talented young warmblood breed that is, however, little known outside its native Hungary.*

# LIPIZZANER

HEIGHT: 15.1–16.2 hh

COLOUR: grey

PERSONALITY TYPE: warm-blooded

TYPICAL USE: High School, riding, show, harness

TEMPERAMENT: intelligent, spirited, kind

ORIGIN: Slovenia

SIMILAR BREEDS: Andalusian, Lusitano

Holy Roman Emperor Maximilian II (1527–76) brought Spanish horses to Austria in 1562, and founded the court stud at Kladruby, in what is now the Czech Republic. His brother, Archduke Charles, established a similar stud with Spanish stock in 1580 at Lipica in Slovenia near the Adriatic Sea. The Kladruby stud became known for its heavy carriage horses, while the Lipica stud produced riding and light carriage types. The two studs sometimes exchanged breeding stock – Kladruby produced Maestoso and Favory, two of the foundation sires of today's Lipizzaner.

## Riding School

The aim was to produce a showy, predominantly grey horse for the ducal stables at Graz and the court stables at Vienna. The famed Spanish Riding School of Vienna was founded in 1572 to teach the nobility, and was so called because it used Spanish horses. There have also been infusions of Neapolitan, Arabian, Danish and German blood. An attempt to

introduce Thoroughbred lines to the breed was not successful.

Interest in the art of classical riding revived during the Renaissance period, when the Spanish horse was considered the most suitable mount because of its exceptional sturdiness, beauty and intelligence. The athletic Lipizzaner was supremely suited to the movements of the *haute école*, or High School.

RIGHT

*The beautiful Lipizzaner horse is perhaps best known for the magical performances it gives with the Spanish Riding School in Vienna.*

## Six Stallions

The Lipizzaner breed is based on six foundation sires, the lines of which still exist today. These stallions were Pluto, a grey Spanish stallion, foaled in 1765 and bought from the Royal Danish Stud;

Conversano, a black Neopolitan stallion (1767); Neapolitano, a brown Neopolitan stallion (1790); Favory, a dun stallion, foaled at the Kladruby stud in 1779; Maestoso, a grey stallion, foaled 1819 at the Hungarian stud of Mezohegyes; and Siglavy, a grey Arabian (1810). Although the Lipizzaner is assumed to be only grey, until the eighteenth century there were Lipizzaners with various coat colours, including dun, spotted and bay. The royal family preferred the light grey horses, however, so breeding was concentrated on this colour.

## Mare Lines

The six foundation sires produced distinctive lines of

Lipizzaner. Conversano stock have strong, ram-like heads and short backs with broad hocks. The Arabian influence is more obvious in Favory horses, which tend to be of

BELOW
*This magnificent breed was on the verge of being wiped out during the Second World War, but was rescued and has since been re-established.*

lighter build, while Maestosos are powerful, with a long back and heavier heads. Neapolitano's progeny are taller, more rangy in appearance, with a high action. Pluto stock is sturdy and has a rectangular build, while Siglavy's is aristocratic, with an elegant head and a relatively short back.

As well as the foundation stallions, there are 18 mare family lines. Each stallion has two names – that of the sire and that of the dam – so horses would have names such as Pluto Theodorosta.

## Edge of Extinction

The history of the Lipizzaner is somewhat stormy, and the breed was almost lost – at the beginning of the twentieth century, there were just 208

purebred Lipizzaners left. The breed was brought to the very edge of extinction during the Second World War, when the stud was forced to leave its premises by the German High Command. It was saved, however, by the Spanish Riding School's then director, Colonel Alois Podhajsky (1898–1973). The stud is now located at Piber, in the Austrian mountains, having been established there in 1920.

Today's Lipizzaner is a magnificent equine, with an attractive head that can show some Arabian influence, but

more usually it has typically Spanish characteristics. Its neck is short and muscular, with flattish withers, a deep chest, sloping shoulders that are suitably conformed for riding or harness, a long back and rounded hindquarters with a well-set tail. Its legs are short and muscular, and they usually have good bone.

Vienna's dancing white horses are a joy to watch, particularly in the opulent splendour of the Spanish Riding School, and their suppleness and athleticism make them especially suited to dressage.

# UKRAINIAN RIDING HORSE

HEIGHT: 15.1–16.1 hh

COLOUR: bay, brown, chestnut, black

PERSONALITY TYPE: warm-blooded

TYPICAL USE: competition, riding

TEMPERAMENT: calm, sensible, intelligent

ORIGIN: Ukraine

SIMILAR BREEDS: all warmbloods

## Fascinating Facts

The Ukrainian Riding Horse Ikhor, ridden by Ivan Kizimov, won the dressage gold medal at the 1968 Olympic Games in Mexico.

RIGHT

*This breed has only been established since the end of the Second World War but has already proved to be a useful and talented sports horse.*

A relatively new breed, the Ukrainian Riding Horse – sometimes also known as the Russian Riding, or Russian Saddle, Horse – was developed after the Second World War to meet the increasing demand for sport horses. It was first developed at the Dnepropetrovsk Stud in the Ukraine. Today, it is bred at the studs of Derkulsk, Yagonitsk and Aleksandriisk. Despite its brief history, the breed is well established in its characteristics because of the highly selective breeding process that is employed.

## Competition Bound

The horse has an attractive head set on a long, muscular neck, with sloping shoulders and a deep chest, although its back has a tendency to be long and hollow. Its croup is long and sloping. The horses are usually bay, chestnut or black in colour, and stand 15.1–16.1 hh.

The horses are kept in a regulated environment. They begin training just before the age of two, and are required to participate in a performance testing as two- and three-year-olds, which includes racing on the track, jumping, and dressage. Only the best are allowed to stand at stud. The most successful have competed at the highest level, including the Olympics.

## Hanoverian Blood

The Ukrainian Riding Horse was based on local mare stock crossed with Trakehner, Hanoverian and Thoroughbred stallions. Some Furioso and Gidran Arabian mares from Hungary were also used. The progeny was then interbred to establish the Ukrainian Riding Horse type. More Hanoverian blood was added to those deemed too fine, while further infusions of Thoroughbred blood refined those that were too heavy. Since the original type was fixed, only Hanoverian and Thoroughbred blood has been used to refine and improve the breed.

# PLEVEN

TEMPERAMENT: calm, obedient, willing

ORIGIN: Bulgaria

SIMILAR BREEDS: Anglo Arab

HEIGHT: 15.2–16 hh

COLOUR: chestnut

PERSONALITY TYPE: warm-blooded

TYPICAL USE: riding, competition

Bulgaria's warmblood breed was developed at the former state stud called Klementina – now the Georgi Dimitrov Agricultural Centre – in 1898. It was the result of crossing local stock with Arabian, Russian Anglo-Arab and Gidran lines. The breed was officially recognized in 1951, and some Thoroughbred blood was introduced for refinement and quality, and to increase the size. The result was a handsome horse with excellent, free-flowing paces and a natural jumping ability.

## Sound Constitution

The Pleven has the calm warmblood temperament, and is willing and obedient, economical to keep and easy to train. It generally has a sound constitution and is tough and enduring. It has a pleasing head with a straight profile, a long, muscular neck and wellformed, nicely sloping shoulders, which give it its very correct action and attractive way of going. It is broad and deep through the chest and has muscular quarters with slightly sloping croup. Its legs are well formed with good bone and excellent feet.

# SYRIAN

TEMPERAMENT: spirited, lively, intelligent

ORIGIN: Syria

SIMILAR BREEDS: Arabian

HEIGHT: 14.2–15.1 hh

COLOUR: chestnut, grey

PERSONALITY TYPE: hot-blooded

TYPICAL USE: riding

Closely related to the Arabian, the Syrian Horse originates from Syria (now the Syrian Arab Republic) in South-West Asia, bordering the Lebanon. Although very rarely standing more than 14.2 hh, the Syrian is regarded as a horse, rather than a pony, and some do reach 15.1 hh. Tough and frugal, having had

to adapt and thrive in its harsh natural climate, it bears a close resemblance to the Arabian and is thought to be a variation of the breed that developed its own distinctive characteristics because of its isolated homeland.

## A Desert Survivor

Like the Arabian, the Syrian is supremely well equipped to survive in desert conditions, being able to withstand high temperatures during the day, as well as the cold of the desert night. It is generally considered less attractive than the Arabian, although it does possess the grace and presence of its close cousin. It is a good keeper, able to thrive on meagre rations. Although it has a tendency to be 'hot', the Syrian is trainable and makes a good riding horse.

# CASPIAN

HEIGHT: 10–12.2 hh

COLOUR: bay, brown, chestnut, grey

PERSONALITY TYPE: hot-blooded

TYPICAL USE: show, driving, riding

TEMPERAMENT: intelligent, lively, brave

ORIGIN: Persia (now Iran)

SIMILAR BREEDS: Arabian

In the 1960s, an American named Louise Firouz discovered about 50 small horses living along the coast of the Caspian Sea, and she wrote: '… that they are so distinctively peculiar to one small region leads one to believe that they were systematically bred for a purpose at one time. Their remarkable characteristics come through so clearly that they are probably throw-backs to a strongly dominant breed.' Ms Firouz is credited with saving the Caspian Horse from the brink of extinction.

## Ancient Lineage

Research into the history and origin of this beguiling little horse proved the ancient lineage of the

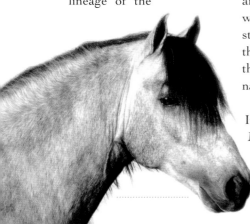

Caspian. It was identified as a royal breed previously thought long extinct. Through examination and research of ancient Persian archeological remains, along with blood type, bone structure and genetic testing, the Caspian was found to be the forerunner of Persia's native wild horses.

It is believed that the Mesopotamians used the Caspian to develop the

---

LEFT

*These extraordinary tiny horses are an ancient breed of enormous quality, and display typical 'desert' features, being tough, fine-skinned and highly intelligent.*

---

Arabian in 3,000 BC, and indeed the elegant Caspian does look like an Arabian in miniature. Identification of the Caspian was aided by several of its unique features, such as its blood haemoglobin composition and its skeletal structure. It is a fine creature with an attractive head and typical 'desert' characteristics, but stands less than 12.2 hh.

## Isolated Horses

Small wild horses roamed the district of Persia around Kermanshah, now known as Bakhatran, in west central Iran. The most common theory of the horse's presence around Kermanshah is that many species were swept southwards ahead of glaciers, retreating to warmer climates. After the glaciers melted, many species returned to their former northern habitats, but some remained within fixed geographical areas forming isolated breeding groups with

distinctive genetic characteristics. This would account for the very early isolated pocket of Caspians in ancient Persia in the Zabras near Kermanshah.

Evidence that a Caspian-type horse existed as early as 3,000 BC can be found in ancient writings and artefacts. A

terracotta plaque from second-millennium Mesopotamia, showing a small horse ridden with a nose ring, can be seen at the British Museum.

## Fascinating Facts

The Persian kings Ardashir I (ruled AD 226–241) and Shapur I (ruled AD 241–272) were depicted on stone reliefs with small horses that stood no more than waist-high.

# PERSIAN ARAB

TEMPERAMENT: spirited, trainable, intelligent

ORIGIN: Persia

SIMILAR BREEDS: Arabian

HEIGHT: 14.2–15.2 hh

COLOUR: grey, bay, chestnut

PERSONALITY TYPE: hot-blooded

TYPICAL USE: riding, racing

Horses are believed to have existed in Persia from around 2,000 BC, which means that the Persian Arab predates the Arabian by about 1,500 years. Although the name 'Persian Arab' is given to all horses from what is now Iran, there is a vast number of different regional strains throughout the country, named after the families that bred them. But they are all of the classical Arabian type, with its refined head with wide forehead and dished profile, and small, alert ears.

## Wiped Out

The south-western region of Khuzestan produces some notable strains of the Persian Arab. There are also very set rules on the selective breeding process in place here, which has helped to keep the strains pure. The Persian Arab is now greatly reduced in numbers, partly due to African horse sickness, which affected Iran in the 1950s and wiped out a vast number of the breed.

The Persian Arab is similar to the Arabian in conformation and characteristics, although it is slightly heavier in build. It is an attractive horse with great presence and natural carriage and bearing. Compact and muscular through the body, it has the Arabian's elegantly arched neck, a broad, deep chest, rounded quarters and a tail that is set and carried high. Generally it is gray, bay, or chestnut in colour, and stands between 14.2 and 15.2 hh. It makes a very good riding horse and is quick and agile, with enormous stamina and spirit.

## New Breeds

Two breeds in Iran have developed from the Persian Arab: the Jaf from Kurdistan and the Darashouri from the Fars region. Both have predominantly Arabian characteristics, and are spirited, quick and have good stamina. The Jaf is considered to have better stamina than the Darashouri and is more able to cope in the extreme desert conditions. The Darashouri is deemed the more attractive and elegant of the two.

---
LEFT

*The Persian Arab exhibits strong Arab characteristics, although it is generally slightly heavier in build and often bigger than its relative.*

# ARABIAN

HEIGHT: 14.2–15 hh

COLOUR: all solid colours except palomino

PERSONALITY TYPE: hot-blooded

TYPICAL USE: riding, racing, endurance

TEMPERAMENT: spirited, brave, affectionate

ORIGIN: Middle East

SIMILAR BREEDS: Akhal-Teke, Barb, Persian Arab

LEFT

*The Arabian is one of the most prepotent horse breeds and has influenced the development of the majority of other horse breeds at some stage.*

Centuries ago, in the inhospitable deserts of the Middle East, there emerged a breed of horse that would influence the equine world beyond all imagination. In the sweet grass oases along the rivers Euphrates and Tigris, in the countries that are now known as Syria, Iraq and Iran, this desert survivor developed into today's glorious Arabian. The Arabian is considered the fountainhead of modern horse breeds, as there are very few that do not have some Arabian blood in their histories.

## Mark of Glory

The Arabian's past was inextricably bound with that of the Bedouins, their religious beliefs, their superstitions and their traditions. To those desert people, the horse was a gift from Allah, to be revered, cherished and almost worshipped.

They believed that their magnificent horse was created by Allah, who said: 'I call you horse; I make you Arabian, and I give you the chestnut colour of the ant. I have hung happiness from your forelock that hangs between your eyes; you shall be the lord of the other animals. Men will follow you wherever you go; you shall be as good for pursuit as for flight. Riches shall be make on your back and fortune shall come through your mediation.'

Allah then blessed the horse with the mark of glory – the white star in the centre of its forehead.

## Mythology and Romance

The Bedouins believed that the Arabian's unique traits were further gifts from Allah. The horse's *jibbah* (the shield-shaped bulge on its forehead) carried the blessings of Allah; the greater the *jibbah*, the greater the blessings. The horse's arched neck with the *mitbah* (the angle at which it joins the head), which makes it incredibly mobile, was a sign of courage. The high-set tail showed pride. All these traits, for which the horses were selectively bred, were held in high esteem and carefully kept *asil*, or pure.

The headmen of the tribes could relate verbally the full histories of each family of horse, and the mythology and romance of the breed grew with each passing century as

## Fascinating Facts

Arabians are often grey, but are seen in all solid colours, except palomino. Bedouin breeders did their best to eliminate black from their prized bloodlines, as it was thought to absorb the desert heat and make the horse less efficient. Black Arabians are, however, seen today.

ABOVE
*The Arab has one fewer vertebrae than other breeds, making it shorter coupled, and has a distinctively high tail carriage.*

stories of courage, endurance and wealth intermingled with the genealogies.

## Enemy Raids

So revered was the Arabian that it would share the tent with its Bedouin owner, and it is thought that this is why the modern breed has such an affinity with humans. To its owner, the Arabian was primarily a weapon of war. Well mounted on a swift Arabian – usually a mare, as they did not whicker to other horses, thus giving away their position – the Bedouin could make a raid on an enemy settlement, capturing herds of camels, goats, sheep and, of course, more horses.

## Universal Breed

The speed and endurance necessary for these raids remain Arabian strengths to this day. And the Arabian's beauty, with its exaggeratedly dished face, tiny, alert ears and dark, liquid eye, make it the most easily recognized of all horse breeds. As well as the *mitbah* and *jibbah*, the Arabian has other unique features: it has 17 ribs, 5 lumbar vertebrae and 16 tail bones. All other equine breeds have 18 ribs, 6 lumbar vertebrae and 18 tail bones.

Fine-boned and lean, the Arabian has the fine silky hair of desert horses with a high sheen. Its mane and tail are long and abundant, with the tail carried gaily high. Its sloping shoulders give it the light, springy action for which it is so prized, and it has a short compact back and long, slender limbs. The ancient Arabian was to provide the foundation for the horse of the sport of kings, the Thoroughbred.

# AKHAL-TEKE

HEIGHT : 14.2–15.2 hh

COLOUR : chestnut, bay, grey, palomino, black, dun

PERSONALITY TYPE: hot-blooded

TYPICAL USE: riding, competition, endurance, racing

TEMPERAMENT: lively, intelligent, stubborn

ORIGIN: Turkmenistan

SIMILAR BREEDS: Turkoman

Exotically beautiful, the Akhal-Teke is an ancient breed that takes its name from a Turkmenian tribe called Teke, which lived at the Akhal oasis in Turkmenistan. It was bred by the Turkmene warriors some 2,500 years ago, but horses very similar to the Akhal-Teke, probably the breed's ancestors, were bred in Ashkhabad as long ago as 1000 BC. It has great endurance and stamina, as well as speed, and is able to cope easily with the extreme heat and intense cold of its Central Asian homeland.

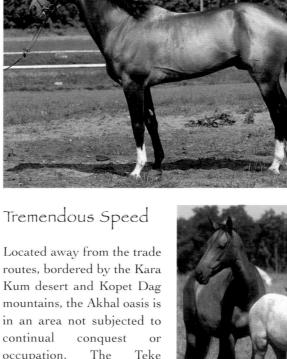

## Metallic Glow

As the chief mount of Turkoman warriors for centuries, the Akhal-Teke developed endless stamina and, with fresh forage available for only three months of the year in the arid desert, the Teke tribespeople

LEFT

*The Akhal-Teke is an elegant and unusual breed, distinguished by its high head and neck carriage.*

## Tremendous Speed

Located away from the trade routes, bordered by the Kara Kum desert and Kopet Dag mountains, the Akhal oasis is in an area not subjected to continual conquest or occupation. The Teke tribespeople took great pleasure in their horses and produced a breed of ancient lineage and great purity. The Akhal-Teke is believed to be related to the Arabian and bears a distinct resemblance to the Munaghi Arabian –

LEFT

*These desert horses can cope with extreme temperatures, and are tough and enduring. They are frequently raced and are incredibly fast.*

both were bred for racing and possessed tremendous speed. The similarities between these ancient breeds have raised the question as to which influenced the other and which one was developed first.

developed their own special methods of horse management. Kept in small bands, tethered to stakes and blanketed, the Akhal-Teke were fed pellets consisting of alfalfa, barley and mutton fat. The result was a horse that can subsist on small amounts of food and water, becomes devoted to its master and is suspicious of strangers.

The blanketing also enhanced the metallic sheen of the horses' coat, which is a source of great pride for their owners – the Akhal-Teke's coat glows like pure gold. It has a unique hair structure that refracts light, producing colours from blazing palominos to electric black

with a distinctive golden sheen. Today's Akhal-Teke retains every quality of endurance, speed, economy, intelligence and beauty that was so prized throughout the centuries by so many different societies.

## Royal Gift

It is widely believed that Bucephalus, the famous favoured mount of Alexander the Great (356–323 BC), was of Turkmenian blood and therefore closely related to the Akhal-Teke. Also said to be fans of the Akhal-Teke were Roman emperors, Genghis Khan (*c.* 1162–1227) and the explorer Marco Polo (1254–1324). Queen Elizabeth II of England was gifted an Akhal-Teke in 1956. Her Majesty's grooms tried to wash off what they thought was polish, but was actually the natural metallic sheen of the stallion's golden dun coat.

The horse is one of great beauty, with an elegant head and graceful neck, high withers, long back and muscular hindquarters. It is very long in the leg and finely boned. It is highly intelligent and possesses a swift turn of foot; it is still used as a racehorse today.

It is also unrivalled in its powers of endurance – 15 Akhal-Tekes travelled from Ashkhabad to Moscow in 1935, a distance of 4,345 km (2,700 miles), crossing 378 km (235 miles) of desert in three days with no water. This feat persuaded breeders of the value of their glorious horse.

## Dressage Medals

There is much speculation about the role the Akhal-Teke played in the development of the Thoroughbred. Careful study of what is known of the Byerley Turk indicates that he was probably an Akhal-Teke and that the Darley Arabian was of the Munighi strain of Arabians and carried a large portion of Akhal-Teke blood.

The Akhal-Teke today is emerging as a sport horse, having won Olympic medals in dressage and possessing a natural jumping ability. Although there are thought to be only about 3,000 left, it is hoped that this beautiful breed will continue to flourish.

# TURKOMAN

HEIGHT: 15 hh

COLOUR: most solid colours

PERSONALITY TYPE: hot-blooded

TYPICAL USE: riding, racing

TEMPERAMENT: intelligent, trainable, hardy

ORIGIN: Turkmenistan

SIMILAR BREEDS: Akhal-Teke

Bred in Iran, the Turkoman – sometimes also called Turkmene – is sometimes considered to be simply another strain of the Akhal-Teke breed. Whatever the case, it is now extinct in its original form, like the Yamud Horse, which was developed in the same region, although horses bred in the region are still called Turkoman. The original Turkoman had the Akhal-Teke's greyhound-like svelteness. It is also documented that some of these horses had the glowing metallic coat of the Akhal-Teke, giving credence to the suggestion that they became the same breed.

## Nomadic Tribes

Modern Turkmenistan, with its population of roughly four million and its economy based largely on cotton and natural gas, was once among the republics of the Soviet Union. In older texts, it is known as Turkmenia. For thousands of years before the 1879 Russian occupation, nomadic tribes and pastoral clans populated the territory, struggling interminably to

graze their herds in the valley of the Amu Darya, Central Asia's longest river, and amid the foothills of the Kopet Mountains that now separate Turkmenistan from Afghanistan and Iran. Nearly every Turkmene family owned at least one or two horses.

## Bred to Race

The horses were bred to race and were raised in an unusual manner, with the mares kept in semi-wild herds that had to fend for themselves against the weather and predators, finding their own food. Colts were caught at six months and kept on long tethers, usually for life. The Turkoman horses were fed a special high-protein diet of chicken, barley, dates, raisins and mutton fat.

Cherished by the nomads, the horses were called Argamaks by the occupying Russians, which meant 'tall and refined'. Swift and hardy, the horses had free-flowing movement and a good temperament, as well as great speed and stamina, characteristics that are seen in the Akhal-Teke today.

# KARABAIR

TEMPERAMENT: brave, intelligent

ORIGIN: Uzbekistan

SIMILAR BREEDS: Arabian, Akhal-Teke, Karabakh

HEIGHT: 14.2–15 hh

COLOUR: bay, chestnut, grey, black

PERSONALITY TYPE: warm-blooded

TYPICAL USE: riding, harness, mounted games

A Central Asian breed, the Karabair is an ancient equine based on stock that is documented as being in the Uzbekistan and northern Tajikistan regions for more than two millennia. It was probably a mix of Arabian and Mongolian blood, later influenced by other desert breeds such as the Turkoman and Akhal-Teke, as well as more Arabian infusions. It has similarities to the Arabian, such as innate toughness, stamina and endurance, but physically it is less graceful.

## Mounted Game

Uzbekistan is still populated by a vast number of nomadic people who have been, through the years, the principal breeders of the Karabair. Their lifestyle accounts for the number of different breeds that have influenced the development of the Karabair.

The horse is fairly central to the lives of the Uzbekistan people – it is used for riding and driving, as well as in the ridden game of kokpar. Kokpar is a ferocious contest which centres on gaining

### LEFT
*The Karabair is a desert breed that is central to the often-nomadic lives of the people of Uzbekistan. It is used for riding and driving and is surefooted, quick and agile.*

possession of the carcass of a dead goat. There are few rules and many injuries, and the Karabair is used almost exclusively to play, due to its bravery and speed.

## Clean-Cut Head

The Karabair had developed in three different types, all of a similar height. The first was a heavy type suitable for light draught, pack and riding. The second was lighter and was mainly used for riding, while the third was better adapted to draught work. There is now less distinction between the three; the heavier type has almost disappeared and the other two types have more or less converged.

The Karabair resembles the Arabian, Persian Arab and Akhal-Teke. It has a medium-sized clean-cut head with a straight or slightly convex profile, wide jaw and high-set medium-long neck. It has wide and well-muscled hindquarters and a sloping croup and shoulders, although the latter can sometimes be too upright. Its chest is well developed, and it has clean, strong legs with good feet.

# KARABAKH

HEIGHT: 14–15 hh

COLOUR: chestnut, bay, dun

PERSONALITY TYPE: warm-blooded

TYPICAL USE: riding, racing

TEMPERAMENT: spirited, courageous

ORIGIN: Azerbaijan

SIMILAR BREEDS: Karabair, Arabian, Akhal-Teke

**D**eveloped in Nagorny Karabakh between the Araks and Kura rivers in Azerbaijan, the Karabakh is another ancient mountain breed formed by crossing local equines with Persian Arabian, Arabian and Turkmenian horses. The Arabian is the most pronounced, with the two breeds having many similarities, although the golden sheen of the Akhal-Teke is also sometimes seen in the Karabakh. The breed is thought to have been in existence since around the fifth century.

## Taken by Conquerors

Some historical sources mention that, during the Arab invasion of Azerbaijan in the eighth and ninth centuries, tens of thousands of horses with golden-chestnut colouring, which were characteristic colours for Karabakhs, were taken by the conquerors. There is some evidence that Karabakh ruler Ibrahim-Khalil Khan (1730–1806) possessed a horse herd numbering 3,000–4,000, mostly consisting of Karabakh.

The breed became increasingly popular in Europe in the nineteenth century; in 1823, an English company purchased 60 purebred Karabakh mares from Mehdi-Kulu Khan, the last ruler of the Karabakh khanate.

## Salvaged

In the early twentieth century, the Karabakh numbers sharply decreased, mostly because of civil and ethnic wars in Azerbaijan.

In 1949, the breed was revived at Agdam Stud, but suffered another setback during Armenian–Azeri conflict. In 1993, most of the Karabakhs were salvaged from the stud. These horses are currently bred in winter pastures in lowland Karabakh plains between Barda and Agjabadi provinces.

Like most mountain breeds, the Karabakh is tough and hardy, able to survive on little feed, a trait vital to the nomadic people of Azerbaijan. It is sure-footed and loyal, but also possesses a good turn of foot.

## **F**ascinating **F**acts

In 2004, a Karabakh horse named Kishmish from Agdam Stud in Azerbaijan set a speed record by running 1,000 m (3,280 ft) in 1 minute 9 seconds and 1,600 m (5,249 ft) in 1 minute 52 seconds.

RIGHT

*This ancient mountain breed shares similarities with the Arab and horses of Turkmenistan, both of which influenced its development.*

# LOKAI

TEMPERAMENT: quiet, willing, obedient

ORIGIN: Tajikistan

SIMILAR BREEDS: Akhal-Teke, Karabair

HEIGHT: 14.3 hh

COLOUR: chestnut, bay, grey, black, palomino

PERSONALITY TYPE: warm-blooded

TYPICAL USE: riding, pack

Despite its diminutive size, the Lokai – found in the region of Tajikistan – is much more of a horse than a pony. It is believed to date back to the sixteenth century and was bred by the Uzbek-Lokai people mainly in the Tajikistan and Kunguz mountains and in the valleys of their rivers. The terrain is rocky, and there is little fresh water – even the rivers have, for the most part, salt water. The horses are kept in herds out at pasture all year round, which makes them extremely tough and enduring.

## Extreme Hardiness

The Lokai is characterized by good action and extreme hardiness. It has great endurance under saddle and pack, and in national games (particularly in the hair-raising kokpar, which demands an agile equine). It reaches maturity late, but responds well to improved feeding and management, and has an excellent temperament. A new breed of saddle horse is being bred in Tajikistan by mating Lokai mares to Arabian and Thoroughbred stallions, to improve their size and refine their appearance, and Tersk blood has been introduced.

## Fascinating Facts

Some Lokais have a curly coat, which can be traced to the stallion Farfor, a curly-coated sorrel which was used for breeding from 1955–70. There are currently experimental breeding projects going on to find out more about the curly coat gene.

BELOW

*Lokai horses are generally quite small in height, but extremely hardy. Often they are plain in the head, and can be prone to cow hocks.*

## Remarkably Agile

The Lokai tends to have a rather plain head with a straight profile, set on a short, muscular neck. Its shoulders are reasonably sloping, and it has a deep, broad chest, wide withers, a short, compact back and very muscular quarters. Its legs are generally strong with well-defined tendons, although the breed does sometimes display conformational defects such as cow hocks and splayed front feet. These defects do not seem to have any adverse effect on the horse's agility or way of going.

# NOVOKIRGHIZ

HEIGHT: 14–15 hh

COLOUR: bay, brown, grey, chestnut

PERSONALITY TYPE: warm-blooded

TYPICAL USE: riding, harness, pack, agriculture

TEMPERAMENT: energetic, tough, honest

ORIGIN: Kyrgyzstan

SIMILAR BREEDS: Don

LEFT

*The Novokirghiz breed is a refinement of the old Kirghiz horse. The breed was systematically improved at the Issyk-Kul Stud farm in Kirghizia.*

# Fascinating Facts

Novokirghiz mares are used for milk, which is fermented and turned into koumiss, a mildly alcoholic drink which is a major staple of the local people's diet and similar to other fermented dairy products found across Central Asia.

**M**ongolian stock was used to create a relatively new breed of horse, developed in the 1930s in Kirghizia, or Kyrgyzstan, a country in Central Asia, bounded to the north by Kazakhstan, to the east by China, to the west by Uzbekistan and to the south by Tajikistan. The new breed was to replace the Old Kirghiz, which was a mountain breed from the high altitudes of Kirghizia and Kazakhstan mainly developed from Mongolian stock. The Novokirghiz is tough and suitable for harness, riding or agricultural work

massive type was the most successful of the three, being the most versatile and well adapted to the environment. The Novokirghiz is strong and frequently used as a packhorse in the mountains. The saddle and basic types were less suited to the mountain climate and lacked stamina.

## Improved Type

More latterly, less of a distinction was made between the three types, with a single,

improved type now in existence. It can cope with any kind of terrain and is tough and strong, with great endurance and an energetic temperament.

The Novokirghiz has a small, neat head, muscular neck, sloping shoulders, pronounced withers, longish back and sloping hindquarters. Its legs are usually quite short and strong and muscular, although sickle hocks are frequently seen.

## Russian Don

The Novokirghiz is faster and more refined than the Old Kirghiz, mainly due to the infusions of Thoroughbred, Russian Don and Budyonny crossed with the older breed. By 1918, 48 Thoroughbreds had been imported to the Issyk-Kul Stud and put to

Old Kirghiz mares. The breed became fixed in the 1930s and 1940s, due to the repeated crossings between the Old Kirghiz, Thoroughbred and Don, and interbreeding of the progeny.

The new breed developed into three types: the saddle, the massive and the basic. The

LEFT

*The Kirghiz horses are well adapted to the mountainous environment, being surefooted and tough, and are used for riding and packing.*

# TERSKY

HEIGHT: 14.3–15.2 hh

COLOUR: predominantly grey, bay, chestnut

PERSONALITY TYPE: warm-blooded

TYPICAL USE: competition, racing, endurance

TEMPERAMENT: easygoing, trainable, gentle

ORIGIN: Russia

SIMILAR BREEDS: Arabian, Streletsky (extinct)

With its distinguishing silver grey colouring and aristocratic pedigree, it is not surprising that, even for a relatively new breed, the Tersky, or Tersk, has so quickly found favour. The Tersky's immediate ancestor was the Streletsky Horse, a favourite among Russian officers for parades and dressage. The Streletsky was developed by crossing Arabian and Anglo-Arab horses with Karabakh, Orlov, Rostopchin, Persian and Turkmenian blood, and named for the Ukrainian farm where it began.

## Fateful Popularity

Unfortunately for the Streletsky, its popularity as a cavalry mount also meant the extinction of the breed, as so many perished in the bloody civil war that followed the 1917 Russian Revolution. But two elegant silver Streletsky stallions remained: Tsenitel, foaled in 1910, and Tsilindr (1911). While just these two horses were not sufficient to resurrect the Streletsky breed, they would found another, equally successful one, the Tersk.

Both Tsilindr and Tsenitel lived long lives – the former, who died at the age of 27, produced several first-class stallions; daughters of the latter, who died at 23, were among the best breeding mares in the new herd.

## Remarkable Journey

Some purebred Streletsky mares were also located and they, as well as mares of complementary breeds such as Don, Kabardin, Arabian and Lipizzaner, were used to expand the breeding herd. This new breed came to be named Tersky, after the farm that received the remnants of the Streletsky herd in 1925. The breed is noted for its cheerful and easy disposition, trainability, longevity, fertility and its characteristic stunning color – described by one devotee as 'silver in the sun'.

A versatile sport horse, it can be found in dressage and endurance, and has achieved success on the world stage in

## Fascinating Facts

During the Second World War, and under the threat of invasion by Germany in 1941, the Tersky herd was removed to western Kazakhstan for its protection, a journey that took 21 days over a distance of 900 km (560 miles). By 1945 and the end of the war, the entire herd was brought back to the Stavropol Farm, in the Northern Caucasus, where it remains to this day.

ABOVE LEFT

*With its muscular, athletic frame and powerful hindquarters, the young Tersk breed has rapidly become very popular.*

competition. Another 'stage' on which Tersky can be found is the circus, where its colour is prized.

# KABARDIN

HEIGHT: 15–15.2 hh

COLOUR: brown, bay, black

PERSONALITY TYPE: warm-blooded

TYPICAL USE: riding, harness, pack

TEMPERAMENT: brave, tractable

ORIGIN: Russia

SIMILAR BREEDS: Karabakh, Karabair

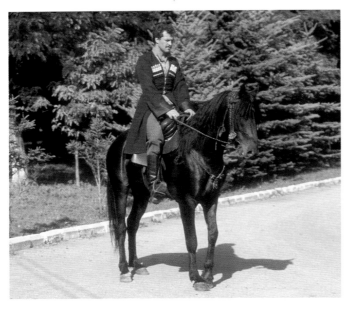

It is called the world's best mountain breed and was developed by the tribespeople of the Northern Caucasus. Like many Russian breeds, it is a product of centuries of primitive selective breeding for survival under the harshest conditions, and is derived from the horses of the people of the steppes, crossed with Karabakh, Persian and Turkmenian strains. Reliable and sure-footed, as well as economical to keep, it has been used to improve native stock in Armenia, Azerbaijan and Georgia.

## Homing Device

The breed has exceptional stamina — in 1935, a group of Kabardins became famous for travelling 2,993 km (1,860 miles) through the Caucasian mountains, in bad weather, in just 37 days. The Kabardin has an extraordinary built-in 'homing device', which helps them to find their way both in the dark and in bad weather.

During the 1917 Russian Revolution and ensuing civil war, numbers of the Kabardin were drastically reduced. Since the 1920s, efforts have been made to re-establish this valuable breed using infusions of Turkmene, Karabakh, Persian and Arabian blood to improve the breed and increase its size.

## Fascinating Facts

In 1946, a major test of the performance of various Soviet breeds was organized in Moscow. It was a 250-km (155-mile) ride with the last mile covered in a gallop. The winner was the Kabardin stallion Ali-Kadym; his time was 25 hours.

BELOW

*The Kabardin does not always have the best conformation, but is however virtually unequalled as a mountain horse.*

## Sure-footed

The best Kabardins are raised at the Karachai and Malka farms – it is sometimes called the Karachai Horse. Since its development in the sixteenth century, the breed has become at home in the mountains and has developed characteristics that are suited to the terrain and the rigours of the climate. It is very sure-footed over rugged ground and can easily cross the treacherous steep mountain passes, negotiating river crossings and deep mountain snow. It rarely stumbles even when trotting or even cantering downhill, and is impervious to cold, mountain showers and hail.

# KUSTANAIR

HEIGHT: 15–15.2 hh

TEMPERAMENT: calm, quiet, alert

COLOUR: chestnut, grey, bay, brown, black, roan

ORIGIN: former USSR

PERSONALITY TYPE: warm-blooded

SIMILAR BREEDS: Karabakh, Karabin

TYPICAL USE: riding, harness, light draught

**W**hen the former USSR wanted a new breed of horse, with two distinct types, the programme began at three state studs, Kustanai, Turgai and Orenburg, which were formally established in 1888, 1887 and 1890, respectively. However, it was the Kustanai Stud that had the earliest and best results, and can be credited with establishing the breed, which was officially recognized in 1951, as well as giving it its name. The Kustanair was not selectively bred into two types until the 1920s.

## Steppe Horses

The foundations for the Kustanair were the native steppe horses crossed with Don, Kazakh, the now-extinct Streletsky and the Thoroughbred. Early crosses were largely unsuccessful; however, by using improved native mares and further infusions of Thoroughbred blood, the fixed characteristics of the Kustanair started to emerge.

Two groups of Kustanair were then taken and raised under different conditions. The first group was stabled, corn-fed and selectively bred, while the second group were kept at pasture all year round and allowed to breed freely. The results were the formation of a distinct saddle horse type with quality and presence, suitable for all riding purposes, and a hardier, tougher creature suitable for both saddle and harness work. By the 1980s, there were more than 40,000 registered Kustanairs.

## Calm and Energetic

Both types of Kustanair are extremely tough, with great stamina and endurance, combined with a calm, quiet and energetic disposition. This in turn makes them highly versatile saddle or harness horses. The Kustanair is an attractive equine, with some being more Thoroughbred in appearance. It has a fine, light head set on a long, muscular neck that is often set quite low. Its withers can be prominent, the shoulders sloping, the back straight and wide, and the croup sloping. It is deep and broad through the chest and has long, muscular legs, which have good joints and hard hooves.

BELOW

*The Kustanair often has prominent withers with the neck set quite low, and an elegant and refined head.*

# LATVIAN

HEIGHT: 15–16 hh

COLOUR: bay, brown, black, chestnut

PERSONALITY TYPE: warm-blooded

TYPICAL USE: competition, riding, harness

TEMPERAMENT: calm, willing, honest

ORIGIN: Latvia

SIMILAR BREEDS: all warmbloods

Probably the best-known example of a Latvian Horse – not to be confused with the Latvian Heavy Draught – is Ulla Salzgeber's dressage World Cup winner Rusty. He was foaled on 2 April 1988 at the Latvian stud farm Burtnieki, and was originally named Rotors. In 1990, the horse was sold to Belarus and later to Germany. Rotors (Rusty) is by Rebuss out of Akra, and three-quarters Hanoverian. He was on the winning German dressage teams at the 1998 World and 1999 European Championships.

## Warmblood Type

Latvia had her own heavy horse breed, which was very successful, and, after the foundation of the Republic of Latvia in 1918, horse breeding became more regulated, with proper registration of stock and selective breeding. There was a shortage of horses in Latvia after the First World War and, at a congress of Latvian horse breeders in 1922, it was decided to breed middle-weight warmblood types, suitable for pleasure and competition riding, using Oldenburg, Hanoverian and Holstein blood. Thorough-bred blood was also used, although to a lesser degree. The new Latvian Horse was recognized as a breed in 1952.

## Competition Horse

The modern Latvian is a successful combination of the features of the utility and saddle horses. Tall, heavy muscled and bony, it has a well-proportioned and solid build, although the joints are sometimes coarse. Muscles are well developed, bone structure solid, chest broad, withers moderately pronounced or high and long, and with a normal slope; its legs are properly set with well-developed knee joints and hocks. Defects include short and ring-boned pasterns and cow hocks. The

commonest colours are bay, brown and black, but chestnut does sometimes occur.

The exploits of Rusty, as well as the show jumper Kasting Horses Vento, ridden by Helena Weinberg, are putting Latvia's warm-blood firmly on the competition horse map.

# RUSSIAN TROTTER

TEMPERAMENT: quiet, trainable, energetic

ORIGIN: Russia

SIMILAR BREEDS: Orlov Trotter

HEIGHT: 15.3–16 hh

COLOUR: bay, black, chestnut, grey

PERSONALITY TYPE: warm-blooded

TYPICAL USE: harness

Following the phenomenal success of the American Standardbred on Russia's harness racing tracks, prize purses were restricted to Russian-bred horses – in effect, the Orlov Trotter. The result of the restrictions was that competitors began to run 'ringers'. In early 1900, the American-bred William CK began racing with false papers as the Orlov Trotter Rassvet. Within a few months, the steel-grey stallion – a colour characteristic in the Orlov, but rare in the Standardbred – had won 20,000 rubles.

Standardbred and Orlov Trotter blood were subsequently added to the best offspring. Periodic infusions of both breeds are still added to this day. The Russian Trotter – sometimes also called the Metis Trotter – became a recognized breed in 1950, and certain standards were set, including a height of no less than 15.3 hh for mares and 16 hh for stallions, to help improve the overall picture.

## Record-Breaker

The modern Russian Trotter is a typical harness horse, generally clean and proportionally built, with well developed muscles and tendons. Its head is light with a straight profile, its neck long, its back and quarters straight and well muscled, and its croup flat, long and broad. The speed of the Russian Trotter is quite high. The 1,600-m (5,249-ft) trot record is 1 min 56.9 seconds. Today, there are thought to be about 27,000 purebred Russian Trotters, produced from 27 studs, the best of them being Elan, Smolensk, Zlynsk, Alexandrov and Dubrovski.

LEFT

*The Russian Trotter was developed from Orlov Trotter and American Standardbred crosses, and is a quality and fast trotting horse.*

## Fascinating Facts

The most outstanding example of the Russian Trotter breed is the bay stallion Zhest, foaled in 1947 at the Kul'tura Stud. At the age of six, he became the first trotter on the European continent to break the two-minute mark.

## Superlative Speed

Russian breeders responded to racing prohibitions against foreign-bred horses by crossing imported American stallions with Orlov Trotters. The result was a horse of superlative speed, but lacking the quality and refinement of the Russian breed. Further breeding produced a larger trotter of better quality, and

# ORLOV TROTTER

HEIGHT: 16 hh

COLOUR: grey, bay, black

PERSONALITY TYPE: warm-blooded

TYPICAL USE: harness, riding

TEMPERAMENT: quiet, intelligent, lively

ORIGIN: Russia

SIMILAR BREEDS: Don, all warmbloods

Russia's most famous horse breed is named for Count Alexei Orlov, who is credited with developing the Orlov Trotter at his Khrenov Stud, established in 1788. In recognition for his services to Catherine the Great (1729–96), he was made Commander of the Russian Fleet and, on winning an important battle, was presented with a grey Arabian stallion, Smetanka. Smetanka was the grandsire of a stallion called Bars I, foaled in 1784, foundation stallion of the Orlov Trotter.

## Fascinating Facts

The Orlov Trotter's robust constitution and high adaptability result in a long life span – the outstanding stallion Kvadrat was used as a sire up to the age of 32.

ABOVE RIGHT

*The magnificent Orlov Trotter is Russia's best-known breed and is a classy, well-conformed trotting horse.*

## Superlative

Moved to the Khrenov Stud, Bars was crossed with mares of Arabian, Dutch, Danish, English and Mecklenburg lines, and the best of the progeny were interbred until fixed characteristics were established. These were to be the Orlov Trotter, a quality carriage horse and a superlative trotter.

The best Orlov Trotters are bred at the Khrenov Stud, Dubrovski, Novotomnikov and Perm, although horses from the different studs tend to have different traits, with the Orlov type the most popular.

## Distinct and Massive

Significant damage to the breed was caused by uncontrolled crossing with the American Standardbred during 1885–1913, as well as by the First World War and the Russian Revolution, following which the breed had to be re-established.

The modern Orlov Trotter is a massive horse of some distinction. Its head is refined and clean cut, its neck long and muscular, and often high-set. Its withers are medium in height and length; its back is long and flat, and sometimes slightly dipped. It has good legs with well-formed feet. It has a quiet but energetic temperament.

The Orlov Trotter is very fertile. At the studs there are 80–85 live births per 100 mares, and the survival rate to one year of age is 78–83 per cent.

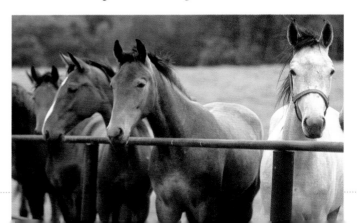

# BUDYONNY

TEMPERAMENT: kind, brave, intelligent

ORIGIN: Russia

SIMILAR BREEDS: Don, Russian Trotter

HEIGHT: 15.1–16 hh

COLOUR: chestnut

PERSONALITY TYPE: warm-blooded

TYPICAL USE: competition, endurance, racing

A Russian hero gave his name to this superb warmblood, created as a cavalry mount to replace horses lost in the First World War and bred by putting Russian Don and Chernomer mares to English Thoroughbreds. The Budyonny breed – sometimes called Budenny, or Budyonovsky – was originally known as the Anglo-Don and was generally chestnut, often with the metallic sheen seen in the Don and in the Akhal-Teke. Arabian blood was later added and the progeny bred back to the Thoroughbred to create a quality horse with stamina and endurance.

## Three Foundation Sires

The Chernomer mares were similar to the Don, but slightly smaller and lighter. Other breeds, particularly the Kazakh and Kirgiz from Mongolia, were not so successful. The required horse from these unions was one with stamina, toughness and endurance, as well as courage, speed and athleticism, combined with an equable temperament.

At the military stud farm at Rostov, Marshal Budyonny experimented with about 70 Thoroughbreds to perfect his equine breed, but only three stallions were accepted into

ABOVE
*These athletic horses reflect their Thoroughbred ancestry in their refined and quality heads, and are versatile sports horses.*

the studbook as foundation sires: Simpatyaga, Inferno and Kokas. Three sons of Simpatyaga, named Sagib, Saksagan and Sagar; two of Inferno, Imam and Islam; and Kokas's son Kagul were to be crucial to the development of the Budyonny.

Progeny of fixed type and characteristics were soon being bred, and the Budyonny was recognized as a breed in 1948 – ironically,

the Russian cavalry was officially disbanded a handful of years later, in 1954.

## Mostly Chestnut

The same faults sometimes seen in the Don's conformation also occur, although to a somewhat lesser extent, in the Budyonny. The Budyonny's head reveals its Thoroughbred ancestry; it has bold, generous eyes and a straight or slightly concave profile. Most Budyonnys are chestnut and, although other colors occur, they are rare. The breed makes an excellent all-round competition horse.

# DON

HEIGHT: 15.2–16.2 hh

COLOUR: chestnut, brown

PERSONALITY TYPE: warm-blooded

TYPICAL USE: riding, competition, harness

TEMPERAMENT: willing, placid

ORIGIN: Russia

SIMILAR BREEDS: Budyonny

Originating from the Russian steppes, in the area between the rivers Don and Olga, the Don Horse is a hardy breed that probably descended from crosses between the steppe-bred Mongolian and Turkoman, Karabakh, Akhal-Teke and Orlovs. It was able to survive where lesser horses might have perished – the Cossack Cavalry, which contributed to Napoleon's defeat in Russia (1812), pursued the French all the way to Paris mounted on Dons. A lot of the French horses died, unable to withstand the extreme cold.

choppy stride, and its quarters can be weak, with a rather straight croup and low-set tail. It sometimes has 'calf' knees and sickle hocks. It has an Oriental-type head of average size, and the neck is generally well formed and muscular. It has a broad, deep chest and long, straight back, and hard, tough hooves.

Despite its shortcomings in conformation, it is very tough with great stamina. In 1951, a stallion named Zenith covered 312 km (193 miles) in 24 hours, resting for only four hours.

## Selective Breeding

It was partly the fame garnered by the Don during these military campaigns that led to a concerted breeding campaign, and selective breeding began in earnest in the 1830s. The Don was bred primarily for the cavalry, for both riding and harness, and was also used in developing and enhancing other breeds, such as the Budyonny.

At the beginning of the twentieth century, Thoroughbred and Arabian blood were added for refinement, but no more outcrosses have been introduced since.

## Great Stamina

The Don does still have conformational faults, despite efforts to breed them out. Its shoulders tend to be rather straight, giving it a

## Fascinating Facts

The Don is still used in harness, often in the traditional *tachanka*, a type of open cart or wagon in which four horses are harnessed side by side.

RIGHT

*The Don is prone to some conformational problems especially in the hindquarters and shoulders, but is a willing and hardy animal.*

# PRZEWALSKI'S HORSE

TEMPERAMENT: aggressive when threatened, sensitive

ORIGIN: Mongolia

SIMILAR BREEDS: Fjord, Exmoor

HEIGHT: 12–14 hh

COLOUR: dun

PERSONALITY TYPE: cold-blooded (arguable)

TYPICAL USE: wild

**M**ongolia's national symbol, Przewalski's Horse, or Przewalski – or the Takh, in its native homeland – is the last surviving genuine wild horse in the world. Sometimes called the Asiatic Wild Horse, it is a dweller of the steppe; until some 15,000 years ago, this immense belt of grasslands stretched away from Manchuria in the East to the Iberian Peninsula in the West. The 30,000-year-old cave drawings found in France and Spain depict a small, stout wild horse with Przewalski-like features.

## Earlier Discovery

It was originally believed that the Przewalski horse was 'discovered' by the Russian explorer Colonel Przhevalsky, for whom it is named, in 1881. More recent information indicates a much earlier encounter. A Scottish doctor who was sent on an embassy to China by Peter the Great (1672–1725) wrote of his experiences in *Journey from St Petersburg to Peking, 1719–1723*, and included an accurate description of this Asiatic Wild Horse.

## **F**ascinating **F**acts

At the end of the twentieth century and the beginning of the twenty-first, small herds of Przewalski's Horse were returned to their native habitat as part of a project to save the wild breed. The Przewalski was previously found only in captivity.

Even earlier, Hans Schiltberger, a Bavarian nobleman, was taken prisoner by the Turks and sold to the famous Tamerlane of the Golden Horde, who in turn gave Schiltberger to a Mongol prince named Egedi. Schiltberger spent several years in the Tien Shan mountains. He wrote of the wild horses he observed in his memoirs *Journey into Heathen Parts*, written in 1427.

## Chromosome Difference

The Przewalski differs from other horses in that it has 66 chromosomes, while all other breeds have 64. The horse is the size of a stocky pony, with dun colouring, black points, dorsal stripe and zebra stripes on its legs. It has a short, bristly mane that stands upright and is shed every summer, so the Przewalski does not grow a long mane and does not have a forelock. Przewalskis are among the most threatened wildlife species in the world. The entire world population consists of no more than 1,500 individual animals.

# ALTAI

HEIGHT: 13–14 hh

COLOUR: chestnut, bay, black, grey, spotted

PERSONALITY TYPE: warm-blooded

TYPICAL USE: pack, meat, trekking

TEMPERAMENT: tough, calm, willing

ORIGIN: Central Asia

SIMILAR BREEDS: none

A mountain breed, the Altai evolved over a long period of time and has been moulded by the harsh climate and conditions of its home in the Altai Mountains in south-west Siberia, where Russia, Mongolia, China and Kazakhstan come together. The word Altai comes from *Al* (gold) and *tau* (mount) – so the horse comes from the 'Mountains of Gold'. Horses have always been important to the tribespeople and nomads in the region, who rely on them for transport and pack.

## Conformational Defects

A sure-footed horse is imperative to the tribespeople of this remote area because they must often travel over steep mountain trails cut from the rock and cross fast-moving streams without slipping. The Altai is a very hardy animal that is indispensable to the people who depend on it.

### BELOW LEFT
*The Altai's hardy constitution, and particularly tough and sound limbs and feet compensate for its occasionally poor conformation.*

Supremely adapted to year-round pasture grazing, it is an economical keeper and fairly even-tempered. It is not the most attractive creature. Its head is rather large and coarse, and its neck has a tendency to be fleshy, rather than muscular. Its back is long and slightly dipped, although its croup is well developed. Its legs are short and sturdy, but conformation defects such as sloping pasterns and bowed hocks do occur. Still, it has excellent feet and a strong constitution. It is most often seen in chestnut, bay, black and grey, although spotted horses sometimes appear.

## Packhorse

Altai Horses cross well with other breeds, such as the Thoroughbred, to make a good performance horse, retaining the Altai's hardy constitution, but being larger and losing some of the conformation defects. The breed has also been crossed with some of the heavy draught breeds to produce animals for meat. The purebred Altai makes a good pack animal, too, due to its endurance and sensible nature.

Today, the Altai is used for trekking in the steppes and in the Altai Mountains.

# MARWARI

TEMPERAMENT: docile, calm, brave

ORIGIN: India

SIMILAR BREEDS: Kathiawari

HEIGHT: up to 14.3 hh

COLOUR: all colours

PERSONALITY TYPE: warm-blooded

TYPICAL USE: riding, military, police

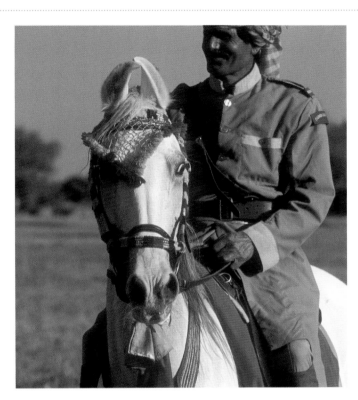

India's Marwari descended from the splendid warhorses that served the ruling families and warriors of feudal India from the beginning of that country's long history. The status of these horses was unparalleled; they were deemed superior to all men. Thus only the Rajput families and the Kshatriyas – a warrior caste – were permitted to ride the Marwari. It was said that, if injured during battle, the Marwari would not fall down until it had carried its rider to safety, and would stand guard over its rider if he were injured.

## Cavalry Mount

The exact origins of the Marwari are not known, although it is believed to have evolved in the state of Marwari and possibly in north-west India near Afghanistan. It developed along similar lines to its neighbour, the Kathiawari, which it resembles, and probably has a high percentage of Arabian blood.

The breed was renowned for its bravery. During the reign of the Moghul Emperor Akbar (1542–1605), the Rajput warriors formed the Imperial Cavalry, employing more than 50,000 horses, most of them Marwari.

## Curling Ears

The Marwari remained popular for many years – it was even used in the First World War – but went into decline in the early twentieth century and was almost extinct by the 1930s. It was saved by the Maharaja Umaid Singhji, who bought some Marwari stallions to breed with the best Marwari mares he could find. There is an ongoing effort by the Indian government to preserve the breed.

It is a noble equine, with tiny ears that curl in towards each other so that they touch – a hallmark also seen in the Kathiawari. Its elegant head is set on a muscular neck of

RIGHT

*The noble Marwari with its tipped ears and majestic bearing is one of India's best-loved horse breeds, along with the Kathiawari.*

good length, with sloping shoulders and deep chest. Its back is compact, and its legs are very strong, with dense bone and hard feet.

# KATHIAWARI

HEIGHT: 14.2–15 hh

COLOUR: predominantly chestnut

PERSONALITY TYPE: warm-blooded

TYPICAL USE: riding, police, polo

TEMPERAMENT: intelligent, affectionate

ORIGIN: India

SIMILAR BREEDS: Marwari, Indian Half-Bred

Although very similar in appearance and characteristics to the Marwari – not least in those tiny, curly ears – the Kathiawari is considered a separate breed. It is thought to date back to the fourteenth century, having evolved from native stock crossed with the Arabian. It takes its name from the Kathiawar peninsula of western Gujarat, on the north-west coast of India. Like the Marwari, the Kathiawari was highly regarded, each royal household having its own horse, which was treated as a favoured pet.

from a shipwreck off the west coast of India, then bred at will with the local pony breeds. It is more likely that Arabians and other Oriental stock were shipped to India during the period of the Moghul emperors, and that these were deliberately crossbred with the indigenous breed, from which evolved the Kathiawari.

It certainly has Arabian characteristics, possessing great endurance and stamina. These abilities made it popular as a warhorse; in the nineteenth century, it was used by both the British and the Mahratta cavalries.

## Arabian Legend

Legend has it that some Arabians swam ashore

## Police Mount

The Kathiawari has the Marwari's elegant head and

graceful neck, and the exaggeratedly turned-in ears. It is narrow and wiry in build, with sloping shoulders, deep chest, long back and sloping croup. Its tail is set and carried high. Its legs are slender but strong, with tough feet, although many Kathiawaris have cow hocks. The horse is hardy and frugal.

Most Kathiawaris are chestnut, although all solid colours appear except black, and some paints. The Kathiawari is a natural pacer, as is the Marwari.

Once bred by wealthy families who would name a strain for the foundation

mare, the Kathiawari is now bred at the government-controlled stud at Junagadh. Today, it is used by the mounted police of Gujarat and for mounted games such as tent pegging and polo.

## Fascinating Facts

The curled ears of Mawaris and Kathiawaris are often known as the 'sting of the scorpion'.

LEFT

*The Kathiawari has similarities with the Marwari, and both breeds exhibit Arabian characteristics in conformation and personality.*

# INDIAN HALF-BRED

TEMPERAMENT: intelligent, sensible

ORIGIN: India

SIMILAR BREEDS: Kathiawari, Marwari,
Australian Stock Horse

HEIGHT: 15–16 hh

COLOUR: all colours

PERSONALITY TYPE:
warm-blooded

TYPICAL USE: riding, military, police

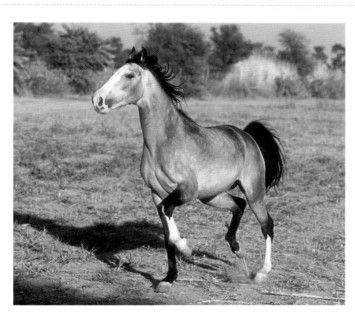

**W**iry and enduring, the Indian Half-Bred was developed in the nineteenth century for the Indian military, which needed a tough and hardy horse that was larger than the country's native breeds, the Marwari and Kathiawari, and their close cousin, the Sindhi. To create the Indian Half-Bred, they used Australian Stock Horses, or Walers, to add bone and substance, and Arabians for refinement. Later Thoroughbred blood was added, perhaps because the native stock already had a proportion of Arabian influence.

## Substantial

Before the development of the Indian Half-Bred, the Indian cavalry used mostly Arabian or part-bred Arabian horses, but the Waler had been imported at the beginning of the twentieth century because it was larger and more suitable.

LEFT

*The Indian Half-Bred was originally developed for the Indian cavalry and is an extremely hardy and sound animal.*

Crossed with the native breeds, the Waler produced a much more substantial equine. The Indian Half-Bred is now produced all over India, particularly at the army remount depot at Saharanpur and the army stud at

Babugarh. As well as being used in the army, the Indian Half-Bred is widely used by the police force in the towns and especially in the rural areas. The Half-Bred can be any colour, and stands between 15 and 16 hh.

## Thoroughbred Benefit

The addition of Thoroughbred blood was to prove of major benefit to the Indian Half-Bred, as it was already well suited to a hot and unforgiving climate. One stallion, called Thomas Jefferson, produced particularly good stock and was used for several years at both Babugarh and Saharanpur.

When the subcontinent was partitioned into India and Pakistan in 1947, India kept eight English and four French Thoroughbreds, which were to form the basis of future breeding stock. Since then, other breeds have been used, including Anglo-Arabs, Bretons and Polish Arabs. The enduring Indian Half-Bred has a rather plain head, but is well formed and sound, with excellent feet.

# BARB

HEIGHT: 14.2–15.2 hh

COLOUR: chestnut, bay, grey, black

PERSONALITY TYPE: hot-blooded

TYPICAL USE: riding, show

TEMPERAMENT: intelligent, brave, fiery

ORIGIN: North Africa

SIMILAR BREEDS: Arabian, Akhal-Teke

There is considerable debate about whether the Arabian came before the Barb, or whether it was the other way around. Certainly, the Barb, or Barbary Horse, as it was sometimes known, is an ancient breed and, like the Arabian, has had a considerable influence on other horse breeds. It is likely that the Barb contains some Arabian blood, and it is a testament to the dominance of the Barb's genes that it has maintained its characteristics. The Barb is sometimes mistaken for an Arabian, but they are two separate breeds.

## Barbarian Warriors

The Barb traces back through antiquity to the time of the Persians and Scythians, in the area of the Fertile Crescent, north-east of the Mediterranean Sea, between the Tigris and Euphrates rivers, then south-east to the Persian Gulf, encompassing

RIGHT

*The Barb is an ancient breed that, like the Arabian, has had considerable influence on the development of many other horse breeds.*

the countries that are now Egypt, Israel, and Lebanon, and parts of Turkey, Jordan, Syria, Iraq and Iran.

King Solomon was given several Barbs in approximately 1950 BC, which is how the Israelites came to have Barbs. The Barb, a desert equine that was extremely tough and enduring, made an excellent warhorse and was used as such by the Israelites, the Ishmaelites and the Berbers. Some believe the name 'Barb' came from the Berber warriors, who were notoriously barbarian in nature, but it is more likely that the name came from the Barbary Coast of North Africa whence the Berbers came.

## Spanish Breeds

The Barb is of great importance to the development of the Spanish horses, of which it is believed to be a direct ancestor. Barbs were introduced to Spain

during the Moorish invasions that began in the eighth century, and influenced the Andalusian and Lusitano breeds. Through them, many other breeds of horse in Europe and the Americas were established.

But perhaps the single most important effect of the Barb was in the development of the English Thoroughbred. One of the three founding stallions of the Thoroughbred was called the Godolphin Arabian, but is widely believed to have been a Barb. The Godolphin Arabian was a small 15-hh bay with a beautiful head, but unnaturally high crest, and was spotted pulling a cart in

Paris by Edward Coke. Mr Coke purchased the horse, took him to England and gave him to a friend, who passed him on to the Earl of Godolphin.

In 1731, he was being used as a teaser on a mare called Roxana, who was to be mated with a stallion called Hobgoblin. It is said that the Godolphin Arabian fought Hobgoblin and covered the mare himself. The resulting foal, Lath, became one of the most famous racehorses of the day, second only to Flying Childers, and founded one of the most successful dynasties of racing.

## Rare Breed

The history of the Barb in England, however, is one that far precedes the Godolphin Arabian, and it is a well-known fact that Barbs were being imported to England for use in the royal studs as long ago as the reign of Richard II (1377–1400).

Along with the Thoroughbred, the Barb is also credited with having had a profound influence on the development of the Camargue horse of France, to which it bears a striking resemblance, the Irish Connemara and various French breeds.

The Barb should not be confused with the Arabian, as it has very distinctive characteristics, such as a convex or Roman profile that is seen in many of the Iberian horses influenced by the Barb.

Today, the number of pure Barb Horses is greatly decreased – the World Organization of the Barb Horse (Organisation Mondiale du Cheval Barbe) was founded in Algeria in 1987 to try to save the breed.

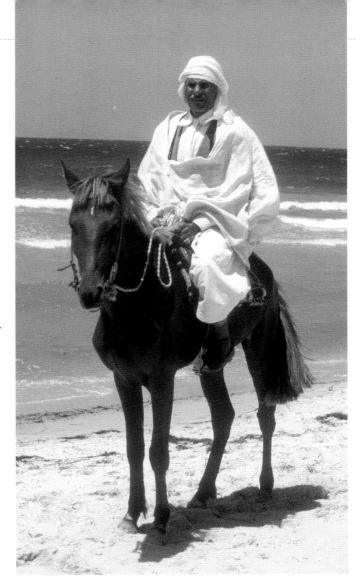

RIGHT

*The Barb, unlike the Arabian, has a distinctly convex profile, and this is seen in many of the Spanish breeds that the Barb influenced.*

## Wise Words

'Never look a gift horse in the mouth.' Saint Jerome (AD 374 –419), on the Epistle to the Ephesians.

# BRUMBY

HEIGHT: 14–15 hh

COLOUR: all colours

PERSONALITY TYPE: warm-blooded

TYPICAL USE: feral

TEMPERAMENT: uncertain temper, unpredictable

ORIGIN: Australia

SIMILAR BREEDS: Australian Stock Horse (Waler)

**H**orses arrived in Australia with the First Fleet that sailed from England in 1788. The journey was long and arduous, for horses as well as humans, and only the toughest survived that dreadful voyage. These horses were probably Thoroughbred and heavy draught breeds, and adapted to the rigours of their harsh new land. Some either escaped or were abandoned, and became feral, forming into natural herds and surviving on what little grazing and fresh water they were able to find. These horses form the basis for what is now known as the Brumby.

## Pest Species

There is some debate about how they came by their name. One theory is that they were named for a farrier, an Englishman called James Brumby who moved to Tasmania in 1804 and left behind some horses. When asked who the horses belonged to, people would say, 'They're Brumby's.' The name may also have come from an Aboriginal word *baroomby*, meaning 'wild', in the language of the Pitjara people on the Warrego and Nogoa rivers in southern Queensland.

The horses thrived in the vast open spaces of Australia, but were quickly seen as being a pest. The Brumby makes a poor riding horse; it often has conformational defects, is not particularly attractive, and is just too wild to be tamed. Although the mane and tail hair of the Brumby is used for musical instruments, brushes and upholstery, the horse is otherwise of little use.

## Protecting the Herd

In the 1960s, a systematic and excessive culling was introduced, using rifles from a helicopter. It was far from exact and often left the wild horses mortally wounded to die a slow, painful death. There was international outcry and, although Brumbies are still culled, it is now carried out far more humanely. This culling is necessary not only to reduce the horses' impact on cattle farming and the natural environment, but also for the protection of the wild herd. In drought conditions, horses could die of starvation and thirst.

# AUSTRALIAN STOCK HORSE

TEMPERAMENT: sensible, intelligent

ORIGIN: Australia

SIMILAR BREEDS: Thoroughbred, Brumby

HEIGHT: 15–16 hh

COLOUR: bay, chestnut, black, brown, grey

PERSONALITY TYPE: warm-blooded

TYPICAL USE: endurance, competition, harness, ranching

As Australia developed rapidly with increasing exploration from the 1830s, knowledgeable horse breeders imported a steady stream of Thoroughbreds to improve the local stock. The use of Thoroughbred stallions on the condition-hardened local mares produced the beautiful strain of tough but stylish equine exemplified by today's Australian Stock Horse, or Waler.

## Working Horses

The horse was originally known as the New South Waler; this was quickly shortened simply to Waler. Early Walers were highly regarded both as working stockhorses and as cavalry mounts, although they were never registered as a breed (it was not until 1971 that the Australian Stock Horse Society was established). Explorers, stockmen, troopers, settlers – all depended upon this reliable and versatile mount, whether they were exploring rough terrain, ploughing land, herding sheep or cattle, or patrolling. The Indian cavalry used Walers extensively; later, during the First World War, Allied forces used them in huge numbers.

By the end of the nineteenth century, the Waler was being exported to India alone at a rate of 5,000 a year, and Australia became the sole supplier of remounts to the British and Indian armies.

## Great Demand

So many horses were exported that, by the end of the Second World War, the Waler had all but disappeared. It was re-established using Thoroughbreds and Arabians, and no further outcrossing has been used since the 1940s. The modern Waler has some similarities to the Thorough-

bred, particularly noticeable in its fine head. Its neck is in proportion to its body and well set on good, sloping shoulders. It has a deep though not excessively wide chest and a strong back. Its quarters are muscular and very powerful, and the legs strong and tough, with well-formed hard hooves.

## Fascinating Facts

Jousting is still practised today: Foligno has an annual jousting tournament – the *Giostra della Quintana* – from a tradition dating back to the fifteenth century.

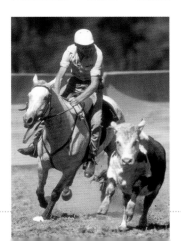

### RIGHT
*Also called Walers, these horses developed from Thoroughbreds and local stock and are noted for their hardy constitution.*

# Heavy Horses

  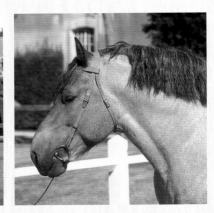

**M**ost draught horse breeds – the word 'draught' comes from the Anglo-Saxon *ᵭragan*, meaning to draw or haul – are thought to have evolved from the ancient Forest Horse, a massive, slow-moving primitive equine from northern Europe. Although now extinct, the Forest Horse was well adapted to its environment, developing broad, flat hooves, which enabled it to live in the widespread swampy areas, and a thick, wiry coat, which may have been dappled to provide camouflage.

Many of today's draught breeds display several characteristics this ancient equine is thought to have had: the blunt, rather heavy head, powerful build and sturdy, short legs. Most are easy and economical keepers, requiring little feed or management, and almost all have a calm, equable nature. Although hot-blooded horses such as the Thoroughbred and the Arabian have often been used in the development of these draughts, the heavy breeds are considered cold-blooded, like their primitive ancestor.

## Long-standing Helpers

These horses have served humankind since time immemorial; they have accompanied us into war – carrying a knight in full armour or pulling the twentieth century's heavy artillery – they have provided transport and they have ploughed the fields and pulled wagons. Uncomplaining, they have worked hard and tirelessly side by side with us, pulling weights that we feeble humans could barely shift an inch for long distances and long hours.

Virtually all draught breeds combine the traits of strength, stamina, health, longevity, patience and a docile temperament, which made them indispensable to generations of farmers before the age of mechanization. They have also provided humankind with sustenance – and even today, when many of us would baulk at eating horse flesh, some heavy horses are bred for their milk and their meat.

It is their committed endeavour and endearing nature, however, for which the world's heavy draught horses are most highly valued.

# SUFFOLK PUNCH

TEMPERAMENT: docile, willing, hard-working

ORIGIN: England

SIMILAR BREEDS: Jutland, Brabant

HEIGHT: 16 hh plus

COLOUR: 'chesnut'

PERSONALITY TYPE: cold-blooded

TYPICAL USE: light draught, harness, riding, show

Now a rare breed, the Suffolk Punch was developed in Suffolk and Norfolk on the east coast of England. The area was bordered on the north, east and south by the North Sea, and on the west by the Fens. Isolated from their neighbors, the farmers of Suffolk developed a breed of horse to suit their special way of life. To plough the heavy clay soil, the horse had to possess not only power, but also stamina, health, longevity and docility. The mighty Suffolk Punch fulfilled all these criteria.

## Pure Breed

As the Suffolk farmer relied on his horses to work his land, he rarely sold them on. This kept the Suffolk Punch relatively unknown out of its fen homeland, but also kept the breed pure. Of all the heavy draught breeds, the Suffolk Punch is thought to be the oldest, with references to the 'Old Breed' – thought to be another name for the Suffolk Punch – dating back to 1506. Crisp's Horse of Ufford, deemed to be the foundation sire of the breed, was foaled in 1768. The first

*RIGHT*

*Suffolks are described as having 'the face of an angel, the body of a beer barrel and the bottom of the farmer's daughter'.*

studbook was produced in 1880 by Herman Biddell, the first secretary of the Suffolk Horse Society.

## Always Chesnut

The Suffolk Punch is always chesnut – and the colour is correctly spelled without the middle 't' – of which there are seven recognized shades: bright, red, golden, yellow, light, dark and dull dark. It has an intelligent head, which is quite fine for a heavy horse breed, with neat ears and a kind eye. Its neck is muscular with a pleasing arch, and it is compact and short-coupled. Its legs are rather short and its body appears too big for them — which has given rise to the 'Punch' part of the breed's name.

Those short legs are exceptionally strong and sound and do not have any feather – this would be a drawback in working the heavy clay soil of East Anglia.

# SHIRE

HEIGHT: 17–18hh

COLOUR: black, bay, brown, grey

PERSONALITY TYPE:
cold-blooded

TYPICAL USE: heavy draught, show

TEMPERAMENT: gentle, docile, willing

ORIGIN: England

SIMILAR BREEDS: Clydesdale, Brabant

**W**illiam the Conqueror is credited with bringing the 'Great Horse' – a sort of equine armoured tank – to England in the eleventh century after the Norman Conquest. Mighty and massive, this imposing creature could easily carry a knight in full armour. The modern breed takes its name from the counties of Derbyshire, Leicestershire and Staffordshire, where it developed. The original Great Horse was crossed with a mixture of Flanders and Friesian horses brought over to England by the Dutch.

## Bakewell Black

Dutch contractors were working on the reclamation of land undertaken in the Fens. Their imported breeds were to have a profound effect on the development of the Shire. Interbreeding between the Great Horse, the Friesian and finally the Flanders produced the English Black, named by Oliver Cromwell. It was much larger than the Great Horse, although it exhibited many of the features of the Flanders Horse and the predominantly black colouring passed down from the Friesian.

Dull in colour, gross and sluggish, it was vastly improved in the Midlands by the renowned breeder of the time, Robert Bakewell (1725–95), and his followers, and for a time it was popularly known as the Bakewell Black.

## Gentle Giant

The Shire's foundation sire is believed to be Packington Blind, which sired the first Shires to appear in the studbook of 1878 – the Shire Horse Society was formed in 1884. The breed was by then known as the English Cart Horse – infusions of different blood had largely bred out the predominantly black colouring, so Bakewell Black became a misnomer, and changed to Shire with the founding of the breed society. The term 'Shire' is thought to come from the Saxon word *schyran*, which means 'divide'.

As news of this gentle giant spread, many stallions were exported, particularly to the United States, where the American Shire Horse Association was founded in 1885.

## Rent-Payers

Meanwhile, in England, ruthless veterinary examination at the London Shire Show virtually eliminated any conformation faults, such as unsound limbs and poor wind. The country's most powerful working horse increased greatly in value, so much so that in the Great Depression of the 1930s, good Shire foals were dubbed the 'rent-payers'.

Mechanization at first had little effect on the fortunes of the Shire Horse; the first motorized vehicles for farm work were inefficient and too expensive, way beyond

## Fascinating Facts

The Shire Horse holds the record for the world's biggest horse – Sampson, foaled in 1846 in Bedfordshire, England, stood 21.2 1/2hh, or 2.2 m (7 ft 2 1/2 in) at the withers and weighed more than 1.5 tonnes.

the means of many during the prolonged Depression. None could match the pulling power of the massive Shire. It was the Second World War that was to have a devastating effect on the breed. It is thought that, in its heyday, there were about a million Shire horses; by the 1960s,

numbers had dwindled to a mere few thousand.

## Breed Revival

It is only in recent years that the breed has enjoyed something of a revival. Many London breweries used the Shire to pull their drays through the city, a wonderful and popular spectacle. Although still a draught horse, ridden classes for Shires have been introduced at British shows.

For all its size, the Shire is a most attractive horse with a charming docile nature. It has a large head with a convex or Roman profile, wide forehead and intelligent, kindly eyes. Its long neck is arched and gives the animal a commanding appearance; its shoulders are deep and oblique, well able to support a collar. Its back is short and compact; its quarters long and sweeping and well muscled. It has long legs with plenty of hard, flat bone and exceptionally good feet, and it has lots of feather. In all, the Shire is a combination of considerable strength and noble beauty.

BELOW

*The Shire horse is considered the largest of the draught breeds, and has a huge pulling capacity. Ploughing competitions such as this are not uncommon.*

# CLYDESDALE

HEIGHT: 17 hh and over

COLOUR: bay, brown, chestnut, roan, black

PERSONALITY TYPE: cold-blooded

TYPICAL USE: draught, harness, riding, show

TEMPERAMENT: kind, docile, willing

ORIGIN: Scotland

SIMILAR BREEDS: Shire, Brabant

Scotland's pride was founded in Lanarkshire, a region formerly known as Clydesdale after the River Clyde, which runs through it. The history of the breed dates back to the middle of the eighteenth century, when native stock in Lanarkshire was bred to Flemish stallions in an effort to produce greater weight and substance. The first Flemish stallion, dark brown in colour, was imported by the 6th Duke of Hamilton, and his tenants were granted its use free of charge.

## Marked Improvement

After this, a John Paterson of Lochlyloch brought a Flemish stallion from England – where these horses were also being used on native mares to produce what would later become the Shire Horse – which was also to prove successful. This stallion was black with a white face and some white on its legs, and Lochlyloch blood soon became highly sought after, as a result of the marked improvement apparent in the region's youngstock.

This horse was followed by a 16.1 hh black stallion called Blaze, which belonged to a Mr Scott of Carstairs and in 1782 took first prize at the Edinburgh Show. Although nothing is known of the latter horse's pedigree, it is thought it was of coaching blood.

## Breed Basis

All modern-day Clydesdales can trace their lineage back to a filly foal bought by a Mr Somerville of Lampits Farm,

# Fascinating Facts

The game horseshoes developed among Grecian soldiers, who could not afford a discus for the playing of quoits, so they modified the game and used old discarded horseshoes instead of a discus.

Carstairs, at a dispersing sale of stock belonging to a Mr Clarkson, who is thought to be a descendant of John Paterson – so it is quite likely this filly was in turn a descendant of the black Flemish stallion. The filly produced a black colt called

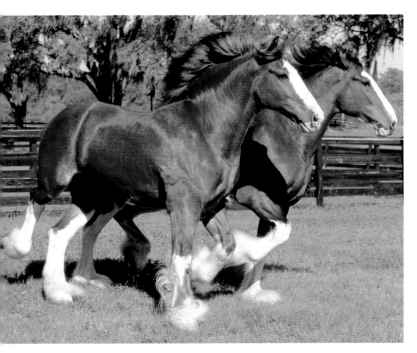

---

**LEFT**

*The Clydesdale breed originated in Scotland, and along with the Shire horse is one of the most elegant draught breeds.*

Glancer – also known as Thompson's Black Horse – which is to be found in the pedigrees of horses today.

The black Glancer had white on both hind legs and is described as 'having a strong neat body set on short thick legs, the clean sharp bones of which were fringed with nice, flowing silken hair'. His dam, known as the Lampits Mare, also foaled Farmers Fancy and Glancer I, and the frequent mating of descendants of these two is thought to have formed the basis of the Clydesdale.

## Formidable

A daughter of Farmers Fancy, Jean, produced a filly foal by Samson in 1860, a powerful dark bay that became the famous Keir Peggy. She produced Darnley, a rich bay with very little white. Among Darnley's most famous sons were MacGregor, Top Gallant and Flashwood. Top Gallant's most prominent son was Sir Everard, which in turn was the sire of Baron's Pride.

Baron's Pride sired one of the breed's most famous sons, Baron of Buchlyvie. In 1911, he was sold for £9,500 – the equivalent today would be about £275,000.

By this time, the Clydesdale was firmly established as a formidable working horse and between 1884 and 1945, more than 20,000 were exported to Australia, New Zealand, the Americas, Russia, Italy and Austria.

## Stylish Trot

After the Second World War, the agricultural industry in the United Kingdom largely replaced its working horses with mechanical power. Clydesdale numbers dwindled and, in 1975, the

horse was categorized by the Rare Breeds Survival Trust as 'vulnerable' – in the years since, and with the increase in breed numbers, it is now categorized as 'at risk'.

Despite its size, the Clydesdale oozes quality, with a straight head which is broad between the eyes, wide muzzle, large nostrils and a bright, clear and intelligent eye. It has a muscular neck (rather long for a draught breed), sloping shoulder and deep body, with supremely sound, long legs and excellent feet. Like the Shire, it has plenty of fine, silky feather. It has a long, easy walk and a springy, stylish trot. A surprisingly active mover for such a large horse, the Clydesdale redefines the term 'horsepower'.

# ARDENNAIS

HEIGHT: 14.3–16hh

COLOUR: bay, roan, chestnut

PERSONALITY TYPE: cold-blooded

TYPICAL USE: draught, meat

TEMPERAMENT: calm, tolerant, hardy

ORIGIN: France

SIMILAR BREEDS: Brabant, Auxois, Trait du Nord

**W**hile there are also a Swedish Ardennes and a Belgian Ardennes, the original breed is from France and is the oldest of them all. It can be traced back to references made by Julius Caesar (100–44 BC) in his account of his conquest of Gaul, *De Bello Gallico*. It is thought that ancestors of this mighty draught horse were bred on the Ardennes – the mountainous region bordering France and Belgium – for more than 2,000 years, and that the Ardennais is descended from the last of the Solutre.

## Paleolithic Horse

The Solutre Horse (*Equus robustus*) was a prehistoric breed found in the area of the same name in the Burgundy region of France during the Paleolithic period in about 50,000 BC, and probably formed the basis for many modern horse breeds.

The old type of Ardennais was probably somewhat lighter than the massive modern horse, and would have been used for riding as well as draught. It is known they were widely used during the French Revolution (1789–99) and afterwards by the French military. During the Napoleonic Wars, the Ardennais was renowned for its great stamina, endurance and ability to survive under the harshest of conditions.

Russia's heavy draught breeds probably evolved from the numbers of Ardennais left behind during the French retreat of 1812.

## Handsome

Today's Ardennais was developed during the nineteenth century by crossing the original with the Boulonnais, Percheron, Thoroughbred and Arabian, to produce a strong, stocky horse with a kind but lively temperament. Despite the infusions of 'hot' blood, however, the Ardennais is still considered cold-blooded, rather than warm-blooded.

The Ardennais is handsome rather than beautiful, with a large head, compact body,

stocky legs and a short mane and tail. It is surefooted enough to cope with rough and hilly terrain, and an economical feeder. Still used for draught work, it is also bred for its meat.

# BRABANT (Belgian Heavy Draught)

TEMPERAMENT: generous, willing, placid

ORIGIN: Belgium

SIMILAR BREEDS: Shire, Clydesdale, Suffolk Punch

HEIGHT: 16–18hh

COLOUR: roan, chestnut

PERSONALITY TYPE: cold-blooded

TYPICAL USE: draught, meat

**T**his breed was originally a warhorse, a Goliath among the heavy draught horse breeds, which owes its sound constitution and robust good health to the lush little corner of Europe where it was developed. Its nearest ancestor was the Flanders, or Flemish, Horse, a huge black powerhouse of an equine feted by the knights of the day, whom it could carry in their full armour with the minimal effort of a man lifting a kitten. Its fame spread – Richard I (1157–99) imported several Belgian horses to England.

## Colossal Horse

Those British imports were in turn to influence the Shire, Clydesdale and Suffolk Punch. As demand for a lighter type of cavalry horse grew, however, the Belgian people resisted the temptation to scale down their massive equine and instead used it for agriculture, its great stature being suited to the rich, heavy soil and the climate.

Until the beginning of the twentieth century, there were three different types of Brabant. The first was the Colossal Horse of Mahaigne, for which the stallion Jean I was responsible; the second was the Big Horse of the Dendre, which was founded by the stallion Orange I; and the last was the Grey Horse of Nivelles, based on the stock produced by the stallion Bayard.

### **F**ascinating **F**acts

In 1866, Dr A.G. van Hoorebeck of Illinois imported the first Brabant into the United States. This breed is now the most popular workhorse in the United States.

## Good Walk

By the twentieth century, the three groups had become indistinguishable. The modern Brabant has a small head on a thick, muscular neck and huge, powerful shoulders. Its rather upright shoulders give it the short, choppy stride often seen in the draught breeds. It does, however, have a good walk. It also has an extremely willing and generous temperament which, combined with its incredible strength, makes it an ideal heavy workhorse.

The Brabant is popular in the United States, where it is known simply as the Belgian Horse and has become much more refined.

LEFT

*The Brabant generally has an excellent walk which, combined with its biddable temperament, makes it a good workhorse.*

# COMTOIS

HEIGHT: 14.1–15.1hh

COLOUR: chestnut

PERSONALITY TYPE: cold-blooded

TYPICAL USE: light draught, meat

TEMPERAMENT: good-natured, trainable, willing

ORIGIN: France

SIMILAR BREEDS: Ardennais

**T**his ancient breed is thought to have existed in France since the fourth century, descending from horses brought to the area by the Burgundians, a people from northern Germany. The Franche-Comté and the Jura Mountains on the border of France and Switzerland are thought to be the original breeding ground of the breed. The Comtois was comparatively small for a draught breed, but its small, stocky stature, with short, hard-boned legs, was ideally suited to its homeland's rough and rocky terrain.

## 'Cobby' Characteristics

In the sixteenth century, the Comtois was used to improve the horses of Burgundy and became famous as a cavalry and artillery horse – Louis XIV (1638–1715) used this breed in his armies for both cavalry and artillery, as did Napoleon on his disastrous campaign into Russia in 1812. In turn, during the nineteenth century, other draught breeds such as the Norman, the Boulonnais and the Percheron were used to improve the Comtois, and since 1905 the use of Ardennais stallions has given the breed greater strength and better legs.

*LEFT*
*These versatile horses were used extensively by Louis XIV for his cavalry and artillery, and by Napoleon during his Russian campaign.*

minimal feather and good strong joints.

## Long-lived

Good-natured, hardy and easy to train, the Comtois is also long-lived. It is now bred in the mountainous regions of the Massif Central, the Pyrenees Mountains and the Alps, for which it is perfectly suited. It is still widely used for hauling wood in the high pine forests of the Jura and for work in the hilly

Today's Comtois is a lightly built draught horse with 'cobby' characteristics. It has a large head set on a short, muscular neck, a broad, deep chest and powerful hindquarters. It has short, strong legs with vineyards of the Arbois area, and is second only to the Breton Horse in numbers in France. Those bred for the meat industry, however, tend to be poorer specimens, as the emphasis is placed on producing bulk.

# BRETON

TEMPERAMENT: sociable, easygoing, willing

ORIGIN: France

SIMILAR BREEDS: Ardennais

HEIGHT: 14.3–16.2hh

COLOUR: bay, grey, chestnut, roan

PERSONALITY TYPE: cold-blooded

TYPICAL USE: draught

A demanding climate and unforgiving land has made the mighty Breton France's premier draught breed. It originated in the province of Bretagne, also known as Brittany, in the north-west of France. Brittany has a history of breeding superb equines, going back to the Middle Ages, and the Breton is the result of evolution over hundreds of years, culminating in a horse of great strength and durability. The Breton became sought after by military leaders around the time of the Crusades (1096–1270).

## Comfortable gait

It is not known how horses first came to the mountains of Breton, although it is known they have been there for thousands of years. The original Breton Horse was thought to be quite small, standing perhaps only about 14hh, but it had a supremely comfortable gait – which was why it was so popular. During the seventeenth century, Breton Horses were sent to New France (now Canada), by the French king Louis XIV, where it was to influence the Canadian Horse, or Cheval Canadien.

## A Dished Face

There are three types of Breton, which come from different districts of Brittany. The Corlay Breton, or Central Mountain Breton, contains Arabian and Thoroughbred blood, and stands between 14.3 and 15.1hh. Considered the true descendant of the original, the Corlay Breton is the smallest of the breed and has a dished face.

The Postier Breton is the result of breeding with Norfolk Trotters and Hackneys during the nineteenth century and has

those breeds' attractive gaits. It stands about 15.1 hh and makes a good coach horse. The Heavy Draught Breton was derived using Ardennais and Percheron blood, and is very strong relative to its size. It can stand up to 16.2 hh and has short but muscular legs.

### ABOVE
*The Breton horse is predominantly chestnut or roan in colour, and generally has a quality head and amenable nature.*

All three types are easygoing, willing workers and tend to be very sociable creatures.

## Fascinating facts

The Canadian Horse, or Cheval Canadien, is descended from Breton Horses sent from the stables of Louis XIV between 1665 and 1670. It also has Barb, Andalusian and Norman blood, and is today recognized as a true breed inherent only to Canada.

# AUXOIS

HEIGHT: 16.3 hh and over

COLOUR: bay, roan, chestnut

PERSONALITY TYPE: cold-blooded

TYPICAL USE: draught, meat

TEMPERAMENT: gentle, willing, biddable

ORIGIN: France

SIMILAR BREEDS: Ardennais, Trait du Nord

**The Auxois is a descendant of the old Burgundian Horse that at one time existed side by side with the Ardennais, to which it is closely related. Compact and powerful, it is known to have been around since the Middle Ages and is therefore probably a distant descendant of the prehistoric Solutre Horse. It was originally from the Côte d'Or and Yonne regions in Burgundy, France, and has the hardiness, strength, stamina and amiable nature of most heavy draught breeds.**

## Free and Fast

In the nineteenth century, infusions of Boulonnais and Percheron blood, as well as Ardennais and Trait du Nord, were added to the Auxois to add height and substance. It most closely resembles the latter two, and selective breeding has resulted in the predominance of bay or red roan colouring. Since the twentieth century, only Ardennais blood has been added and, although the Auxois is considerably larger than its close cousin, it is finer in the legs and has smaller quarters.

Despite its bulk, the Auxois can move surprisingly freely and quickly, thanks to a well-sloped shoulder.

## Breed Revival

The Auxois has a relatively light head for a draught breed, with a broad forehead and small, alert ears. It is stoutly built, with a short, thick neck, flattish withers and a deep, wide chest. It is broad through the back and has a long, sloping, muscular croup with a low-set tail. Although slender for its size, the Auxois has particularly powerful legs.

---
LEFT

*Unlike many draught breeds, the Auxois often has a good slope to its shoulder, which allows it to move freely at speed.*

---

Its kind, biddable nature combines with its superb pulling power to produce a strong, durable equine. Its bulk means that the Auxois is also bred for its meat.

Today, very few of these excellent equines remain, although efforts are being made to maintain the breed, particularly around the Cluny Stud and the fertile areas of Yonne and Saône-et-Loire.

# TRAIT DU NORD

TEMPERAMENT: kind, gentle, easygoing

ORIGIN: France

SIMILAR BREEDS: Ardennais, Auxois

HEIGHT: 15.2–16.2hh

COLOUR: bay, roan

PERSONALITY TYPE: cold-blooded

TYPICAL USE: draught, agriculture, harness, meat

Considered, incorrectly, by many to be a 'branch' of the Ardennais, the Trait du Nord is a fairly new breed – the studbook was opened in 1903. *Trait* is the French word for 'draught', and *nord* refers to 'north', which is the region in France whence this horse comes. The Trait du Nord is the result of crossbreeding Ardennais and Flemish horses with the Belgian Brabant. Constitutionally strong, calm and enduring, it was formerly used in the vast cereal and sugarbeet farms in the north of France.

## Briefly Popular

The horse is still bred in the areas around Lille, the Sommes, the Aisne and the Pas-de-Calais, although its numbers are declining – the breed enjoyed a brief period of popularity after the studbook was established in the early twentieth century, but has since gone into decline. This is a shame because it possesses that vigour and energy necessary to enable it to trot at a remarkable pace, while at walking speed it has proved a well-balanced draught horse with the mass and thrust to create the maximum of power and ease of work. It also has great pulling power and hardiness, combined with a calm disposition.

## Energetic Trot

The Trait du Nord has a rather heavy head with a straight profile set on a short, muscular neck, flat withers

BELOW

*The short coupled and massive frame of this horse is typical of the Trait du Nord, a hardy, useful draught breed, whose numbers are sadly declining.*

and a broad, deep chest. Its sloping shoulders give it the energetic trot, and it has a short, straight back. It has broad loins and a wide, muscular croup, which is nicely sloping. It legs are short and strong, well muscled and feathered below the knee and hock, with broad, well-formed joints. It is ideally suited to heavy draught work and for agricultural work in hilly and rough terrains, which it can cross with ease. It makes a good harness horse, but is also bred for its meat.

### Fascinating Facts

The word 'chivalry' comes from the French word for horse, *cheval*; the term became associated with the knights who gallantly rode on horseback and the ideal standard of behaviour for such noblemen.

# NORMANDY COB

HEIGHT: 15.2–16.3hh

COLOUR: chestnut, bay

PERSONALITY TYPE: warm-blooded

TYPICAL USE: light draught, riding, harness

TEMPERAMENT: docile, gentle, lively

ORIGIN: France

SIMILAR BREEDS: warmbloods

This light draught breed has a long history dating back to the small but tough Bidet Horse that existed before the Roman Empire some 2,000 years ago. During Roman rule, the Romans crossed the Bidet with their heavyweight pack mares to produce a strong horse of more quality that was suitable for military use. The Bidet was a tough and enduring creature, probably brought to France from Asia by the Celts and, as well as Mongolian influences, likely contained Eastern blood.

## Warm-blooded

Later, in the sixteenth and seventeenth centuries, some Arabian and Barb blood was added, followed by that of

## Fascinating Facts

The phrase 'straight from the horse's mouth' is actually misquoted from the Bible. In the book of Numbers (22:28), God speaks a prophecy through the mouth of a donkey, which would have made the original phrase 'straight from the donkey's mouth'.

Thoroughbred and Norfolk Roadster. This means that, although a draught breed, the Normandy Cob is essentially a warmblood.

During the eighteenth and nineteenth centuries, two royal studs were established in France, at Le Pin in 1728 and at Saint-Lô in 1806, the

latter becoming the centre of breeding for the Normandy Cob. By 1976, the Saint-Lô stud was standing 60 Normandy Cob stallions. By the twentieth century, two distinct types of Cob had developed: a lighter version suitable for riding and a heavier type for light draught, carriage and farm work. The second type is most common today.

## Classy Horse

The modern Normandy Cob is a classy equine with great presence and an energetic, extravagant gait. While docile and gentle, it has tremendous presence and activity. It has a plain but not

unattractive head, a shortish neck set on good shoulders and a wide, deep chest. It has a short back and compact body, with a round croup and excellent legs with minimal feather. Although the breed was traditionally docked, the practice is now prohibited in some countries, so its tail is plaited and bound instead.

There is no studbook for the Normandy Cob, although its breeding is documented, and in some cases performance testing is carried out.

LEFT
*The Norman Cob is one of the classiest of draught breeds due to the influence of Thoroughbred and Arab blood, and is extremely versatile.*

# POITEVIN

**HEIGHT:** 16–16.2hh

**TEMPERAMENT:** placid, docile

**ORIGIN:** France

**SIMILAR BREEDS:** Auxois

**COLOUR:** dun, grey, bay, black, palomino

**PERSONALITY TYPE:** cold-blooded

**TYPICAL USE:** donkey/mule production, meat

**LEFT**

*The Poitevin is used most widely for the production of the Poitevin mule by crossing Poitevin mares with Baudet de Poitou donkeys.*

comparison to its body and somewhat thick, with coarse feathering. Its feet are large and flat, and its body hair coarse. Most Poitevins are dun – a throwback to its primitive roots – but grey, bay, black and palomino also occur.

Sometimes also known as the Mulassier, the Poitevin Horse originates in the Poitou region of France and is believed to be related to the ancient primitive Forest Horse of Northern Europe, a huge creature also known as *Equus ferus silvaticus*, or the Diluvial Horse. The Poitevin itself is a rather unprepossessing creature, unpleasing to the eye, with poor conformation and poor performance. It is the least known of the nine heavy French breeds and the most endangered.

In appearance, the Poitevin has a coarse, heavy head with a straight or convex profile, set on a rather stumpy, muscular neck. Its shoulders are quite straight and are poorly conformed, and it is long through the body, with a straight back and sloping croup. Its legs are short in

## Enduring

The Poitevin's biggest claim to fame is as a producer of the Baudet de Poitou, a donkey breed that can stand up to 16hh. Hardy and tough, the latter has an amazingly quick, energetic stride for a donkey and shares its studbook with that of the Poitevin, which was started in 1885. Breeding Baudet de Poitou jackasses to Poitevin mares produces the Poitevin mule, a strong, tough and enduring animal with a long working life and a good disposition and constitution. Although the demand for mules has declined, they are enjoying greater popularity once again. The Poitevin itself is also bred for meat.

## Primitive Roots

The Poitevin is believed to have descended from various Danish and Norwegian heavy breeds that were probably imported to the regions during the land reclamation work of the seventeenth century. It was used as a draught horse and for working the land.

# PERCHERON

HEIGHT: 15.2–17hh

COLOUR: grey, black

PERSONALITY TYPE: cold-blooded

TYPICAL USE: draught, agriculture, harness, riding

TEMPERAMENT: sensible, gentle, willing

ORIGIN: France

SIMILAR BREEDS: Boulonnais

Perhaps the best known of all France's heavy breeds, the Percheron takes its name from the La Perche district of northern France, but can be found worldwide. It is a breed of great antiquity; evidence has been recovered of a type of horse, very similar to the Percheron, having existed in the La Perche area since the Ice Age, although its exact roots are unknown. It is thought to be related, distantly, to the Boulonnais, with which it shares its elegance and considerable beauty.

## Free-flowing Stride

Arabian blood was crossed with the native mares of La Perche following the invasion of the Moors, who were defeated at the Battle of Tours

### Fascinating Facts

W.C. Fields, American comedian and actor, once joked and admired that 'Horse sense is the thing a horse has which keeps it from betting on people.'

in 732. Their abandoned hot-blooded horses were bred to existing heavy Flemish stock. The influence of the Arabian blood is indicated particularly in the unusually free-flowing and active stride of the Percheron.

Further infusions of Arabian blood were introduced during the Middle Ages. By the time of the Crusades, the Percheron was widely recognized as outstanding for its substance and soundness, as well as for its beauty and grace.

## Amazing Stamina

The renowned stud at Le Pin was a central breeding area for the Percheron and, in 1760, it imported an Arabian stallion called Gallipoli. He in turn sired one of the most famous Percheron stallions, Jean le Blanc, foaled in 1830, and all modern Percheron

---
RIGHT

*There is a high margin of Arab blood in the popular French Percheron, which is reflected in its versatility as a riding and draught animal.*

bloodlines trace back to him. The Percheron was first imported to the United States in 1839, by an Edward Harris from Moorestown, New Jersey. Just over 20 years later, two stallions, Normandy and Louis Napoleon, were imported to Ohio. The latter was sold to Illinois and into the ownership of the Dunham family, who were later instrumental in forming the breed society.

## French Imports

During the 1870s and 1880s, literally thousands of heavy draught horses were imported to the United States from Europe, particularly stallions from France and Great Britain. Once the importers found the old province of La Perche – and noted the superiority of its heavy horses – it became the primary source of imports.

During the winter of 1875–76, the National

Association of Importers and Breeders of Norman Horses was launched in Chicago, Illinois. The name was soon altered to Percheron-Norman and, within a few years, had been shortened simply to 'Percheron'.

## American Favourite

The financial downturn of 1893 halted the importations; between 1894 and 1898 there were virtually none, and breeding of stock was greatly curtailed. The former association went bust.

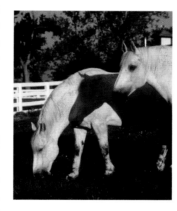

But recovery was swift. Importations were resumed in 1898 and between that time and 1905, they averaged about 700 head a year. The new Percheron Horse Association of America was formed in 1902 and by 1906, there were 13,000 stallions registered. By 1930, the Percheron had become so popular that there were three times as many registered Percherons as other draught breeds combined.

Following the Second World War, the breed was badly affected by mechanization as the tractor overtook the horse. A handful of farmers – including Amish, who were great supporters of the breed – kept the Percheron alive through the next 20 years and it continues to thrive in the United States today.

## Fine Head

The Percheron has an exceptionally fine head, which is attributed to the Arabian blood, a well-made neck set onto good withers, deep chest, strong back and muscled quarters. It has short, clean legs with minimal feathering and good, hard bone. The Percheron has been used to improve other breeds.

For a heavy horse, the Percheron has grace, freedom of movement and amazing stamina – it is able to travel in trot for an incredible 57 km (35 miles) a day.

# BOULONNAIS

HEIGHT: 15–15.3hh

COLOUR: mostly grey, chestnut, black, bay

PERSONALITY TYPE: cold-blooded

TYPICAL USE: draught, meat

TEMPERAMENT: gentle, kind

ORIGIN: France

SIMILAR BREEDS: Percheron

Called the 'Thorough-bred of draught breeds', the Boulonnais combines the elegance of the hotblood with the strength of the cold. One of the most beautiful of all the draughts, the 'White Marble Horse' can be traced back to the native stock of the Numidian army occupation of Boulogne in northern France in 55–54 BC. During the Crusades, two breeders concentrated on creating a warhorse that would be fast and agile, yet still strong enough to carry a knight in full armour through a rigorous battle.

## Horse of the Tide

Eustache, Comte de Boulogne, and Robert, Comte d'Artois, crossed the heavy Northern stallions with German Mecklenberg mares, similar to modern Hanoverians, for the base warhorse. The Spanish occupation of nearby Flanders during the seventeenth century brought in Spanish Barb, Andalusian and Arabian horses, and the distinctive Boulonnais emerged, of which there were two types.

## Fascinating Facts

Today, the annual race still known as the Route du Poisson commemorates the now-extinct *mareyeur* type of Boulonnais, in recognition of the horse's role in bringing fresh seafood to Paris.

The smaller *mareyeur* variety – the name means 'Horse of the Tide' – was used to pull heavy carts of fish from Boulogne to Paris, a distance of almost 340 km (200 miles). The Route du Poisson was traversed in under 18 hours, allowing Parisians to have fresh fish for their dining table.

## Mostly Grey

With better roads and rail transportation, the *mareyeur* type was allowed to die out. The larger Boulonnais, direct heir to the warhorse bloodlines, is still bred in

small numbers, but two world wars almost destroyed the breed. In the early twentieth century, there were thought to be 600,000 Boulonnais in France. There are now only an estimated 700 Boulonnais in France, 150 in Germany and fewer than 75 in Belgium. Most Boulonnais today are grey – about 15 per cent are chestnut, black or bay. It is said to resemble a small 'wide-awake' Percheron.

RIGHT

*The Boulonnais, like the Percheron, contains Arab blood, and is noted for its particularly attractive head and great stamina.*

# ITALIAN HEAVY DRAUGHT
## (Tiro Pesante Rapido)

**TEMPERAMENT:** quiet, biddable, sociable

**ORIGIN:** Italy

**SIMILAR BREEDS:** Breton

**HEIGHT:** 15–16hh
**COLOUR:** mostly chestnut, bay, roan
**PERSONALITY TYPE:** cold-blooded
**TYPICAL USE:** draught, agriculture, meat

Experimental breeding led to the development of the Italian Heavy Draught – known in Italian as the Tiro Pesante Rapido, which means 'quick heavy draught'. It originated in the northern regions of Italy, but was popular throughout the country. The breed began with native stock being crossed with Brabant, Percheron and Boulonnais; many of these early experiments were unsuccessful. When the Breton was bred to the local mares, however, the Italian Heavy Draught was born.

## A Distinctive Brand

Originally, Neapolitan, Arabian and Hackney horses were crossed with the native mares of Ferrara in northern Italy to produce a lightweight, active workhorse. But a need arose for a heavier farm and a heavy artillery breed. The earlier crossings with the Boulonnais produced what came to be known as the Agricultural Heavy Horse, but then the Breton was added and the new name coined, and the studbook was opened in 1926. Horses that are accepted to the studbook are branded with a five-runged ladder with a shield on the near side of their hindquarters.

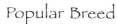

*These predominantly chestnut horses are versatile, useful agricultural animals known for their particularly good trot.*

## Popular Breed

The Breton passed to the Italian Heavy Draught its fast, active trot, which gave rise to the latter's nickname, and it resembles the Breton quite closely in appearance. It is almost always chestnut with flaxen mane and tail, although bays and roans

also appear. It is a highly attractive, cobby little horse, with a quality head for a draught breed, a powerful neck, excellent shoulders and compact, muscular body. Its legs are sometimes poor, and rather light in bone, but the overall picture is a pleasing one. It is an economical and easy keeper, and matures quickly.

The Italian Heavy Draught is still used in its homeland for farm work and remains popular – a third of all breeding stallions in the modern Italy are her native heavy horse.

# FREIBERGER (Franches-Montagne)

HEIGHT: 14.3–15.3hh

COLOUR: chestnut, bay

PERSONALITY TYPE: cold-blooded

TYPICAL USE: farm, pack, military, light draught, riding

TEMPERAMENT: kind, calm, willing

ORIGIN: Switzerland

SIMILAR BREEDS: none

*LEFT*
*The Freiberger breed originally developed into two types, a heavier pure draught animal and a lighter strain suitable for riding.*

Also known as the Franches-Montagne, the Freiberger was developed in the Jura Mountains of Switzerland – this small range, north of the Alps, is sometimes called the Freiberger Mountains – at the end of the nineteenth century. It was created by crossing the native Bernese Jura Horse with the English Thoroughbred and the Anglo-Norman, with some influences from the Ardennais and the Arabian. It is highly versatile, being used for light draught, farm work, riding and competition.

## Upland Farmers

As a mountain breed, the Freiberger is naturally sure-footed and tough, and far more suited to working the hilly mountainous areas than a tractor. It is still widely used by the upland farmers of Jura and by the Swiss Army, which favours it as a pack and patrol animal. The Freiberger is also found all over Europe.

There are two distinct types within the Freiberger breed: a broader, heavier stamp with greater muscle development and a lighter, finer type. Today, the continuing demands for a competition horse as well as a leisure riding animal mean that there is a trend towards breeding the lighter type.

## Founding Sire

Many modern Freibergers trace back to one stallion called Vaillant, foaled in 1891, which was a mix of Norfolk Roadster, Anglo-Norman and English hunter blood. Valliant was a great-grandson of a half-bred English hunter stallion called Leo H, which had some Norfolk Roadster blood and was imported to Switzerland in 1865. Poulette, Vaillant's grandam on both sides, was thought to be of Thoroughbred and Anglo-Norman stock. Imprévu, an Anglo-Norman imported in 1889, produced a second important line through his great-grandson Chasseur.

Other outcrosses to French, English and Belgian horses had no lasting effect, and it was not until after the Second World War that a new bloodline emerged from Urus, another stallion with Norman blood. Since then, further outcrosses have been carefully monitored. Anglo-Normans are usually selected, but Arabian blood has also been added.

## Fascinating Facts

Horse enthusiast, Winston Churchill once proclaimed, 'No hour of life is wasted that is spent in the saddle…There is something about the outside of a horse that is good for the inside of a man.'

## Swiss Cross

The Freiberger today is bred at the federal Swiss stud at Avenches, where breeding is strictly regulated

and highly selective. A Freiberger that has been bred at Avenches is branded with a Swiss cross.

The Freiberger matures quickly into a well-balanced, active and calm equine which is a willing and easy worker with equable temperament. In the past few years,

experiments have begun with crossing the Freiberger with the Swiss Half-Blood, or Schweizer Halbblut, to make a lighter, more elegant competition horse. It has an

active stride that makes it successful in dressage and natural athleticism that allows it to hold its own in the show-jumping arena.

## Pony-like

The pure Freiberger has a small, almost pony-like head that can be a little heavy, with a pronounced jawline and a broad forehead. Its neck is muscular and arching, with a good sloping shoulder, broad and pronounced withers, and a straight and powerful back. The Freiberger does not, like so many draught breeds, suffer conformational faults in its legs, which in this breed are invariably good and clean, with strong joints, plenty of bone and good, hard feet. It sometimes has a small amount of feathering, although modern breeding

has largely bred this out. Sometimes a finer head is seen, with an almost Arabian outlook, although this is not necessarily desirable.

The Freiberger is always bay or chestnut, but variations of shades do occur, and it stands between 14.3 and 15.3 hh. Sure-footed, agile and good-natured, the Freiberger is an energetic little horse with power, sweet temper, endurance and agility. In all, it is a triumph for its breeders, who continue to produce this superb mountain draught. Although the lighter type is still more popular, it is more a draught breed than a light horse.

# NORIKER

HEIGHT: 16–17hh

COLOUR: chestnut, bay, roan, dun

PERSONALITY TYPE: cold-blooded

TYPICAL USE: draught, harness, riding, agriculture

TEMPERAMENT: calm, placid, willing

ORIGIN: Austria

SIMILAR BREEDS: Brabant, Black Forest Chestnut, Haflinger

The name of this breed comes from the ancient Roman state of Noricum, high in the Alpine regions of Austria. The Romans constructed an extensive road system in Noricum and, as old relics show, horses closely resembling the Noriker – also known as the Norisches Kaltbult, or Pinzgauer – were used to pull wagons and as pack animals. The breed is renowned for being sure-footed as well as tough and constitutionally sound, and it is capable of pulling considerable loads over long distances.

## Strict Guidelines

The Romans established studs, and it is likely that the Noriker developed from the heavy warhorse that was being selectively bred in the Salzburg region. During the Middle Ages, the Noriker continued to be bred, but by then in studs attached to monasteries. Today it is widely bred throughout southern Germany, where it is known as the South German Coldblood, as well as in Austria. It is likely that Haflinger and also Spanish, Neapolitan and Burgundian horses feature in its history.

The Prince-Archbishop of Salzburg is credited with forming the Noriker studbook some 400 years ago, and strict guidelines were drawn up to which the breed had to conform.

## All-rounder

The breeding of the Noriker is currently based on five bloodlines: Volcano, Nero, Diamand, Schaunitz and Elmar. The aim was to breed a sturdy, amiable, enduring sort of horse, one that was sound and sure-footed – in other words, an ideal all-round workhorse for a mountainous terrain. Half of these horses were bay, although chestnut also appeared. The leopard spot markings seen in early Norikers – the Pinzgauer strain of Noriker, once considered a separate breed, was spotted – became increasingly rare. Today the most common colour is liver chestnut with flaxen mane and tail, which contributes to the breed's overall good looks.

Noriker breeding stallions are required to pass demanding tests that measure their strength and speed.

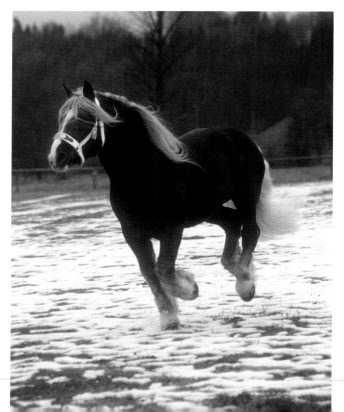

RIGHT

*These attractive horses are predominantly liver chestnut in colour with a striking flaxen mane and tail.*

# SCHWARZWÄLDER FÜCHSE
## (Black Forest Chestnut)

TEMPERAMENT: good-natured, gentle, lively

ORIGIN: Germany

SIMILAR BREEDS: Noriker, Breton

HEIGHT: 14.3–15hh

COLOUR: sorrel to dark chestnut, occasionally grey

PERSONALITY TYPE: cold-blooded

TYPICAL USE: agriculture, forestry, harness, riding

### Fascinating Facts

The name Schwarzwälder Füchse translates as 'Black Forest Sorrel', but the last word has been changed to 'Chestnut'. The breed is also sometimes called Schwarzwälder Kaltblut, which means 'Black Forest Coldblood'.

In its German homeland, the Schwarzwälder Füchse, Black Forest Chestnut, is known as the 'Pearl of the Black Forest', and this active, lively little horse is one of the most attractive of the draught breeds. It comes from the Black Forest in Baden-Wurttemberg in southern Germany and is small and hardy, well able to cope with the long winters of the region and sure-footed enough to traverse the hilly regions of its woodland home with ease. The farmers of the region have used it for centuries.

## Forged Papers

Horses existed in the Black Forest as long ago as the Middle Ages, and more recently the Noriker draught has had a major influence on the Schwarzwälder Füchse. Indeed, the Schwarzwälder Füchse resembles a small Noriker, or a larger Haflinger. Infusions of Breton blood have, latterly, also had some impact on the breed, but attempts to use the Brabant, or Belgian Heavy Draught, to increase size have been largely unsuccessful.

When the breed association was formed in 1896 and a studbook was established, breeders were instructed to use only Belgian stallions.

The traditional farmers secretly used native stallions, however, and forged the resulting foals' identity papers. By the First World War, the authorities finally realized that the Belgians were not suitable for the Schwarzwäld farmers, and so lifted the restrictions.

## Striking Colour

Lively and agile, long-lived and fertile, the Schwarzwälder Füchse stands about 15hh. It has a refined head for a draught breed, with a wide forehead and tapering muzzle. Its neck is strong and its shoulders muscular and powerful. Its legs are quite fine, but strong, with little feathering, and it has good feet. Its colour varies from sorrel to dark chestnut, usually with flaxen mane and tail, although a striking dark silver dapple – known in Germany as Kohlfuchs – is sometimes seen.

ABOVE

*This relatively small draught breed is highly attractive and particularly hardy. It is sure-footed and well adapted to hilly terrain.*

# SCHLESWIG HEAVY DRAUGHT

HEIGHT: 15.2–16hh

COLOUR: chestnut

PERSONALITY TYPE: cold-blooded

TYPICAL USE: agriculture, harness, riding

TEMPERAMENT: willing, kind, active

ORIGIN: Germany

SIMILAR BREEDS: Jutland

## Fascinating Facts

Barbara Jo Rubin was the first female jockey to win a race in 1969.

The Schleswig Heavy Draught takes its name from the Schleswig-Holstein region of northern Germany, which borders on Denmark and, at times, has been part of that country. It is therefore not surprising that the Schleswig resembles the Jutland, the Danish heavy horse to which it is closely related. A relatively new breed, the

**Schleswig Heavy Draught was developed during the second half of the nineteenth century as a draught breed of medium stature; the breed society was established in 1891.**

### Severely Depleted

The breed is based on the Jutland and can be traced back to one stallion, Aldrup Munkedal, and his descendants, Hovding and Prins af Jylland. Infusions of lighter blood, including Yorkshire Coach Horse and Thoroughbred, are thought to have had little lasting effect. Later, a Suffolk Punch stallion named Oppenheim LXII was used, and traces of his influence remain.

By the end of the nineteenth century, the Schleswig was in demand for pulling trams and buses, and working the land. The breed survived the First World War – during which its homeland was under Danish rule – although numbers were severely depleted. Breton and Boulonnais blood was introduced, with great success.

### Ten Stallions Left

The Second World War had a more devastating effect, and the surviving Schleswig horses were bred back to Jutlands to re-establish the breed. Still, it is thought there are only about 10 purebred stallions left today.

**LEFT**

*As the Schleswig breed developed, Cleveland Bay (pictured) blood was introduced to lighten the stock in frame and make it suitable for use in the artillery.*

The Schleswig is an attractive cobby type of draught horse, with a good-looking head, short, crested neck, powerful shoulders, a body that tends to be long, but with good depth through the girth, and strong limbs with a fair amount of feather. It is most usually chestnut with flaxen mane and tail. A second type of Schleswig has been developed that is rather lighter and makes a good riding horse.

**ABOVE**

*The Schleswig Heavy Draught developed from the Jutland breed. This photograph of a magnificent Jutland stallion reflects the qualities that were stamped onto the Schleswig through careful breeding.*

# RHINELAND HEAVY DRAUGHT

TEMPERAMENT: quiet, willing, docile

ORIGIN: Germany

SIMILAR BREEDS: Brabant

HEIGHT: 16–17hh

COLOUR: chestnut, sorrel, roan

PERSONALITY TYPE: cold-blooded

TYPICAL USE: agriculture, draught, harness

**K**nown variously as the Rhenisch-Deutsches Kaltblut, Rhenish-Belgian, Rhenish-German or German Coldblood, the Rhineland Heavy Draught is also called different things in different regions of its homeland, such as Westphalian Draught, Altmarker Draught, Saxon-Thuringian Draught, Renish Draught and Mecklenburg Draught. It was developed during the last half of the nineteenth century for agricultural and draught purposes, and enjoyed a fairly brief period of popularity.

## Highly Efficient

The breed was once the most common horse in Germany – the studbook was opened in 1876 – but is now quite rare,

---

LEFT

*Percheron blood, such as the horse pictured, was also used to refine and improve the Rhineland Heavy Draught.*

---

with a total population of some 2,000. Since the age of mechanization, particularly, the numbers of the Rhineland Heavy Draught have dramatically decreased and now only about 2 per cent of the German horse population are draught breeds.

---

LEFT

*The Rhineland Heavy Draught breed developed from the Ardennes breed, like the horse pictured, crossed with other draught breeds.*

---

The Rhineland Heavy Draught was developed largely from the Brabant (Belgian Heavy Draught), with infusions from the Ardennais, Clydesdale, Percheron and Boulonnais, to produce a heavyweight but attractive animal of great power. It made an excellent farm and draught horse, and was highly efficient at both.

## Low to the Ground

For its size, it has a small but well-shaped head with a heavy jaw, set on an extremely powerful, well-arched neck with a pronounced crest. It generally has rather low

withers, but its shoulders are likely to be massive and it has a broad, deep chest. Its back is short and wide, its quarters rounded and muscular, its legs short and strong with good joints and very hard feet. It stands between 16 and 17 hh, and is most usually sorrel, chestnut or roan in colour, although the occasional bay and black do occur.

The Rhineland appears low to the ground, due to the shortness of its leg in comparison to the bulk of the body, but it is not unattractive. It has an excellent temperament, being quiet, yet willing and energetic when required.

# DUTCH HEAVY DRAUGHT

HEIGHT: 16–17hh

COLOUR: chestnut, bay, grey

PERSONALITY TYPE: cold-blooded

TYPICAL USE: agriculture, draught

TEMPERAMENT: intelligent, gentle, willing

ORIGIN: The Netherlands

SIMILAR BREEDS: Brabant

**D**eveloped in the Netherlands after 1918, the Dutch Heavy Draught is a relatively new breed and the heaviest of all the country's horses. It was developed by crossbreeding the Belgian Brabant, Zeeland-type Dutch mares and the Ardennais, and still bears a resemblance to the Brabant. The aim was to produce a massive, powerful horse of strong and solid build. It was most popular in the provinces of Zeeland and North Brabant, where it worked the large arable farms in the heavy marine clay.

ABOVE

*These powerful horses with their massive frame are capable of pulling huge loads and are well equipped to deal with the heavy clay ground of their homelands.*

## Long Working Life

Although the Dutch Draught is a huge, solid horse, it is surprisingly active and tends to have a long working life. Before mechanization, it was invaluable to the Dutch farmer, and was found extensively throughout Gelderland, North Brabant and Limburg, due to its phenomenal strength and gentle temperament. It was also found on the large farms in the clay areas of the Groningen, but it did not succeed in ousting the region's eponymous breed. When the Royal Dutch Heavy Draught Society was formed on 22 December 1914, its aim was to produce a handsome, strong horse with power, particularly suited to prolonged and heavy haulage or traction.

## Free and Easy

The Dutch Heavy Draught is indeed a massive creature, but its head is far from coarse, with a straight rather than convex profile, short, lively ears and a kind, intelligent eye. It has a short neck, often set on loaded shoulders, good well-formed withers, muscular chest and hind quarters and a wide, strong back. It has a sloping croup and low-set tail, strong legs with plenty of muscle and good, hard bone and excellent feet. Despite its size, its movement should be free and easy. It is generally intelligent, a good doer and economical to keep.

Since mechanization, numbers have suffered serious decline, but a few good breeding animals still exist.

# JUTLAND

TEMPERAMENT: quiet, willing, biddable

ORIGIN: Denmark

SIMILAR BREEDS: Schleswig, Suffolk Punch

HEIGHT: 15.3hh

COLOUR: generally chestnut

PERSONALITY TYPE: cold-blooded

TYPICAL USE: draught, parade

Ninth-century pictures of Danish warriors show them riding horses that appear quite similar to the modern Jutland, although the breed is thought to have started in the twelfth century. The Jutland was used not only as a draught horse, but also as a popular mount of the knights of medieval times, having both the strength and stamina to carry a knight in full armour. The modern version of the breed is not used for riding, however, and is thought to have been developed around 1850.

## Suffolk Connection

It is generally accepted that one stallion, Oppenheim LXII, had a major influence on the Jutland. He was imported to the region in 1860 by the well-known horse trader Oppenheimer of Hamburg, who specialized in Suffolk Punches – Oppenheim is thought to be a Shire–Suffolk Punch cross. Six generations after Oppenheim came the stallion Aldrup Menkedal, which is considered the foundation sire of the breed. Almost all Jutland breeding can now be traced back to Hovding and Prins af Jylland, two of his sons. These horses also appear in the pedigree of the Schleswig Heavy Draught, which is closely related to the Jutland.

There is a theory that the Vikings took Danish horses into Britain and that the Suffolk Punch developed from these, and there are certainly similarities between the modern Jutland and the Suffolk Punch.

## Cleveland Bay

The Jutland is a compact, heavy horse with short, stocky legs and some feathering, although breeders are trying to eliminate this. In the past, the breed has been criticized as having weak joints, which, again, breeders have been trying to improve. Its head tends to be rather plain, but not unattractive. It is thought to have some Cleveland Bay and Yorkshire Coach Horse blood in its lineage, which has added some refinement, and Frederiksborg blood was added to improve its paces.

### Fascinating Facts

Since 1928, the Jutland has had a close association with the Carlsberg brewery, which uses Jutlands to haul brewery wagons. At one time there were 210 Jutland horses with Carlsberg, and today about 20 are still used for beer transportation in Copenhagen, Denmark.

LEFT

*The impressive Jutland breed was used both as a draught animal and for riding, and was one of the favourite mounts of the medieval knights.*

# DOLE GUDBRANDSDAL

HEIGHT: 14–15hh

COLOUR: black, bay, brown

PERSONALITY TYPE: cold-blooded

TYPICAL USE: pack, light draught, harness

TEMPERAMENT: gentle, honest, calm

ORIGIN: Norway

SIMILAR BREEDS: Friesian, Fell, Dales

**A**lthough the National Dolehorse Association was not established until 1967, the Dole Gudbrandsdal is actually an ancient breed, originating in the great central valley of Gudbrandsdal that connects the Oslo region of Norway with the North Sea coast. It is one of the smallest coldbloods and, in appearance, it much resembles Britain's Fell and Dales ponies. The strong similarity is hardly surprising, as all three breeds would have derived from the same prehistoric wild stock.

## Trade Routes

Between the fourth and eighth centuries, Friesian merchants from the Netherlands introduced their own black horses to both Norway and the British Isles. Later, between the years 800 and 1066, there was much influence back and forth between western Norway and the north of England.

The Dole Gudbrandsdal was developed as a pack animal, carrying goods along Norway's overland trade routes. But in the nineteenth century, experiments were made with the breed, crossing the Dole with Swedish Warmbloods and English Thoroughbreds to produce a lighter type of riding horse. One particular stallion, Odin, thought to be a Thoroughbred–Norfolk Trotter cross imported in 1834, was to have considerable influence. The Dole Gudbrundsdal, in turn, was influenced by the stallion Brimen 825.

---

**LEFT**

*This ancient draught breed evolved from the same prehistoric stock that gave rise to the British Fell and Dales ponies, and the similarity is still marked.*

## Luxuriant Mane

Two types of Dole were developed, the heavy draught Gudbrandsdal and the Dole Trotter. Despite the fact that the first cross of warmblood and Dole produced good riding animals, the practice of crossbreeding with Dole has more or less ceased, and use of the Thoroughbred has been restricted.

The Gudbrandsdal has the luxuriant mane and tail seen in the Fell, Dales and Friesian horses, and is a powerful little horse with strong legs and feet. The Gudbrandsdal undergoes testing and

## Fascinating Facts

Before the Gudbrandsdal may be used for breeding purposes, its lower legs and feet are routinely X-rayed to ensure that there are no weaknesses.

grading, judged on its pulling power and trot. Trotters used for racing must have a good performance record to be allowed to be used for breeding.

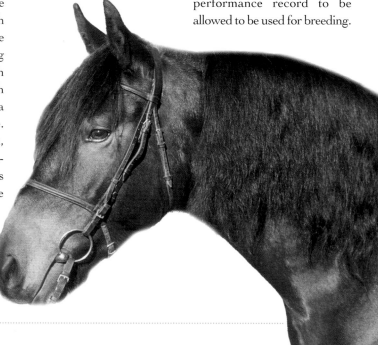

# NORTH SWEDISH

TEMPERAMENT: willing, calm, biddable

ORIGIN: Sweden

SIMILAR BREEDS: Dole Gudbrandsdal,
Swedish Ardennes

HEIGHT: 15–15.3 hh

COLOUR: most solid colours

PERSONALITY TYPE:
cold-blooded

TYPICAL USE: forestry, draught

A lighter type of draught horse, the North Swedish, is ideally suited to the forest and lumber work in the Swedish woodlands for which it was principally bred and at which it is more efficient than any machinery. It is related to the Dole Gudbrandsdal, having both developed from the ancient native horses of Sweden and Norway. It is a smallish, stocky creature, with incredible strength, draught capability, stamina and endurance, and is notably long-lived, appearing relatively immune to many equine diseases.

## Young Breed

As a breed, the North Swedish is still young, its studbook having been established in 1909. Infusions of Friesian and Oldenburg, as well as some of the heavier European draught breeds, have been introduced. Since 1903, however, there have been stringent breeding regulations, in an effort to stabilize its type and retain its admirable characteristics. Foremost in this has been the Stallion Rearing Institute of Wangen in Jamtland, which is now one of the principal North Swedish studs.

## Rigorously Tested

This is probably one of the most rigorously tested breeds in the world, having to undergo testing on its pulling power, action and fertility. Its lower legs are X-rayed to ensure no defects are bred on.

County Horse Days events are held annually, where stallions and mares are examined in a number of different situations, and particular attention is paid to temperament.

The North Swedish Horse is willing and co-operative. It has a pony-like head (which can be a little heavy), muscular and crested neck,

### ABOVE

*This is a relatively young, and very versatile draught breed, whose qualities have been maintained through rigorous breed standards.*

and sloping shoulders that give it a long, springy stride. Recognized colours are brown, black, chestnut, buckskin, palomino, smoky and grey. This latter colour, however, is acceptable only where descent is verifiable back to the Norwegian 'blue horse'.

A lighter version of the breed, the Swedish Trotter, has also been developed.

# SWEDISH ARDENNES

HEIGHT: 15.2–16hh

COLOUR: black, brown, bay, chestnut

PERSONALITY TYPE: cold-blooded

TYPICAL USE: agriculture, draught, forestry

TEMPERAMENT: kind, gentle, calm

ORIGIN: Sweden

SIMILAR BREEDS: Ardennais

In the late nineteenth century, it was felt that existing Swedish native breeds were unsuited to the heavy agricultural work required. The large Ardennais was therefore introduced to Sweden in 1872; by 1880, most of

ABOVE/RIGHT

*The Swedish Ardennes developed from the French Ardennes, pictured, and are popular agricultural horses especially in the timber industry.*

south and central Sweden had imported or crossed Ardennais.

These heavier horses were bred with native stock, and conformation was now given priority. By 1874, examinations were required before a Swedish Warmblood, Swedish Ardennes or North Swedish Horse could be entered into the studbook. The Swedish Ardennes studbook was opened in 1901.

## Frugal Rations

The Swedish Ardennes remains popular as a carthorse, and is also used for hauling timber in inaccessible mountain areas. It can withstand extreme variations in climate, is a strong and exceptionally eager worker and can survive on frugal rations. A muscular, compact horse known for its longevity and overall good health, it has a heavy head, short, thick

neck, wide chest, well-muscled shoulders and short back. Its short legs have a little feathering.

# SOKOLSKY

HEIGHT: 15–16hh

COLOUR: chestnut, bay, brown

PERSONALITY TYPE: cold-blooded

TYPICAL USE: draught, agricultural, pack, trek

TEMPERAMENT: kind, willing, even-tempered

ORIGIN: Poland

SIMILAR BREEDS: Dole Gudbrandsdal, Brabant

Developed in the 1900s, the Sokolsky was produced using crosses of Brabant, Belgian Ardennes, Norfolk, Dole Gudbrandsdal and Anglo-Norman stock. The result is a versatile draught horse of great strength that is not excessively heavy. Tough and hardy, with free, active gaits, it is an excellent worker and economical feeder.

These traits have ensured the Sokolsky's popularity. Its home, Sokolka in north-east Poland, is on the edge of the Knyszyn Primeval Forest, bordering Belarus. The area

includes both river valleys and glacial hills, and the Sokolsky is also used as a pack animal and for trekking.

## Growing reputation

The Sokolsky has a slightly heavy head, straight profile, large, kind eyes and alert ears. Its neck is quite long, but very

muscular and broad at the base. Its well-constructed shoulders are reasonably sloping. It has a deep chest and pronounced withers, and a short, straight back, with a sloping, muscular croup. Its legs are strong with well-formed hard hooves. The Sokolsky's reputation has spread, and it is now also bred in parts of Russia.

# LATVIAN HARNESS HORSE

TEMPERAMENT: patient, kind, willing

ORIGIN: Latvia

SIMILAR BREEDS: Dole Gudbrandsdal, Oldenburg

HEIGHT: 15–16hh

COLOUR: bay, black, chestnut

PERSONALITY TYPE: cold-blooded

TYPICAL USE: light draught, riding

Three types of horse were developed in Latvia, then part of the Soviet Union, in the nineteenth century. These were the Latvian Light Harness Horse, the lightweight Latvian and the heavier version of the harness type. This last is thought to have descended from the old Forest Horse, a primitive creature considered the root of most cold-blooded draught breeds in the world today. The Latvian Harness Horse was established in 1952.

## Influential Infusion

It is thought that continuing infusions of Dole Gudbrandsdal, North Swedish, Zemaituka, Finnish Universal and Oldenburg, as well as other heavy European breeds, were added. The most influential infusions – in all versions of the Latvian horse – were those from the Oldenburg, Hanoverian and Holstein. During the early

RIGHT

*There are three types of the Latvian Harness Horse, with the lightest strain, pictured, making a useful riding and light draught horse.*

half of the twentieth century, 65 Oldenburg stallions and 42 Oldenburg mares were imported from the Netherlands, which became the base for developing the breed. Further crosses were made using Hanoverian, Norfolk Roadster, East Friesian and Ardennais.

## Patient and Willing

The resulting equine was a plain but good-looking animal with a slightly large but pleasing head, expressive eyes and small, rather neat ears. It has a long muscular neck set on high withers – a trait not often seen in a draught breed – desirably sloping shoulders and a deep, broad chest. Its back can be rather straight, and other conformational defects are a tendency towards cow hocks and a predisposition to ring bone. That being said, the Latvian Harness Horse is generally well structured and muscular, with good legs and hard joints, plenty of stamina and endurance, as well as a patient and willing disposition.

Today, the riding version of the Latvian is most common as pleasure and competition riding continue to grow in popularity, and the heavier type is rarely seen.

## Fascinating Facts

Horses cannot vomit. Therefore whatever a horse consumes must pass through the digestive system. This inability to vomit is the most common reason for colic, a big problem with horses.

# LITHUANIAN HEAVY DRAUGHT

HEIGHT: 15–16hh

COLOUR: chestnut, bay, black, grey, roan

PERSONALITY TYPE: cold-blooded

TYPICAL USE: draught

TEMPERAMENT: gentle, quiet, willing

ORIGIN: Lithuania

SIMILAR BREEDS: Latvian Harness Horse

Although the Lithuanian Heavy Draught originated in Lithuania at the end of the nineteenth century, the breed has been registered only since 1963 (when Lithuania was still part of the Soviet Union). But there is no denying its popularity – by 1964, there were an estimated 62,000 Lithuanian Heavy Draughts in the breed's homeland, a testament to its versatility, its demand and its fertility. The breed was developed by crossing the Zemaituka, or Zhumd, ponies with the Swedish Ardennes and the Finnish Universal Horse.

## Highly Fertile

To ensure the breed is preserved, potential stallions

have to pass a series of rigorous performance tests before being allowed to be used as breeding stock. The Lithuanian enjoys considerable longevity and is also highly fertile – at the best studs, such as Nyamun, Sudav and Zhagar, the foal crop is 80 per cent, with a

survival rate up to one year of age of 76–79 per cent.

Immensely strong and enduring, with a quiet temperament, the Lithuanian is suitable for heavy draught and agricultural work. It thrives in harsh and extreme landscapes, and seems impervious to cold.

## Fascinating Facts

Horse whisperers are said to be able to communicate with the horse in its own language. Some have used this ability to train horses whilst others use it to 'heal' with their hands.

## Setting Records

The Lithuanian Heavy Draught is renowned for its excellent walk and trot – fairly rare in draught horses – and has set several records.

### LEFT
This draught breed has a particularly good walk and trot which, combined with its extreme hardiness, has made it an extremely popular horse in its home country.

It can pull a weight of 150 kg (330 lb) for a distance of 2,000 m (6,561 ft) in 13 minutes 20 seconds, and trot the same distance pulling 50 kg (110 lb) in 4 minutes 45 seconds.

It is a nicely proportioned horse, with a large head that is clean-cut, but sometimes a little coarse. It has a short and well muscled neck, reasonably pronounced withers and a wide, deep chest. Its back is short and powerful, with a rounded croup and a high-set tail. The legs are short with well formed feet. Similarities can be found between the Lithuanian Heavy Draught and the heavier Latvian Harness Horse, in both conformation and paces.

# TORIC

TEMPERAMENT: calm, sensible

ORIGIN: Estonia

SIMILAR BREEDS: Postier Breton

HEIGHT: 15–15.2hh

COLOUR: chestnut, bay, brown, grey

PERSONALITY TYPE: cold-blooded

TYPICAL USE: all-round utility

An all-purpose utility breed, the Toric, also known as Tori, was developed in Estonia at the Tori Stud between 1890 and 1950. To develop the breed, native Estonian mares, thought to be Klepper, were crossed with European warmblood stallions. A draught horse of great quality, the Toric is also sometimes referred to as the Estonian Klepper or Double Klepper.

## Taking Shape

The Toric's founding stallion was called Hetman, and was a son of a sire called Stewart. Stewart – it is possible this name was that of the horse's owner – was known to be a cross between a Norfolk Trotter and an Anglo-Norman mare. He bred Hetman from an undocumented hunter mare.

The Tori Stud was established in 1856 in Estonia's Pärnu county, largely because the horses of the region were near extinction. There followed various experimental crossings – the stud had been established with 47 mares and

7 stallions, plus imported Finnish horses, three Arabian stallions and two trotters. But it was not until the arrival of Hetman, foaled in 1886, that the new breed began to take shape.

## Valuable Nucleus

Using Hetman and subsequently his sons, a valuable nucleus was formed, but by 1930 detrimental signs of inbreeding were recorded. Hence, in 1937, the number of lines was increased with

### ABOVE
*The modern Toric is a light draught horse of extreme elegance and refinement, and is surprisingly athletic, with an aptitude for jumping.*

the introduction of imported Postier Breton stallions.

The modern Toric is a light draught and harness type with a clean, solid build. It has a large or medium-sized head, with a straight profile, a long, muscular neck, massive shoulders and a broad, deep chest. Its back

has a tendency to be long, but is wide with muscular quarters and a well-set tail. The legs are short and strong, with good joints and strong tendons. Recently, emphasis has been on producing a good all-round sport horse.

# MURÄKOZI

HEIGHT: up to 16hh

COLOUR: chestnut with flaxen mane and tail, brown, bay, black, grey

PERSONALITY TYPE: cold-blooded

TYPICAL USE: draught, agriculture

TEMPERAMENT: willing, honest, biddable

ORIGIN: Hungary

SIMILAR BREEDS: Ardennais

Hungary's heavy draught horse was developed in the area of the River Mura in the southern part of the country and continues to be bred there today, as well as in Poland and in the countries of the former Yugoslavia. It was developed by putting native Hungarian mares called Mur-Insulan – which translates as 'from the Mura region' – to Ardennais, Noriker and Percheron stallions. Some Thoroughbred and Arabian blood was added, although the Murakozi is considered a coldblood.

## Great Demand

This combination has produced a useful, quality draught horse that is extremely strong, good-looking and swift for such a heavy breed. In the years between the two world wars, the Muräkozi was extremely popular in Hungary and was employed extensively on farms. Arable farming in Hungary increased after the First World War, and the Muräkozi was in great demand – by the 1920s, it made up about 20 per cent of the country's entire equine population.

By the end of the Second World War, however, the breeding stock of the Muräkozi was severely depleted and outside blood was introduced to re-establish the horse. Between 1947 and 1949, 17 Ardennais stallions from France and 59 from Belgian were imported.

## Farmer's Friend

The Muräkozi is an economical keeper, able to thrive on frugal pickings, and tends to mature early, so is capable of going into work at the age of two. It is hard-

ABOVE

*The Muräkozi typically has very little feathering on its legs, and its legs are generally relatively fine in comparison to the bulk of its frame.*

working and biddable, a boon to the farmers of Hungary.

It has the plain head of many of the draught breeds, with a convex profile and large kindly eye. It has generally good conformation, with a short, muscular neck, low, broad withers and powerful sloping shoulders. Its chest is

deep and wide, and its body compact with a well-sprung rib cage. Its legs can be rather light for its frame, and there is little feather.

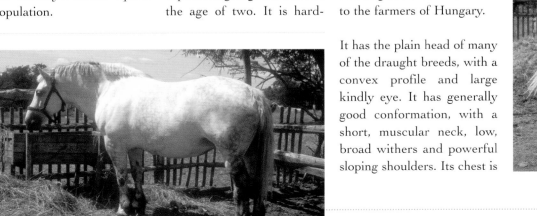

# RUSSIAN HEAVY DRAUGHT

TEMPERAMENT: willing, trainable, calm

ORIGIN: former Soviet Union

SIMILAR BREEDS: Ardennais,
Soviet Heavy Draught

HEIGHT: about 14.3hh

COLOUR: chestnut, roan, bay

PERSONALITY TYPE: cold-blooded

TYPICAL USE:
light draught, agriculture

Systematic breeding of a small draught horse that was strong, fast, easy to handle and economic to feed began in Russia in the 1860s, using Ardennais, Brabant and Orlov lines on native Ukrainian mares. The two main centres of breeding were the state studs of Khrenov and Derkul, as well as Chesma, Kochubei and Chaplits. In 1875, there were nine Ardennais stallions in Russia; by 1915, there were almost 600. Once there was a small nucleus of the new breed, they were backbred to fix type.

## Active Stride

The Orlov Trotter blood was thought to give the Russian Heavy Draught its swift, active stride, but the Ardennais blood was so influential that, for a time, the breed was known as the Russian Ardennes. During this period, the breeding centres at Chesma and the Dubrovsk, and subsequently the Pershino and Khrenov studs, played a major role in developing the new draught.

The Russian Heavy Draught was introduced to the world's

zootechnical public at the Paris Exhibition of 1900. But the First World War, followed by the Russian Revolution, all but wiped the breed out.

## Longevity and Fertility

Efforts were made to re-establish the breed, even though, in 1924, only 92 Ardennais stallions could be located. The year before, breeding stock at Dubrovsk was moved to the Novoalexandrov Stud in the Voroshilovgrad region, while the Khrenov stock was moved first to Pershino and

subsequently to Uralsk and Kuedin studs. By 1937 the stock of purebreds was reconstituted, and the Russian Heavy Draught was registered as a breed in 1952. It is small for a draught horse, standing only about 14.3hh,

LEFT

*The Russian Heavy Draught is an attractive small draught horse that is typically highly fertile and long-lived.*

but enjoys both longevity and continued fertility. The stallion Kolodnik, foaled in 1952, was still being used for breeding up to 1978, while the mare Logika, foaled 1962, produced 18 foals in as many years and was still going strong in 1989.

# Fascinating Facts

Horses and ponies can rest and even sleep standing up because of a stay apparatus in their patella or kneecap.

# SOVIET HEAVY DRAUGHT

HEIGHT: 15–16hh

COLOUR: chestnut, brown, bay

PERSONALITY TYPE: cold-blooded

TYPICAL USE: draught, meat

TEMPERAMENT: gentle, willing, honest

ORIGIN: former Soviet Union

SIMILAR BREEDS: Brabant

LEFT

The Percheron, pictured, has been influential in the development of many draught breeds, including the Soviet Heavy Draught, and generally improves on the stock it is crossed with.

**Percheron and Brabant stallions used on the native mares were to produce the Soviet Heavy Draught at the end of the nineteenth century. The breeding area was quite extensive, including Yaroslavl, Vladimir, Gorki, Penza, Ryazan, Tula, Tambov, Voronezh and Orel regions and Mordovia. These regions had a developed agricultural industry, requiring strong and sufficiently fast horses of ample size, muscle and power. The Soviet Heavy Draught answered every call.**

## Breeding Centres

Three state breeding centres – Pochinkovsk, Mordovian and Gavrilovo-Posad – were established in 1936 in what was then the Soviet Union. Alexandroz farm in Vladimir region and Yaroslavl farm branched off from Gavrilovo-Posadsk, and subsequently the Pochinkovsk and the Mordovian facilities were transformed into studs. These latter two are still the two leading breeding areas.

In the Baltic zone, new breeds, the Lithuanian and the Estonian Heavy Draught, began to be formed on a different local mare basis.

## Solid Build

The Soviet Heavy Draught is a massive horse of solid build that matures quickly, but is less resistant to equine diseases than some other draught breeds. Despite their substantial size, they have surprisingly free movement at the walk and trot.

The horse has a well-proportioned head with a pronounced jaw and straight or slightly convex profile. Its neck is muscular with a tendency to be short and its shoulders are straight and strong – this straightness does not seem to have an adverse effect on the horse's action. It has low withers and a long back, sometimes occasionally dipped – again, this conformational fault does not appear to be detrimental to the breed, nor do its often pigeon-toed front legs and sickle-hocked hind. The Soviet Heavy Draught is a good milk and meat producer, and a new line is being developed that will hopefully eliminate the conformational defects.

# VLADIMIR HEAVY DRAUGHT

TEMPERAMENT: willing, gentle, kind

ORIGIN: former Soviet Union

SIMILAR BREEDS: Clydesdale

HEIGHT: up to 16hh

COLOUR: most solid colours

PERSONALITY TYPE: cold-blooded

TYPICAL USE: light draught, harness

is muscular but longer than in other draught breeds, and powerful shoulders. Its chest is broad and more developed than that of the Clydesdale; it has pronounced withers and is tremendously deep in the girth. Its back can be rather long and sometimes weak, but it has sloping muscular quarters. Its legs are long like those of the Clydesdale, with plenty of feathering.

This breed, officially recognized only since 1946, was developed at the collective and state breeding establishments in the Vladimir and Ivanovo regions of Russia; the state stables of Gavrilovo-Posadsk – instrumental in the development of the Russian Heavy Draught – also played a role. The Vladimir Heavy Draught was established primarily through crosses between Clydesdale and Shire sires with local mares, with the aim of producing a middleweight draught breed with good pulling power and speed.

## Clydesdale Sires

The foundation sires can be traced back to three Clydesdales: Lord James and Border Brand, both foaled in 1910, and Glen Albin, born in 1923. Infusions of Cleveland Bay, Percheron and Suffolk Punch blood were also added, as well as some from the Ardennais. From 1925, however, no further outcrosses were permitted, and the breed was further evolved by taking the best of the progeny and interbreeding to produce the standard Vladimir of today. There are currently four lines of Vladimir Heavy Draught, with modern breeding being carried out at the Yuryev-Polski stud.

## Quality and Presence

The Vladimir Heavy Draught owes much to its Clydesdale roots, with the Shire influence being less apparent. It has a large head with a straight or convex profile, a well-proportioned neck that

The breed has considerable quality and presence, as well possessing the typical gentle and willing temperament found in other draught breeds, which makes it easy to handle. It is used for pulling the traditional Russian troika, or horse-drawn sled.

# Useful Addresses

**British Horse Society**
Stoneleigh Park
Kenilworth
Warwickshire, CV8 2XZ
UK
Tel: +44 (0)8701 202 244
www.bhs.org.uk

**Association of British Riding Schools**
Queen's Chambers,
38–40 Queen Street
Penzance
Cornwall,TR18 4BH
UK
Tel: +44 (0)1736 369 440
www.abrs-info.org

**British Dressage**
Stoneleigh Park
Kenilworth
Warwickshire, CV8 2RJ
UK
Tel: +44 (0)2476 698 830
www.britishdressage.co.uk

**British Show Jumping Association**
National Agricultural Centre,
Stoneleigh Park
Kenilworth
Warwickshire
CV8 2LR
UK
Tel: +44 (0)2476 698 800
www.bsja.co.uk

**British Eventing**
Stoneleigh Park
Kenilworth
Warwickshire, CV8 2RN
UK
Tel: +44 (0)2476 698 856.
www.britisheventing.com

**British Equine Veterinary Association**
Mulberry House
31 Market Street
Fordham, Ely
Cambridgeshire, CB7 5LQ
UK
Tel: + 44 (0)1638 723 555
www.beva.org.uk

**International League for the Protection of Horses**
Anne Colvin House
Snetterton
Norfolk, NR16 2LR
UK
Tel: +44 (0)1953 498 682
www.ilph.org

**Rare Breeds Survival**
Stoneleigh Park
Kenilworth
Warwickshire, CV8 2LG
UK
Tel: +44 (0)2476 696 551
www.rbst.org.uk

**American Association of Equine Practitioners**
4075 Iron Works Parkway
Lexington
Kentucky 40511
USA
Tel: +1 859 233 0147
www.aaep.org

**American Association of Riding Schools**
8375 Coldwater Road
Davison
Michigan 48423-8966
USA
Tel: +1 810 496 0360
www.ucanride.com

**United States Dressage Federation**
4047 Iron Works Parkway
Lexington
Kentucky 40511
USA
Tel: +1 859 971 7722
www.usdf.org

**United States Equestrian Federation**
4047 Iron Works Parkway
Lexington
Kentucky 40511
USA
Tel: +1 859 258 2472
www.usef.org

**United States Eventing Association**
525 Old Waterford Road, NW
Leesburg
Virginia 20176
USA
Tel: +1 703 779 0440
www.useventing.com

**Publications:**

*Horse & Hound*
9th Floor Blue Fin Building
110 Southwark Street
London, SE1 0SU
UK
Tel: +44 (0)20 3148 4562
www.horseandhound.co.uk

*Equine Journal*
103 Roxbury Street
Keene
New Hampshire 03431
USA
Tel: +1 800 742 9171
www.equinejournal.com

# Further Reading

Baskett, John, *The Horse in Art*, Yale University Press (New Haven, Conneticut), 2006

Bowen, Edward, *Horse Racing's Greatest Moments*, Eclipse Press (Lexington, Kentucky), 2001

Burn, D. and Fitzsimons, C., *Identification Guide: Horses & Ponies*, Flame Tree Publishing (London, UK), 2008

Draper, Judith, *The Ultimate Encyclopedia of Horse Breeds and Horse Care*, Hermes House (London, UK), 2003

Draper, Judith, *The Book of Horses: An Encyclopedia of Horse Breeds of the World*, Southwater Publishing (London, UK), 2003

Johns, Catherine, *Horses: History, Myth, Art*, Harvard University Press (Cambridge, Massachusetts), 2007

Frape, David, *Equine Nutrition and Feeding*, Wiley-Blackwell (Hoboken, New Jersey), 2004

Giffin, James M. and Gore, Tom, *Horse Owner's Veterinary Handbook*, Howell Book House (Hoboken, New Jersey), 1997

Green, John, *Horse Anatomy*, Dover Publications (Mineola, New Jersey), 2006

Hakola, Susan E., *The Equus Illustrated Handbook of Equine Anatomy*, Primedia Equine Network (Gaithersburg, Maryland), 2006

Harris, Susan E., *Horse Gaits, Balance and Movement*, Howell Book House (Hoboken, New Jersey), 2005

Harris, Susan E., *Grooming to Win: How to Groom, Trim, Braid and Prepare Your Horse for Show*, Howell Book House (Hoboken, New Jersey), 1991

Hausman, Gerald and Hausman, Loretta, *The Mythology of Horses: Horse Legend and Lore Throughout the Ages*, Three Rivers Press (New York, New York), 2003

Hedge, Juliet and Wagoner, Don (Ed.s), *Horse Conformation: Structure, Soundness and Performance*, The Lyons Press (Guilford, Conneticut), 2004

Hendricks, Bonnie L., *International Encyclopedia of Horse Breeds*, University of Oklahoma Press (Norman, Oklahoma), 2007

Hill, Cherry, *Horse Handling & Grooming*, Storey Publishing (North Adams, Massachusetts), 1997

Jahiel, Jessica, *The Rider's Problem Solver*, Storey Publishing (North Adams, Massachusetts), 2006

Lewis, Lon D.; Knight, Anthony; Lewis, Bart; and Lewis, Corey, *Feeding and Care of the Horse*, Wiley-Blackwell (Hoboken, New Jersey), 1996

Lucas, Sharon, *The New Encyclopedia of the Horse*, Dorling Kindersley (London, UK), 2001

McBane, Susan, *The Illustrated Encyclopedia of Horse Breeds*, Wellfleet Press (Seacaucus, New Jersey), 1997

Micklem, William, *Complete Horse Riding Manual*, Dorling Kindersley (London, UK), 2003

Murdoch, Wendy, *Simplify Your Riding*, Carriage House Publishing (Middleton, New Hampshire), 2004

Pavord, Tony and Pavord, Marcy, *The Complete Equine Veterinary Manual*, David & Charles Publishers (Newton Abbot, Devon, UK), 2004

Pickeral, Tamsin, *The Horse: 30,000 Years of the Horse in Art*, Merrell Publishers (London, UK), 2006

Self-Bucklin, Gincy, *How Your Horse Wants You to Ride*, Howell Book House (Hoboken, New Jersey), 2006

Sly, Debby, *The Ultimate Book of the Horse and Rider*, Hermes House (London, UK), 2004

Smith, Mike, *Getting the Most from Riding Lessons*, Storey Publishing (North Adams, Massachusetts), 1998

Swinney, Nicola Jane, *Horse Breeds of the World*, The Lyons Press (Guilford, Conneticut), 2006

Vogel, Colin, *Complete Horse Care Manual*, Dorling Kindersley (London, UK), 2003

# Glossary

**action**
The way a horse moves at various gaits, also reflected in head, neck and tail carriage.

**aids**
Signals from the rider or handler to the horse that imparts to the animal what the rider/handler wants it to do. They can be natural (such as mind, seat, weight, body) or artificial (such as whips and spurs).

**airs**
Movements of the High School (*Haute École*), associated with advanced or classical equitation, such as 'airs above the ground', where the horse leaves the ground.

**appendicular skeleton**
Bones in horse's legs, shoulders and hindquarters.

**axial skeleton**
Skull, backbone and ribcage.

**back at the knee**
A conformational fault in which the forelegs curve back below the knee. Opposite of over at the knee.

**bay**
Brown horse with black points.

**brand**
Marks put on horse's coat for identification.

**breed (n.)**
Subspecies of horse that has a defined set of distinguishing characteristics, which may have been encouraged and developed by man.

**blaze**
Wide white mark on horse's face.

**bone**
Measured round the circumference of the horse's leg, just below the knee. Dictates how much weight the horse can carry. Hard bone is desirable as it enables horses to carry heavier weights.

**bowed hocks**
Hocks turn out, with feet turning in. *See also* 'cow hocks'; 'sickle hocks'.

**buckskin**
Colour similar to dun, but generally brighter and darker; the colour of a tanned hide.

**bull neck**
Short, thick neck.

**calf knees**
Also known as 'back at the knee'.

**canines**
Four teeth in the interdental space, usually found only in male horses (also called 'tushes').

**cardiac sphincter**
Muscle at entrance to horse's stomach.

**carriage driving**
Driving a two- or four-wheeled carriage using one, two or four horses. Modern carriage driving trials are three day events.

**carriage horse**
Horse used to pull carriages – usually relatively light and elegant and used in carriage driving competition.

**carthorse**
Large, strong, cold-blooded draught horse used for pulling carts or other heavy loads.

**chestnut**
Horse with an orange or reddish brown coat, of varying shades.

**coach horse**
Horse used to pull a coach or carriage, usually powerfully built for fairly heavy loads.

**cob**
Small, stocky horses with compact bodies, short legs and steady dispositions. A type, rather than a breed, usually of unknown or mixed breeding.

**coffin joint**
Between pedal bone and short pastern in horse's foot.

**coldblood (n.), cold-blooded (adj.)**
Large horse with calm, gentle disposition; suitable for slow, hard work. Draught horses are considered coldbloods.

**colt**
Uncastrated male horse or pony under the age of four.

**conformation**
A horses' shape and 'composition'; particularly determined by the body parts' proportion and relationship to one another.

**coronet band**
At the top of horse's foot.

**cow hocks**
Hocks turn in, with feet turning out. *See also* 'bowed hocks'; 'sickle hocks'.

**croup**
Topline of a horse measured from the point of the hip to the point of the buttock.

**dam**
The horse's female parent.

**depth of girth**
The measurement from the horse's withers to the elbow.

**dental star**
Black mark found on front of tables of teeth.

**destrier**
This word described the finest and strongest medieval warhorse ridden by knights. A type of horse, rather than a breed.

**digital cushion**
Large piece of tissue at back of horse's foot (also called 'plantar cushion').

**dished face**
A concave profile, such as that of the Arabian.

**dock**
The part of the horse's tail on which the hair grows.

**dorsal stripe**
A line of darker hair extending from the horse's neck to the tail, seen in the 'primitive' breeds. Also called 'eel stripe'.

**draught**
Heavy horse, or a term applied to a horse drawing any vehicle.

**dressage**
Training a horse to the highest possible level, so that it accurately performs a number of movements at different paces in a relaxed way in response to the rider's subtle aids.

**dun**
Horse with a yellowy brown coat and black points, often with a dorsal stripe.

**endocrine system**
Releases hormones into horse's body.

**English saddle**
Saddle with a steel cantle and pommel and no horn (unlike a Western saddle), designed to allow freedom of movement.

**ermine marks**
Patches of colour in horse's white socks or stockings.

**eventing**
Eventing is a complete competition combining dressage, show jumping and cross-country. Events take place over one, two or three days.

**ewe neck**
Well-developed muscle underneath the neck and weak topline.

**feather**
Long hair on the lower legs and fetlocks, common in heavy draught breeds.

**flaxen**
White mane and tail on chestnut.

**filly**
Female horse or pony under the age of four.

**five-gaited**
A horse that can demonstrate five gaits, three natural (walk, trot, canter) and two 'man-made' (slow and rack).

**freezemark**
White numbers on horse's coat, put on with chilled markers, for identification.

**frog**
Horny, V-shaped part of bottom of horse's foot.

**gait**
The horse's action, such as walk, trot or canter; also applied to the American gaited horses.

**gaited horse**
Horse that performs a foot fall pattern outside the normal walk, trot, canter sequence.

**Galvayne's Groove**
Develops down the outside of upper corner incisors; can be used to help with judging a horse's age.

**gelding**
Castrated male horse.

**goose-rump**
When the quarters slope sharply from croup to dock.

**hack**
General riding horse. Show quality hacks have flawless manners and looks.

**hand**
Traditional unit of measurement for horses. One hand equals 4 in (10.16 cm). The symbol for this unit is 'hh' (standing for 'hands high').

**harness horse**
Horse used for pulling vehicles.

*Haute École*
High School, the classical art of advanced riding, seen, for example, in the Spanish Riding School of Vienna.

**heavy horse**
Any large draught breed.

**herring-gutted**
When the underside of the body slopes steeply upwards towards the stifle.

**hindquarters**
The back quarters of a horse, from the flank to the tail.

**hollow back**
Dipped back; can develop with age. Also called 'sway back'.

**hotblood (n.), hot-blooded (adj.)**
Light saddle horse such as the Thoroughbred and the Arabian, with highly-strung, fiery-tempered nature.

**hunter**
Horse bred and trained to be ridden for hunting. Can either be show hunters, or working/field hunters.

**incisors**
The 12 biting teeth at front of a horse's mouth.

**infundibulum**
Large dark hole found in centre of tables of teeth.

**interdental space**
Gap between the incisors and premolars.

**jibbah**
A shield-shaped bulge on the forehead, unique to the Arabian.

**Isabella**
Another term for palomino.

**jumper's bump**
When the horse has a pronounced croup.

**laminae**
Leaves of tissue between hoof wall and pedal bone.

**light horse**
Any equine over 15 hh that is not one of the heavy draught breeds.

**light of bone**
A conformation fault where the amount of bone below the knee is too small in comparison to the size of the horse.

**loaded shoulder**
Excessive muscle formation; a conformational fault.

**lungeing**
(Also called 'lunging' or 'longeing'). Where a horse is held on a long rope and made to circle round its trainer for training and exercise.

**lymphatic system**
Drains excess fluid and helps horse's body to fight infection.

**mare**
Adult female horse or pony.

**mealy muzzle**
Oatmeal-coloured muzzle seen on the Exmoor Pony.

**mitbah**
The angle at which the Arabian's head meets the neck; unique to the breed.

**molars**
The 12 chewing teeth at back of a horse's mouth.

**navicular bone**
Small bone in horse's foot.

**over at the knee**
A conformational fault; the opposite of back at the knee.

**pacer**
A horse that performs a lateral action, rather than diagonal like the trot.

**palomino**
Horse with a yellowy gold coat and white mane and tail.

**pastern bone**
Extends from horse's lower leg into top of the foot.

**pedal bone**
Large bone in horse's foot.

**perlino**
Cream-coloured horse with blue eyes.

**piebald**
Horse with black-and-white patches.

**pigeon toes**
When the toes turn in.

**plantar cushion**
Large piece of tissue at back of horse's foot (also called 'digital cushion').

**points of the horse**
Specific external parts of the horse. In relation to colour, the points of the horse refer to the mane, tail, muzzle, tips of the ears and lower legs.

**polo pony**
Fast, agile and quick-thinking horse used to play the game of polo, even if it is taller then the maximum height for a pony (14.2 hands).

**pony**
Small horse, usually under 14.2 hands. However, ponies are not necessarily simply a small or miniature horse as they tend to differ from horses in other ways. For example they may have thicker manes, tails and coat; proportionally shorter legs, wider barrels, shorter and thicker necks; and sometimes calmer temperaments.

**posting**
In rising trot, when the rider rises from the saddle for one beat and sits in the saddle for the alternate beat.

**premolars**
The 12 chewing teeth at back of a horse's mouth.

**prepotency**
The ability to pass on characteristics to the progeny.

**presence**
The 'sparkle' seen in show horses and competition horses that says, 'Look at me.'

**primitive**
The term used to describe the early horse breeds, such as Przewalski's, Tarpan and Solutre.

**prophet's thumb mark**
Muscular indentation, usually on neck or shoulder; considered lucky.

**quarters**
*See* hindquarters.

**rack**
A four-beat gait known as the fifth gait in some North American breeds. Also called 'single-foot'.

**remount**
A horse used for service in an army or the police force.

**roach back**
Back curves upwards towards and over loins.

**Roman nose**
Nose that is convex in profile.

**saddle horse**
Horse bred or trained for riding.

**sickle hocks**
Hocks that are too bent and weak. *See also* 'bowed hocks'; 'cow hocks'.

**sire**
The horse's male parent.

**skewbald**
Horse with patches of white and any colour other than black.

**snip**
White on horse's nose.

**sock**
White on a horse's leg extending from the foot to the fetlock or below.

**sole**
Bottom of horse's foot.

**sport horse**
Type of horse – purebred or crossbred – that is used for equestrian disciplines such as dressage, jumping, eventing or endurance.

**stallion**
Adult male horse that has not been castrated (gelded).

**star**
White mark on horse's forehead or between eyes.

**stocking**
White on horse's leg extending from the foot to between the fetlock and knee or hock (or sometimes higher, known as 'white legs').

**stripe**
Narrow white mark on horse's face.

**studbook**
Book in which the pedigree of purebred stock are officially recorded.

**swan neck**
Long neck which is dipped in front of the withers, then arched, with the highest point further back, then the poll.

**sway back**
Dipped back; can develop with age. Also called 'hollow back'.

**tables**
Top surface of lower incisors.

**tack**
The various saddles, bridles and other equipment used in horse riding, driving and management.

**teaser**
A substitute stallion used to test whether a mare is ready to be mated.

***tölt***
The lateral gait seen in the Icelandic Horse.

**trotting horse; trotter**
Horse that has been trained to trot, for example in harness racing.

**tushes**
Four teeth in the interdental space, usually found only in male horses (also called 'canines').

**type**
'Types' of horses are not breeds, but usually a group of breeds that share similar characteristics or are used for a particular activity such as polo or hunting.

**wall**
Outside of horse's foot.

**warmblood (n.), warm-blooded (adj.)**
Generally, a half-bred or part-bred horse of an even temperament, usually crossed out from Arabian or Thoroughbred stock, or the result of a cross between hot-blooded and cold-blooded breeds to create a sturdy, athletic horse.

**Western pleasure**
Western-style competition, in particular judging conformation and temperament, gait cadence and speed.

**Western saddle**
Saddle used for western riding and for working on horse and cattle ranches, a distinctive feature of which is the horn.

**withers**
The highest part of a horse's back, on the ridge behind the neck and between the shoulders.

**white face**
When the white on a horse's face covers the eyes, forehead and much of the muzzle.

**whorls**
Places where the hair swirls and grows in different directions.

**wolf teeth**
Remnants of defunct first premolars; one or more found in some horses.

**zebra stripes**
Dark stripes on the horse's lower legs, a primitive feature.

# Picture Credits

Illustrations by **Ann Biggs**.

All photographs are courtesy of **Bob Langrish** except:

**Animal Photography:** Venyamin Nikiforov: 179 (tr, ct), 288 (tl, b), 291 (tr, c), 336 (tl, c); Sally Anne Thompson: 179 (b, cr), 248, 267, 270 (c), 273, 285, (tr), 336 (b), 337

**Ardea:** Hans Dossenbach: 125 (bl), 127 (tl), 178 (tl, c), 183 (b); Chris Knights: 334 (cl, b)

**Corbis:** 24 (t), 29 (b), 182 (tl, cr); James L. Amos: 76 (c); Araldo de Luca: 23 (b); The Art Archive: 23 (c); Asian Art & Archaeology, Inc.: 23 (t); Bettmann: 12 (cl), 14 (bl), 24 (bl), 24 (cr), 28 (br), 29 (tr); Stefano Bianchetti: 24 (br); Bureau L.A. Collection: 5 (ctl), 28 (t); Burstein Collection: 22 (cl); Christie's Images: 26 (t, b); The Gallery Collection: 27 (tl); Gianni Dagli Orti: 12 (cl); Lindsay Hebberd: 182 (cl); Historical Picture Archive: 12 (b); John Noble: 19 (c); John Springer Collection: 28 (bl); Barry Lewis: 21 (t); Leo Mason: 17 (b); Stewart Mike: 16 (br); National Gallery, London: 27 (tl); Galen Rowell: 183 (tr); Skyscan: 22 (b); Stapleton Collection: 25 (t); The State Russian Museum: 22 (tl), 25 (b); Graham Tim: 8, 13 (tl, tr); Underwood & Underwood: 15 (tr); Patrick Ward: 13 (b); Nik Wheeler: 27 (b); Bo Zaunders: 74 (t); Jim Zuckerman: 21 (c)

**FLPA:** Mark Newman: 130 (t), 133 (b); Jurgen & Christine Sohns: 133 (t); Frank Stober: 131 (t); Zhinong Xi; 133 (c)

**Foundry Arts:** 180 (b), 184 (tl, cr), 277 (tr, cl), 291 (b), 328 (tl, bl), 329 (tr, br), 340 (tl, b)

**Kit Houghton:** 150, 167, 183 (cr), 184 (cl, br), 249 (tr, ctr), 270 (tl, b), 272 (tl, c, bl), 276 (tl, b)

**Shutterstock:** Terry Alexander: 88 (tl), 93 (b); Joy Brown: 85 (c); Gabriel Moisa: 79 (b) Cheryl Ann Quigley: 103 (b); Virtuelle: 74 (bl);

**TopFoto:** 22 (cr), 29 (tl), 288 (c)

Every effort has been made to contact copyright holders and we apologise in advance for any omissions. We will be pleased to insert appropriate acknowledgments in subsequent editions of this publication.

# Index